ANCIENT HISTORY

This mystic maze all started as a map of the Old Valley with roads, rivers, etc. As we progressed it simply degenerated into memorable impressions and "atmosphere" of long gone days, places and people. Geographical locations are approximate. Viewers can place themselves on hills back of Los Gatos looking north. The plentiful "corn", caricatures and cartoons are not greatly exaggerated. While local "historians" and old-timers enjoy spotting the errors and omissions, here are a few boiled down keynotes:

(1) Actually it wasn't Portola but a couple of his deer hunting soldiers that from about this point in 1769 accidentally had the first view of the Old Valley through Spanish eyes. (2) Nature was kind to our First Citizens, the Valley Indians. Life was easy with a temperate climate and natural food at hand. Advent of the Americanos brought work and new diseases with almost final extinction of some of the local tribes. (3) Leland Stanford brought higher education westward with his magnificent Stanford University. (4) Firewood, pickets and tan bark for Eberhardt's Tannery (S.C.) were hauled from these mountains by four horse wagons. (5) Capt. Elisha Stevens (creek and "boulevard") settled in these western mountains ten years before the Civil War. (6) The medicinal spring waters from Congress Springs and Alum Rock claimed cures from hangnails to senility. (7) Moody's Gulch furnished limited gas for early autos and unlimited stock buying opportunities. (8) Mtn. Charley road is named for Charley McKiernon who in 1854 tangled with a female bear in this locale. He survived but his punctured skull was patched with two silver 50 cents pieces. (9) On the good ship Alviso one could take daily trips to San Francisco for a fare of 50 cents. (10) Yes, there actually was a Battle of Santa Clara. It was fought in 1846 near present Lawrence Road and Highway 101. There were extremely few casualties. We won. (11) The author, 1901, debating attendance at Doyle School. (12) Subdivisions and apartment beehives have left too few blossoms for the annual Festival. (13) Forbes Mill and Lyndon Hotel long survived Progress and destruction. (14) New Chicago was an early and marshy subdivision. Some mail order buyers might find their lots by row boat at high tide. (15) James Lick built a flour mill and endowed Lick Observatory. (16) The Sarah Winchester we knew (at a distance) was shy, charitable and furnished never ending employment. (17) James Dunham in 1896 really cooked up an unsolved Alfred Hitchcock thriller. For unknown reasons he murdered six of his family and on horseback disappeared into the Mount Hamilton range—forever. (18) President T. R. planted a redwood here in 1903. (19) Lumbering was an active industry and Old Valley residences were built from native redwood or pine. (20) Spanish grants of vast acreage dwindled. (21) We give prominence to the Old San Jose Electric Tower, 1881-1916. It *did* provide illumination and at least a certain municipal Distinction, (with which the present metropolis is no longer overburdened). (22) Sour childhood memories almost prevented this touching horticultural scene depicting the prune industry, little changed over the years. (23) Lone Hill? Try and find this landmark! (24) Tiburcio Vasquez, our own prize bandit, rivalled Murietta in ferocious exploits. He was tried and convicted upon circumstantial evidence. (25) New Almaden Mines were world second to the original Almaden in Spain. (26) Stone quarried here for the old Post Office, Hall of Records, Stanford, etc. (27) Once a dinkey steam train ran to Alum Rock past Flickinger's Cannery (28) where once all fruit cans were hand soldered. (29) Who was Manly? He was the '49 rescuer of the Bennett party stranded in Death Valley. Farmed at about this spot and had a home on Stockton Avenue in San Jose. (Hist. Marker). (30) This original, palatial Hayes mansion burned but the forty acres of landscaped grounds (80's) have been preserved and once provided an authentic Frontier Village Amusement Park.

There's more,—if you have a magnifying glass and a long memory.

Cartoon
PEN & INKLINGS OF THE OLD
SANTA CLARA VALLEY

Pen and Inklings

This limited edition was printed as a membership premium by
THE SAN JOSE HISTORICAL MUSEUM ASSOCIATION
635 Phelan Avenue
San Jose, California 95112

Printed in USA by
The Rosicrucian Press
76 Notre Dame Avenue
San Jose, California 95110

Dust Jacket design by Ralph Rambo.

Limited first edition, 1984
Published by the San Jose Historical Museum Association

DEDICATION

To my Mother
Dora Butler Rambo
Who lived and loved those
peaceful, forgotten days.
1870 - 1939

ACKNOWLEDGMENTS

For the welcome offer to produce this anthology I sincerely thank the San Jose Historical Museum Association. Publication of *Pen & Inklings* reaches my topmost goal.

Its contents are selections from writings and drawings through some twenty retirement years. I wish that I could list the great number of helpful, encouraging friends that kept company with this enjoyable period. I do thank them all.

Instead, and relating directly with *Pen & Inklings,* I shall list a few distinguished authors, editors and publishers who gave valuable services and advice: Roberta Jamison, Kathleen Muller, Mignon Gibson, Frances and Theron Fox, Helen and Clyde Arbuckle, Paul D. Anderson, Elizabeth Ribble, and Pamela Rowe. They, with a host of other true friends have proven that years of hopeful wishing can become a happy reality!

CONTENTS

Page No.

I. Introduction: Ralph Rambo — The Book 9

II. Foreword: Ralph Rambo — The Man 11

III. Ralph Rambo the Author 15

    A. Excerpts from *Me & Cy* 17

    B. *Lady of Mystery* 47

    C. *Sierra Santa* 63

    D. *The Little House* 79

    E. Excerpts from *Almost Forgotten* 95

    F. Excerpts from *Remember When* 123

IV. Ralph Rambo the Artist 145

    A. Cartoons of the Period 147

    B. Dog Days 152

    C. The Butterfly-Better Fly 153

    D. A Weaver's Dream 153

    E. Almost Forgotten Pioneers 154

    F. Memory Lane 155

    G. Winchester Mystery House in 1900 156

    H. Doyle School Group 157

    I. Almost Forgotten Words 158

    J. Do You Remember Game 159

    K. The Biographer and a Few Pioneer Friends ... 160

    L. Famous Outhouses 161

    M. Old Valley Ads 162

    N. Dingbats 163

    O. Vasquez the Bandit 164

Page No.

V. Ralph Rambo the Poet 173

    A.   Mystery Valley 175

    B.   "The Night Before . . . !" .... 176 & 177

    C.   Ode to the Prune 178

    D.   Tempus Fugit 179

    E.   1981 Greetings 180

VI. Ralph Rambo the Cartographer 181

    A.   Diseño of the Rancho Santa Teresa 183

    B.   Map of Santa Clara County Ranchos .... 184 & 185

    C.   Pueblo de San José de Guadalupe — Location Map .... 186 & 187

    D.   Pueblo de San José de Guadalupe — Scenic Map .... 188 & 189

    E.   Santa Clara County Country Schools circa 1887 .... 190 & 191

    F.   California Map .... Rear Pocket

VII. Epilogue 192

INTRODUCTION
RALPH RAMBO—THE BOOK

Each year the San Jose Historical Museum Association publishes a quality, hardbound volume of local history as a membership premium and as a way of promoting and preserving local history. The search for the annual volume solicits ideas from a variety of sources and writers. At a meeting of the Board of Directors of the San Jose Historical Museum Association in early 1983, Ralph Rambo's name was suggested as a possibility with a tinge of awe and admiration. It was noted that Rambo would be celebrating his 90th birthday in 1984 and a Rambo book would be a wonderful way to commemorate all he had done for local history. The Board members were unanimous in their desire to produce a volume of the collected works of this local living legend.

Advisory Board member Roberta Jamison agreed to help us approach Rambo with the idea. Roberta had developed a deep friendship with Rambo ever since their work on the Peralta Adobe project began in 1975. As fate would have it, this type of publication fulfills a dream for Ralph Rambo. Previous works were softcover and of this major hardcover publication Rambo states, "Only a few of us have the privilege of realizing, literally, a dream become a reality. To this writer, the publication of *Pen & Inklings* is just such a realization." To be a part of helping someone realize a dream is an overwhelming benefit of this project.

After the approval from Rambo, the real work of publishing began. Although he had been producing this material for 20 years, the task of compiling and editing was lengthy. Kathy Muller, employed by the Association to coordinate all their services, was responsible for seeing this book through all the stages of production. Along with Roberta Jamison, Kathy met regularly with Rambo to select materials, to take his recommendations on what and how to edit, and to include as much as possible of Rambo's favorite published works while introducing new items. The task of trimming this volume was difficult but the variety of Rambo's work is well represented.

Rambo calls himself a "nostalgician" and Kathy and Roberta helped him illustrate this through the book sections that show off his versatility. The sections are titled, Ralph Rambo the Writer, Ralph Rambo the Artist, Ralph Rambo the Poet, and Ralph Rambo the Cartographer, and include a wealth of entertainment and talent.

Another overwhelming by-product of the project is the correspondence that both Kathy and Roberta received from Rambo. Ralph was in touch with the production of the book with every decision and volumes of mail—entertaining, reflective, and illustrated mail—arrived at the Museum almost daily to ensure the progress of this publication. Much of the content of these letters was included in the "Dear Reader" letters from Rambo that introduce each section of the book. The "Dear Reader" material is new and unique to this publication and gives the reader insight into Ralph Rambo and his works.

Kathy Muller and Roberta Jamison ensured that this publication would fulfill Rambo's dream of a permanent gift of nostalgic history to the citizens of his beloved Santa Clara Valley. Special touches such as the Map of California, which is included in a pocket in the back, the autographed bookplate, and the quality of paper and selection of type were all details that they coordinated.

I wish to acknowledge the Stella B. Gross Charitable Trust for their overwhelming support of this project in granting half the production costs. I would also like to acknowledge both the Hugh Stuart Center Charitable Trust and the Sourisseau Academy of San Jose State University for their important financial assistance as well. I would like to thank the Junior League of San Jose for permission to include materials on the Peralta Adobe. Frances and Theron Fox are thanked for their generous donation of services in writing the Foreword. Both Ted Livingston and the Rosicrucian Press were wonderful for the editors and the Museum Association to work with on this project.

Recognition is given to the 1983 and 1984 San Jose Historical Museum Association Boards for their selection and support of this important historical publication and for fulfilling Ralph Rambo's dream.

I would like to acknowledge and thank both of the editors, Roberta Jamison and Kathy Muller, for this evidence of their labor of love and dedication to quality. And finally I would like to thank RALPH RAMBO for allowing us to participate with him in preserving his memories of San Jose and the Santa Clara Valley.

Happy 90th Birthday, Ralph!

Mignon Gibson
Museum Director

FOREWORD
RALPH RAMBO—THE MAN

When tall, trim, seventy-year old Ralph Rambo walked into the Rosicrucian Press office, manuscript in hand, late in 1963, he had the ideal story to publish, *Almost Forgotten,* a history of our valley. It was hand-lettered with hundreds of cartoons and vignette caricatures which he modestly referred to as his "Pen and Inklings".

Being history buffs and pioneer residents who lived and experienced this enviable period he was writing about, we became very enthusiastic and excited, and from this business encounter evolved an enriching friendship for both of us.

The affable Rambo explained, "Facing retirement I needed something to do so I wrote a book, *Looking Backward, 1900,* for my granddaughters, Katherine and Ann, to show the valley at the turn-of-the-century and the unforgettable characters who lived in it. I made about fifty mimeographed copies to give to old friends, who in turn passed the copies to others. Their reaction was astounding. They insisted I write more. Here lay an untouched field of opportunity—old-timers to be awakened and newcomers to initiate."

Ralph Rambo, born at 10 Sunol Street, San Jose, in 1894, later moved to a ten-acre prune orchard on Miller Avenue near Cupertino. There he attended the one-room Doyle School with one teacher and 23 pupils, and Santa Clara High School where he completed his education in 1912. Blackboard decorations at Doyle School were the first evidence of Rambo's talent as an artist. That was back in early 1900.

As a youngster with boyish indifference, Rambo watched the thousands of acres surrounding him planted with millions of fruit trees and vineyards. But for him it was more fun to run a quarter of a mile down Miller Avenue to see his first automobile chugging loudly down the dusty two-lane Stevens Creek Road, which is today Stevens Creek Boulevard. (Henry Ford was just beginning to put America on wheels.) Rambo was curious and observant, with an excellent memory which came in handy 60 years later.

When he was 21 he married Katherine Coker, a childhood sweetheart, who had helped him through his mathematics

11

classes. They enjoyed 37 happy years of marriage before her death in 1952. Their two sons, Bill and Jim, both rose to the tops of their professions. The latter, curator of the San Francisco Palace of the Legion of Honor for twenty years, died in 1981. Bill, Professor Emeritus, former Associate Dean for Research in Stanford School of Engineering, resides in Palo Alto.

We printed 2000 copies of Rambo's first published book, *Almost Forgotten,* in 1964 and before the year ended the book was in its third edition and 8,000 copies had been sold. Meanwhile Rambo was busy working on a sequel, *Remember When,* which met with similar success.

No sooner was the ink dry on one book than he began on another until he produced ten hand-lettered books filled with Santa Clara Valley lore absorbed over the years.

While the bulwark of his successful books is comprehensive research, much of it is augmented by personal anecdotes, perceptive humorous observations illustrated with sketches. His characters are people who qualified by interest rather than the movers and shakers of importance. He is frequently referred to as an historian although he prefers to be known as a "nostalgician".

Rambo had disliked the way history was taught in school as a youngster. He adds, "It was too dry, memorizing dates, naming battles, without any amusing description of people or the way of life."

This dislike was an asset as it formed the basis of his books, the atmosphere of the old valley, the intimate nostalgia.

"I couldn't believe how anxious people were for the history. I call mine "sugar-coated" because it's easy to swallow." His reminiscences, laced with humor, characterize his soft-cover books.

All of his work was done on a large roll top desk using a hand-held magnifying glass and special pen point. The cartoons were sketched separately on imported scratch board. Cartooning found its place without disturbing factual information.

"I avoid cold printed type and besides, I enjoy hand-lettering my books. Although I first type out my story two or three times before I start the lettering."

To this prolific author this was not WORK but pure unhurried pleasure. While beginning his legendary career as a nostalgician at age 70 when most people are retired, Rambo was still going strong when he became an octogenarian. With his 90th birthday on May 16, 1984 he has graduated to the nonagenarian status and is still a six foot-two imposing figure.

Besides his books, Rambo has sketched six different large maps, some out of print, as well as poetry which has been unpublished until this time. He has drawn a series of postcards, illustrated numerous books for other people and designed historical medallions for organizations.

"One of the things that was always in the back of my mind was drawing a cartoon map of the valley. Before I retired I worked out an historical cartoon map of the valley filled with the atmosphere of long-gone days, places and people. I had to wait fifty years to draw this map, but once I got started, it took me three months to complete it." Today thousands of his Pen & Inklings

Cartoon Maps of the old Santa Clara Valley have been sold.

One of the highlights of Ralph Rambo's career was when the City of San Jose presented the former President Gerald Ford with his map of California. Rambo says, "I had lived under 15 Presidents when I had the honor of shaking hands with President Ford in 1976 and seeing him leave with my map in one hand and a copy of the *Luis Maria Peralta* book, which I illustrated for Frances, in the other." The map of California is included as a special feature in the pocket of this book.

However, he adds, "My proudest achievements were the translations of all my books into Braille and Audio Cassettes which have been used extensively by the blind, the Veterans Hospital in Palo Alto and retirement homes." Variety Audio Inc. taped all his books on Audio Cassettes for the blind.

When Roberta Jamison, Chairman of the Advisory Board of the Forbes Mill Regional Museum in Los Gatos, suggested to Alessandro Baccari, Museum Curator, that the Museum provide a Rambo exhibit dedicated to the preservation of Santa Clara Valley history, he agreed this would be a rare opportunity to involve a living part of the valley in the museum display. As a result, the Forbes Mill Regional Museum featured a popular six-month exhibition in the fall of 1983 *Old Valley Rambolings* which documented Rambo's career throughout his productive years with a variety of his works, including cartoon maps, his books and tapes and his numerous comments.

Today this living legend, who qualifies as an historian, calligrapher, poet and cartographer, remains a lifelong booster for the Valley of Hearts Delight and continues to share his memories from his Palo Alto retirement home suite. The result of his works will prove useful to generations to come. It is indeed a privilege to be associated with Ralph Rambo.

Frances and Theron Fox

EDITOR'S NOTE

Frances and Theron Fox, both natives of the Santa Clara Valley, are local historians in their own right.

Frances is the author of *Luis Maria Peralta and His Adobe* and *Land Grant to Landmarks,* both of which were illustrated by her friend, Ralph Rambo. She has also authored numerous booklets of local interest and magazine articles that have seen national circulation. Frances has been a regularly featured teacher at the California History Center, DeAnza College, and was a recipient of the highly prestigious Award of Merit from the California Historical Society in 1982. She is also a former President of the San Jose Landmarks Commission and presently serves as Parliamentarian on the Board of Directors of the San Jose Historical Museum Association.

Theron is Commissioner Emeritus of the San Jose Landmarks Commission and the man whose leadership and drive originally convinced the City of San Jose to allocate the space and funds for an Historical Museum. He was also instrumental in the preservation of the Peralta and Roberto Adobes. Theron was employed as sales manager for The Rosicrucian Press from 1934 to 1971 and has enjoyed a life-long interest in printing. Today the Print Shop at the San Jose Historical Museum is dedicated in his honor.

Dear Reader,

My first book was called *Looking Backward 1900*. You might call it the "fuse" that started the collection of Old Valley Nostalgia that followed in the next fifteen years. It was never published. Only about fifty homemade and handmade copies were given away free to friends and relatives long ago. Why did I write it? I was about to terminate my 50 years of employment by a printing firm, so it was actually the first time I had the opportunity to fulfill my long pent-up desire to record memories of the Old Valley. The "book" was dedicated and directly written to my two granddaughters, Ann and Katherine, and contained about 95 pages, including 14 full page illustrations or cartoons.

I have been asked why *Looking Backward 1900* was not published in quantity along with the others that followed. But it was only the test, the first tremulous step toward more detailed Old Valley coverage. Remember that I had no writing experience whatever. The content of *Looking Backward 1900* was not lost; 80% of it was later incorporated in *Almost Forgotten* and *Remember When,* especially the illustration pages. They have been reduced, used and borrowed for years.

Why did I hand-letter 90% of my books? It happens that I *enjoyed* lettering. And one more reason, I could take my choice between hand-lettering or paying (in those days) $15.00 an hour to have type set. So, I, loaded with time, hand-lettered.

Let's take a single page. I have already done my often lengthy research. I have written and retyped maybe two or three times. Now for the lettering, which must be precise. An average page (8½ x 11″) might require from ten to fifteen hours to produce, and of course the illustrations or cartoons thereon could take whatever their size or detail required. A "thumbnail" vignette might take two hours, a 3 x 5″, about six to eight hours. A full page cartoon, eight to ten hours.

Do you see the enormous advantage I had in reducing production costs? I simply handed the lithographer a book full of these handmade pages, and he, just as simply, tacked them on his camera board and shot them, made his negatives or positives and printing plate, and fastened them to his high speed press. I had books selling in Books, Inc. in a week!

One last request to any reader. Some of the stories in this book were written twenty years ago and you do not need to be reminded that the Old Santa Clara Valley was "overnight" changed to Silicon Valley in more than name only. I am a nonagenarian—born in 1894. Therefore, I must ask for your tolerant indulgence in overlooking errors in dates, places, and names. Please let slippery nostalgia hold full sway. This is not a reference book.

Yours Truly
Ralph Rambo

A story of the old Santa Clara Valley

Me and Cy

and a "retirement colony" in the Alviso garbage dumps

Written and illustrated by
Ralph Rambo

Dear Reader,

Yes, it's *Me & Cy,* not *Cy & Me.* Just like the Small Boy with few manners and little education would title it.

Of the ten books I wrote, this was, by far, the most enjoyable to create. Perhaps because I was personally acquainted with just such a contemporary group of turn-of-the-century characters. I was 10 or 12 years old, an *impressionable age.*

A little plot accidentally appeared somehow, much to my pleased surprise. Alas, I confess it's fiction as far as plot is concerned, but you *must* enjoy the O. Henry ending.

The scene still exists untouched, garbage and hog farm removed. My friends, the characters, were fully capable of every one of their actions and the parts they played. Even if it sounds like fiction I assure you that I simply made puppets out of some dear, old, long-gone intimate friends. And how I enjoyed it! Kindly shed *one* tear.

Readers in surprising numbers believe that it was one of my personal experiences, a true story. I have had many adults, besides small children, ask me if I married little Sophy! Why not? I have grown to believe almost every word of the story myself.

Except for hogs and original actors, the scenario remains, awaiting a T.V. camera and an imaginative director.

Yours Truly
Ralph Rambo

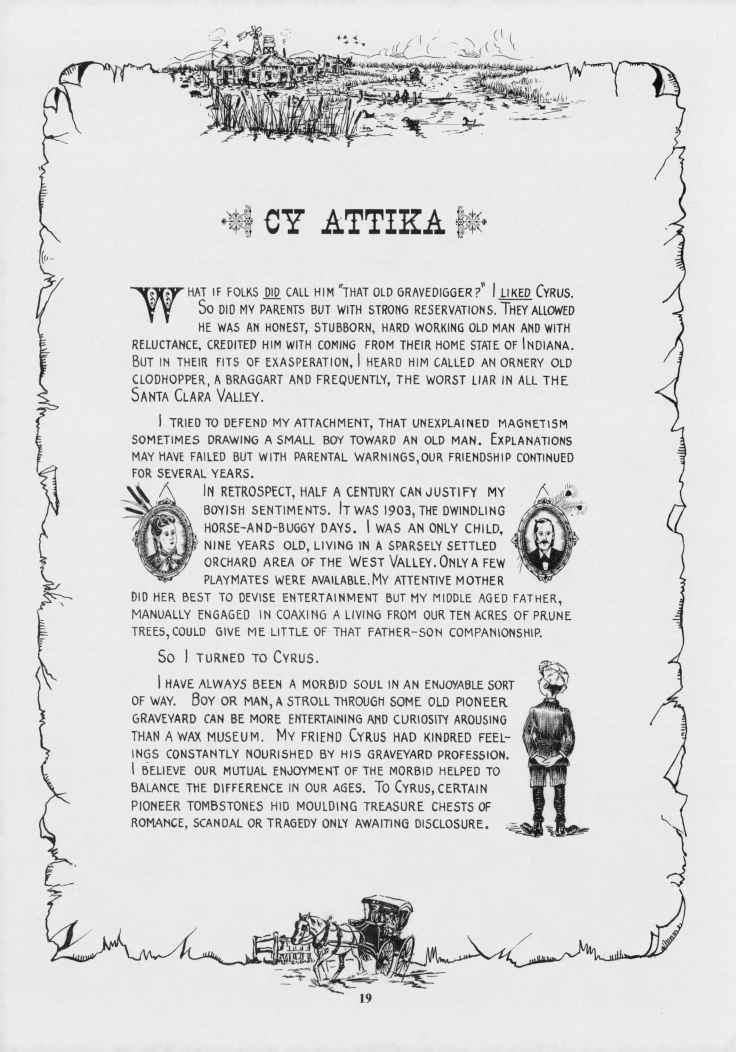

✤ CY ATTIKA ✤

WHAT IF FOLKS _DID_ CALL HIM "THAT OLD GRAVEDIGGER?" I _LIKED_ CYRUS. SO DID MY PARENTS BUT WITH STRONG RESERVATIONS. THEY ALLOWED HE WAS AN HONEST, STUBBORN, HARD WORKING OLD MAN AND WITH RELUCTANCE, CREDITED HIM WITH COMING FROM THEIR HOME STATE OF INDIANA. BUT IN THEIR FITS OF EXASPERATION, I HEARD HIM CALLED AN ORNERY OLD CLODHOPPER, A BRAGGART AND FREQUENTLY, THE WORST LIAR IN ALL THE SANTA CLARA VALLEY.

I TRIED TO DEFEND MY ATTACHMENT, THAT UNEXPLAINED MAGNETISM SOMETIMES DRAWING A SMALL BOY TOWARD AN OLD MAN. EXPLANATIONS MAY HAVE FAILED BUT WITH PARENTAL WARNINGS, OUR FRIENDSHIP CONTINUED FOR SEVERAL YEARS.

IN RETROSPECT, HALF A CENTURY CAN JUSTIFY MY BOYISH SENTIMENTS. IT WAS 1903, THE DWINDLING HORSE-AND-BUGGY DAYS. I WAS AN ONLY CHILD, NINE YEARS OLD, LIVING IN A SPARSELY SETTLED ORCHARD AREA OF THE WEST VALLEY. ONLY A FEW PLAYMATES WERE AVAILABLE. MY ATTENTIVE MOTHER DID HER BEST TO DEVISE ENTERTAINMENT BUT MY MIDDLE AGED FATHER, MANUALLY ENGAGED IN COAXING A LIVING FROM OUR TEN ACRES OF PRUNE TREES, COULD GIVE ME LITTLE OF THAT FATHER-SON COMPANIONSHIP.

SO I TURNED TO CYRUS.

I HAVE ALWAYS BEEN A MORBID SOUL IN AN ENJOYABLE SORT OF WAY. BOY OR MAN, A STROLL THROUGH SOME OLD PIONEER GRAVEYARD CAN BE MORE ENTERTAINING AND CURIOSITY AROUSING THAN A WAX MUSEUM. MY FRIEND CYRUS HAD KINDRED FEELINGS CONSTANTLY NOURISHED BY HIS GRAVEYARD PROFESSION. I BELIEVE OUR MUTUAL ENJOYMENT OF THE MORBID HELPED TO BALANCE THE DIFFERENCE IN OUR AGES. TO CYRUS, CERTAIN PIONEER TOMBSTONES HID MOULDING TREASURE CHESTS OF ROMANCE, SCANDAL OR TRAGEDY ONLY AWAITING DISCLOSURE.

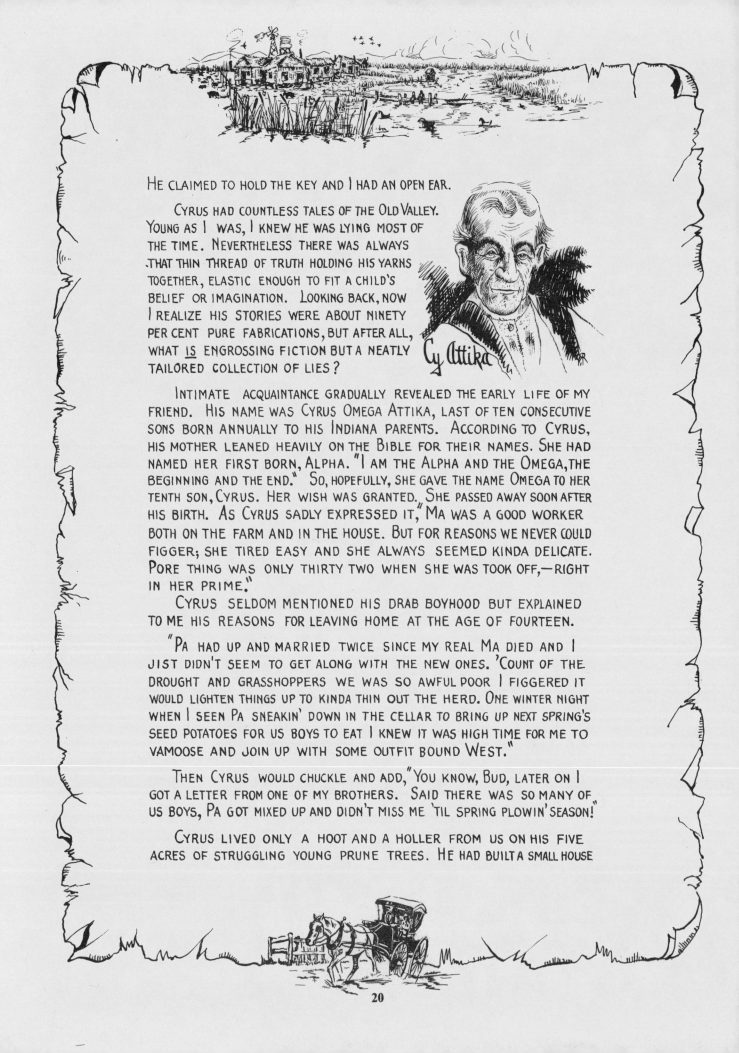

He claimed to hold the key and I had an open ear.

Cyrus had countless tales of the Old Valley. Young as I was, I knew he was lying most of the time. Nevertheless there was always that thin thread of truth holding his yarns together, elastic enough to fit a child's belief or imagination. Looking back, now I realize his stories were about ninety per cent pure fabrications, but after all, what IS engrossing fiction but a neatly tailored collection of lies?

Cy Attika

Intimate acquaintance gradually revealed the early life of my friend. His name was Cyrus Omega Attika, last of ten consecutive sons born annually to his Indiana parents. According to Cyrus, his mother leaned heavily on the Bible for their names. She had named her first born, Alpha. "I am the Alpha and the Omega, the beginning and the end." So, hopefully, she gave the name Omega to her tenth son, Cyrus. Her wish was granted. She passed away soon after his birth. As Cyrus sadly expressed it, "Ma was a good worker both on the farm and in the house. But for reasons we never could figger; she tired easy and she always seemed kinda delicate. Pore thing was only thirty two when she was took off,—right in her prime."

Cyrus seldom mentioned his drab boyhood but explained to me his reasons for leaving home at the age of fourteen.

"Pa had up and married twice since my real Ma died and I jist didn't seem to get along with the new ones. 'Count of the drought and grasshoppers we was so awful poor I figgered it would lighten things up to kinda thin out the herd. One winter night when I seen Pa sneakin' down in the cellar to bring up next spring's seed potatoes for us boys to eat I knew it was high time for me to vamoose and join up with some outfit bound West."

Then Cyrus would chuckle and add, "You know, Bud, later on I got a letter from one of my brothers. Said there was so many of us boys, Pa got mixed up and didn't miss me 'til spring plowin' season!"

Cyrus lived only a hoot and a holler from us on his five acres of struggling young prune trees. He had built a small house

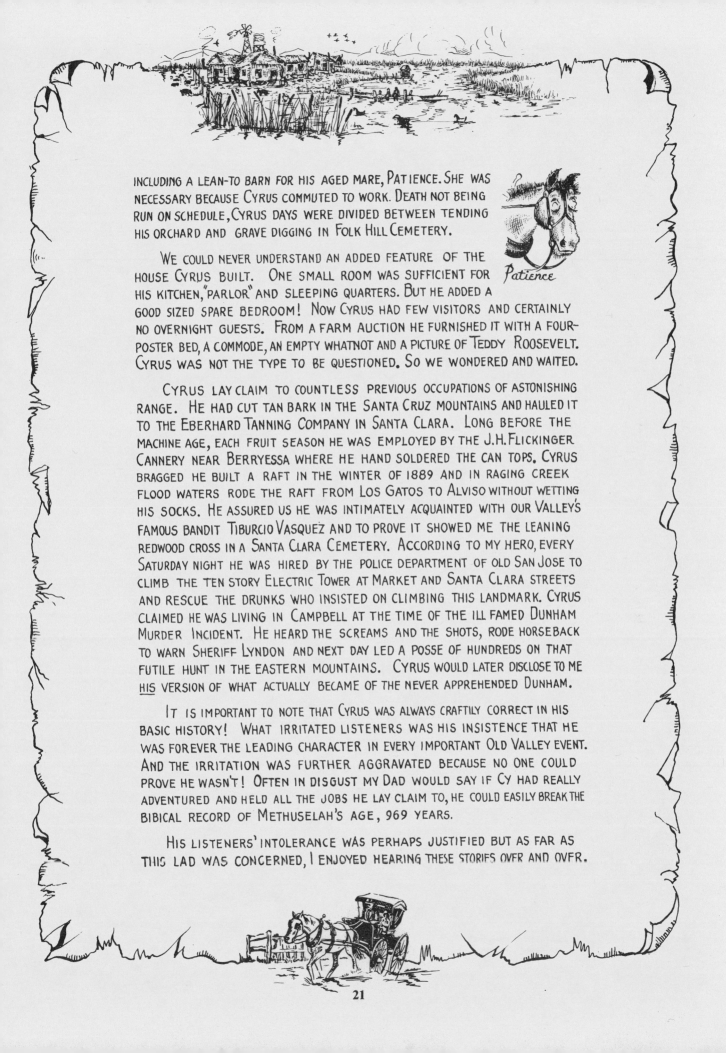

INCLUDING A LEAN-TO BARN FOR HIS AGED MARE, PATIENCE. SHE WAS
NECESSARY BECAUSE CYRUS COMMUTED TO WORK. DEATH NOT BEING
RUN ON SCHEDULE, CYRUS DAYS WERE DIVIDED BETWEEN TENDING
HIS ORCHARD AND GRAVE DIGGING IN FOLK HILL CEMETERY.

Patience

WE COULD NEVER UNDERSTAND AN ADDED FEATURE OF THE
HOUSE CYRUS BUILT. ONE SMALL ROOM WAS SUFFICIENT FOR
HIS KITCHEN, "PARLOR" AND SLEEPING QUARTERS. BUT HE ADDED A
GOOD SIZED SPARE BEDROOM! NOW CYRUS HAD FEW VISITORS AND CERTAINLY
NO OVERNIGHT GUESTS. FROM A FARM AUCTION HE FURNISHED IT WITH A FOUR-
POSTER BED, A COMMODE, AN EMPTY WHATNOT AND A PICTURE OF TEDDY ROOSEVELT.
CYRUS WAS NOT THE TYPE TO BE QUESTIONED. SO WE WONDERED AND WAITED.

CYRUS LAY CLAIM TO COUNTLESS PREVIOUS OCCUPATIONS OF ASTONISHING
RANGE. HE HAD CUT TAN BARK IN THE SANTA CRUZ MOUNTAINS AND HAULED IT
TO THE EBERHARD TANNING COMPANY IN SANTA CLARA. LONG BEFORE THE
MACHINE AGE, EACH FRUIT SEASON HE WAS EMPLOYED BY THE J.H.FLICKINGER
CANNERY NEAR BERRYESSA WHERE HE HAND SOLDERED THE CAN TOPS. CYRUS
BRAGGED HE BUILT A RAFT IN THE WINTER OF 1889 AND IN RAGING CREEK
FLOOD WATERS RODE THE RAFT FROM LOS GATOS TO ALVISO WITHOUT WETTING
HIS SOCKS. HE ASSURED US HE WAS INTIMATELY ACQUAINTED WITH OUR VALLEY'S
FAMOUS BANDIT TIBURCIO VASQUEZ AND TO PROVE IT SHOWED ME THE LEANING
REDWOOD CROSS IN A SANTA CLARA CEMETERY. ACCORDING TO MY HERO, EVERY
SATURDAY NIGHT HE WAS HIRED BY THE POLICE DEPARTMENT OF OLD SAN JOSE TO
CLIMB THE TEN STORY ELECTRIC TOWER AT MARKET AND SANTA CLARA STREETS
AND RESCUE THE DRUNKS WHO INSISTED ON CLIMBING THIS LANDMARK. CYRUS
CLAIMED HE WAS LIVING IN CAMPBELL AT THE TIME OF THE ILL FAMED DUNHAM
MURDER INCIDENT. HE HEARD THE SCREAMS AND THE SHOTS, RODE HORSEBACK
TO WARN SHERIFF LYNDON AND NEXT DAY LED A POSSE OF HUNDREDS ON THAT
FUTILE HUNT IN THE EASTERN MOUNTAINS. CYRUS WOULD LATER DISCLOSE TO ME
HIS VERSION OF WHAT ACTUALLY BECAME OF THE NEVER APPREHENDED DUNHAM.

IT IS IMPORTANT TO NOTE THAT CYRUS WAS ALWAYS CRAFTILY CORRECT IN HIS
BASIC HISTORY! WHAT IRRITATED LISTENERS WAS HIS INSISTENCE THAT HE
WAS FOREVER THE LEADING CHARACTER IN EVERY IMPORTANT OLD VALLEY EVENT.
AND THE IRRITATION WAS FURTHER AGGRAVATED BECAUSE NO ONE COULD
PROVE HE WASN'T! OFTEN IN DISGUST MY DAD WOULD SAY IF CY HAD REALLY
ADVENTURED AND HELD ALL THE JOBS HE LAY CLAIM TO, HE COULD EASILY BREAK THE
BIBICAL RECORD OF METHUSELAH'S AGE, 969 YEARS.

HIS LISTENERS' INTOLERANCE WAS PERHAPS JUSTIFIED BUT AS FAR AS
THIS LAD WAS CONCERNED, I ENJOYED HEARING THESE STORIES OVER AND OVER.

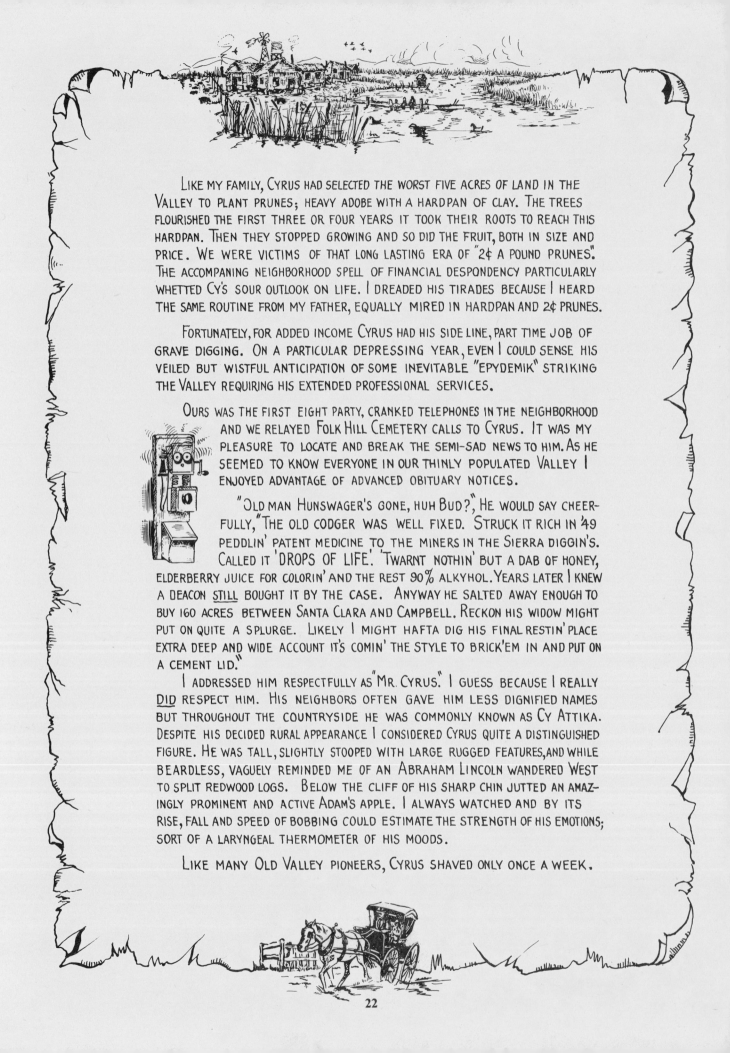

LIKE MY FAMILY, CYRUS HAD SELECTED THE WORST FIVE ACRES OF LAND IN THE VALLEY TO PLANT PRUNES; HEAVY ADOBE WITH A HARDPAN OF CLAY. THE TREES FLOURISHED THE FIRST THREE OR FOUR YEARS IT TOOK THEIR ROOTS TO REACH THIS HARDPAN. THEN THEY STOPPED GROWING AND SO DID THE FRUIT, BOTH IN SIZE AND PRICE. WE WERE VICTIMS OF THAT LONG LASTING ERA OF "2¢ A POUND PRUNES". THE ACCOMPANING NEIGHBORHOOD SPELL OF FINANCIAL DESPONDENCY PARTICULARLY WHETTED CY'S SOUR OUTLOOK ON LIFE. I DREADED HIS TIRADES BECAUSE I HEARD THE SAME ROUTINE FROM MY FATHER, EQUALLY MIRED IN HARDPAN AND 2¢ PRUNES.

FORTUNATELY, FOR ADDED INCOME CYRUS HAD HIS SIDE LINE, PART TIME JOB OF GRAVE DIGGING. ON A PARTICULAR DEPRESSING YEAR, EVEN I COULD SENSE HIS VEILED BUT WISTFUL ANTICIPATION OF SOME INEVITABLE "EPYDEMIK" STRIKING THE VALLEY REQUIRING HIS EXTENDED PROFESSIONAL SERVICES.

OURS WAS THE FIRST EIGHT PARTY, CRANKED TELEPHONES IN THE NEIGHBORHOOD AND WE RELAYED FOLK HILL CEMETERY CALLS TO CYRUS. IT WAS MY PLEASURE TO LOCATE AND BREAK THE SEMI-SAD NEWS TO HIM. AS HE SEEMED TO KNOW EVERYONE IN OUR THINLY POPULATED VALLEY I ENJOYED ADVANTAGE OF ADVANCED OBITUARY NOTICES.

"OLD MAN HUNSWAGER'S GONE, HUH BUD?", HE WOULD SAY CHEERFULLY, "THE OLD CODGER WAS WELL FIXED. STRUCK IT RICH IN '49 PEDDLIN' PATENT MEDICINE TO THE MINERS IN THE SIERRA DIGGIN'S. CALLED IT 'DROPS OF LIFE'. 'TWARNT NOTHIN' BUT A DAB OF HONEY, ELDERBERRY JUICE FOR COLORIN' AND THE REST 90% ALKYHOL. YEARS LATER I KNEW A DEACON STILL BOUGHT IT BY THE CASE. ANYWAY HE SALTED AWAY ENOUGH TO BUY 160 ACRES BETWEEN SANTA CLARA AND CAMPBELL. RECKON HIS WIDOW MIGHT PUT ON QUITE A SPLURGE. LIKELY I MIGHT HAFTA DIG HIS FINAL RESTIN' PLACE EXTRA DEEP AND WIDE ACCOUNT IT'S COMIN' THE STYLE TO BRICK'EM IN AND PUT ON A CEMENT LID."

I ADDRESSED HIM RESPECTFULLY AS "MR. CYRUS." I GUESS BECAUSE I REALLY DID RESPECT HIM. HIS NEIGHBORS OFTEN GAVE HIM LESS DIGNIFIED NAMES BUT THROUGHOUT THE COUNTRYSIDE HE WAS COMMONLY KNOWN AS CY ATTIKA. DESPITE HIS DECIDED RURAL APPEARANCE I CONSIDERED CYRUS QUITE A DISTINGUISHED FIGURE. HE WAS TALL, SLIGHTLY STOOPED WITH LARGE RUGGED FEATURES, AND WHILE BEARDLESS, VAGUELY REMINDED ME OF AN ABRAHAM LINCOLN WANDERED WEST TO SPLIT REDWOOD LOGS. BELOW THE CLIFF OF HIS SHARP CHIN JUTTED AN AMAZINGLY PROMINENT AND ACTIVE ADAM'S APPLE. I ALWAYS WATCHED AND BY ITS RISE, FALL AND SPEED OF BOBBING COULD ESTIMATE THE STRENGTH OF HIS EMOTIONS; SORT OF A LARYNGEAL THERMOMETER OF HIS MOODS.

LIKE MANY OLD VALLEY PIONEERS, CYRUS SHAVED ONLY ONCE A WEEK.

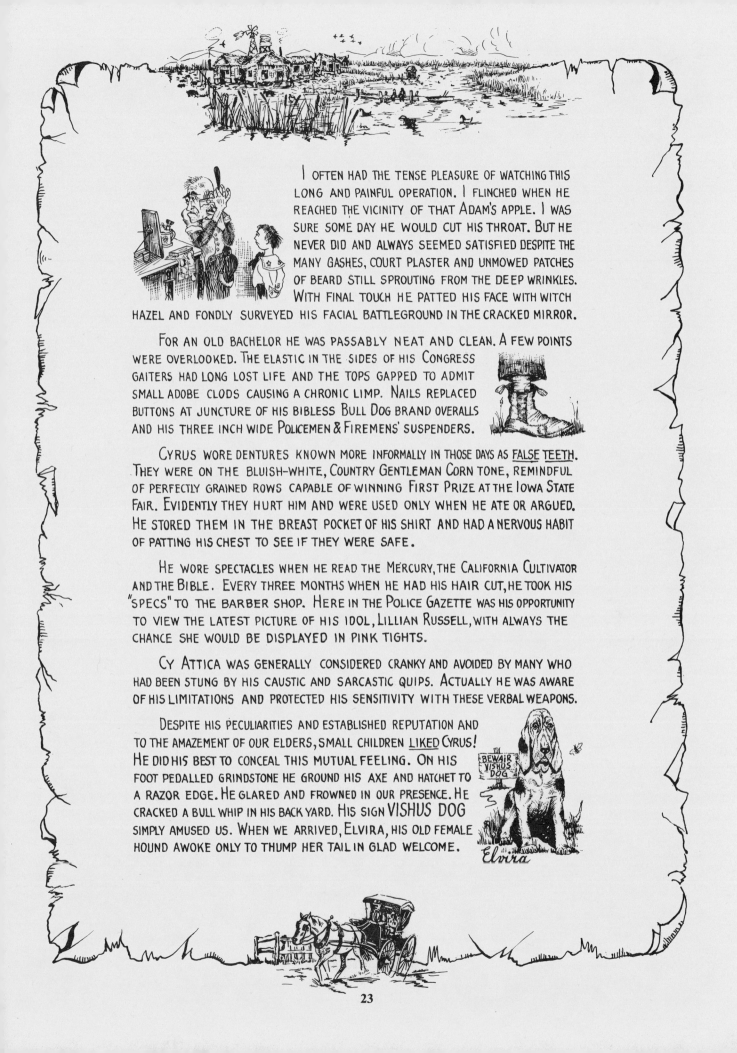

I OFTEN HAD THE TENSE PLEASURE OF WATCHING THIS LONG AND PAINFUL OPERATION. I FLINCHED WHEN HE REACHED THE VICINITY OF THAT ADAM'S APPLE. I WAS SURE SOME DAY HE WOULD CUT HIS THROAT. BUT HE NEVER DID AND ALWAYS SEEMED SATISFIED DESPITE THE MANY GASHES, COURT PLASTER AND UNMOWED PATCHES OF BEARD STILL SPROUTING FROM THE DEEP WRINKLES. WITH FINAL TOUCH HE PATTED HIS FACE WITH WITCH HAZEL AND FONDLY SURVEYED HIS FACIAL BATTLEGROUND IN THE CRACKED MIRROR.

FOR AN OLD BACHELOR HE WAS PASSABLY NEAT AND CLEAN. A FEW POINTS WERE OVERLOOKED. THE ELASTIC IN THE SIDES OF HIS CONGRESS GAITERS HAD LONG LOST LIFE AND THE TOPS GAPPED TO ADMIT SMALL ADOBE CLODS CAUSING A CHRONIC LIMP. NAILS REPLACED BUTTONS AT JUNCTURE OF HIS BIBLESS BULL DOG BRAND OVERALLS AND HIS THREE INCH WIDE POLICEMEN & FIREMENS' SUSPENDERS.

CYRUS WORE DENTURES KNOWN MORE INFORMALLY IN THOSE DAYS AS FALSE TEETH. THEY WERE ON THE BLUISH-WHITE, COUNTRY GENTLEMAN CORN TONE, REMINDFUL OF PERFECTLY GRAINED ROWS CAPABLE OF WINNING FIRST PRIZE AT THE IOWA STATE FAIR. EVIDENTLY THEY HURT HIM AND WERE USED ONLY WHEN HE ATE OR ARGUED. HE STORED THEM IN THE BREAST POCKET OF HIS SHIRT AND HAD A NERVOUS HABIT OF PATTING HIS CHEST TO SEE IF THEY WERE SAFE.

HE WORE SPECTACLES WHEN HE READ THE MERCURY, THE CALIFORNIA CULTIVATOR AND THE BIBLE. EVERY THREE MONTHS WHEN HE HAD HIS HAIR CUT, HE TOOK HIS "SPECS" TO THE BARBER SHOP. HERE IN THE POLICE GAZETTE WAS HIS OPPORTUNITY TO VIEW THE LATEST PICTURE OF HIS IDOL, LILLIAN RUSSELL, WITH ALWAYS THE CHANCE SHE WOULD BE DISPLAYED IN PINK TIGHTS.

CY ATTICA WAS GENERALLY CONSIDERED CRANKY AND AVOIDED BY MANY WHO HAD BEEN STUNG BY HIS CAUSTIC AND SARCASTIC QUIPS. ACTUALLY HE WAS AWARE OF HIS LIMITATIONS AND PROTECTED HIS SENSITIVITY WITH THESE VERBAL WEAPONS.

DESPITE HIS PECULIARITIES AND ESTABLISHED REPUTATION AND TO THE AMAZEMENT OF OUR ELDERS, SMALL CHILDREN LIKED CYRUS! HE DID HIS BEST TO CONCEAL THIS MUTUAL FEELING. ON HIS FOOT PEDALLED GRINDSTONE HE GROUND HIS AXE AND HATCHET TO A RAZOR EDGE. HE GLARED AND FROWNED IN OUR PRESENCE. HE CRACKED A BULL WHIP IN HIS BACK YARD. HIS SIGN VISHUS DOG SIMPLY AMUSED US. WHEN WE ARRIVED, ELVIRA, HIS OLD FEMALE HOUND AWOKE ONLY TO THUMP HER TAIL IN GLAD WELCOME.

BEWAIR VISHUS DOG

Elvira

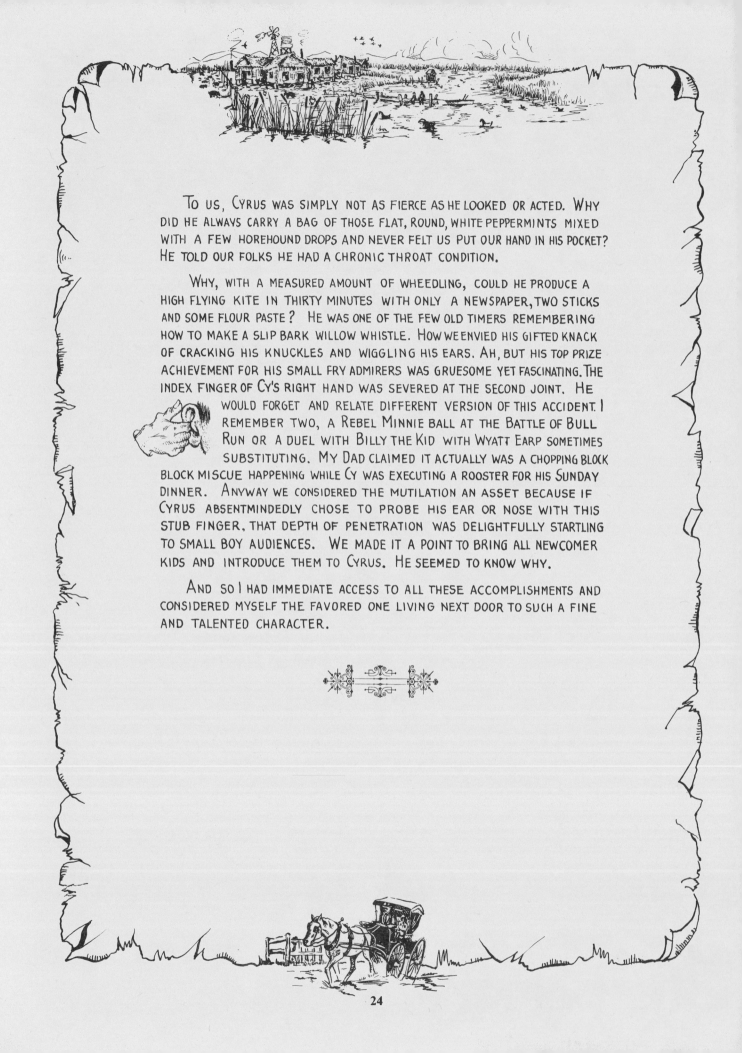

To us, Cyrus was simply not as fierce as he looked or acted. Why did he always carry a bag of those flat, round, white peppermints mixed with a few horehound drops and never felt us put our hand in his pocket? He told our folks he had a chronic throat condition.

Why, with a measured amount of wheedling, could he produce a high flying kite in thirty minutes with only a newspaper, two sticks and some flour paste? He was one of the few old timers remembering how to make a slip bark willow whistle. How we envied his gifted knack of cracking his knuckles and wiggling his ears. Ah, but his top prize achievement for his small fry admirers was gruesome yet fascinating. The index finger of Cy's right hand was severed at the second joint. He would forget and relate different version of this accident. I remember two, a Rebel Minnie ball at the Battle of Bull Run or a duel with Billy the Kid with Wyatt Earp sometimes substituting. My Dad claimed it actually was a chopping block block miscue happening while Cy was executing a rooster for his Sunday dinner. Anyway we considered the mutilation an asset because if Cyrus absentmindedly chose to probe his ear or nose with this stub finger, that depth of penetration was delightfully startling to small boy audiences. We made it a point to bring all newcomer kids and introduce them to Cyrus. He seemed to know why.

And so I had immediate access to all these accomplishments and considered myself the favored one living next door to such a fine and talented character.

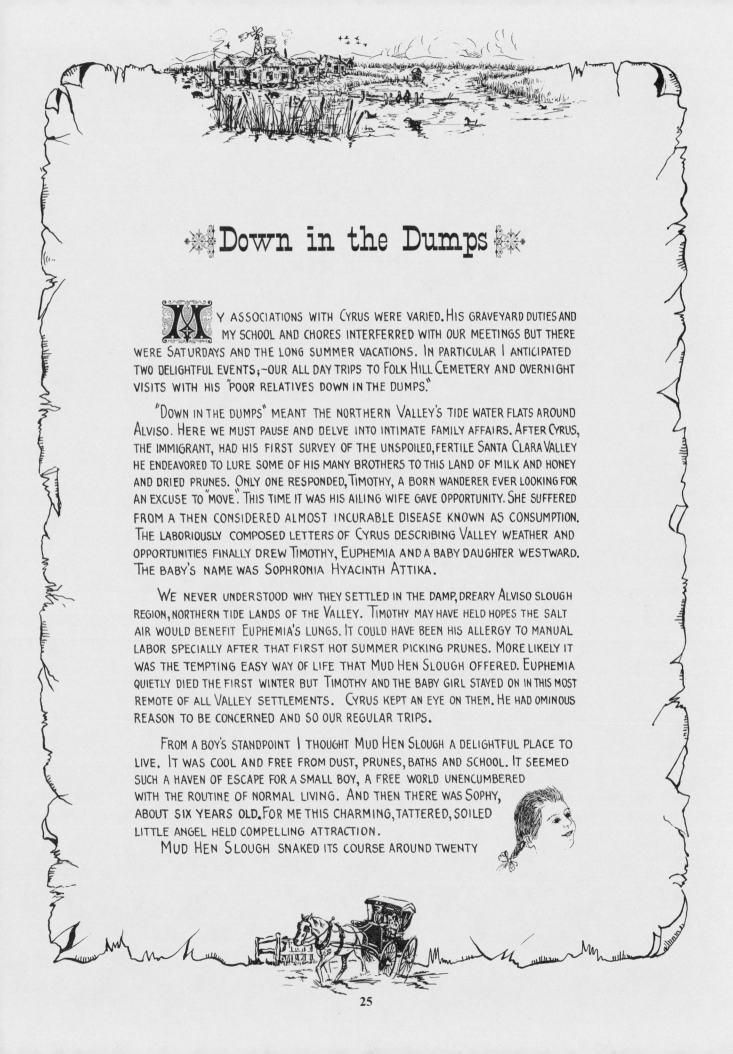

❊Down in the Dumps❊

MY ASSOCIATIONS WITH CYRUS WERE VARIED. HIS GRAVEYARD DUTIES AND MY SCHOOL AND CHORES INTERFERRED WITH OUR MEETINGS BUT THERE WERE SATURDAYS AND THE LONG SUMMER VACATIONS. IN PARTICULAR I ANTICIPATED TWO DELIGHTFUL EVENTS;—OUR ALL DAY TRIPS TO FOLK HILL CEMETERY AND OVERNIGHT VISITS WITH HIS "POOR RELATIVES DOWN IN THE DUMPS."

"DOWN IN THE DUMPS" MEANT THE NORTHERN VALLEY'S TIDE WATER FLATS AROUND ALVISO. HERE WE MUST PAUSE AND DELVE INTO INTIMATE FAMILY AFFAIRS. AFTER CYRUS, THE IMMIGRANT, HAD HIS FIRST SURVEY OF THE UNSPOILED, FERTILE SANTA CLARA VALLEY HE ENDEAVORED TO LURE SOME OF HIS MANY BROTHERS TO THIS LAND OF MILK AND HONEY AND DRIED PRUNES. ONLY ONE RESPONDED, TIMOTHY, A BORN WANDERER EVER LOOKING FOR AN EXCUSE TO "MOVE". THIS TIME IT WAS HIS AILING WIFE GAVE OPPORTUNITY. SHE SUFFERED FROM A THEN CONSIDERED ALMOST INCURABLE DISEASE KNOWN AS CONSUMPTION. THE LABORIOUSLY COMPOSED LETTERS OF CYRUS DESCRIBING VALLEY WEATHER AND OPPORTUNITIES FINALLY DREW TIMOTHY, EUPHEMIA AND A BABY DAUGHTER WESTWARD. THE BABY'S NAME WAS SOPHRONIA HYACINTH ATTIKA.

WE NEVER UNDERSTOOD WHY THEY SETTLED IN THE DAMP, DREARY ALVISO SLOUGH REGION, NORTHERN TIDE LANDS OF THE VALLEY. TIMOTHY MAY HAVE HELD HOPES THE SALT AIR WOULD BENEFIT EUPHEMIA'S LUNGS. IT COULD HAVE BEEN HIS ALLERGY TO MANUAL LABOR SPECIALLY AFTER THAT FIRST HOT SUMMER PICKING PRUNES. MORE LIKELY IT WAS THE TEMPTING EASY WAY OF LIFE THAT MUD HEN SLOUGH OFFERED. EUPHEMIA QUIETLY DIED THE FIRST WINTER BUT TIMOTHY AND THE BABY GIRL STAYED ON IN THIS MOST REMOTE OF ALL VALLEY SETTLEMENTS. CYRUS KEPT AN EYE ON THEM. HE HAD OMINOUS REASON TO BE CONCERNED AND SO OUR REGULAR TRIPS.

FROM A BOY'S STANDPOINT I THOUGHT MUD HEN SLOUGH A DELIGHTFUL PLACE TO LIVE. IT WAS COOL AND FREE FROM DUST, PRUNES, BATHS AND SCHOOL. IT SEEMED SUCH A HAVEN OF ESCAPE FOR A SMALL BOY, A FREE WORLD UNENCUMBERED WITH THE ROUTINE OF NORMAL LIVING. AND THEN THERE WAS SOPHY, ABOUT SIX YEARS OLD. FOR ME THIS CHARMING, TATTERED, SOILED LITTLE ANGEL HELD COMPELLING ATTRACTION.
MUD HEN SLOUGH SNAKED ITS COURSE AROUND TWENTY

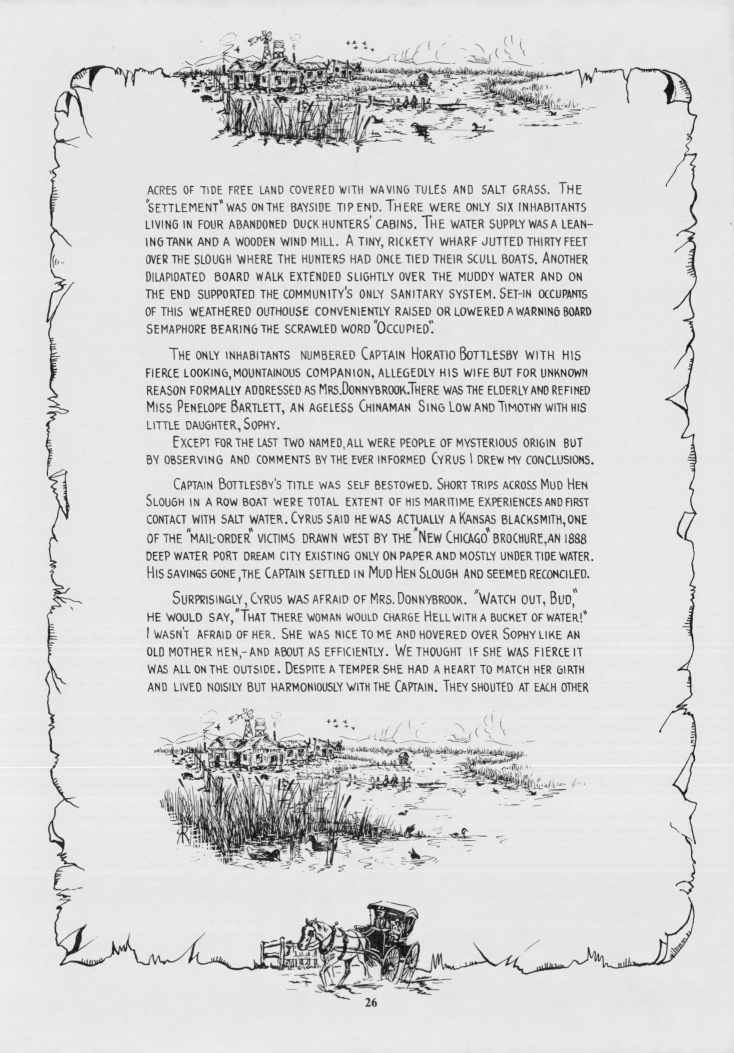

ACRES OF TIDE FREE LAND COVERED WITH WAVING TULES AND SALT GRASS. THE "SETTLEMENT" WAS ON THE BAYSIDE TIP END. THERE WERE ONLY SIX INHABITANTS LIVING IN FOUR ABANDONED DUCK HUNTERS' CABINS. THE WATER SUPPLY WAS A LEANING TANK AND A WOODEN WIND MILL. A TINY, RICKETY WHARF JUTTED THIRTY FEET OVER THE SLOUGH WHERE THE HUNTERS HAD ONCE TIED THEIR SCULL BOATS. ANOTHER DILAPIDATED BOARD WALK EXTENDED SLIGHTLY OVER THE MUDDY WATER AND ON THE END SUPPORTED THE COMMUNITY'S ONLY SANITARY SYSTEM. SET-IN OCCUPANTS OF THIS WEATHERED OUTHOUSE CONVENIENTLY RAISED OR LOWERED A WARNING BOARD SEMAPHORE BEARING THE SCRAWLED WORD "OCCUPIED".

THE ONLY INHABITANTS NUMBERED CAPTAIN HORATIO BOTTLESBY WITH HIS FIERCE LOOKING, MOUNTAINOUS COMPANION, ALLEGEDLY HIS WIFE BUT FOR UNKNOWN REASON FORMALLY ADDRESSED AS MRS. DONNYBROOK. THERE WAS THE ELDERLY AND REFINED MISS PENELOPE BARTLETT, AN AGELESS CHINAMAN SING LOW AND TIMOTHY WITH HIS LITTLE DAUGHTER, SOPHY.

EXCEPT FOR THE LAST TWO NAMED, ALL WERE PEOPLE OF MYSTERIOUS ORIGIN BUT BY OBSERVING AND COMMENTS BY THE EVER INFORMED CYRUS I DREW MY CONCLUSIONS.

CAPTAIN BOTTLESBY'S TITLE WAS SELF BESTOWED. SHORT TRIPS ACROSS MUD HEN SLOUGH IN A ROW BOAT WERE TOTAL EXTENT OF HIS MARITIME EXPERIENCES AND FIRST CONTACT WITH SALT WATER. CYRUS SAID HE WAS ACTUALLY A KANSAS BLACKSMITH, ONE OF THE "MAIL-ORDER" VICTIMS DRAWN WEST BY THE "NEW CHICAGO" BROCHURE, AN 1888 DEEP WATER PORT DREAM CITY EXISTING ONLY ON PAPER AND MOSTLY UNDER TIDE WATER. HIS SAVINGS GONE, THE CAPTAIN SETTLED IN MUD HEN SLOUGH AND SEEMED RECONCILED.

SURPRISINGLY, CYRUS WAS AFRAID OF MRS. DONNYBROOK. "WATCH OUT, BUD," HE WOULD SAY, "THAT THERE WOMAN WOULD CHARGE HELL WITH A BUCKET OF WATER!" I WASN'T AFRAID OF HER. SHE WAS NICE TO ME AND HOVERED OVER SOPHY LIKE AN OLD MOTHER HEN,—AND ABOUT AS EFFICIENTLY. WE THOUGHT IF SHE WAS FIERCE IT WAS ALL ON THE OUTSIDE. DESPITE A TEMPER SHE HAD A HEART TO MATCH HER GIRTH AND LIVED NOISILY BUT HARMONIOUSLY WITH THE CAPTAIN. THEY SHOUTED AT EACH OTHER

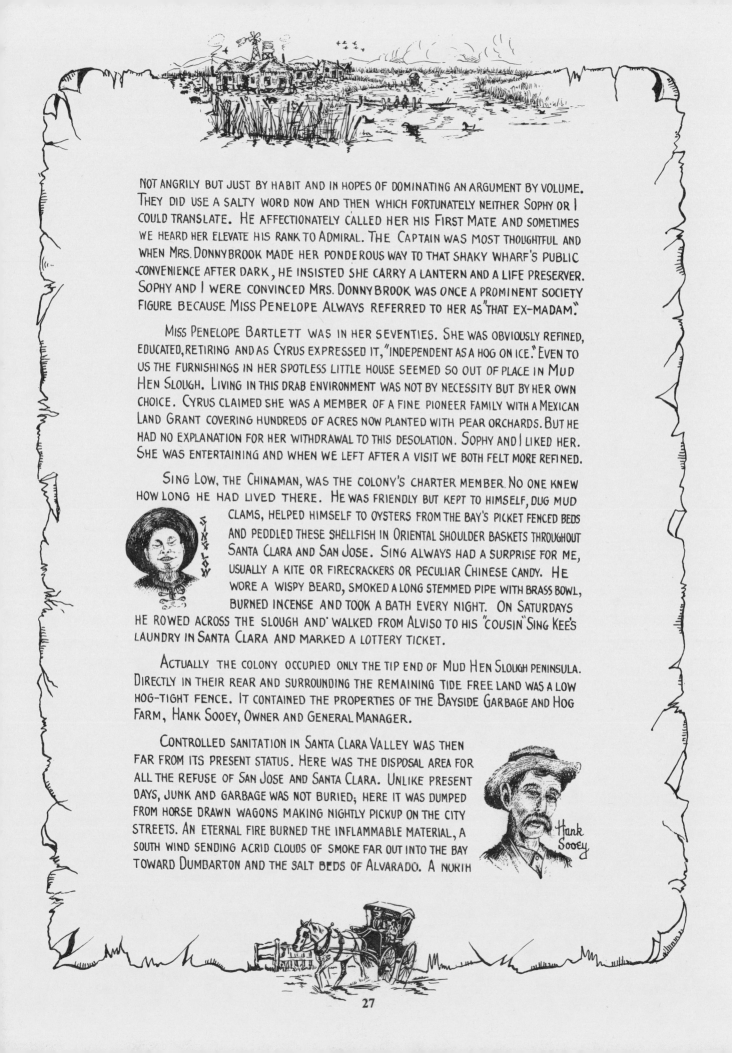

NOT ANGRILY BUT JUST BY HABIT AND IN HOPES OF DOMINATING AN ARGUMENT BY VOLUME. THEY DID USE A SALTY WORD NOW AND THEN WHICH FORTUNATELY NEITHER SOPHY OR I COULD TRANSLATE. HE AFFECTIONATELY CALLED HER HIS FIRST MATE AND SOMETIMES WE HEARD HER ELEVATE HIS RANK TO ADMIRAL. THE CAPTAIN WAS MOST THOUGHTFUL AND WHEN MRS. DONNYBROOK MADE HER PONDEROUS WAY TO THAT SHAKY WHARF'S PUBLIC CONVENIENCE AFTER DARK, HE INSISTED SHE CARRY A LANTERN AND A LIFE PRESERVER. SOPHY AND I WERE CONVINCED MRS. DONNYBROOK WAS ONCE A PROMINENT SOCIETY FIGURE BECAUSE MISS PENELOPE ALWAYS REFERRED TO HER AS "THAT EX-MADAM."

MISS PENELOPE BARTLETT WAS IN HER SEVENTIES. SHE WAS OBVIOUSLY REFINED, EDUCATED, RETIRING AND AS CYRUS EXPRESSED IT, "INDEPENDENT AS A HOG ON ICE." EVEN TO US THE FURNISHINGS IN HER SPOTLESS LITTLE HOUSE SEEMED SO OUT OF PLACE IN MUD HEN SLOUGH. LIVING IN THIS DRAB ENVIRONMENT WAS NOT BY NECESSITY BUT BY HER OWN CHOICE. CYRUS CLAIMED SHE WAS A MEMBER OF A FINE PIONEER FAMILY WITH A MEXICAN LAND GRANT COVERING HUNDREDS OF ACRES NOW PLANTED WITH PEAR ORCHARDS. BUT HE HAD NO EXPLANATION FOR HER WITHDRAWAL TO THIS DESOLATION. SOPHY AND I LIKED HER. SHE WAS ENTERTAINING AND WHEN WE LEFT AFTER A VISIT WE BOTH FELT MORE REFINED.

SING LOW, THE CHINAMAN, WAS THE COLONY'S CHARTER MEMBER. NO ONE KNEW HOW LONG HE HAD LIVED THERE. HE WAS FRIENDLY BUT KEPT TO HIMSELF, DUG MUD CLAMS, HELPED HIMSELF TO OYSTERS FROM THE BAY'S PICKET FENCED BEDS AND PEDDLED THESE SHELLFISH IN ORIENTAL SHOULDER BASKETS THROUGHOUT SANTA CLARA AND SAN JOSE. SING ALWAYS HAD A SURPRISE FOR ME, USUALLY A KITE OR FIRECRACKERS OR PECULIAR CHINESE CANDY. HE WORE A WISPY BEARD, SMOKED A LONG STEMMED PIPE WITH BRASS BOWL, BURNED INCENSE AND TOOK A BATH EVERY NIGHT. ON SATURDAYS HE ROWED ACROSS THE SLOUGH AND WALKED FROM ALVISO TO HIS "COUSIN" SING KEE'S LAUNDRY IN SANTA CLARA AND MARKED A LOTTERY TICKET.

ACTUALLY THE COLONY OCCUPIED ONLY THE TIP END OF MUD HEN SLOUGH PENINSULA. DIRECTLY IN THEIR REAR AND SURROUNDING THE REMAINING TIDE FREE LAND WAS A LOW HOG-TIGHT FENCE. IT CONTAINED THE PROPERTIES OF THE BAYSIDE GARBAGE AND HOG FARM, HANK SOOEY, OWNER AND GENERAL MANAGER.

CONTROLLED SANITATION IN SANTA CLARA VALLEY WAS THEN FAR FROM ITS PRESENT STATUS. HERE WAS THE DISPOSAL AREA FOR ALL THE REFUSE OF SAN JOSE AND SANTA CLARA. UNLIKE PRESENT DAYS, JUNK AND GARBAGE WAS NOT BURIED; HERE IT WAS DUMPED FROM HORSE DRAWN WAGONS MAKING NIGHTLY PICKUP ON THE CITY STREETS. AN ETERNAL FIRE BURNED THE INFLAMMABLE MATERIAL, A SOUTH WIND SENDING ACRID CLOUDS OF SMOKE FAR OUT INTO THE BAY TOWARD DUMBARTON AND THE SALT BEDS OF ALVARADO. A NORTH

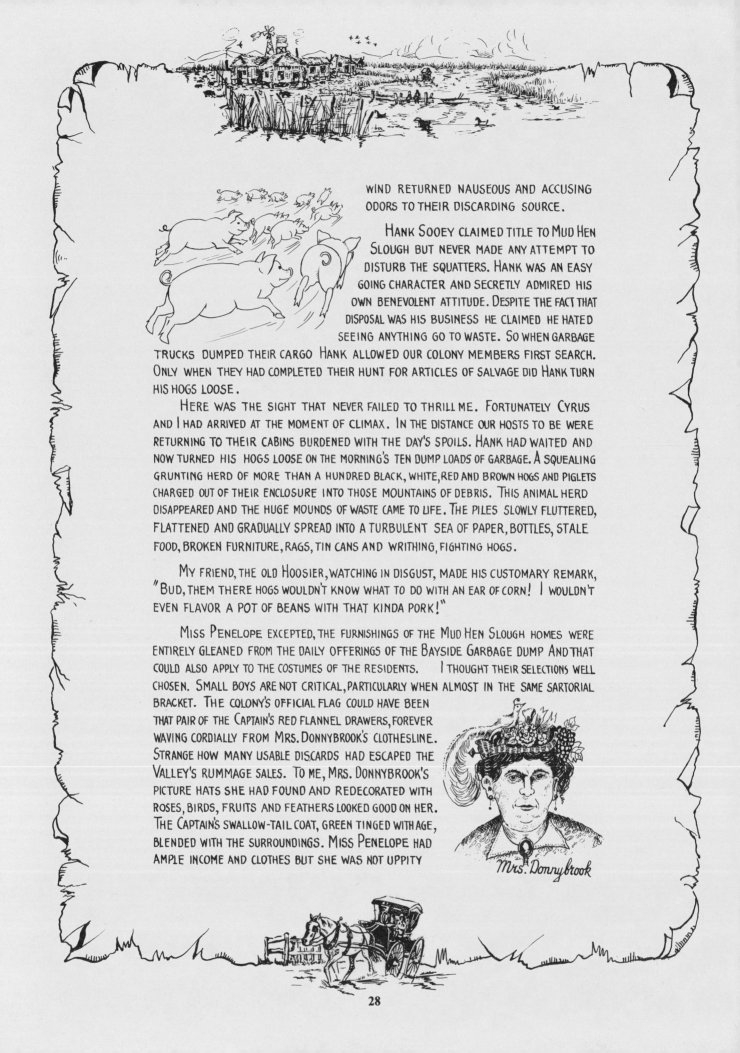

WIND RETURNED NAUSEOUS AND ACCUSING ODORS TO THEIR DISCARDING SOURCE.

HANK SOOEY CLAIMED TITLE TO MUD HEN SLOUGH BUT NEVER MADE ANY ATTEMPT TO DISTURB THE SQUATTERS. HANK WAS AN EASY GOING CHARACTER AND SECRETLY ADMIRED HIS OWN BENEVOLENT ATTITUDE. DESPITE THE FACT THAT DISPOSAL WAS HIS BUSINESS HE CLAIMED HE HATED SEEING ANYTHING GO TO WASTE. SO WHEN GARBAGE TRUCKS DUMPED THEIR CARGO HANK ALLOWED OUR COLONY MEMBERS FIRST SEARCH. ONLY WHEN THEY HAD COMPLETED THEIR HUNT FOR ARTICLES OF SALVAGE DID HANK TURN HIS HOGS LOOSE.

HERE WAS THE SIGHT THAT NEVER FAILED TO THRILL ME. FORTUNATELY CYRUS AND I HAD ARRIVED AT THE MOMENT OF CLIMAX. IN THE DISTANCE OUR HOSTS TO BE WERE RETURNING TO THEIR CABINS BURDENED WITH THE DAY'S SPOILS. HANK HAD WAITED AND NOW TURNED HIS HOGS LOOSE ON THE MORNING'S TEN DUMP LOADS OF GARBAGE. A SQUEALING GRUNTING HERD OF MORE THAN A HUNDRED BLACK, WHITE, RED AND BROWN HOGS AND PIGLETS CHARGED OUT OF THEIR ENCLOSURE INTO THOSE MOUNTAINS OF DEBRIS. THIS ANIMAL HERD DISAPPEARED AND THE HUGE MOUNDS OF WASTE CAME TO LIFE. THE PILES SLOWLY FLUTTERED, FLATTENED AND GRADUALLY SPREAD INTO A TURBULENT SEA OF PAPER, BOTTLES, STALE FOOD, BROKEN FURNITURE, RAGS, TIN CANS AND WRITHING, FIGHTING HOGS.

MY FRIEND, THE OLD HOOSIER, WATCHING IN DISGUST, MADE HIS CUSTOMARY REMARK, "BUD, THEM THERE HOGS WOULDN'T KNOW WHAT TO DO WITH AN EAR OF CORN! I WOULDN'T EVEN FLAVOR A POT OF BEANS WITH THAT KINDA PORK!"

MISS PENELOPE EXCEPTED, THE FURNISHINGS OF THE MUD HEN SLOUGH HOMES WERE ENTIRELY GLEANED FROM THE DAILY OFFERINGS OF THE BAYSIDE GARBAGE DUMP AND THAT COULD ALSO APPLY TO THE COSTUMES OF THE RESIDENTS. I THOUGHT THEIR SELECTIONS WELL CHOSEN. SMALL BOYS ARE NOT CRITICAL, PARTICULARLY WHEN ALMOST IN THE SAME SARTORIAL BRACKET. THE COLONY'S OFFICIAL FLAG COULD HAVE BEEN THAT PAIR OF THE CAPTAIN'S RED FLANNEL DRAWERS, FOREVER WAVING CORDIALLY FROM MRS. DONNYBROOK'S CLOTHESLINE. STRANGE HOW MANY USABLE DISCARDS HAD ESCAPED THE VALLEY'S RUMMAGE SALES. TO ME, MRS. DONNYBROOK'S PICTURE HATS SHE HAD FOUND AND REDECORATED WITH ROSES, BIRDS, FRUITS AND FEATHERS LOOKED GOOD ON HER. THE CAPTAIN'S SWALLOW-TAIL COAT, GREEN TINGED WITH AGE, BLENDED WITH THE SURROUNDINGS. MISS PENELOPE HAD AMPLE INCOME AND CLOTHES BUT SHE WAS NOT UPPITY

Mrs. Donnybrook

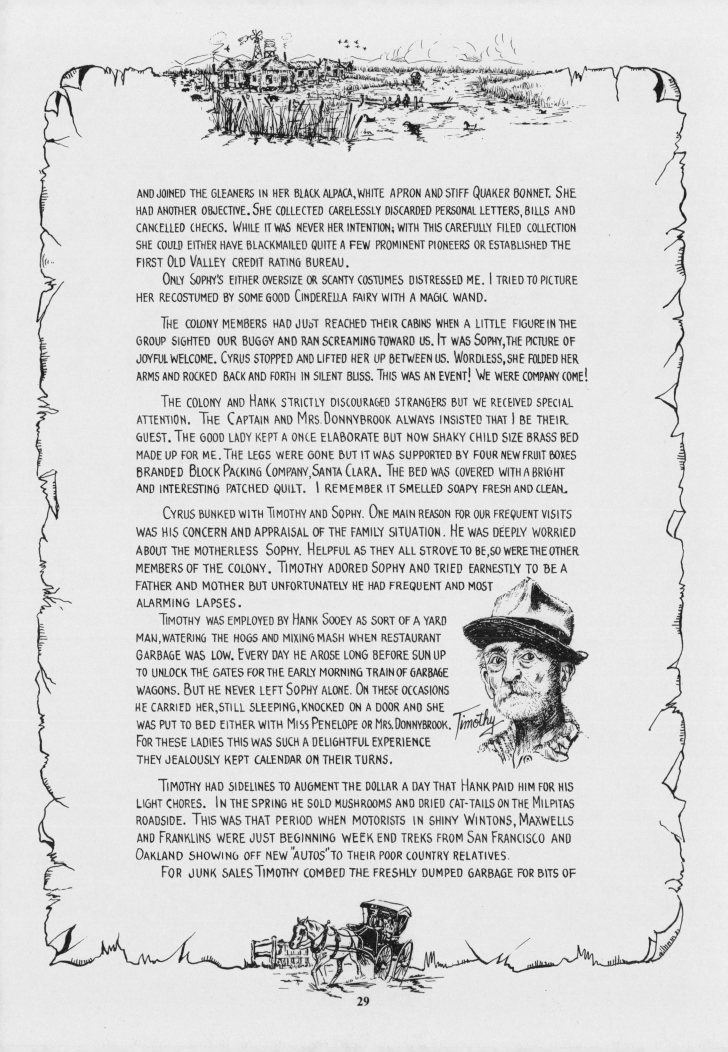

AND JOINED THE GLEANERS IN HER BLACK ALPACA, WHITE APRON AND STIFF QUAKER BONNET. SHE HAD ANOTHER OBJECTIVE. SHE COLLECTED CARELESSLY DISCARDED PERSONAL LETTERS, BILLS AND CANCELLED CHECKS. WHILE IT WAS NEVER HER INTENTION; WITH THIS CAREFULLY FILED COLLECTION SHE COULD EITHER HAVE BLACKMAILED QUITE A FEW PROMINENT PIONEERS OR ESTABLISHED THE FIRST OLD VALLEY CREDIT RATING BUREAU.

ONLY SOPHY'S EITHER OVERSIZE OR SCANTY COSTUMES DISTRESSED ME. I TRIED TO PICTURE HER RECOSTUMED BY SOME GOOD CINDERELLA FAIRY WITH A MAGIC WAND.

THE COLONY MEMBERS HAD JUST REACHED THEIR CABINS WHEN A LITTLE FIGURE IN THE GROUP SIGHTED OUR BUGGY AND RAN SCREAMING TOWARD US. IT WAS SOPHY, THE PICTURE OF JOYFUL WELCOME. CYRUS STOPPED AND LIFTED HER UP BETWEEN US. WORDLESS, SHE FOLDED HER ARMS AND ROCKED BACK AND FORTH IN SILENT BLISS. THIS WAS AN EVENT! WE WERE COMPANY COME!

THE COLONY AND HANK STRICTLY DISCOURAGED STRANGERS BUT WE RECEIVED SPECIAL ATTENTION. THE CAPTAIN AND MRS. DONNYBROOK ALWAYS INSISTED THAT I BE THEIR GUEST. THE GOOD LADY KEPT A ONCE ELABORATE BUT NOW SHAKY CHILD SIZE BRASS BED MADE UP FOR ME. THE LEGS WERE GONE BUT IT WAS SUPPORTED BY FOUR NEW FRUIT BOXES BRANDED BLOCK PACKING COMPANY, SANTA CLARA. THE BED WAS COVERED WITH A BRIGHT AND INTERESTING PATCHED QUILT. I REMEMBER IT SMELLED SOAPY FRESH AND CLEAN.

CYRUS BUNKED WITH TIMOTHY AND SOPHY. ONE MAIN REASON FOR OUR FREQUENT VISITS WAS HIS CONCERN AND APPRAISAL OF THE FAMILY SITUATION. HE WAS DEEPLY WORRIED ABOUT THE MOTHERLESS SOPHY. HELPFUL AS THEY ALL STROVE TO BE, SO WERE THE OTHER MEMBERS OF THE COLONY. TIMOTHY ADORED SOPHY AND TRIED EARNESTLY TO BE A FATHER AND MOTHER BUT UNFORTUNATELY HE HAD FREQUENT AND MOST ALARMING LAPSES.

TIMOTHY WAS EMPLOYED BY HANK SOOEY AS SORT OF A YARD MAN, WATERING THE HOGS AND MIXING MASH WHEN RESTAURANT GARBAGE WAS LOW. EVERY DAY HE AROSE LONG BEFORE SUN UP TO UNLOCK THE GATES FOR THE EARLY MORNING TRAIN OF GARBAGE WAGONS. BUT HE NEVER LEFT SOPHY ALONE. ON THESE OCCASIONS HE CARRIED HER, STILL SLEEPING, KNOCKED ON A DOOR AND SHE WAS PUT TO BED EITHER WITH MISS PENELOPE OR MRS. DONNYBROOK. FOR THESE LADIES THIS WAS SUCH A DELIGHTFUL EXPERIENCE THEY JEALOUSLY KEPT CALENDAR ON THEIR TURNS.

Timothy

TIMOTHY HAD SIDELINES TO AUGMENT THE DOLLAR A DAY THAT HANK PAID HIM FOR HIS LIGHT CHORES. IN THE SPRING HE SOLD MUSHROOMS AND DRIED CAT-TAILS ON THE MILPITAS ROADSIDE. THIS WAS THAT PERIOD WHEN MOTORISTS IN SHINY WINTONS, MAXWELLS AND FRANKLINS WERE JUST BEGINNING WEEK END TREKS FROM SAN FRANCISCO AND OAKLAND SHOWING OFF NEW "AUTOS" TO THEIR POOR COUNTRY RELATIVES.

FOR JUNK SALES TIMOTHY COMBED THE FRESHLY DUMPED GARBAGE FOR BITS OF

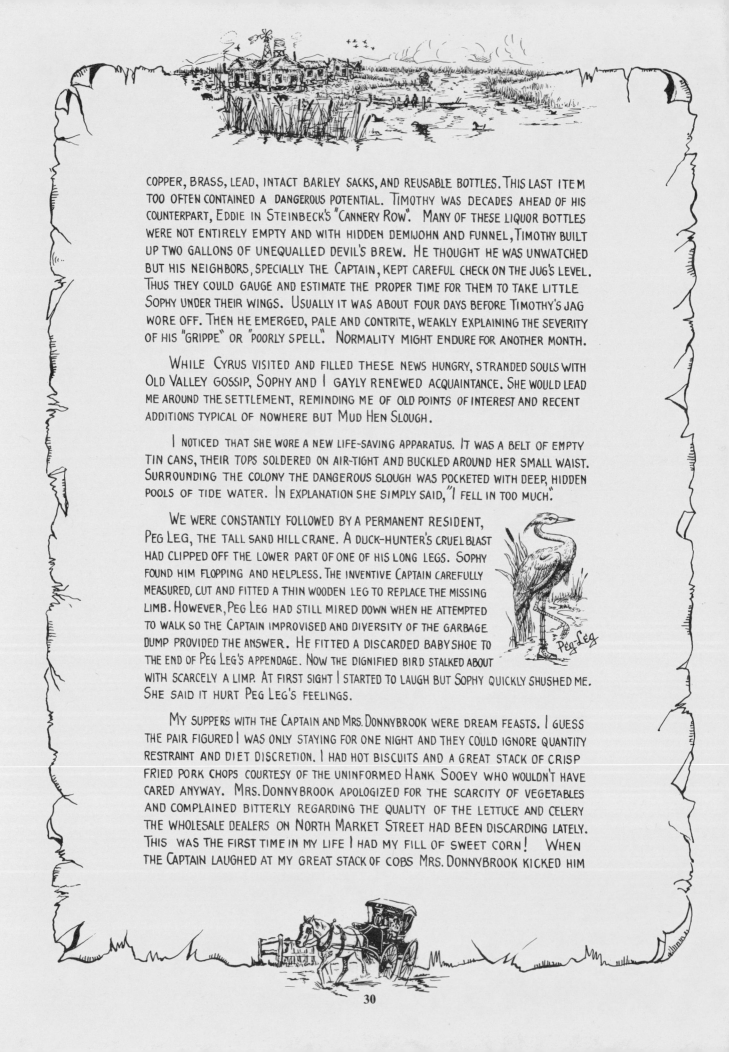

COPPER, BRASS, LEAD, INTACT BARLEY SACKS, AND REUSABLE BOTTLES. THIS LAST ITEM
TOO OFTEN CONTAINED A DANGEROUS POTENTIAL. TIMOTHY WAS DECADES AHEAD OF HIS
COUNTERPART, EDDIE IN STEINBECK'S "CANNERY ROW". MANY OF THESE LIQUOR BOTTLES
WERE NOT ENTIRELY EMPTY AND WITH HIDDEN DEMIJOHN AND FUNNEL, TIMOTHY BUILT
UP TWO GALLONS OF UNEQUALLED DEVIL'S BREW. HE THOUGHT HE WAS UNWATCHED
BUT HIS NEIGHBORS, SPECIALLY THE CAPTAIN, KEPT CAREFUL CHECK ON THE JUG'S LEVEL.
THUS THEY COULD GAUGE AND ESTIMATE THE PROPER TIME FOR THEM TO TAKE LITTLE
SOPHY UNDER THEIR WINGS. USUALLY IT WAS ABOUT FOUR DAYS BEFORE TIMOTHY'S JAG
WORE OFF. THEN HE EMERGED, PALE AND CONTRITE, WEAKLY EXPLAINING THE SEVERITY
OF HIS "GRIPPE" OR "POORLY SPELL". NORMALITY MIGHT ENDURE FOR ANOTHER MONTH.

WHILE CYRUS VISITED AND FILLED THESE NEWS HUNGRY, STRANDED SOULS WITH
OLD VALLEY GOSSIP, SOPHY AND I GAYLY RENEWED ACQUAINTANCE. SHE WOULD LEAD
ME AROUND THE SETTLEMENT, REMINDING ME OF OLD POINTS OF INTEREST AND RECENT
ADDITIONS TYPICAL OF NOWHERE BUT MUD HEN SLOUGH.

I NOTICED THAT SHE WORE A NEW LIFE-SAVING APPARATUS. IT WAS A BELT OF EMPTY
TIN CANS, THEIR TOPS SOLDERED ON AIR-TIGHT AND BUCKLED AROUND HER SMALL WAIST.
SURROUNDING THE COLONY THE DANGEROUS SLOUGH WAS POCKETED WITH DEEP, HIDDEN
POOLS OF TIDE WATER. IN EXPLANATION SHE SIMPLY SAID, "I FELL IN TOO MUCH."

WE WERE CONSTANTLY FOLLOWED BY A PERMANENT RESIDENT,
PEG LEG, THE TALL SAND HILL CRANE. A DUCK-HUNTER'S CRUEL BLAST
HAD CLIPPED OFF THE LOWER PART OF ONE OF HIS LONG LEGS. SOPHY
FOUND HIM FLOPPING AND HELPLESS. THE INVENTIVE CAPTAIN CAREFULLY
MEASURED, CUT AND FITTED A THIN WOODEN LEG TO REPLACE THE MISSING
LIMB. HOWEVER, PEG LEG HAD STILL MIRED DOWN WHEN HE ATTEMPTED
TO WALK SO THE CAPTAIN IMPROVISED AND DIVERSITY OF THE GARBAGE
DUMP PROVIDED THE ANSWER. HE FITTED A DISCARDED BABY SHOE TO
THE END OF PEG LEG'S APPENDAGE. NOW THE DIGNIFIED BIRD STALKED ABOUT

Peg-Leg

WITH SCARCELY A LIMP. AT FIRST SIGHT I STARTED TO LAUGH BUT SOPHY QUICKLY SHUSHED ME.
SHE SAID IT HURT PEG LEG'S FEELINGS.

MY SUPPERS WITH THE CAPTAIN AND MRS. DONNYBROOK WERE DREAM FEASTS. I GUESS
THE PAIR FIGURED I WAS ONLY STAYING FOR ONE NIGHT AND THEY COULD IGNORE QUANTITY
RESTRAINT AND DIET DISCRETION. I HAD HOT BISCUITS AND A GREAT STACK OF CRISP
FRIED PORK CHOPS COURTESY OF THE UNINFORMED HANK SOOEY WHO WOULDN'T HAVE
CARED ANYWAY. MRS. DONNYBROOK APOLOGIZED FOR THE SCARCITY OF VEGETABLES
AND COMPLAINED BITTERLY REGARDING THE QUALITY OF THE LETTUCE AND CELERY
THE WHOLESALE DEALERS ON NORTH MARKET STREET HAD BEEN DISCARDING LATELY.
THIS WAS THE FIRST TIME IN MY LIFE I HAD MY FILL OF SWEET CORN! WHEN
THE CAPTAIN LAUGHED AT MY GREAT STACK OF COBS MRS. DONNYBROOK KICKED HIM

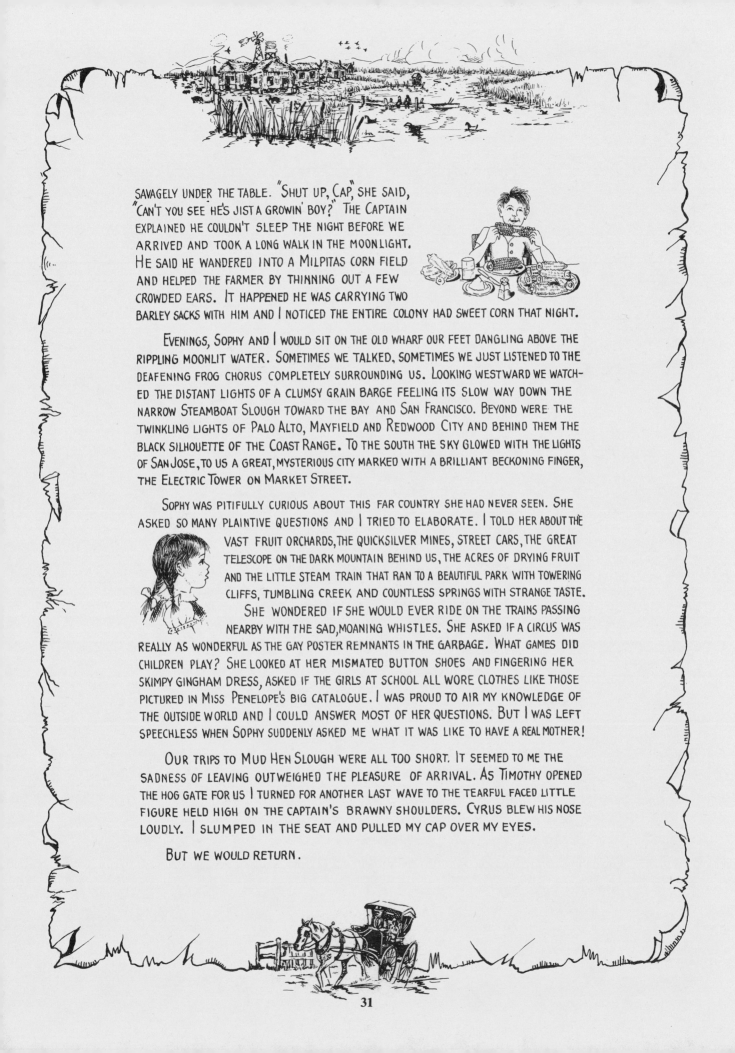

SAVAGELY UNDER THE TABLE. "SHUT UP, CAP," SHE SAID,
"CAN'T YOU SEE HE'S JIST A GROWIN' BOY?" THE CAPTAIN
EXPLAINED HE COULDN'T SLEEP THE NIGHT BEFORE WE
ARRIVED AND TOOK A LONG WALK IN THE MOONLIGHT.
HE SAID HE WANDERED INTO A MILPITAS CORN FIELD
AND HELPED THE FARMER BY THINNING OUT A FEW
CROWDED EARS. IT HAPPENED HE WAS CARRYING TWO
BARLEY SACKS WITH HIM AND I NOTICED THE ENTIRE COLONY HAD SWEET CORN THAT NIGHT.

EVENINGS, SOPHY AND I WOULD SIT ON THE OLD WHARF OUR FEET DANGLING ABOVE THE
RIPPLING MOONLIT WATER. SOMETIMES WE TALKED, SOMETIMES WE JUST LISTENED TO THE
DEAFENING FROG CHORUS COMPLETELY SURROUNDING US. LOOKING WESTWARD WE WATCH-
ED THE DISTANT LIGHTS OF A CLUMSY GRAIN BARGE FEELING ITS SLOW WAY DOWN THE
NARROW STEAMBOAT SLOUGH TOWARD THE BAY AND SAN FRANCISCO. BEYOND WERE THE
TWINKLING LIGHTS OF PALO ALTO, MAYFIELD AND REDWOOD CITY AND BEHIND THEM THE
BLACK SILHOUETTE OF THE COAST RANGE. TO THE SOUTH THE SKY GLOWED WITH THE LIGHTS
OF SAN JOSE, TO US A GREAT, MYSTERIOUS CITY MARKED WITH A BRILLIANT BECKONING FINGER,
THE ELECTRIC TOWER ON MARKET STREET.

SOPHY WAS PITIFULLY CURIOUS ABOUT THIS FAR COUNTRY SHE HAD NEVER SEEN. SHE
ASKED SO MANY PLAINTIVE QUESTIONS AND I TRIED TO ELABORATE. I TOLD HER ABOUT THE
VAST FRUIT ORCHARDS, THE QUICKSILVER MINES, STREET CARS, THE GREAT
TELESCOPE ON THE DARK MOUNTAIN BEHIND US, THE ACRES OF DRYING FRUIT
AND THE LITTLE STEAM TRAIN THAT RAN TO A BEAUTIFUL PARK WITH TOWERING
CLIFFS, TUMBLING CREEK AND COUNTLESS SPRINGS WITH STRANGE TASTE.

SHE WONDERED IF SHE WOULD EVER RIDE ON THE TRAINS PASSING
NEARBY WITH THE SAD, MOANING WHISTLES. SHE ASKED IF A CIRCUS WAS
REALLY AS WONDERFUL AS THE GAY POSTER REMNANTS IN THE GARBAGE. WHAT GAMES DID
CHILDREN PLAY? SHE LOOKED AT HER MISMATED BUTTON SHOES AND FINGERING HER
SKIMPY GINGHAM DRESS, ASKED IF THE GIRLS AT SCHOOL ALL WORE CLOTHES LIKE THOSE
PICTURED IN MISS PENELOPE'S BIG CATALOGUE. I WAS PROUD TO AIR MY KNOWLEDGE OF
THE OUTSIDE WORLD AND I COULD ANSWER MOST OF HER QUESTIONS. BUT I WAS LEFT
SPEECHLESS WHEN SOPHY SUDDENLY ASKED ME WHAT IT WAS LIKE TO HAVE A REAL MOTHER!

OUR TRIPS TO MUD HEN SLOUGH WERE ALL TOO SHORT. IT SEEMED TO ME THE
SADNESS OF LEAVING OUTWEIGHED THE PLEASURE OF ARRIVAL. AS TIMOTHY OPENED
THE HOG GATE FOR US I TURNED FOR ANOTHER LAST WAVE TO THE TEARFUL FACED LITTLE
FIGURE HELD HIGH ON THE CAPTAIN'S BRAWNY SHOULDERS. CYRUS BLEW HIS NOSE
LOUDLY. I SLUMPED IN THE SEAT AND PULLED MY CAP OVER MY EYES.

BUT WE WOULD RETURN.

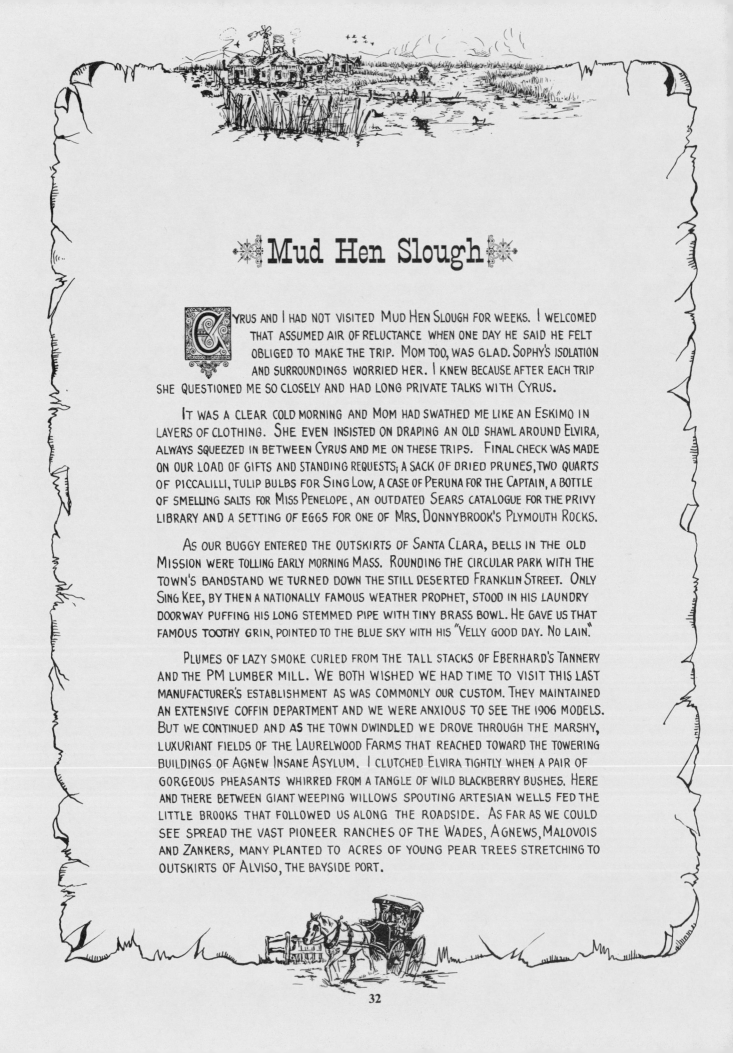

❊Mud Hen Slough❊

CYRUS AND I HAD NOT VISITED MUD HEN SLOUGH FOR WEEKS. I WELCOMED THAT ASSUMED AIR OF RELUCTANCE WHEN ONE DAY HE SAID HE FELT OBLIGED TO MAKE THE TRIP. MOM TOO, WAS GLAD. SOPHY'S ISOLATION AND SURROUNDINGS WORRIED HER. I KNEW BECAUSE AFTER EACH TRIP SHE QUESTIONED ME SO CLOSELY AND HAD LONG PRIVATE TALKS WITH CYRUS.

IT WAS A CLEAR COLD MORNING AND MOM HAD SWATHED ME LIKE AN ESKIMO IN LAYERS OF CLOTHING. SHE EVEN INSISTED ON DRAPING AN OLD SHAWL AROUND ELVIRA, ALWAYS SQUEEZED IN BETWEEN CYRUS AND ME ON THESE TRIPS. FINAL CHECK WAS MADE ON OUR LOAD OF GIFTS AND STANDING REQUESTS; A SACK OF DRIED PRUNES, TWO QUARTS OF PICCALILLI, TULIP BULBS FOR SING LOW, A CASE OF PERUNA FOR THE CAPTAIN, A BOTTLE OF SMELLING SALTS FOR MISS PENELOPE, AN OUTDATED SEARS CATALOGUE FOR THE PRIVY LIBRARY AND A SETTING OF EGGS FOR ONE OF MRS. DONNYBROOK'S PLYMOUTH ROCKS.

AS OUR BUGGY ENTERED THE OUTSKIRTS OF SANTA CLARA, BELLS IN THE OLD MISSION WERE TOLLING EARLY MORNING MASS. ROUNDING THE CIRCULAR PARK WITH THE TOWN'S BANDSTAND WE TURNED DOWN THE STILL DESERTED FRANKLIN STREET. ONLY SING KEE, BY THEN A NATIONALLY FAMOUS WEATHER PROPHET, STOOD IN HIS LAUNDRY DOORWAY PUFFING HIS LONG STEMMED PIPE WITH TINY BRASS BOWL. HE GAVE US THAT FAMOUS TOOTHY GRIN, POINTED TO THE BLUE SKY WITH HIS "VELLY GOOD DAY. NO LAIN."

PLUMES OF LAZY SMOKE CURLED FROM THE TALL STACKS OF EBERHARD'S TANNERY AND THE PM LUMBER MILL. WE BOTH WISHED WE HAD TIME TO VISIT THIS LAST MANUFACTURER'S ESTABLISHMENT AS WAS COMMONLY OUR CUSTOM. THEY MAINTAINED AN EXTENSIVE COFFIN DEPARTMENT AND WE WERE ANXIOUS TO SEE THE 1906 MODELS. BUT WE CONTINUED AND AS THE TOWN DWINDLED WE DROVE THROUGH THE MARSHY, LUXURIANT FIELDS OF THE LAURELWOOD FARMS THAT REACHED TOWARD THE TOWERING BUILDINGS OF AGNEW INSANE ASYLUM. I CLUTCHED ELVIRA TIGHTLY WHEN A PAIR OF GORGEOUS PHEASANTS WHIRRED FROM A TANGLE OF WILD BLACKBERRY BUSHES. HERE AND THERE BETWEEN GIANT WEEPING WILLOWS SPOUTING ARTESIAN WELLS FED THE LITTLE BROOKS THAT FOLLOWED US ALONG THE ROADSIDE. AS FAR AS WE COULD SEE SPREAD THE VAST PIONEER RANCHES OF THE WADES, AGNEWS, MALOVOIS AND ZANKERS, MANY PLANTED TO ACRES OF YOUNG PEAR TREES STRETCHING TO OUTSKIRTS OF ALVISO, THE BAYSIDE PORT.

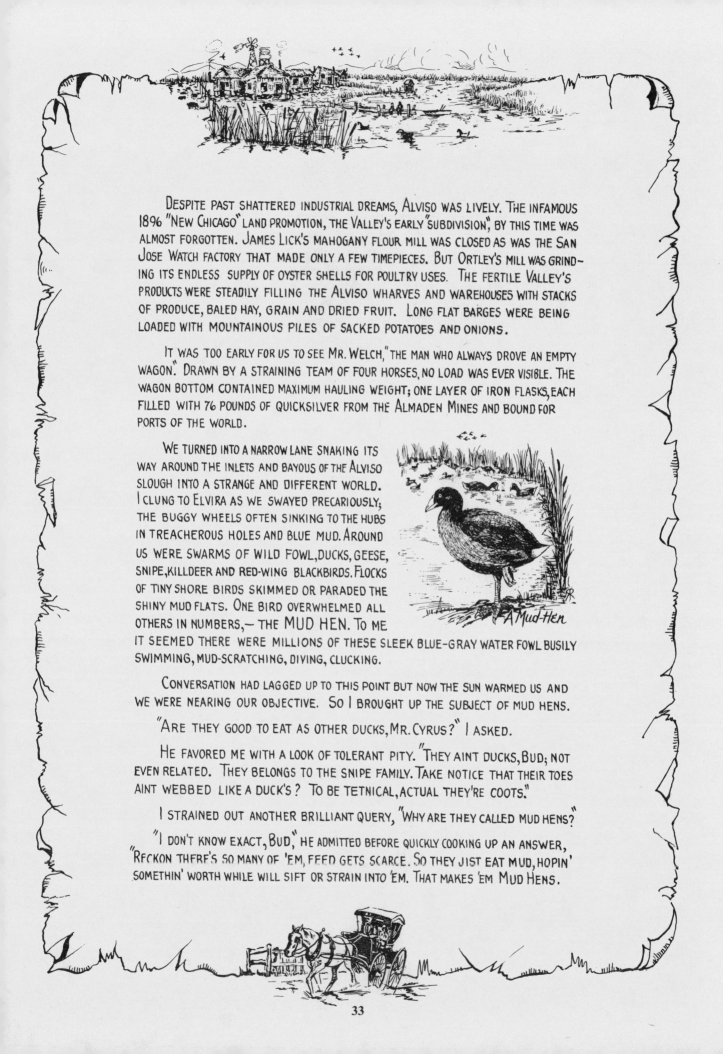

Despite past shattered industrial dreams, Alviso was lively. The infamous 1896 "New Chicago" land promotion, the Valley's early "subdivision", by this time was almost forgotten. James Lick's mahogany flour mill was closed as was the San Jose Watch factory that made only a few timepieces. But Ortley's mill was grinding its endless supply of oyster shells for poultry uses. The fertile Valley's products were steadily filling the Alviso wharves and warehouses with stacks of produce, baled hay, grain and dried fruit. Long flat barges were being loaded with mountainous piles of sacked potatoes and onions.

It was too early for us to see Mr. Welch, "the man who always drove an empty wagon". Drawn by a straining team of four horses, no load was ever visible. The wagon bottom contained maximum hauling weight; one layer of iron flasks, each filled with 76 pounds of quicksilver from the Almaden Mines and bound for ports of the world.

We turned into a narrow lane snaking its way around the inlets and bayous of the Alviso Slough into a strange and different world. I clung to Elvira as we swayed precariously; the buggy wheels often sinking to the hubs in treacherous holes and blue mud. Around us were swarms of wild fowl, ducks, geese, snipe, killdeer and red-wing blackbirds. Flocks of tiny shore birds skimmed or paraded the shiny mud flats. One bird overwhelmed all others in numbers,— the MUD HEN. To me it seemed there were millions of these sleek blue-gray water fowl busily swimming, mud-scratching, diving, clucking.

F A Mud-Hen

Conversation had lagged up to this point but now the sun warmed us and we were nearing our objective. So I brought up the subject of mud hens.

"Are they good to eat as other ducks, Mr. Cyrus?" I asked.

He favored me with a look of tolerant pity. "They aint ducks, Bud; not even related. They belongs to the snipe family. Take notice that their toes aint webbed like a duck's? To be tetnical, actual they're coots."

I strained out another brilliant query, "Why are they called mud hens?"

"I don't know exact, Bud," he admitted before quickly cooking up an answer, "Reckon there's so many of 'em, feed gets scarce. So they jist eat mud, hopin' somethin' worth while will sift or strain into 'em. That makes 'em Mud Hens.

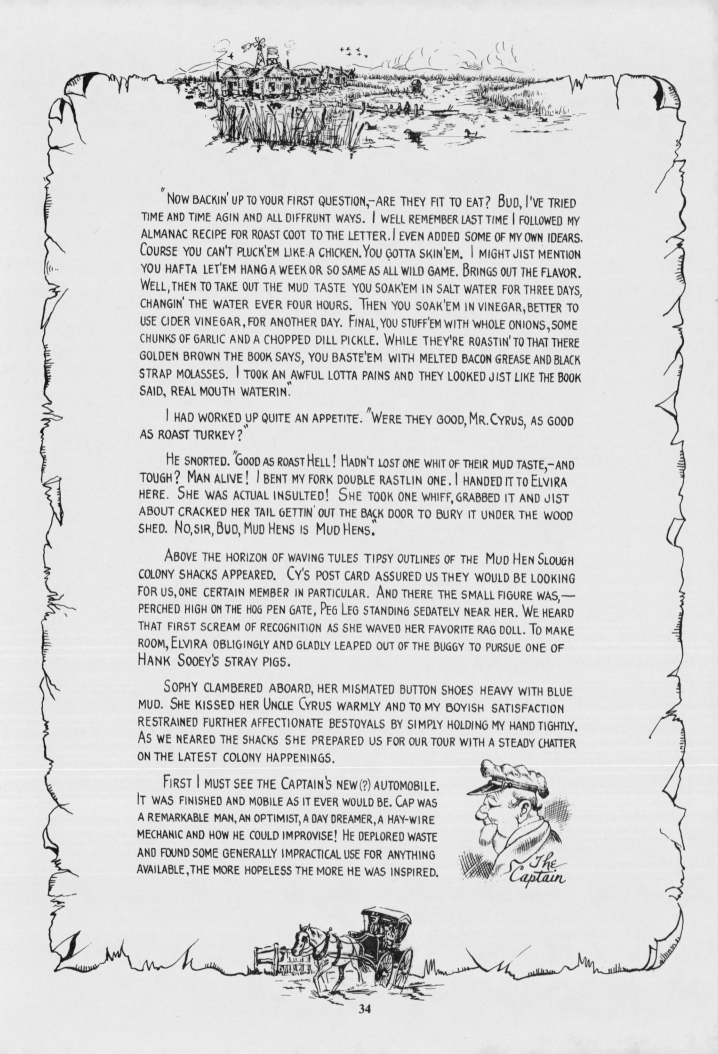

"Now backin' up to your first question,—are they fit to eat? Bud, I've tried time and time agin and all diffrunt ways. I well remember last time I followed my almanac recipe for roast coot to the letter. I even added some of my own idears. Course you can't pluck'em like a chicken. You gotta skin'em. I might jist mention you hafta let'em hang a week or so same as all wild game. Brings out the flavor. Well, then to take out the mud taste you soak'em in salt water for three days, changin' the water ever four hours. Then you soak'em in vinegar, better to use cider vinegar, for another day. Final, you stuff'em with whole onions, some chunks of garlic and a chopped dill pickle. While they're roastin' to that there golden brown the book says, you baste'em with melted bacon grease and black strap molasses. I took an awful lotta pains and they looked jist like the book said, real mouth waterin."

I had worked up quite an appetite. "Were they good, Mr. Cyrus, as good as roast turkey?"

He snorted. "Good as roast Hell! Hadn't lost one whit of their mud taste,—and tough? Man alive! I bent my fork double rastlin one. I handed it to Elvira here. She was actual insulted! She took one whiff, grabbed it and jist about cracked her tail gettin' out the back door to bury it under the wood shed. No, sir, Bud, Mud Hens is Mud Hens."

Above the horizon of waving tules tipsy outlines of the Mud Hen Slough colony shacks appeared. Cy's post card assured us they would be looking for us, one certain member in particular. And there the small figure was,— perched high on the hog pen gate, Peg Leg standing sedately near her. We heard that first scream of recognition as she waved her favorite rag doll. To make room, Elvira obligingly and gladly leaped out of the buggy to pursue one of Hank Sooey's stray pigs.

Sophy clambered aboard, her mismated button shoes heavy with blue mud. She kissed her Uncle Cyrus warmly and to my boyish satisfaction restrained further affectionate bestoyals by simply holding my hand tightly. As we neared the shacks she prepared us for our tour with a steady chatter on the latest colony happenings.

First I must see the Captain's new (?) automobile. It was finished and mobile as it ever would be. Cap was a remarkable man, an optimist, a day dreamer, a hay-wire mechanic and how he could improvise! He deplored waste and found some generally impractical use for anything available, the more hopeless the more he was inspired.

The Captain

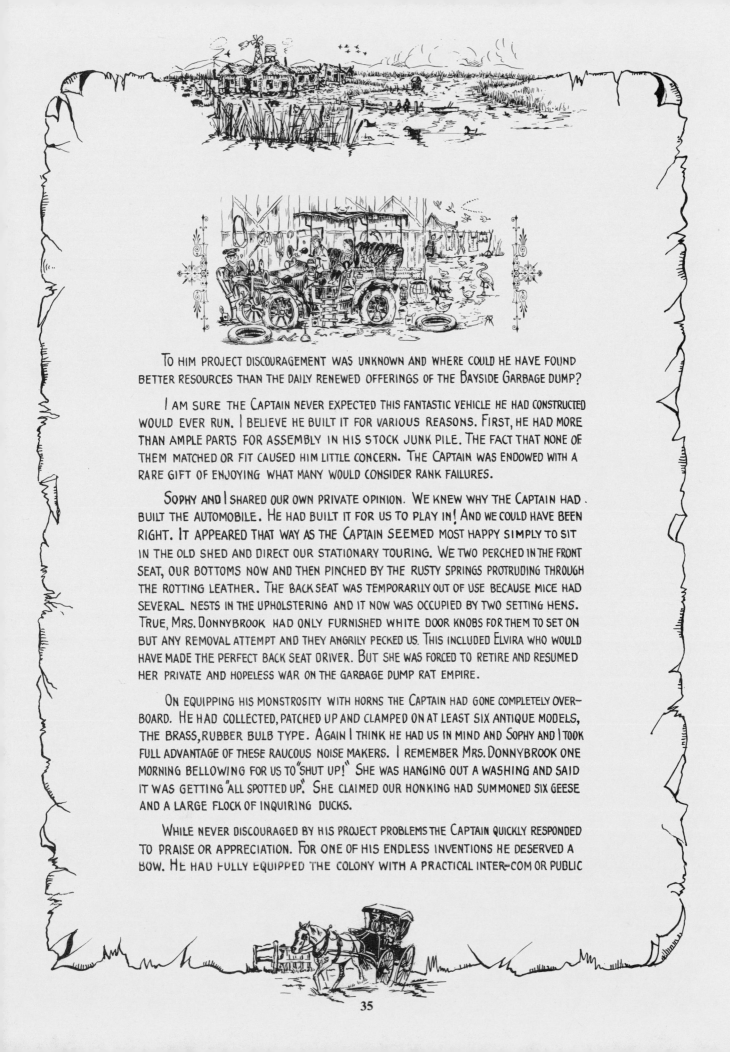

To him project discouragement was unknown and where could he have found better resources than the daily renewed offerings of the Bayside Garbage dump?

I am sure the Captain never expected this fantastic vehicle he had constructed would ever run. I believe he built it for various reasons. First, he had more than ample parts for assembly in his stock junk pile. The fact that none of them matched or fit caused him little concern. The Captain was endowed with a rare gift of enjoying what many would consider rank failures.

Sophy and I shared our own private opinion. We knew why the Captain had built the automobile. He had built it for us to play in! And we could have been right. It appeared that way as the Captain seemed most happy simply to sit in the old shed and direct our stationary touring. We two perched in the front seat, our bottoms now and then pinched by the rusty springs protruding through the rotting leather. The back seat was temporarily out of use because mice had several nests in the upholstering and it now was occupied by two setting hens. True, Mrs. Donnybrook had only furnished white door knobs for them to set on but any removal attempt and they angrily pecked us. This included Elvira who would have made the perfect back seat driver. But she was forced to retire and resumed her private and hopeless war on the garbage dump rat empire.

On equipping his monstrosity with horns the Captain had gone completely over-board. He had collected, patched up and clamped on at least six antique models, the brass, rubber bulb type. Again I think he had us in mind and Sophy and I took full advantage of these raucous noise makers. I remember Mrs. Donnybrook one morning bellowing for us to "shut up!" She was hanging out a washing and said it was getting "all spotted up". She claimed our honking had summoned six geese and a large flock of inquiring ducks.

While never discouraged by his project problems the Captain quickly responded to praise or appreciation. For one of his endless inventions he deserved a bow. He had fully equipped the colony with a practical inter-com or public

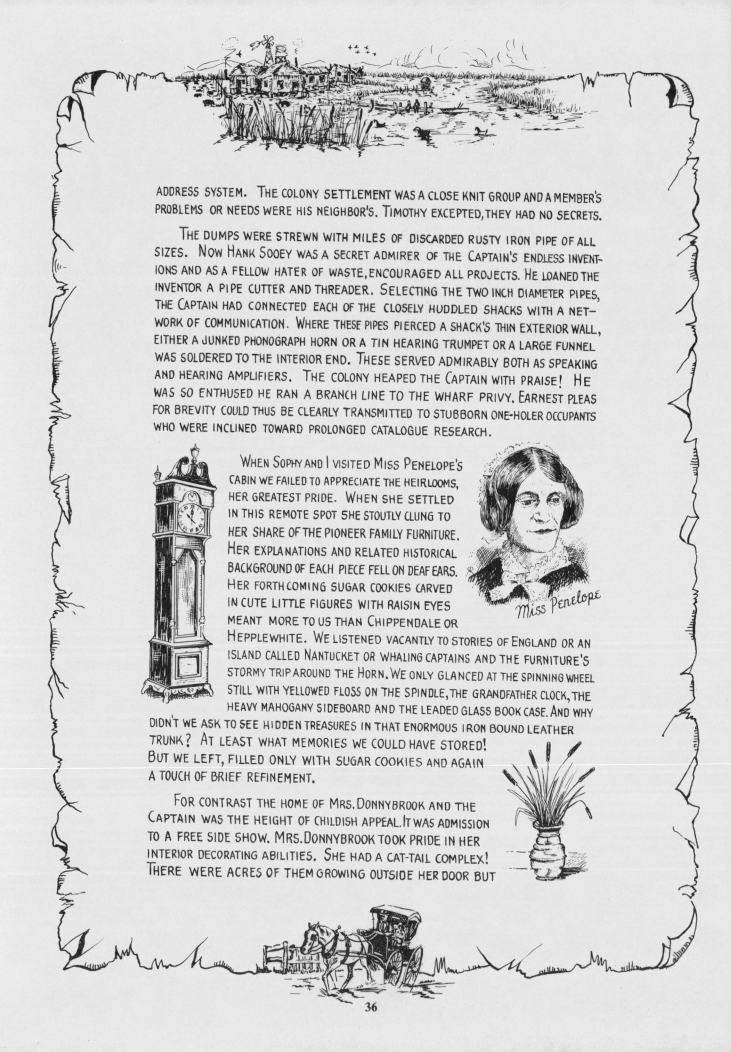

ADDRESS SYSTEM. THE COLONY SETTLEMENT WAS A CLOSE KNIT GROUP AND A MEMBER'S PROBLEMS OR NEEDS WERE HIS NEIGHBOR'S. TIMOTHY EXCEPTED, THEY HAD NO SECRETS.

THE DUMPS WERE STREWN WITH MILES OF DISCARDED RUSTY IRON PIPE OF ALL SIZES. NOW HANK SOOEY WAS A SECRET ADMIRER OF THE CAPTAIN'S ENDLESS INVENTIONS AND AS A FELLOW HATER OF WASTE, ENCOURAGED ALL PROJECTS. HE LOANED THE INVENTOR A PIPE CUTTER AND THREADER. SELECTING THE TWO INCH DIAMETER PIPES, THE CAPTAIN HAD CONNECTED EACH OF THE CLOSELY HUDDLED SHACKS WITH A NETWORK OF COMMUNICATION. WHERE THESE PIPES PIERCED A SHACK'S THIN EXTERIOR WALL, EITHER A JUNKED PHONOGRAPH HORN OR A TIN HEARING TRUMPET OR A LARGE FUNNEL WAS SOLDERED TO THE INTERIOR END. THESE SERVED ADMIRABLY BOTH AS SPEAKING AND HEARING AMPLIFIERS. THE COLONY HEAPED THE CAPTAIN WITH PRAISE! HE WAS SO ENTHUSED HE RAN A BRANCH LINE TO THE WHARF PRIVY. EARNEST PLEAS FOR BREVITY COULD THUS BE CLEARLY TRANSMITTED TO STUBBORN ONE-HOLER OCCUPANTS WHO WERE INCLINED TOWARD PROLONGED CATALOGUE RESEARCH.

WHEN SOPHY AND I VISITED MISS PENELOPE'S CABIN WE FAILED TO APPRECIATE THE HEIRLOOMS, HER GREATEST PRIDE. WHEN SHE SETTLED IN THIS REMOTE SPOT SHE STOUTLY CLUNG TO HER SHARE OF THE PIONEER FAMILY FURNITURE. HER EXPLANATIONS AND RELATED HISTORICAL BACKGROUND OF EACH PIECE FELL ON DEAF EARS. HER FORTHCOMING SUGAR COOKIES CARVED IN CUTE LITTLE FIGURES WITH RAISIN EYES MEANT MORE TO US THAN CHIPPENDALE OR HEPPLEWHITE. WE LISTENED VACANTLY TO STORIES OF ENGLAND OR AN ISLAND CALLED NANTUCKET OR WHALING CAPTAINS AND THE FURNITURE'S STORMY TRIP AROUND THE HORN. WE ONLY GLANCED AT THE SPINNING WHEEL STILL WITH YELLOWED FLOSS ON THE SPINDLE, THE GRANDFATHER CLOCK, THE HEAVY MAHOGANY SIDEBOARD AND THE LEADED GLASS BOOK CASE. AND WHY DIDN'T WE ASK TO SEE HIDDEN TREASURES IN THAT ENORMOUS IRON BOUND LEATHER TRUNK? AT LEAST WHAT MEMORIES WE COULD HAVE STORED! BUT WE LEFT, FILLED ONLY WITH SUGAR COOKIES AND AGAIN A TOUCH OF BRIEF REFINEMENT.

Miss Penelope

FOR CONTRAST THE HOME OF MRS. DONNYBROOK AND THE CAPTAIN WAS THE HEIGHT OF CHILDISH APPEAL. IT WAS ADMISSION TO A FREE SIDE SHOW. MRS. DONNYBROOK TOOK PRIDE IN HER INTERIOR DECORATING ABILITIES. SHE HAD A CAT-TAIL COMPLEX! THERE WERE ACRES OF THEM GROWING OUTSIDE HER DOOR BUT

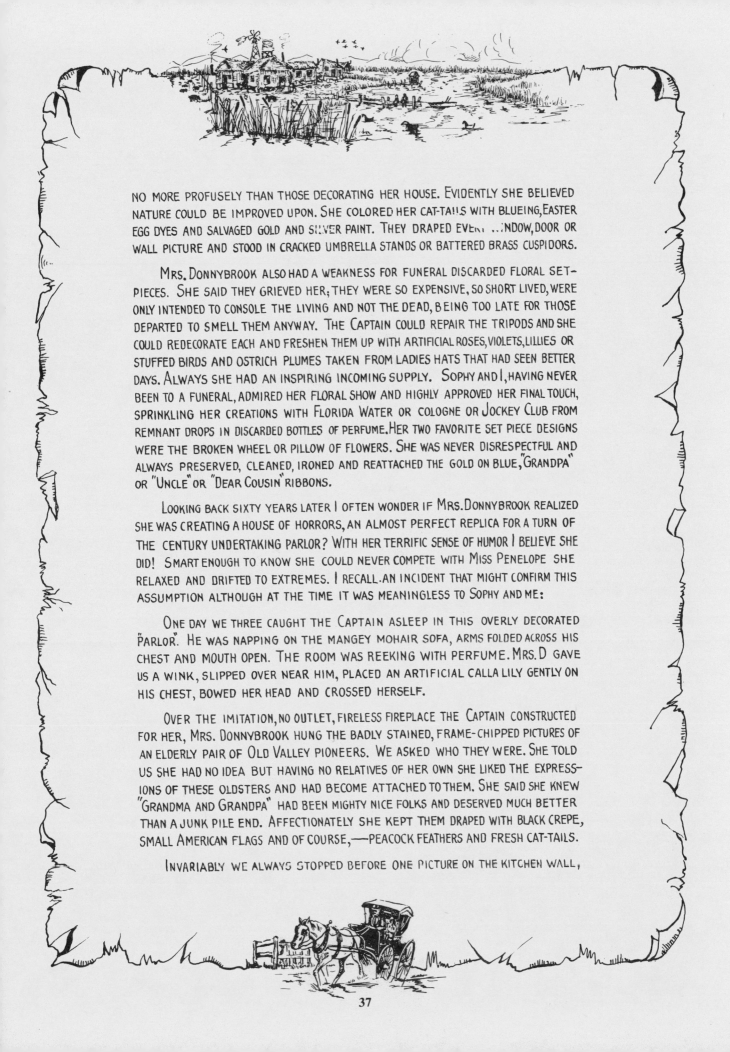

NO MORE PROFUSELY THAN THOSE DECORATING HER HOUSE. EVIDENTLY SHE BELIEVED NATURE COULD BE IMPROVED UPON. SHE COLORED HER CAT-TAILS WITH BLUEING, EASTER EGG DYES AND SALVAGED GOLD AND SILVER PAINT. THEY DRAPED EVERY WINDOW, DOOR OR WALL PICTURE AND STOOD IN CRACKED UMBRELLA STANDS OR BATTERED BRASS CUSPIDORS.

MRS. DONNYBROOK ALSO HAD A WEAKNESS FOR FUNERAL DISCARDED FLORAL SET-PIECES. SHE SAID THEY GRIEVED HER; THEY WERE SO EXPENSIVE, SO SHORT LIVED, WERE ONLY INTENDED TO CONSOLE THE LIVING AND NOT THE DEAD, BEING TOO LATE FOR THOSE DEPARTED TO SMELL THEM ANYWAY. THE CAPTAIN COULD REPAIR THE TRIPODS AND SHE COULD REDECORATE EACH AND FRESHEN THEM UP WITH ARTIFICIAL ROSES, VIOLETS, LILLIES OR STUFFED BIRDS AND OSTRICH PLUMES TAKEN FROM LADIES HATS THAT HAD SEEN BETTER DAYS. ALWAYS SHE HAD AN INSPIRING INCOMING SUPPLY. SOPHY AND I, HAVING NEVER BEEN TO A FUNERAL, ADMIRED HER FLORAL SHOW AND HIGHLY APPROVED HER FINAL TOUCH, SPRINKLING HER CREATIONS WITH FLORIDA WATER OR COLOGNE OR JOCKEY CLUB FROM REMNANT DROPS IN DISCARDED BOTTLES OF PERFUME. HER TWO FAVORITE SET PIECE DESIGNS WERE THE BROKEN WHEEL OR PILLOW OF FLOWERS. SHE WAS NEVER DISRESPECTFUL AND ALWAYS PRESERVED, CLEANED, IRONED AND REATTACHED THE GOLD ON BLUE, "GRANDPA" OR "UNCLE" OR "DEAR COUSIN" RIBBONS.

LOOKING BACK SIXTY YEARS LATER I OFTEN WONDER IF MRS. DONNYBROOK REALIZED SHE WAS CREATING A HOUSE OF HORRORS, AN ALMOST PERFECT REPLICA FOR A TURN OF THE CENTURY UNDERTAKING PARLOR? WITH HER TERRIFIC SENSE OF HUMOR I BELIEVE SHE DID! SMART ENOUGH TO KNOW SHE COULD NEVER COMPETE WITH MISS PENELOPE SHE RELAXED AND DRIFTED TO EXTREMES. I RECALL AN INCIDENT THAT MIGHT CONFIRM THIS ASSUMPTION ALTHOUGH AT THE TIME IT WAS MEANINGLESS TO SOPHY AND ME:

ONE DAY WE THREE CAUGHT THE CAPTAIN ASLEEP IN THIS OVERLY DECORATED "PARLOR". HE WAS NAPPING ON THE MANGEY MOHAIR SOFA, ARMS FOLDED ACROSS HIS CHEST AND MOUTH OPEN. THE ROOM WAS REEKING WITH PERFUME. MRS. D GAVE US A WINK, SLIPPED OVER NEAR HIM, PLACED AN ARTIFICIAL CALLA LILY GENTLY ON HIS CHEST, BOWED HER HEAD AND CROSSED HERSELF.

OVER THE IMITATION, NO OUTLET, FIRELESS FIREPLACE THE CAPTAIN CONSTRUCTED FOR HER, MRS. DONNYBROOK HUNG THE BADLY STAINED, FRAME-CHIPPED PICTURES OF AN ELDERLY PAIR OF OLD VALLEY PIONEERS. WE ASKED WHO THEY WERE. SHE TOLD US SHE HAD NO IDEA BUT HAVING NO RELATIVES OF HER OWN SHE LIKED THE EXPRESS-IONS OF THESE OLDSTERS AND HAD BECOME ATTACHED TO THEM. SHE SAID SHE KNEW "GRANDMA AND GRANDPA" HAD BEEN MIGHTY NICE FOLKS AND DESERVED MUCH BETTER THAN A JUNK PILE END. AFFECTIONATELY SHE KEPT THEM DRAPED WITH BLACK CREPE, SMALL AMERICAN FLAGS AND OF COURSE, —PEACOCK FEATHERS AND FRESH CAT-TAILS.

INVARIABLY WE ALWAYS STOPPED BEFORE ONE PICTURE ON THE KITCHEN WALL,

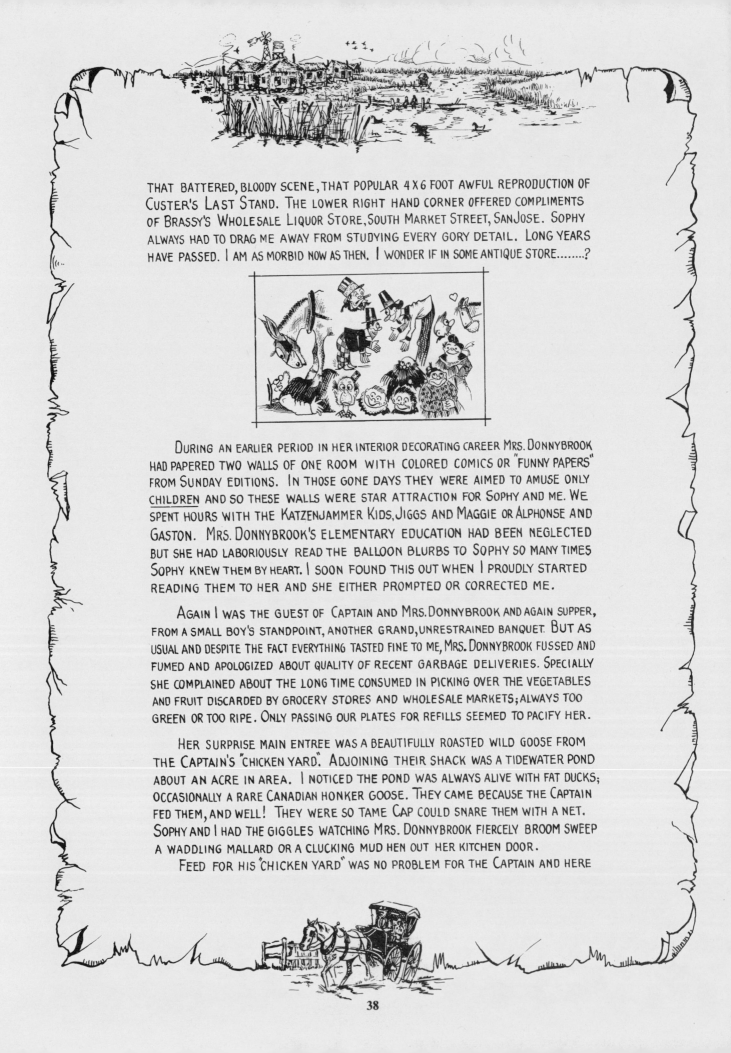

THAT BATTERED, BLOODY SCENE, THAT POPULAR 4 X 6 FOOT AWFUL REPRODUCTION OF CUSTER'S LAST STAND. THE LOWER RIGHT HAND CORNER OFFERED COMPLIMENTS OF BRASSY'S WHOLESALE LIQUOR STORE, SOUTH MARKET STREET, SAN JOSE. SOPHY ALWAYS HAD TO DRAG ME AWAY FROM STUDYING EVERY GORY DETAIL. LONG YEARS HAVE PASSED. I AM AS MORBID NOW AS THEN. I WONDER IF IN SOME ANTIQUE STORE........?

DURING AN EARLIER PERIOD IN HER INTERIOR DECORATING CAREER MRS. DONNYBROOK HAD PAPERED TWO WALLS OF ONE ROOM WITH COLORED COMICS OR "FUNNY PAPERS" FROM SUNDAY EDITIONS. IN THOSE GONE DAYS THEY WERE AIMED TO AMUSE ONLY CHILDREN AND SO THESE WALLS WERE STAR ATTRACTION FOR SOPHY AND ME. WE SPENT HOURS WITH THE KATZENJAMMER KIDS, JIGGS AND MAGGIE OR ALPHONSE AND GASTON. MRS. DONNYBROOK'S ELEMENTARY EDUCATION HAD BEEN NEGLECTED BUT SHE HAD LABORIOUSLY READ THE BALLOON BLURBS TO SOPHY SO MANY TIMES SOPHY KNEW THEM BY HEART. I SOON FOUND THIS OUT WHEN I PROUDLY STARTED READING THEM TO HER AND SHE EITHER PROMPTED OR CORRECTED ME.

AGAIN I WAS THE GUEST OF CAPTAIN AND MRS. DONNYBROOK AND AGAIN SUPPER, FROM A SMALL BOY'S STANDPOINT, ANOTHER GRAND, UNRESTRAINED BANQUET. BUT AS USUAL AND DESPITE THE FACT EVERYTHING TASTED FINE TO ME, MRS. DONNYBROOK FUSSED AND FUMED AND APOLOGIZED ABOUT QUALITY OF RECENT GARBAGE DELIVERIES. SPECIALLY SHE COMPLAINED ABOUT THE LONG TIME CONSUMED IN PICKING OVER THE VEGETABLES AND FRUIT DISCARDED BY GROCERY STORES AND WHOLESALE MARKETS; ALWAYS TOO GREEN OR TOO RIPE. ONLY PASSING OUR PLATES FOR REFILLS SEEMED TO PACIFY HER.

HER SURPRISE MAIN ENTREE WAS A BEAUTIFULLY ROASTED WILD GOOSE FROM THE CAPTAIN'S "CHICKEN YARD". ADJOINING THEIR SHACK WAS A TIDEWATER POND ABOUT AN ACRE IN AREA. I NOTICED THE POND WAS ALWAYS ALIVE WITH FAT DUCKS; OCCASIONALLY A RARE CANADIAN HONKER GOOSE. THEY CAME BECAUSE THE CAPTAIN FED THEM, AND WELL! THEY WERE SO TAME CAP COULD SNARE THEM WITH A NET. SOPHY AND I HAD THE GIGGLES WATCHING MRS. DONNYBROOK FIERCELY BROOM SWEEP A WADDLING MALLARD OR A CLUCKING MUD HEN OUT HER KITCHEN DOOR.

FEED FOR HIS "CHICKEN YARD" WAS NO PROBLEM FOR THE CAPTAIN AND HERE

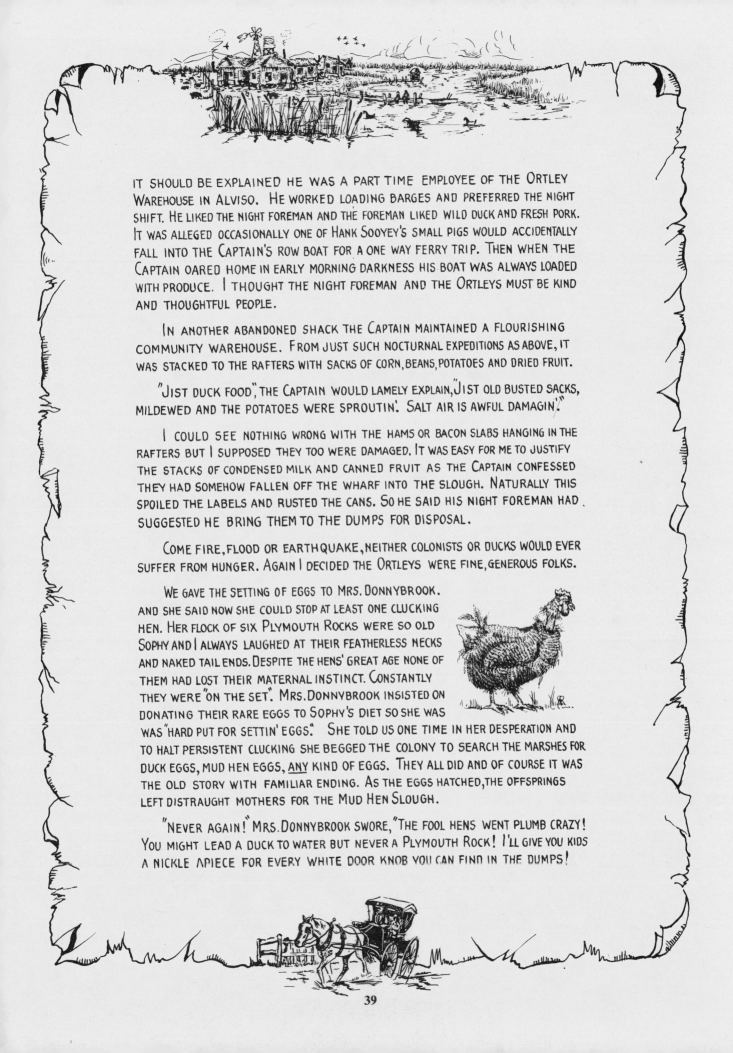

IT SHOULD BE EXPLAINED HE WAS A PART TIME EMPLOYEE OF THE ORTLEY WAREHOUSE IN ALVISO. HE WORKED LOADING BARGES AND PREFERRED THE NIGHT SHIFT. HE LIKED THE NIGHT FOREMAN AND THE FOREMAN LIKED WILD DUCK AND FRESH PORK. IT WAS ALLEGED OCCASIONALLY ONE OF HANK SOOYEY'S SMALL PIGS WOULD ACCIDENTALLY FALL INTO THE CAPTAIN'S ROW BOAT FOR A ONE WAY FERRY TRIP. THEN WHEN THE CAPTAIN OARED HOME IN EARLY MORNING DARKNESS HIS BOAT WAS ALWAYS LOADED WITH PRODUCE. I THOUGHT THE NIGHT FOREMAN AND THE ORTLEYS MUST BE KIND AND THOUGHTFUL PEOPLE.

IN ANOTHER ABANDONED SHACK THE CAPTAIN MAINTAINED A FLOURISHING COMMUNITY WAREHOUSE. FROM JUST SUCH NOCTURNAL EXPEDITIONS AS ABOVE, IT WAS STACKED TO THE RAFTERS WITH SACKS OF CORN, BEANS, POTATOES AND DRIED FRUIT.

"JIST DUCK FOOD", THE CAPTAIN WOULD LAMELY EXPLAIN, "JIST OLD BUSTED SACKS, MILDEWED AND THE POTATOES WERE SPROUTIN'. SALT AIR IS AWFUL DAMAGIN'."

I COULD SEE NOTHING WRONG WITH THE HAMS OR BACON SLABS HANGING IN THE RAFTERS BUT I SUPPOSED THEY TOO WERE DAMAGED. IT WAS EASY FOR ME TO JUSTIFY THE STACKS OF CONDENSED MILK AND CANNED FRUIT AS THE CAPTAIN CONFESSED THEY HAD SOMEHOW FALLEN OFF THE WHARF INTO THE SLOUGH. NATURALLY THIS SPOILED THE LABELS AND RUSTED THE CANS. SO HE SAID HIS NIGHT FOREMAN HAD SUGGESTED HE BRING THEM TO THE DUMPS FOR DISPOSAL.

COME FIRE, FLOOD OR EARTHQUAKE, NEITHER COLONISTS OR DUCKS WOULD EVER SUFFER FROM HUNGER. AGAIN I DECIDED THE ORTLEYS WERE FINE, GENEROUS FOLKS.

WE GAVE THE SETTING OF EGGS TO MRS. DONNYBROOK. AND SHE SAID NOW SHE COULD STOP AT LEAST ONE CLUCKING HEN. HER FLOCK OF SIX PLYMOUTH ROCKS WERE SO OLD SOPHY AND I ALWAYS LAUGHED AT THEIR FEATHERLESS NECKS AND NAKED TAIL ENDS. DESPITE THE HENS' GREAT AGE NONE OF THEM HAD LOST THEIR MATERNAL INSTINCT. CONSTANTLY THEY WERE "ON THE SET". MRS. DONNYBROOK INSISTED ON DONATING THEIR RARE EGGS TO SOPHY'S DIET SO SHE WAS WAS "HARD PUT FOR SETTIN' EGGS." SHE TOLD US ONE TIME IN HER DESPERATION AND TO HALT PERSISTENT CLUCKING SHE BEGGED THE COLONY TO SEARCH THE MARSHES FOR DUCK EGGS, MUD HEN EGGS, ANY KIND OF EGGS. THEY ALL DID AND OF COURSE IT WAS THE OLD STORY WITH FAMILIAR ENDING. AS THE EGGS HATCHED, THE OFFSPRINGS LEFT DISTRAUGHT MOTHERS FOR THE MUD HEN SLOUGH.

"NEVER AGAIN!" MRS. DONNYBROOK SWORE, "THE FOOL HENS WENT PLUMB CRAZY! YOU MIGHT LEAD A DUCK TO WATER BUT NEVER A PLYMOUTH ROCK! I'LL GIVE YOU KIDS A NICKLE APIECE FOR EVERY WHITE DOOR KNOB YOU CAN FIND IN THE DUMPS!

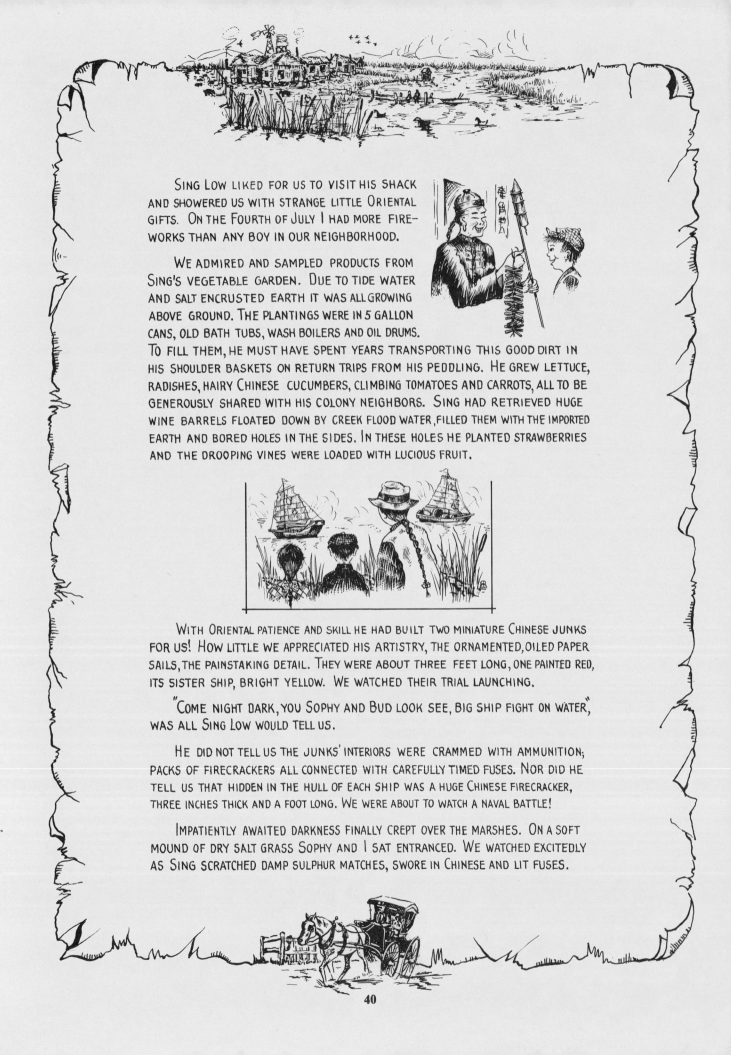

Sing Low liked for us to visit his shack and showered us with strange little Oriental gifts. On the Fourth of July I had more fireworks than any boy in our neighborhood.

We admired and sampled products from Sing's vegetable garden. Due to tide water and salt encrusted earth it was all growing above ground. The plantings were in 5 gallon cans, old bath tubs, wash boilers and oil drums. To fill them, he must have spent years transporting this good dirt in his shoulder baskets on return trips from his peddling. He grew lettuce, radishes, hairy Chinese cucumbers, climbing tomatoes and carrots, all to be generously shared with his colony neighbors. Sing had retrieved huge wine barrels floated down by creek flood water, filled them with the imported earth and bored holes in the sides. In these holes he planted strawberries and the drooping vines were loaded with lucious fruit.

With Oriental patience and skill he had built two miniature Chinese junks for us! How little we appreciated his artistry, the ornamented, oiled paper sails, the painstaking detail. They were about three feet long, one painted red, its sister ship, bright yellow. We watched their trial launching.

"Come night dark, you Sophy and Bud look see, big ship fight on water", was all Sing Low would tell us.

He did not tell us the junks' interiors were crammed with ammunition; packs of firecrackers all connected with carefully timed fuses. Nor did he tell us that hidden in the hull of each ship was a huge Chinese firecracker, three inches thick and a foot long. We were about to watch a naval battle!

Impatiently awaited darkness finally crept over the marshes. On a soft mound of dry salt grass Sophy and I sat entranced. We watched excitedly as Sing scratched damp sulphur matches, swore in Chinese and lit fuses.

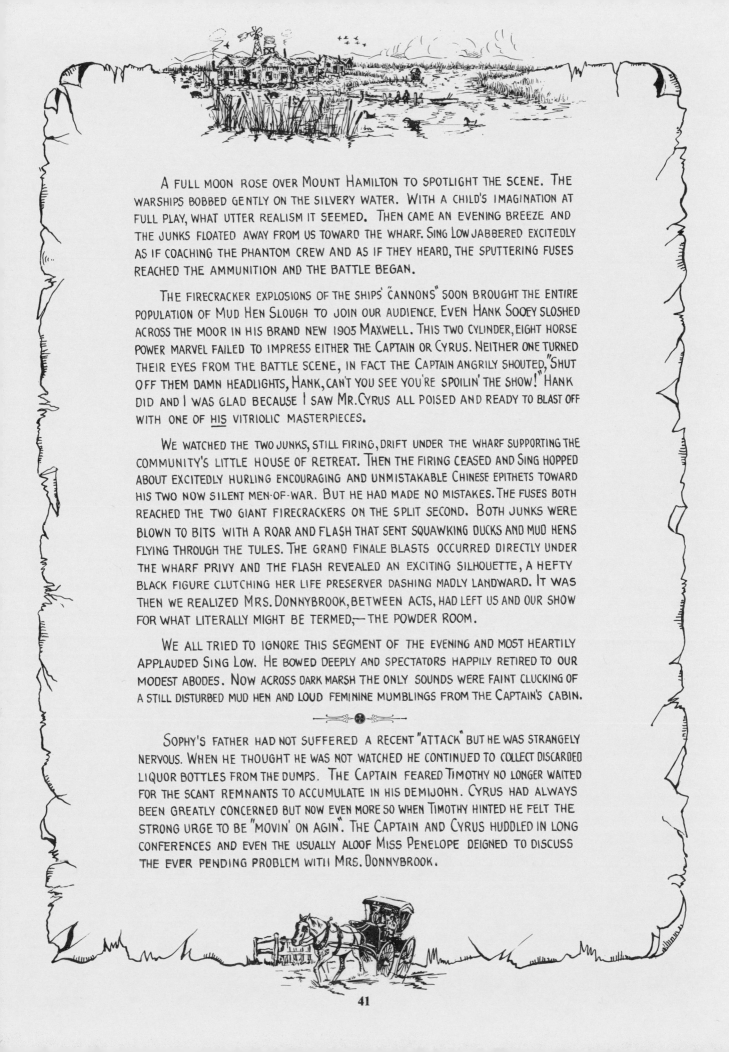

A full moon rose over Mount Hamilton to spotlight the scene. The warships bobbed gently on the silvery water. With a child's imagination at full play, what utter realism it seemed. Then came an evening breeze and the junks floated away from us toward the wharf. Sing Low jabbered excitedly as if coaching the phantom crew and as if they heard, the sputtering fuses reached the ammunition and the battle began.

The firecracker explosions of the ships' "cannons" soon brought the entire population of Mud Hen Slough to join our audience. Even Hank Sooey sloshed across the moor in his brand new 1905 Maxwell. This two cylinder, eight horse power marvel failed to impress either the Captain or Cyrus. Neither one turned their eyes from the battle scene, in fact the Captain angrily shouted, "Shut off them damn headlights, Hank, can't you see you're spoilin' the show!" Hank did and I was glad because I saw Mr. Cyrus all poised and ready to blast off with one of HIS vitriolic masterpieces.

We watched the two junks, still firing, drift under the wharf supporting the community's little house of retreat. Then the firing ceased and Sing hopped about excitedly hurling encouraging and unmistakable Chinese epithets toward his two now silent men-of-war. But he had made no mistakes. The fuses both reached the two giant firecrackers on the split second. Both junks were blown to bits with a roar and flash that sent squawking ducks and mud hens flying through the tules. The grand finale blasts occurred directly under the wharf privy and the flash revealed an exciting silhouette, a hefty black figure clutching her life preserver dashing madly landward. It was then we realized Mrs. Donnybrook, between acts, had left us and our show for what literally might be termed,—the powder room.

We all tried to ignore this segment of the evening and most heartily applauded Sing Low. He bowed deeply and spectators happily retired to our modest abodes. Now across dark marsh the only sounds were faint clucking of a still disturbed mud hen and loud feminine mumblings from the Captain's cabin.

Sophy's father had not suffered a recent "attack" but he was strangely nervous. When he thought he was not watched he continued to collect discarded liquor bottles from the dumps. The Captain feared Timothy no longer waited for the scant remnants to accumulate in his demijohn. Cyrus had always been greatly concerned but now even more so when Timothy hinted he felt the strong urge to be "movin' on agin". The Captain and Cyrus huddled in long conferences and even the usually aloof Miss Penelope deigned to discuss the ever pending problem with Mrs. Donnybrook.

41

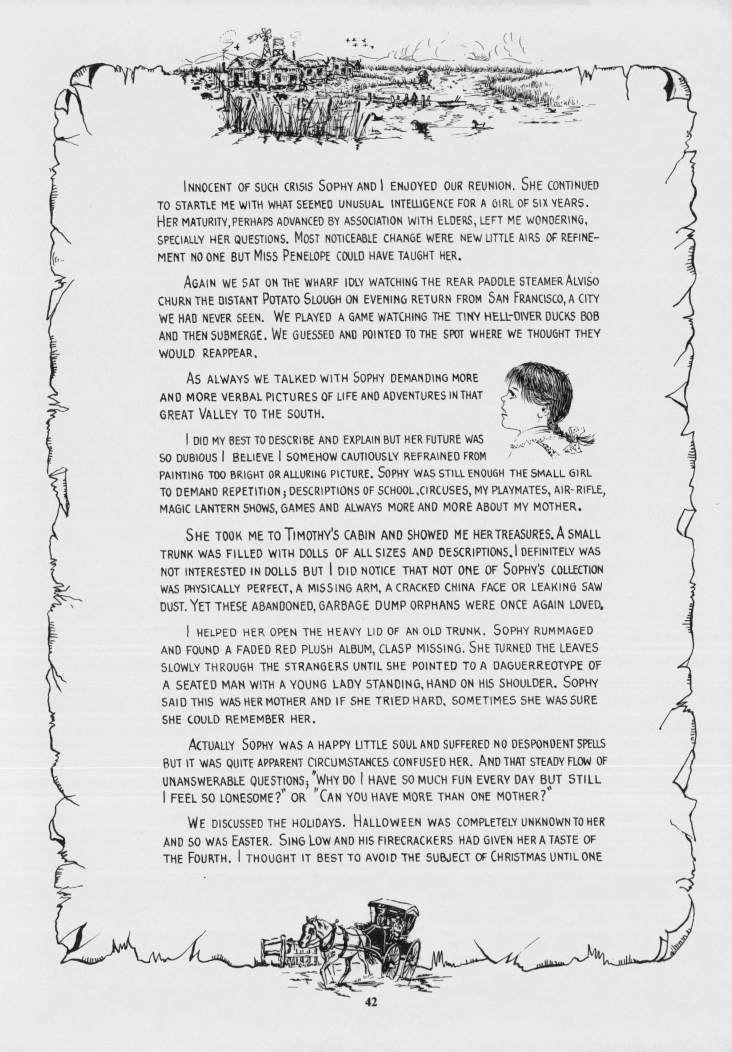

INNOCENT OF SUCH CRISIS SOPHY AND I ENJOYED OUR REUNION. SHE CONTINUED TO STARTLE ME WITH WHAT SEEMED UNUSUAL INTELLIGENCE FOR A GIRL OF SIX YEARS. HER MATURITY, PERHAPS ADVANCED BY ASSOCIATION WITH ELDERS, LEFT ME WONDERING, SPECIALLY HER QUESTIONS. MOST NOTICEABLE CHANGE WERE NEW LITTLE AIRS OF REFINEMENT NO ONE BUT MISS PENELOPE COULD HAVE TAUGHT HER.

AGAIN WE SAT ON THE WHARF IDLY WATCHING THE REAR PADDLE STEAMER ALVISO CHURN THE DISTANT POTATO SLOUGH ON EVENING RETURN FROM SAN FRANCISCO, A CITY WE HAD NEVER SEEN. WE PLAYED A GAME WATCHING THE TINY HELL-DIVER DUCKS BOB AND THEN SUBMERGE. WE GUESSED AND POINTED TO THE SPOT WHERE WE THOUGHT THEY WOULD REAPPEAR.

AS ALWAYS WE TALKED WITH SOPHY DEMANDING MORE AND MORE VERBAL PICTURES OF LIFE AND ADVENTURES IN THAT GREAT VALLEY TO THE SOUTH.

I DID MY BEST TO DESCRIBE AND EXPLAIN BUT HER FUTURE WAS SO DUBIOUS I BELIEVE I SOMEHOW CAUTIOUSLY REFRAINED FROM PAINTING TOO BRIGHT OR ALLURING PICTURE. SOPHY WAS STILL ENOUGH THE SMALL GIRL TO DEMAND REPETITION; DESCRIPTIONS OF SCHOOL, CIRCUSES, MY PLAYMATES, AIR-RIFLE, MAGIC LANTERN SHOWS, GAMES AND ALWAYS MORE AND MORE ABOUT MY MOTHER.

SHE TOOK ME TO TIMOTHY'S CABIN AND SHOWED ME HER TREASURES. A SMALL TRUNK WAS FILLED WITH DOLLS OF ALL SIZES AND DESCRIPTIONS. I DEFINITELY WAS NOT INTERESTED IN DOLLS BUT I DID NOTICE THAT NOT ONE OF SOPHY'S COLLECTION WAS PHYSICALLY PERFECT, A MISSING ARM, A CRACKED CHINA FACE OR LEAKING SAW DUST. YET THESE ABANDONED, GARBAGE DUMP ORPHANS WERE ONCE AGAIN LOVED.

I HELPED HER OPEN THE HEAVY LID OF AN OLD TRUNK. SOPHY RUMMAGED AND FOUND A FADED RED PLUSH ALBUM, CLASP MISSING. SHE TURNED THE LEAVES SLOWLY THROUGH THE STRANGERS UNTIL SHE POINTED TO A DAGUERREOTYPE OF A SEATED MAN WITH A YOUNG LADY STANDING, HAND ON HIS SHOULDER. SOPHY SAID THIS WAS HER MOTHER AND IF SHE TRIED HARD, SOMETIMES SHE WAS SURE SHE COULD REMEMBER HER.

ACTUALLY SOPHY WAS A HAPPY LITTLE SOUL AND SUFFERED NO DESPONDENT SPELLS BUT IT WAS QUITE APPARENT CIRCUMSTANCES CONFUSED HER. AND THAT STEADY FLOW OF UNANSWERABLE QUESTIONS; "WHY DO I HAVE SO MUCH FUN EVERY DAY BUT STILL I FEEL SO LONESOME?" OR "CAN YOU HAVE MORE THAN ONE MOTHER?"

WE DISCUSSED THE HOLIDAYS. HALLOWEEN WAS COMPLETELY UNKNOWN TO HER AND SO WAS EASTER. SING LOW AND HIS FIRECRACKERS HAD GIVEN HER A TASTE OF THE FOURTH. I THOUGHT IT BEST TO AVOID THE SUBJECT OF CHRISTMAS UNTIL ONE

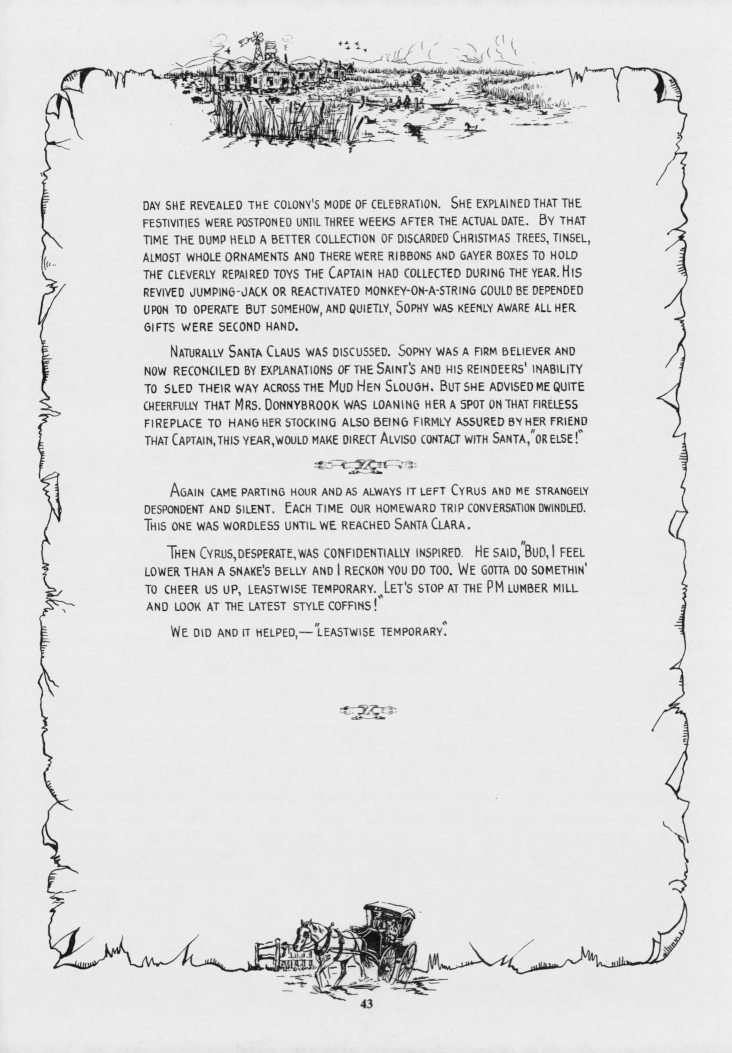

DAY SHE REVEALED THE COLONY'S MODE OF CELEBRATION. SHE EXPLAINED THAT THE FESTIVITIES WERE POSTPONED UNTIL THREE WEEKS AFTER THE ACTUAL DATE. BY THAT TIME THE DUMP HELD A BETTER COLLECTION OF DISCARDED CHRISTMAS TREES, TINSEL, ALMOST WHOLE ORNAMENTS AND THERE WERE RIBBONS AND GAYER BOXES TO HOLD THE CLEVERLY REPAIRED TOYS THE CAPTAIN HAD COLLECTED DURING THE YEAR. HIS REVIVED JUMPING-JACK OR REACTIVATED MONKEY-ON-A-STRING COULD BE DEPENDED UPON TO OPERATE BUT SOMEHOW, AND QUIETLY, SOPHY WAS KEENLY AWARE ALL HER GIFTS WERE SECOND HAND.

NATURALLY SANTA CLAUS WAS DISCUSSED. SOPHY WAS A FIRM BELIEVER AND NOW RECONCILED BY EXPLANATIONS OF THE SAINT'S AND HIS REINDEERS' INABILITY TO SLED THEIR WAY ACROSS THE MUD HEN SLOUGH. BUT SHE ADVISED ME QUITE CHEERFULLY THAT MRS. DONNYBROOK WAS LOANING HER A SPOT ON THAT FIRELESS FIREPLACE TO HANG HER STOCKING ALSO BEING FIRMLY ASSURED BY HER FRIEND THAT CAPTAIN, THIS YEAR, WOULD MAKE DIRECT ALVISO CONTACT WITH SANTA, "OR ELSE!"

AGAIN CAME PARTING HOUR AND AS ALWAYS IT LEFT CYRUS AND ME STRANGELY DESPONDENT AND SILENT. EACH TIME OUR HOMEWARD TRIP CONVERSATION DWINDLED. THIS ONE WAS WORDLESS UNTIL WE REACHED SANTA CLARA.

THEN CYRUS, DESPERATE, WAS CONFIDENTIALLY INSPIRED. HE SAID, "BUD, I FEEL LOWER THAN A SNAKE'S BELLY AND I RECKON YOU DO TOO. WE GOTTA DO SOMETHIN' TO CHEER US UP, LEASTWISE TEMPORARY. LET'S STOP AT THE PM LUMBER MILL AND LOOK AT THE LATEST STYLE COFFINS!"

WE DID AND IT HELPED,—"LEASTWISE TEMPORARY."

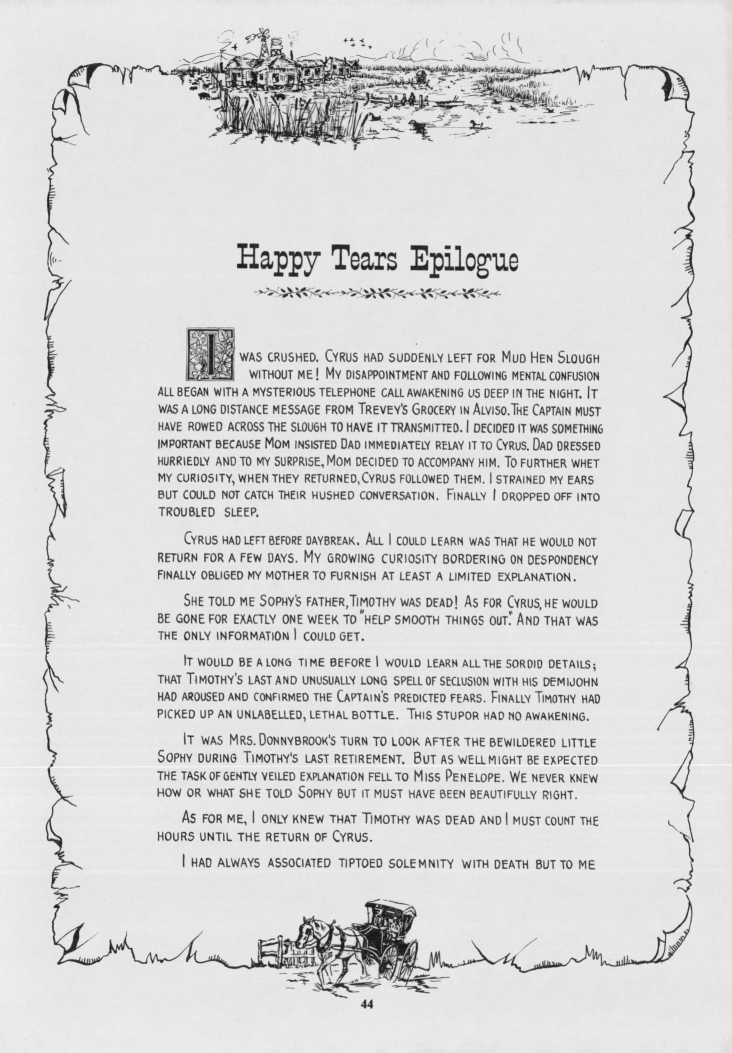

Happy Tears Epilogue

I WAS CRUSHED. CYRUS HAD SUDDENLY LEFT FOR MUD HEN SLOUGH WITHOUT ME! MY DISAPPOINTMENT AND FOLLOWING MENTAL CONFUSION ALL BEGAN WITH A MYSTERIOUS TELEPHONE CALL AWAKENING US DEEP IN THE NIGHT. IT WAS A LONG DISTANCE MESSAGE FROM TREVEY'S GROCERY IN ALVISO. THE CAPTAIN MUST HAVE ROWED ACROSS THE SLOUGH TO HAVE IT TRANSMITTED. I DECIDED IT WAS SOMETHING IMPORTANT BECAUSE MOM INSISTED DAD IMMEDIATELY RELAY IT TO CYRUS. DAD DRESSED HURRIEDLY AND TO MY SURPRISE, MOM DECIDED TO ACCOMPANY HIM. TO FURTHER WHET MY CURIOSITY, WHEN THEY RETURNED, CYRUS FOLLOWED THEM. I STRAINED MY EARS BUT COULD NOT CATCH THEIR HUSHED CONVERSATION. FINALLY I DROPPED OFF INTO TROUBLED SLEEP.

CYRUS HAD LEFT BEFORE DAYBREAK. ALL I COULD LEARN WAS THAT HE WOULD NOT RETURN FOR A FEW DAYS. MY GROWING CURIOSITY BORDERING ON DESPONDENCY FINALLY OBLIGED MY MOTHER TO FURNISH AT LEAST A LIMITED EXPLANATION.

SHE TOLD ME SOPHY'S FATHER, TIMOTHY WAS DEAD! AS FOR CYRUS, HE WOULD BE GONE FOR EXACTLY ONE WEEK TO "HELP SMOOTH THINGS OUT." AND THAT WAS THE ONLY INFORMATION I COULD GET.

IT WOULD BE A LONG TIME BEFORE I WOULD LEARN ALL THE SORDID DETAILS; THAT TIMOTHY'S LAST AND UNUSUALLY LONG SPELL OF SECLUSION WITH HIS DEMIJOHN HAD AROUSED AND CONFIRMED THE CAPTAIN'S PREDICTED FEARS. FINALLY TIMOTHY HAD PICKED UP AN UNLABELLED, LETHAL BOTTLE. THIS STUPOR HAD NO AWAKENING.

IT WAS MRS. DONNYBROOK'S TURN TO LOOK AFTER THE BEWILDERED LITTLE SOPHY DURING TIMOTHY'S LAST RETIREMENT. BUT AS WELL MIGHT BE EXPECTED THE TASK OF GENTLY VEILED EXPLANATION FELL TO MISS PENELOPE. WE NEVER KNEW HOW OR WHAT SHE TOLD SOPHY BUT IT MUST HAVE BEEN BEAUTIFULLY RIGHT.

AS FOR ME, I ONLY KNEW THAT TIMOTHY WAS DEAD AND I MUST COUNT THE HOURS UNTIL THE RETURN OF CYRUS.

I HAD ALWAYS ASSOCIATED TIPTOED SOLEMNITY WITH DEATH BUT TO ME

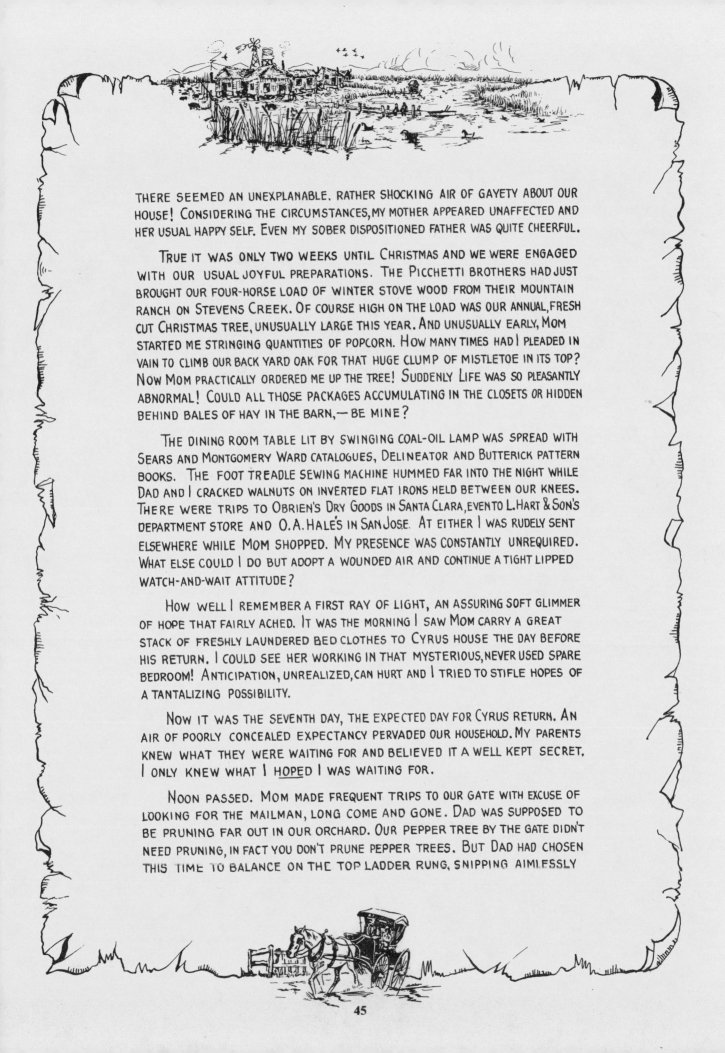

THERE SEEMED AN UNEXPLANABLE, RATHER SHOCKING AIR OF GAYETY ABOUT OUR HOUSE! CONSIDERING THE CIRCUMSTANCES, MY MOTHER APPEARED UNAFFECTED AND HER USUAL HAPPY SELF. EVEN MY SOBER DISPOSITIONED FATHER WAS QUITE CHEERFUL.

TRUE IT WAS ONLY TWO WEEKS UNTIL CHRISTMAS AND WE WERE ENGAGED WITH OUR USUAL JOYFUL PREPARATIONS. THE PICCHETTI BROTHERS HAD JUST BROUGHT OUR FOUR-HORSE LOAD OF WINTER STOVE WOOD FROM THEIR MOUNTAIN RANCH ON STEVENS CREEK. OF COURSE HIGH ON THE LOAD WAS OUR ANNUAL, FRESH CUT CHRISTMAS TREE, UNUSUALLY LARGE THIS YEAR. AND UNUSUALLY EARLY, MOM STARTED ME STRINGING QUANTITIES OF POPCORN. HOW MANY TIMES HAD I PLEADED IN VAIN TO CLIMB OUR BACK YARD OAK FOR THAT HUGE CLUMP OF MISTLETOE IN ITS TOP? NOW MOM PRACTICALLY ORDERED ME UP THE TREE! SUDDENLY LIFE WAS SO PLEASANTLY ABNORMAL! COULD ALL THOSE PACKAGES ACCUMULATING IN THE CLOSETS OR HIDDEN BEHIND BALES OF HAY IN THE BARN,— BE MINE?

THE DINING ROOM TABLE LIT BY SWINGING COAL-OIL LAMP WAS SPREAD WITH SEARS AND MONTGOMERY WARD CATALOGUES, DELINEATOR AND BUTTERICK PATTERN BOOKS. THE FOOT TREADLE SEWING MACHINE HUMMED FAR INTO THE NIGHT WHILE DAD AND I CRACKED WALNUTS ON INVERTED FLAT IRONS HELD BETWEEN OUR KNEES. THERE WERE TRIPS TO OBRIEN'S DRY GOODS IN SANTA CLARA, EVEN TO L. HART & SON'S DEPARTMENT STORE AND O. A. HALE'S IN SAN JOSE. AT EITHER I WAS RUDELY SENT ELSEWHERE WHILE MOM SHOPPED. MY PRESENCE WAS CONSTANTLY UNREQUIRED. WHAT ELSE COULD I DO BUT ADOPT A WOUNDED AIR AND CONTINUE A TIGHT LIPPED WATCH-AND-WAIT ATTITUDE?

HOW WELL I REMEMBER A FIRST RAY OF LIGHT, AN ASSURING SOFT GLIMMER OF HOPE THAT FAIRLY ACHED. IT WAS THE MORNING I SAW MOM CARRY A GREAT STACK OF FRESHLY LAUNDERED BED CLOTHES TO CYRUS HOUSE THE DAY BEFORE HIS RETURN. I COULD SEE HER WORKING IN THAT MYSTERIOUS, NEVER USED SPARE BEDROOM! ANTICIPATION, UNREALIZED, CAN HURT AND I TRIED TO STIFLE HOPES OF A TANTALIZING POSSIBILITY.

NOW IT WAS THE SEVENTH DAY, THE EXPECTED DAY FOR CYRUS RETURN. AN AIR OF POORLY CONCEALED EXPECTANCY PERVADED OUR HOUSEHOLD. MY PARENTS KNEW WHAT THEY WERE WAITING FOR AND BELIEVED IT A WELL KEPT SECRET, I ONLY KNEW WHAT I HOPED I WAS WAITING FOR.

NOON PASSED. MOM MADE FREQUENT TRIPS TO OUR GATE WITH EXCUSE OF LOOKING FOR THE MAILMAN, LONG COME AND GONE. DAD WAS SUPPOSED TO BE PRUNING FAR OUT IN OUR ORCHARD. OUR PEPPER TREE BY THE GATE DIDN'T NEED PRUNING, IN FACT YOU DON'T PRUNE PEPPER TREES. BUT DAD HAD CHOSEN THIS TIME TO BALANCE ON THE TOP LADDER RUNG, SNIPPING AIMLESSLY

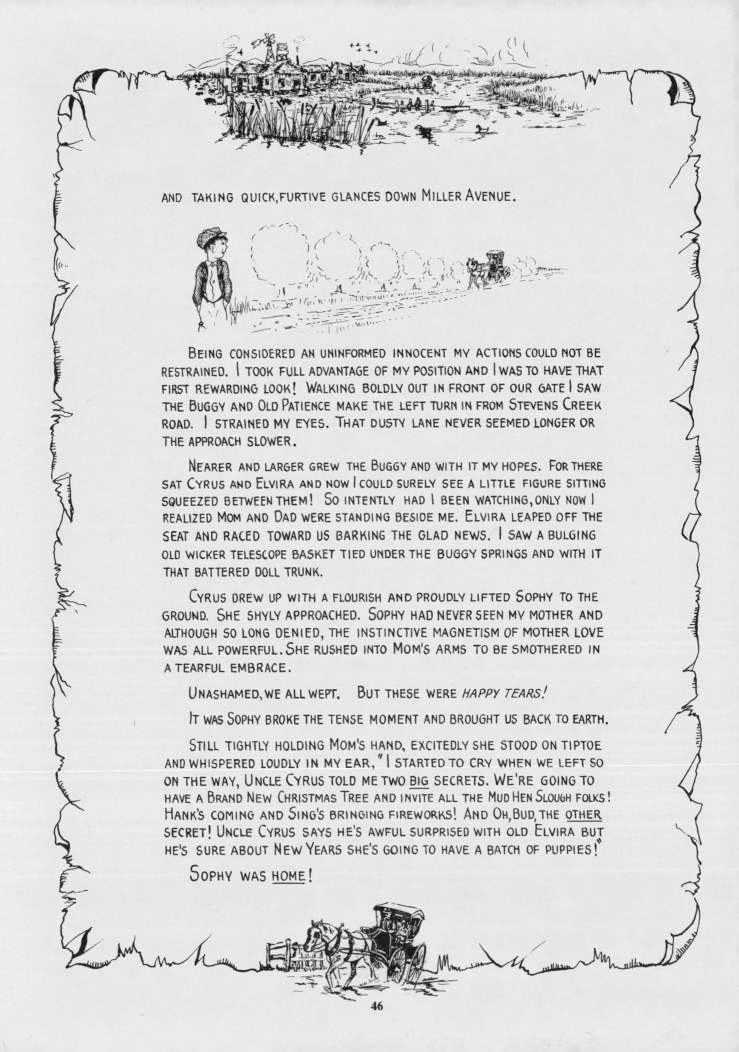

AND TAKING QUICK, FURTIVE GLANCES DOWN MILLER AVENUE.

BEING CONSIDERED AN UNINFORMED INNOCENT MY ACTIONS COULD NOT BE RESTRAINED. I TOOK FULL ADVANTAGE OF MY POSITION AND I WAS TO HAVE THAT FIRST REWARDING LOOK! WALKING BOLDLY OUT IN FRONT OF OUR GATE I SAW THE BUGGY AND OLD PATIENCE MAKE THE LEFT TURN IN FROM STEVENS CREEK ROAD. I STRAINED MY EYES. THAT DUSTY LANE NEVER SEEMED LONGER OR THE APPROACH SLOWER.

NEARER AND LARGER GREW THE BUGGY AND WITH IT MY HOPES. FOR THERE SAT CYRUS AND ELVIRA AND NOW I COULD SURELY SEE A LITTLE FIGURE SITTING SQUEEZED BETWEEN THEM! SO INTENTLY HAD I BEEN WATCHING, ONLY NOW I REALIZED MOM AND DAD WERE STANDING BESIDE ME. ELVIRA LEAPED OFF THE SEAT AND RACED TOWARD US BARKING THE GLAD NEWS. I SAW A BULGING OLD WICKER TELESCOPE BASKET TIED UNDER THE BUGGY SPRINGS AND WITH IT THAT BATTERED DOLL TRUNK.

CYRUS DREW UP WITH A FLOURISH AND PROUDLY LIFTED SOPHY TO THE GROUND. SHE SHYLY APPROACHED. SOPHY HAD NEVER SEEN MY MOTHER AND ALTHOUGH SO LONG DENIED, THE INSTINCTIVE MAGNETISM OF MOTHER LOVE WAS ALL POWERFUL. SHE RUSHED INTO MOM'S ARMS TO BE SMOTHERED IN A TEARFUL EMBRACE.

UNASHAMED, WE ALL WEPT. BUT THESE WERE *HAPPY TEARS!*

IT WAS SOPHY BROKE THE TENSE MOMENT AND BROUGHT US BACK TO EARTH.

STILL TIGHTLY HOLDING MOM'S HAND, EXCITEDLY SHE STOOD ON TIPTOE AND WHISPERED LOUDLY IN MY EAR, "I STARTED TO CRY WHEN WE LEFT SO ON THE WAY, UNCLE CYRUS TOLD ME TWO BIG SECRETS. WE'RE GOING TO HAVE A BRAND NEW CHRISTMAS TREE AND INVITE ALL THE MUD HEN SLOUGH FOLKS! HANK'S COMING AND SING'S BRINGING FIREWORKS! AND OH, BUD, THE OTHER SECRET! UNCLE CYRUS SAYS HE'S AWFUL SURPRISED WITH OLD ELVIRA BUT HE'S SURE ABOUT NEW YEARS SHE'S GOING TO HAVE A BATCH OF PUPPIES!"

SOPHY WAS HOME!

lady of
MYSTERY
(Sarah Winchester)

BY RALPH RAMBO

*The story of Santa Clara Valley's
most famous lady, Sarah Winchester,
and her fabulous mystery mansion*

Dear Reader,

This book was written because of my desire to minimize some of the grotesque, misconceived, sometimes false, legends built around this gracious and distinguished character, Sarah Winchester. In fact, or at least in my estimation, she was the Old Valley's most famous lady.

My book was composed with little or no research. My impressions were acquired mainly in my youthful days by listening to my elders.

We were "neighbors" only in distance. We had no close personal or verbal contact, although there were significant exceptions. My father's first work upon his 1885 California arrival was helping in the landscaping and fruit tree planting of her 40-acre orchard. Naturally he had chances for observation. My uncle, Edward B. Rambo, was her appointed first head of the West Coast branch of the Winchester Repeating Arms Company in San Francisco. He had direct business and financial connection with the Lady. From him we gained information often of more than "casual interest". To our Uncle Ned, Sarah was "quite peculiar at times" but far, far from "crazy" as so often reported by Valley natives.

My booklet first describes the mansion in detail. I believe in the public's enjoying visits and tours of the world famous MYSTERY HOUSE. I have written nothing to greatly dispel their expectations, but actually to me no great mystery ever existed. The explanation seems so simple. Sarah owned a conventional mansion up the Peninsula! Sarah loved the study of architecture. Sarah had untold millions, untaxed. SO—this became a gigantic game of building blocks—adding, tearing down, replacing and totally ignoring Valley intolerants' opinions. It was a never-ending engrossing game for 35 years. (This is only the writer's *personal* opinion.)

In the section "Tall Tales" I relate the birth and long-lived legends that grew like mushrooms around our Valley's celebrated Lady. Then the pages labeled "Short Facts" refute each of these Tall Tales.

In the pages on "Mystery Lady" I expose her true personality with intimate accounts of her activities in and outside the mansion, especially her beneficence, her unrestrained charity and her love of children.

Since this booklet was written, the "House" has enjoyed extensive restoration, including restored landscaping. No tour of the New Santa Clara Valley is complete without a visit to this castle-sized mysterious abode of our Lady of Mystery. Has the dwelling place of one tiny lady, in all this world, ever enjoyed such millions of visitors?

To this retired writer there will always be the Old Valley's BIG THREE, forever unmatched in character of achievement; namely, HENRY MILLER, JAMES LICK, and SARAH WINCHESTER. (And I think I can hear a loud "AMEN!" from the Valley's greatest Historian.)

Yours Truly
Ralph Rambo

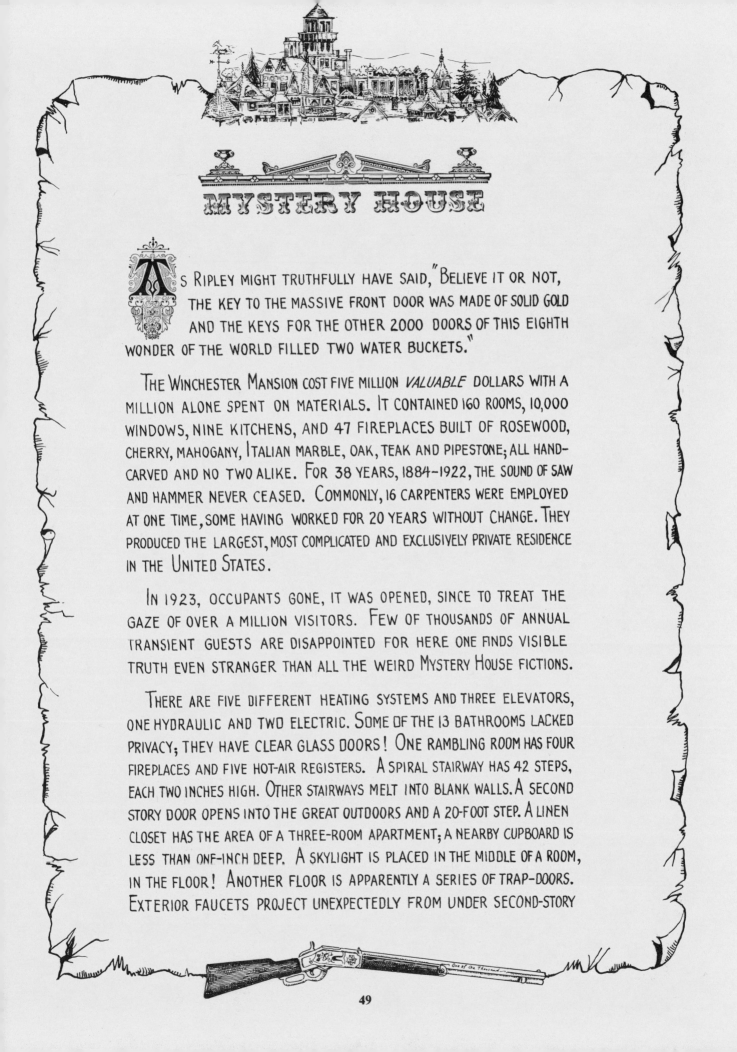

MYSTERY HOUSE

As Ripley might truthfully have said, "Believe it or not, the key to the massive front door was made of solid gold and the keys for the other 2000 doors of this eighth wonder of the world filled two water buckets."

The Winchester Mansion cost five million *valuable* dollars with a million alone spent on materials. It contained 160 rooms, 10,000 windows, nine kitchens, and 47 fireplaces built of rosewood, cherry, mahogany, Italian marble, oak, teak and pipestone; all hand-carved and no two alike. For 38 years, 1884-1922, the sound of saw and hammer never ceased. Commonly, 16 carpenters were employed at one time, some having worked for 20 years without change. They produced the largest, most complicated and exclusively private residence in the United States.

In 1923, occupants gone, it was opened, since to treat the gaze of over a million visitors. Few of thousands of annual transient guests are disappointed for here one finds visible truth even stranger than all the weird Mystery House fictions.

There are five different heating systems and three elevators, one hydraulic and two electric. Some of the 13 bathrooms lacked privacy; they have clear glass doors! One rambling room has four fireplaces and five hot-air registers. A spiral stairway has 42 steps, each two inches high. Other stairways melt into blank walls. A second story door opens into the great outdoors and a 20-foot step. A linen closet has the area of a three-room apartment; a nearby cupboard is less than one-inch deep. A skylight is placed in the middle of a room, in the floor! Another floor is apparently a series of trap-doors. Exterior faucets project unexpectedly from under second-story

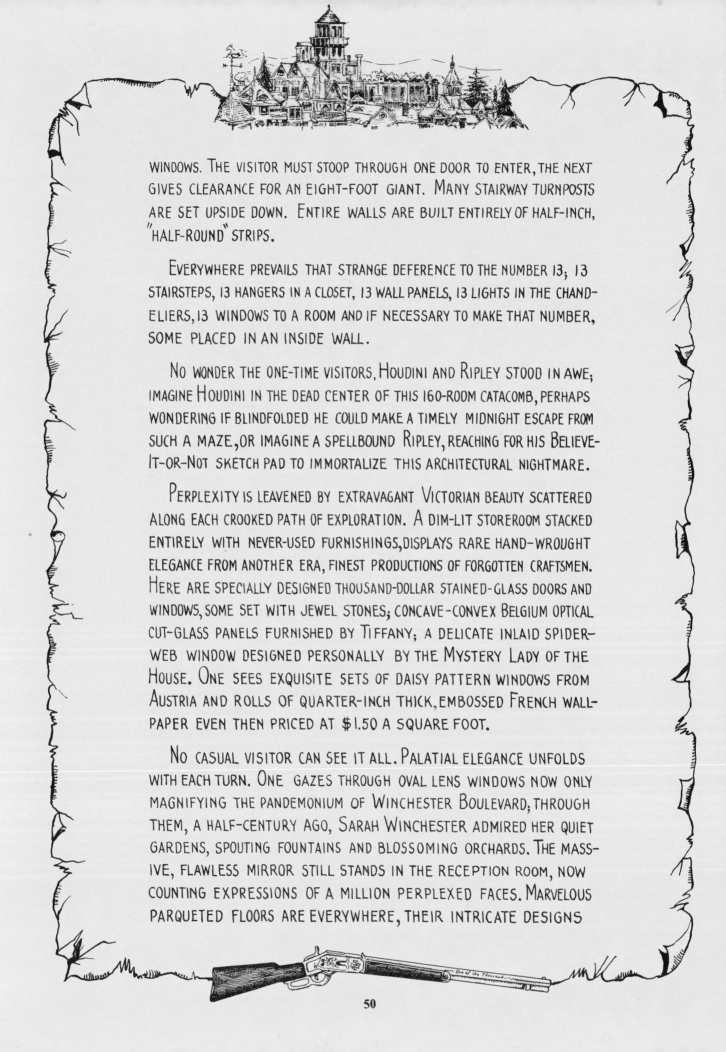

WINDOWS. THE VISITOR MUST STOOP THROUGH ONE DOOR TO ENTER, THE NEXT GIVES CLEARANCE FOR AN EIGHT-FOOT GIANT. MANY STAIRWAY TURNPOSTS ARE SET UPSIDE DOWN. ENTIRE WALLS ARE BUILT ENTIRELY OF HALF-INCH, "HALF-ROUND" STRIPS.

EVERYWHERE PREVAILS THAT STRANGE DEFERENCE TO THE NUMBER 13; 13 STAIRSTEPS, 13 HANGERS IN A CLOSET, 13 WALL PANELS, 13 LIGHTS IN THE CHANDELIERS, 13 WINDOWS TO A ROOM AND IF NECESSARY TO MAKE THAT NUMBER, SOME PLACED IN AN INSIDE WALL.

NO WONDER THE ONE-TIME VISITORS, HOUDINI AND RIPLEY STOOD IN AWE; IMAGINE HOUDINI IN THE DEAD CENTER OF THIS 160-ROOM CATACOMB, PERHAPS WONDERING IF BLINDFOLDED HE COULD MAKE A TIMELY MIDNIGHT ESCAPE FROM SUCH A MAZE, OR IMAGINE A SPELLBOUND RIPLEY, REACHING FOR HIS BELIEVE-IT-OR-NOT SKETCH PAD TO IMMORTALIZE THIS ARCHITECTURAL NIGHTMARE.

PERPLEXITY IS LEAVENED BY EXTRAVAGANT VICTORIAN BEAUTY SCATTERED ALONG EACH CROOKED PATH OF EXPLORATION. A DIM-LIT STOREROOM STACKED ENTIRELY WITH NEVER-USED FURNISHINGS, DISPLAYS RARE HAND-WROUGHT ELEGANCE FROM ANOTHER ERA, FINEST PRODUCTIONS OF FORGOTTEN CRAFTSMEN. HERE ARE SPECIALLY DESIGNED THOUSAND-DOLLAR STAINED-GLASS DOORS AND WINDOWS, SOME SET WITH JEWEL STONES; CONCAVE-CONVEX BELGIUM OPTICAL CUT-GLASS PANELS FURNISHED BY TIFFANY; A DELICATE INLAID SPIDER-WEB WINDOW DESIGNED PERSONALLY BY THE MYSTERY LADY OF THE HOUSE. ONE SEES EXQUISITE SETS OF DAISY PATTERN WINDOWS FROM AUSTRIA AND ROLLS OF QUARTER-INCH THICK, EMBOSSED FRENCH WALLPAPER EVEN THEN PRICED AT $1.50 A SQUARE FOOT.

NO CASUAL VISITOR CAN SEE IT ALL. PALATIAL ELEGANCE UNFOLDS WITH EACH TURN. ONE GAZES THROUGH OVAL LENS WINDOWS NOW ONLY MAGNIFYING THE PANDEMONIUM OF WINCHESTER BOULEVARD; THROUGH THEM, A HALF-CENTURY AGO, SARAH WINCHESTER ADMIRED HER QUIET GARDENS, SPOUTING FOUNTAINS AND BLOSSOMING ORCHARDS. THE MASSIVE, FLAWLESS MIRROR STILL STANDS IN THE RECEPTION ROOM, NOW COUNTING EXPRESSIONS OF A MILLION PERPLEXED FACES. MARVELOUS PARQUETED FLOORS ARE EVERYWHERE, THEIR INTRICATE DESIGNS

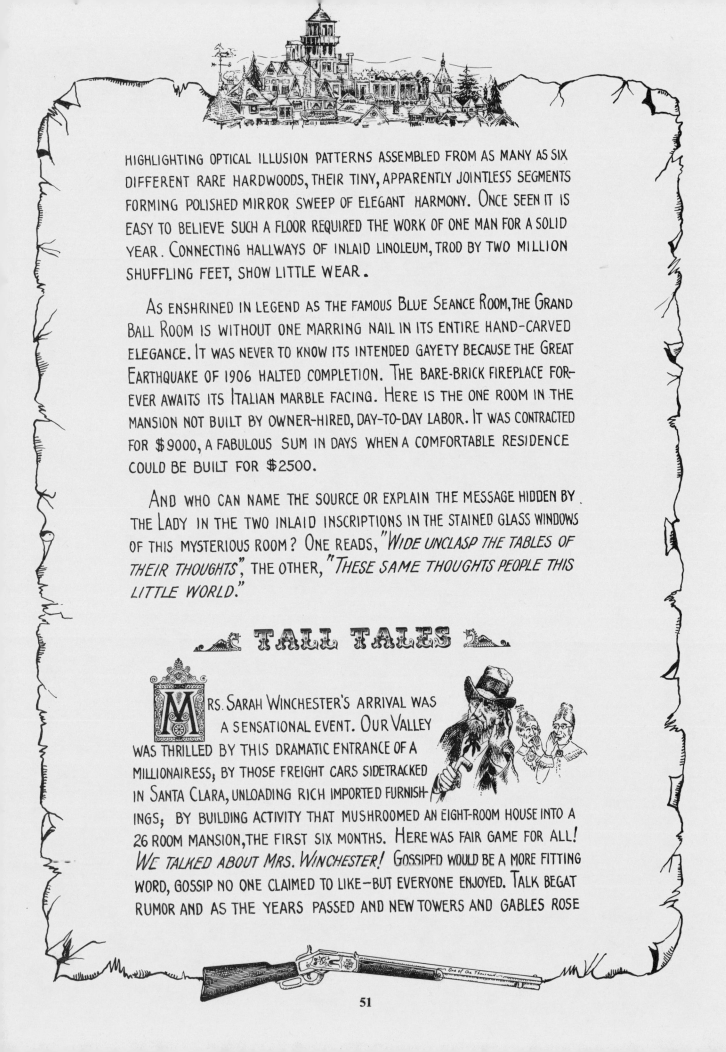

HIGHLIGHTING OPTICAL ILLUSION PATTERNS ASSEMBLED FROM AS MANY AS SIX DIFFERENT RARE HARDWOODS, THEIR TINY, APPARENTLY JOINTLESS SEGMENTS FORMING POLISHED MIRROR SWEEP OF ELEGANT HARMONY. ONCE SEEN IT IS EASY TO BELIEVE SUCH A FLOOR REQUIRED THE WORK OF ONE MAN FOR A SOLID YEAR. CONNECTING HALLWAYS OF INLAID LINOLEUM, TROD BY TWO MILLION SHUFFLING FEET, SHOW LITTLE WEAR.

AS ENSHRINED IN LEGEND AS THE FAMOUS BLUE SEANCE ROOM, THE GRAND BALL ROOM IS WITHOUT ONE MARRING NAIL IN ITS ENTIRE HAND-CARVED ELEGANCE. IT WAS NEVER TO KNOW ITS INTENDED GAYETY BECAUSE THE GREAT EARTHQUAKE OF 1906 HALTED COMPLETION. THE BARE-BRICK FIREPLACE FOREVER AWAITS ITS ITALIAN MARBLE FACING. HERE IS THE ONE ROOM IN THE MANSION NOT BUILT BY OWNER-HIRED, DAY-TO-DAY LABOR. IT WAS CONTRACTED FOR $9000, A FABULOUS SUM IN DAYS WHEN A COMFORTABLE RESIDENCE COULD BE BUILT FOR $2500.

AND WHO CAN NAME THE SOURCE OR EXPLAIN THE MESSAGE HIDDEN BY THE LADY IN THE TWO INLAID INSCRIPTIONS IN THE STAINED GLASS WINDOWS OF THIS MYSTERIOUS ROOM? ONE READS, *"WIDE UNCLASP THE TABLES OF THEIR THOUGHTS"*, THE OTHER, *"THESE SAME THOUGHTS PEOPLE THIS LITTLE WORLD."*

TALL TALES

MRS. SARAH WINCHESTER'S ARRIVAL WAS A SENSATIONAL EVENT. OUR VALLEY WAS THRILLED BY THIS DRAMATIC ENTRANCE OF A MILLIONAIRESS; BY THOSE FREIGHT CARS SIDETRACKED IN SANTA CLARA, UNLOADING RICH IMPORTED FURNISHINGS; BY BUILDING ACTIVITY THAT MUSHROOMED AN EIGHT-ROOM HOUSE INTO A 26 ROOM MANSION, THE FIRST SIX MONTHS. HERE WAS FAIR GAME FOR ALL! *WE TALKED ABOUT MRS. WINCHESTER!* GOSSIPED WOULD BE A MORE FITTING WORD, GOSSIP NO ONE CLAIMED TO LIKE—BUT EVERYONE ENJOYED. TALK BEGAT RUMOR AND AS THE YEARS PASSED AND NEW TOWERS AND GABLES ROSE

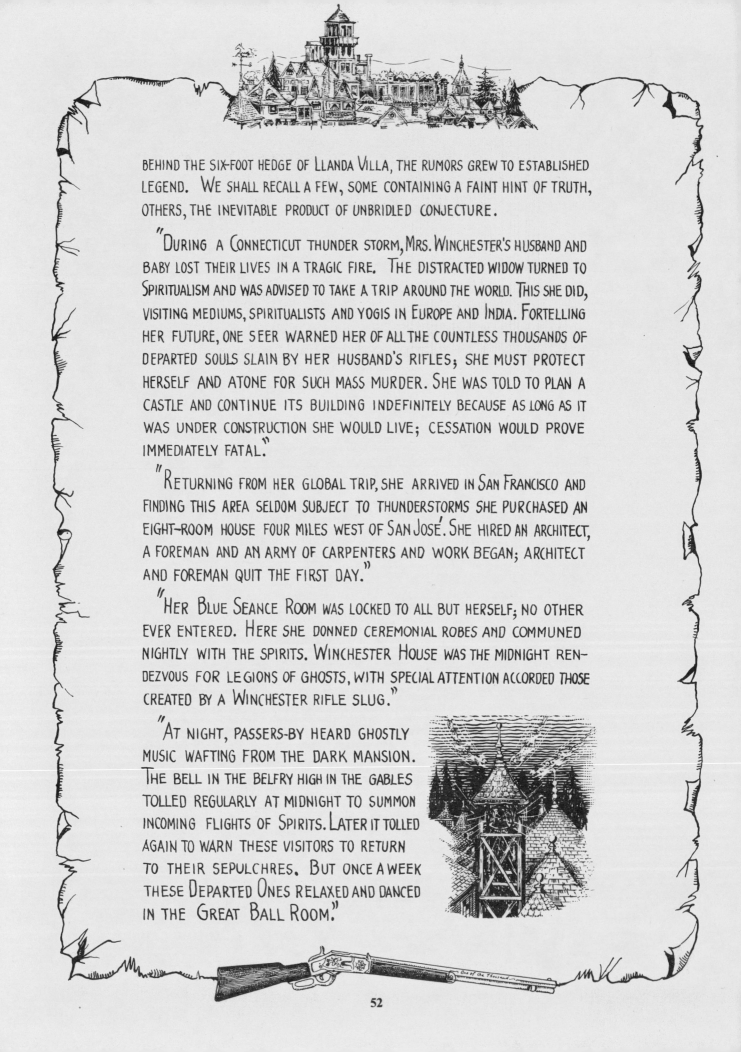

BEHIND THE SIX-FOOT HEDGE OF LLANDA VILLA, THE RUMORS GREW TO ESTABLISHED LEGEND. WE SHALL RECALL A FEW, SOME CONTAINING A FAINT HINT OF TRUTH, OTHERS, THE INEVITABLE PRODUCT OF UNBRIDLED CONJECTURE.

"DURING A CONNECTICUT THUNDER STORM, MRS. WINCHESTER'S HUSBAND AND BABY LOST THEIR LIVES IN A TRAGIC FIRE. THE DISTRACTED WIDOW TURNED TO SPIRITUALISM AND WAS ADVISED TO TAKE A TRIP AROUND THE WORLD. THIS SHE DID, VISITING MEDIUMS, SPIRITUALISTS AND YOGIS IN EUROPE AND INDIA. FORETELLING HER FUTURE, ONE SEER WARNED HER OF ALL THE COUNTLESS THOUSANDS OF DEPARTED SOULS SLAIN BY HER HUSBAND'S RIFLES; SHE MUST PROTECT HERSELF AND ATONE FOR SUCH MASS MURDER. SHE WAS TOLD TO PLAN A CASTLE AND CONTINUE ITS BUILDING INDEFINITELY BECAUSE AS LONG AS IT WAS UNDER CONSTRUCTION SHE WOULD LIVE; CESSATION WOULD PROVE IMMEDIATELY FATAL."

"RETURNING FROM HER GLOBAL TRIP, SHE ARRIVED IN SAN FRANCISCO AND FINDING THIS AREA SELDOM SUBJECT TO THUNDERSTORMS SHE PURCHASED AN EIGHT-ROOM HOUSE FOUR MILES WEST OF SAN JOSÉ. SHE HIRED AN ARCHITECT, A FOREMAN AND AN ARMY OF CARPENTERS AND WORK BEGAN; ARCHITECT AND FOREMAN QUIT THE FIRST DAY."

"HER BLUE SEANCE ROOM WAS LOCKED TO ALL BUT HERSELF; NO OTHER EVER ENTERED. HERE SHE DONNED CEREMONIAL ROBES AND COMMUNED NIGHTLY WITH THE SPIRITS. WINCHESTER HOUSE WAS THE MIDNIGHT RENDEZVOUS FOR LEGIONS OF GHOSTS, WITH SPECIAL ATTENTION ACCORDED THOSE CREATED BY A WINCHESTER RIFLE SLUG."

"AT NIGHT, PASSERS-BY HEARD GHOSTLY MUSIC WAFTING FROM THE DARK MANSION. THE BELL IN THE BELFRY HIGH IN THE GABLES TOLLED REGULARLY AT MIDNIGHT TO SUMMON INCOMING FLIGHTS OF SPIRITS. LATER IT TOLLED AGAIN TO WARN THESE VISITORS TO RETURN TO THEIR SEPULCHRES. BUT ONCE A WEEK THESE DEPARTED ONES RELAXED AND DANCED IN THE GREAT BALL ROOM."

52

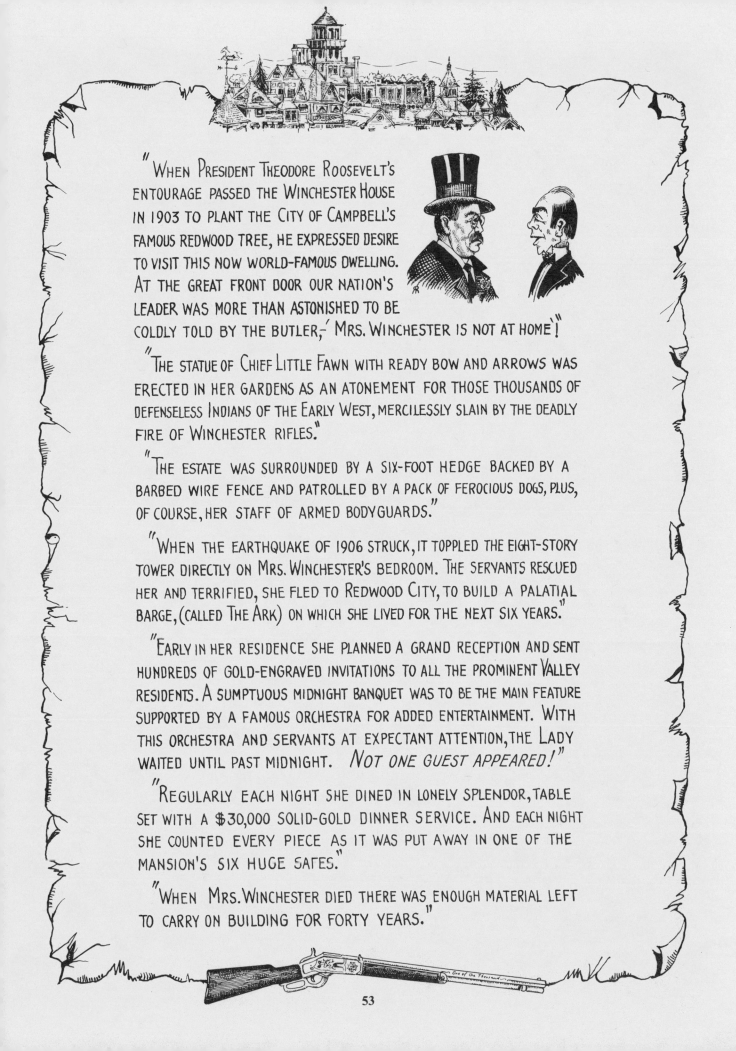

"WHEN PRESIDENT THEODORE ROOSEVELT'S ENTOURAGE PASSED THE WINCHESTER HOUSE IN 1903 TO PLANT THE CITY OF CAMPBELL'S FAMOUS REDWOOD TREE, HE EXPRESSED DESIRE TO VISIT THIS NOW WORLD-FAMOUS DWELLING. AT THE GREAT FRONT DOOR OUR NATION'S LEADER WAS MORE THAN ASTONISHED TO BE COLDLY TOLD BY THE BUTLER,—' MRS. WINCHESTER IS NOT AT HOME'!"

"THE STATUE OF CHIEF LITTLE FAWN WITH READY BOW AND ARROWS WAS ERECTED IN HER GARDENS AS AN ATONEMENT FOR THOSE THOUSANDS OF DEFENSELESS INDIANS OF THE EARLY WEST, MERCILESSLY SLAIN BY THE DEADLY FIRE OF WINCHESTER RIFLES."

"THE ESTATE WAS SURROUNDED BY A SIX-FOOT HEDGE BACKED BY A BARBED WIRE FENCE AND PATROLLED BY A PACK OF FEROCIOUS DOGS, PLUS, OF COURSE, HER STAFF OF ARMED BODYGUARDS."

"WHEN THE EARTHQUAKE OF 1906 STRUCK, IT TOPPLED THE EIGHT-STORY TOWER DIRECTLY ON MRS. WINCHESTER'S BEDROOM. THE SERVANTS RESCUED HER AND TERRIFIED, SHE FLED TO REDWOOD CITY, TO BUILD A PALATIAL BARGE, (CALLED THE ARK) ON WHICH SHE LIVED FOR THE NEXT SIX YEARS."

"EARLY IN HER RESIDENCE SHE PLANNED A GRAND RECEPTION AND SENT HUNDREDS OF GOLD-ENGRAVED INVITATIONS TO ALL THE PROMINENT VALLEY RESIDENTS. A SUMPTUOUS MIDNIGHT BANQUET WAS TO BE THE MAIN FEATURE SUPPORTED BY A FAMOUS ORCHESTRA FOR ADDED ENTERTAINMENT. WITH THIS ORCHESTRA AND SERVANTS AT EXPECTANT ATTENTION, THE LADY WAITED UNTIL PAST MIDNIGHT. *NOT ONE GUEST APPEARED!*"

"REGULARLY EACH NIGHT SHE DINED IN LONELY SPLENDOR, TABLE SET WITH A $30,000 SOLID-GOLD DINNER SERVICE. AND EACH NIGHT SHE COUNTED EVERY PIECE AS IT WAS PUT AWAY IN ONE OF THE MANSION'S SIX HUGE SAFES."

"WHEN MRS. WINCHESTER DIED THERE WAS ENOUGH MATERIAL LEFT TO CARRY ON BUILDING FOR FORTY YEARS."

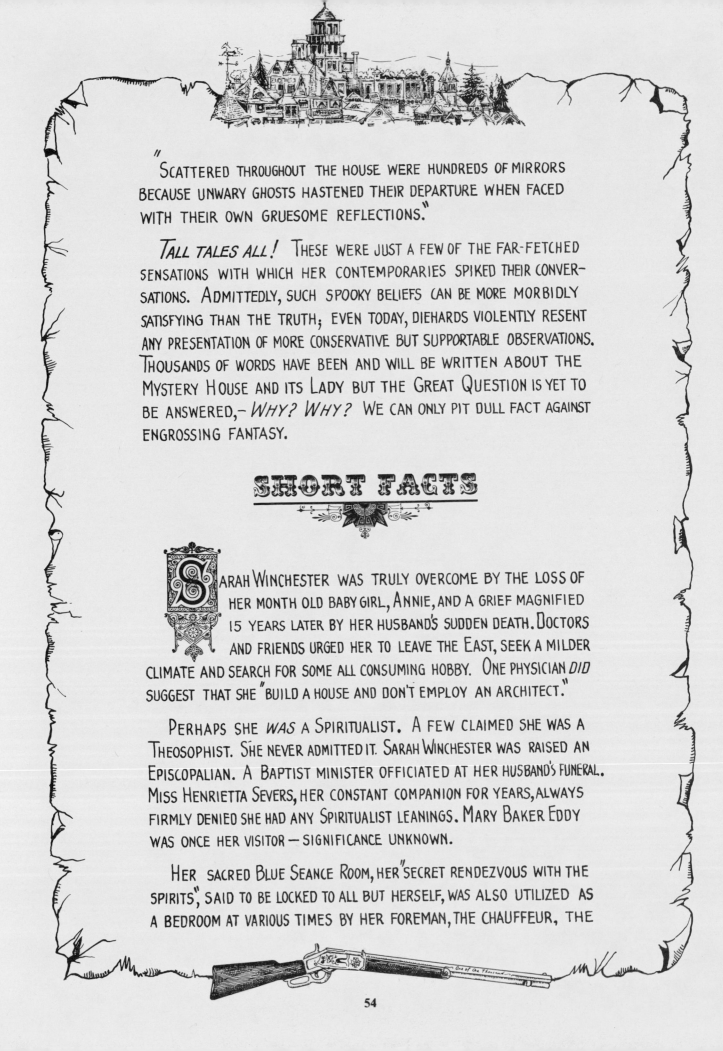

"Scattered throughout the house were hundreds of mirrors because unwary ghosts hastened their departure when faced with their own gruesome reflections."

Tall tales all! These were just a few of the far-fetched sensations with which her contemporaries spiked their conversations. Admittedly, such spooky beliefs can be more morbidly satisfying than the truth; even today, diehards violently resent any presentation of more conservative but supportable observations. Thousands of words have been and will be written about the Mystery House and its Lady but the great question is yet to be answered,— *Why? Why?* We can only pit dull fact against engrossing fantasy.

Short Facts

Sarah Winchester was truly overcome by the loss of her month old baby girl, Annie, and a grief magnified 15 years later by her husband's sudden death. Doctors and friends urged her to leave the East, seek a milder climate and search for some all consuming hobby. One physician *did* suggest that she "build a house and don't employ an architect."

Perhaps she *was* a Spiritualist. A few claimed she was a Theosophist. She never admitted it. Sarah Winchester was raised an Episcopalian. A Baptist minister officiated at her husband's funeral. Miss Henrietta Severs, her constant companion for years, always firmly denied she had any Spiritualist leanings. Mary Baker Eddy was once her visitor — significance unknown.

Her sacred Blue Seance Room, her "secret rendezvous with the spirits", said to be locked to all but herself, was also utilized as a bedroom at various times by her foreman, the chauffeur, the

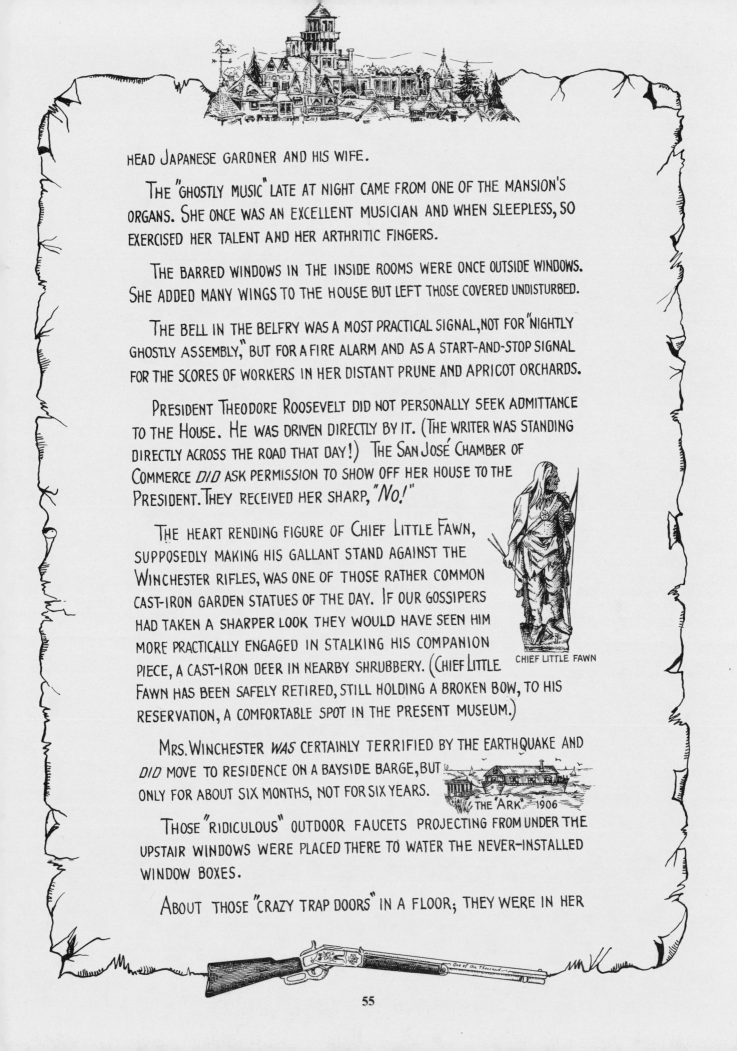

HEAD JAPANESE GARDNER AND HIS WIFE.

THE "GHOSTLY MUSIC" LATE AT NIGHT CAME FROM ONE OF THE MANSION'S ORGANS. SHE ONCE WAS AN EXCELLENT MUSICIAN AND WHEN SLEEPLESS, SO EXERCISED HER TALENT AND HER ARTHRITIC FINGERS.

THE BARRED WINDOWS IN THE INSIDE ROOMS WERE ONCE OUTSIDE WINDOWS. SHE ADDED MANY WINGS TO THE HOUSE BUT LEFT THOSE COVERED UNDISTURBED.

THE BELL IN THE BELFRY WAS A MOST PRACTICAL SIGNAL, NOT FOR "NIGHTLY GHOSTLY ASSEMBLY," BUT FOR A FIRE ALARM AND AS A START-AND-STOP SIGNAL FOR THE SCORES OF WORKERS IN HER DISTANT PRUNE AND APRICOT ORCHARDS.

PRESIDENT THEODORE ROOSEVELT DID NOT PERSONALLY SEEK ADMITTANCE TO THE HOUSE. HE WAS DRIVEN DIRECTLY BY IT. (THE WRITER WAS STANDING DIRECTLY ACROSS THE ROAD THAT DAY!) THE SAN JOSÉ CHAMBER OF COMMERCE *DID* ASK PERMISSION TO SHOW OFF HER HOUSE TO THE PRESIDENT. THEY RECEIVED HER SHARP, "NO!"

THE HEART RENDING FIGURE OF CHIEF LITTLE FAWN, SUPPOSEDLY MAKING HIS GALLANT STAND AGAINST THE WINCHESTER RIFLES, WAS ONE OF THOSE RATHER COMMON CAST-IRON GARDEN STATUES OF THE DAY. IF OUR GOSSIPERS HAD TAKEN A SHARPER LOOK THEY WOULD HAVE SEEN HIM MORE PRACTICALLY ENGAGED IN STALKING HIS COMPANION PIECE, A CAST-IRON DEER IN NEARBY SHRUBBERY. (CHIEF LITTLE

CHIEF LITTLE FAWN

FAWN HAS BEEN SAFELY RETIRED, STILL HOLDING A BROKEN BOW, TO HIS RESERVATION, A COMFORTABLE SPOT IN THE PRESENT MUSEUM.)

MRS. WINCHESTER *WAS* CERTAINLY TERRIFIED BY THE EARTHQUAKE AND *DID* MOVE TO RESIDENCE ON A BAYSIDE BARGE, BUT ONLY FOR ABOUT SIX MONTHS, NOT FOR SIX YEARS.

THE "ARK" 1906

THOSE "RIDICULOUS" OUTDOOR FAUCETS PROJECTING FROM UNDER THE UPSTAIR WINDOWS WERE PLACED THERE TO WATER THE NEVER-INSTALLED WINDOW BOXES.

ABOUT THOSE "CRAZY TRAP DOORS" IN A FLOOR; THEY WERE IN HER

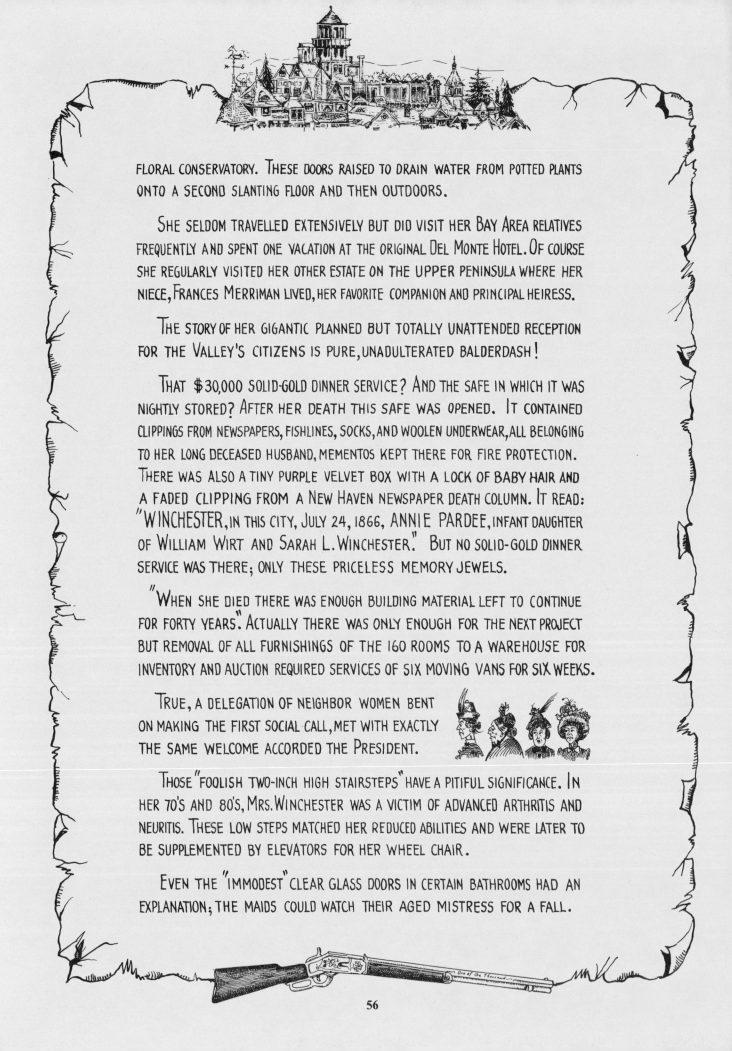

FLORAL CONSERVATORY. THESE DOORS RAISED TO DRAIN WATER FROM POTTED PLANTS ONTO A SECOND SLANTING FLOOR AND THEN OUTDOORS.

SHE SELDOM TRAVELLED EXTENSIVELY BUT DID VISIT HER BAY AREA RELATIVES FREQUENTLY AND SPENT ONE VACATION AT THE ORIGINAL DEL MONTE HOTEL. OF COURSE SHE REGULARLY VISITED HER OTHER ESTATE ON THE UPPER PENINSULA WHERE HER NIECE, FRANCES MERRIMAN LIVED, HER FAVORITE COMPANION AND PRINCIPAL HEIRESS.

THE STORY OF HER GIGANTIC PLANNED BUT TOTALLY UNATTENDED RECEPTION FOR THE VALLEY'S CITIZENS IS PURE, UNADULTERATED BALDERDASH!

THAT $30,000 SOLID-GOLD DINNER SERVICE? AND THE SAFE IN WHICH IT WAS NIGHTLY STORED? AFTER HER DEATH THIS SAFE WAS OPENED. IT CONTAINED CLIPPINGS FROM NEWSPAPERS, FISHLINES, SOCKS, AND WOOLEN UNDERWEAR, ALL BELONGING TO HER LONG DECEASED HUSBAND, MEMENTOS KEPT THERE FOR FIRE PROTECTION. THERE WAS ALSO A TINY PURPLE VELVET BOX WITH A LOCK OF BABY HAIR AND A FADED CLIPPING FROM A NEW HAVEN NEWSPAPER DEATH COLUMN. IT READ: "WINCHESTER, IN THIS CITY, JULY 24, 1866, ANNIE PARDEE, INFANT DAUGHTER OF WILLIAM WIRT AND SARAH L. WINCHESTER." BUT NO SOLID-GOLD DINNER SERVICE WAS THERE; ONLY THESE PRICELESS MEMORY JEWELS.

"WHEN SHE DIED THERE WAS ENOUGH BUILDING MATERIAL LEFT TO CONTINUE FOR FORTY YEARS." ACTUALLY THERE WAS ONLY ENOUGH FOR THE NEXT PROJECT BUT REMOVAL OF ALL FURNISHINGS OF THE 160 ROOMS TO A WAREHOUSE FOR INVENTORY AND AUCTION REQUIRED SERVICES OF SIX MOVING VANS FOR SIX WEEKS.

TRUE, A DELEGATION OF NEIGHBOR WOMEN BENT ON MAKING THE FIRST SOCIAL CALL, MET WITH EXACTLY THE SAME WELCOME ACCORDED THE PRESIDENT.

THOSE "FOOLISH TWO-INCH HIGH STAIRSTEPS" HAVE A PITIFUL SIGNIFICANCE. IN HER 70'S AND 80'S, MRS. WINCHESTER WAS A VICTIM OF ADVANCED ARTHRITIS AND NEURITIS. THESE LOW STEPS MATCHED HER REDUCED ABILITIES AND WERE LATER TO BE SUPPLEMENTED BY ELEVATORS FOR HER WHEEL CHAIR.

EVEN THE "IMMODEST" CLEAR GLASS DOORS IN CERTAIN BATHROOMS HAD AN EXPLANATION; THE MAIDS COULD WATCH THEIR AGED MISTRESS FOR A FALL.

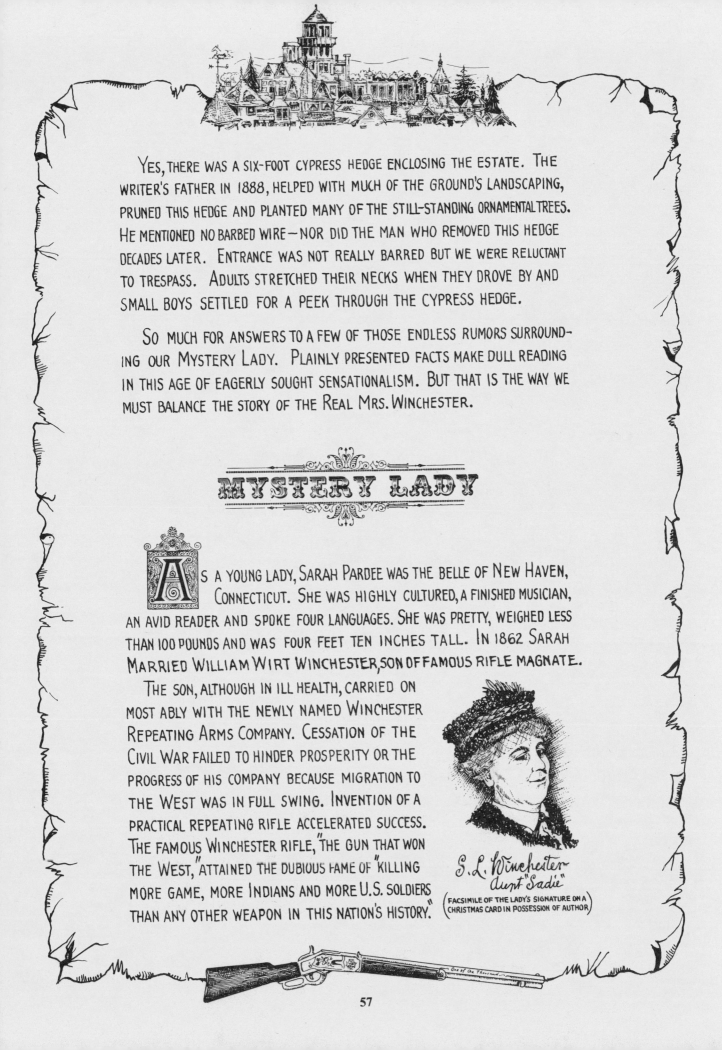

YES, THERE WAS A SIX-FOOT CYPRESS HEDGE ENCLOSING THE ESTATE. THE WRITER'S FATHER IN 1888, HELPED WITH MUCH OF THE GROUND'S LANDSCAPING, PRUNED THIS HEDGE AND PLANTED MANY OF THE STILL-STANDING ORNAMENTAL TREES. HE MENTIONED NO BARBED WIRE — NOR DID THE MAN WHO REMOVED THIS HEDGE DECADES LATER. ENTRANCE WAS NOT REALLY BARRED BUT WE WERE RELUCTANT TO TRESPASS. ADULTS STRETCHED THEIR NECKS WHEN THEY DROVE BY AND SMALL BOYS SETTLED FOR A PEEK THROUGH THE CYPRESS HEDGE.

SO MUCH FOR ANSWERS TO A FEW OF THOSE ENDLESS RUMORS SURROUNDING OUR MYSTERY LADY. PLAINLY PRESENTED FACTS MAKE DULL READING IN THIS AGE OF EAGERLY SOUGHT SENSATIONALISM. BUT THAT IS THE WAY WE MUST BALANCE THE STORY OF THE REAL MRS. WINCHESTER.

MYSTERY LADY

AS A YOUNG LADY, SARAH PARDEE WAS THE BELLE OF NEW HAVEN, CONNECTICUT. SHE WAS HIGHLY CULTURED, A FINISHED MUSICIAN, AN AVID READER AND SPOKE FOUR LANGUAGES. SHE WAS PRETTY, WEIGHED LESS THAN 100 POUNDS AND WAS FOUR FEET TEN INCHES TALL. IN 1862 SARAH MARRIED WILLIAM WIRT WINCHESTER, SON OF FAMOUS RIFLE MAGNATE.

THE SON, ALTHOUGH IN ILL HEALTH, CARRIED ON MOST ABLY WITH THE NEWLY NAMED WINCHESTER REPEATING ARMS COMPANY. CESSATION OF THE CIVIL WAR FAILED TO HINDER PROSPERITY OR THE PROGRESS OF HIS COMPANY BECAUSE MIGRATION TO THE WEST WAS IN FULL SWING. INVENTION OF A PRACTICAL REPEATING RIFLE ACCELERATED SUCCESS. THE FAMOUS WINCHESTER RIFLE, "THE GUN THAT WON THE WEST," ATTAINED THE DUBIOUS FAME OF "KILLING MORE GAME, MORE INDIANS AND MORE U.S. SOLDIERS THAN ANY OTHER WEAPON IN THIS NATION'S HISTORY."

S. L. Winchester
Aunt "Sadie"
(FACSIMILE OF THE LADY'S SIGNATURE ON A CHRISTMAS CARD IN POSSESSION OF AUTHOR)

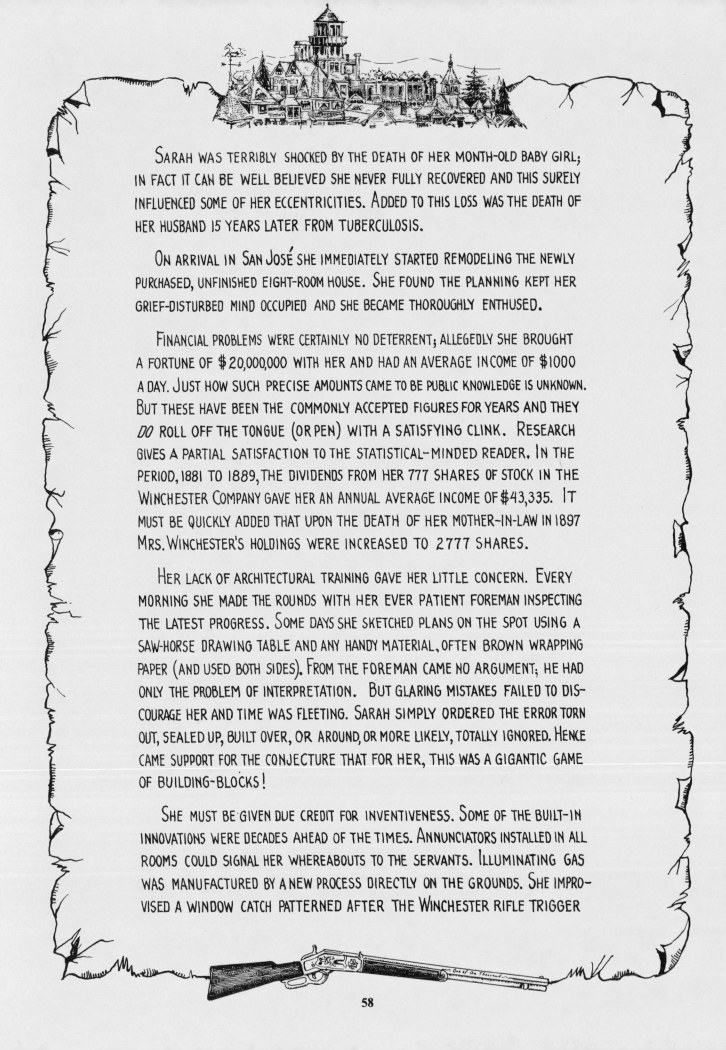

SARAH WAS TERRIBLY SHOCKED BY THE DEATH OF HER MONTH-OLD BABY GIRL; IN FACT IT CAN BE WELL BELIEVED SHE NEVER FULLY RECOVERED AND THIS SURELY INFLUENCED SOME OF HER ECCENTRICITIES. ADDED TO THIS LOSS WAS THE DEATH OF HER HUSBAND 15 YEARS LATER FROM TUBERCULOSIS.

ON ARRIVAL IN SAN JOSÉ SHE IMMEDIATELY STARTED REMODELING THE NEWLY PURCHASED, UNFINISHED EIGHT-ROOM HOUSE. SHE FOUND THE PLANNING KEPT HER GRIEF-DISTURBED MIND OCCUPIED AND SHE BECAME THOROUGHLY ENTHUSED.

FINANCIAL PROBLEMS WERE CERTAINLY NO DETERRENT; ALLEGEDLY SHE BROUGHT A FORTUNE OF $20,000,000 WITH HER AND HAD AN AVERAGE INCOME OF $1000 A DAY. JUST HOW SUCH PRECISE AMOUNTS CAME TO BE PUBLIC KNOWLEDGE IS UNKNOWN. BUT THESE HAVE BEEN THE COMMONLY ACCEPTED FIGURES FOR YEARS AND THEY *DO* ROLL OFF THE TONGUE (OR PEN) WITH A SATISFYING CLINK. RESEARCH GIVES A PARTIAL SATISFACTION TO THE STATISTICAL-MINDED READER. IN THE PERIOD, 1881 TO 1889, THE DIVIDENDS FROM HER 777 SHARES OF STOCK IN THE WINCHESTER COMPANY GAVE HER AN ANNUAL AVERAGE INCOME OF $43,335. IT MUST BE QUICKLY ADDED THAT UPON THE DEATH OF HER MOTHER-IN-LAW IN 1897 MRS. WINCHESTER'S HOLDINGS WERE INCREASED TO 2777 SHARES.

HER LACK OF ARCHITECTURAL TRAINING GAVE HER LITTLE CONCERN. EVERY MORNING SHE MADE THE ROUNDS WITH HER EVER PATIENT FOREMAN INSPECTING THE LATEST PROGRESS. SOME DAYS SHE SKETCHED PLANS ON THE SPOT USING A SAW-HORSE DRAWING TABLE AND ANY HANDY MATERIAL, OFTEN BROWN WRAPPING PAPER (AND USED BOTH SIDES). FROM THE FOREMAN CAME NO ARGUMENT; HE HAD ONLY THE PROBLEM OF INTERPRETATION. BUT GLARING MISTAKES FAILED TO DIS- COURAGE HER AND TIME WAS FLEETING. SARAH SIMPLY ORDERED THE ERROR TORN OUT, SEALED UP, BUILT OVER, OR AROUND, OR MORE LIKELY, TOTALLY IGNORED. HENCE CAME SUPPORT FOR THE CONJECTURE THAT FOR HER, THIS WAS A GIGANTIC GAME OF BUILDING-BLOCKS!

SHE MUST BE GIVEN DUE CREDIT FOR INVENTIVENESS. SOME OF THE BUILT-IN INNOVATIONS WERE DECADES AHEAD OF THE TIMES. ANNUNCIATORS INSTALLED IN ALL ROOMS COULD SIGNAL HER WHEREABOUTS TO THE SERVANTS. ILLUMINATING GAS WAS MANUFACTURED BY A NEW PROCESS DIRECTLY ON THE GROUNDS. SHE IMPRO- VISED A WINDOW CATCH PATTERNED AFTER THE WINCHESTER RIFLE TRIGGER

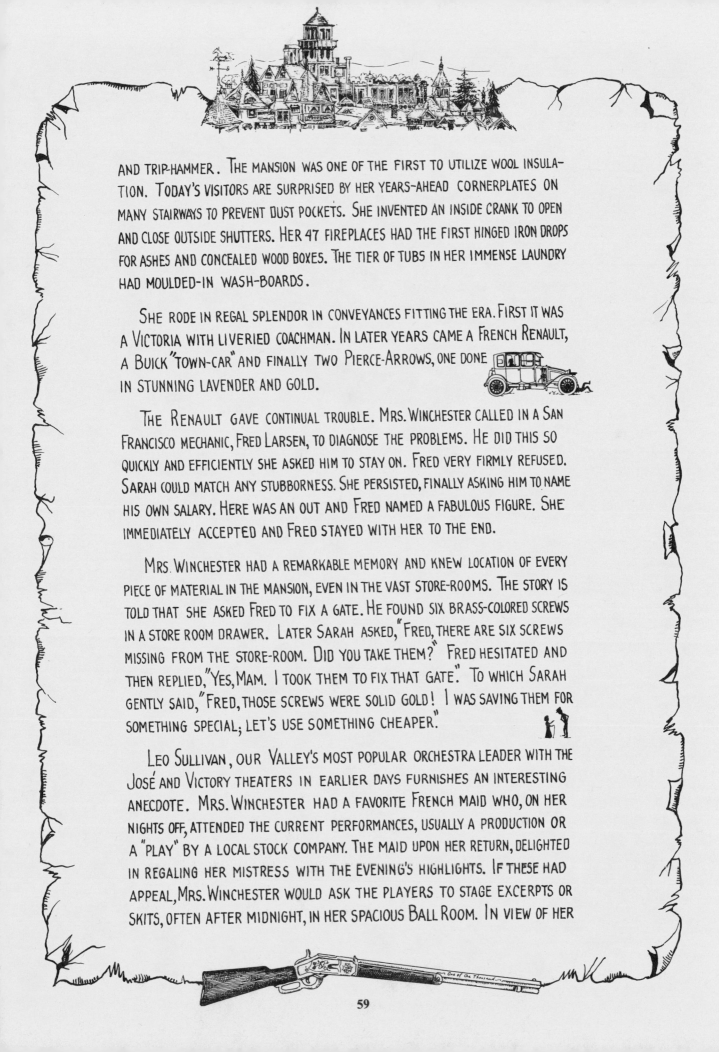

AND TRIP-HAMMER. THE MANSION WAS ONE OF THE FIRST TO UTILIZE WOOL INSULATION. TODAY'S VISITORS ARE SURPRISED BY HER YEARS-AHEAD CORNERPLATES ON MANY STAIRWAYS TO PREVENT DUST POCKETS. SHE INVENTED AN INSIDE CRANK TO OPEN AND CLOSE OUTSIDE SHUTTERS. HER 47 FIREPLACES HAD THE FIRST HINGED IRON DROPS FOR ASHES AND CONCEALED WOOD BOXES. THE TIER OF TUBS IN HER IMMENSE LAUNDRY HAD MOULDED-IN WASH-BOARDS.

SHE RODE IN REGAL SPLENDOR IN CONVEYANCES FITTING THE ERA. FIRST IT WAS A VICTORIA WITH LIVERIED COACHMAN. IN LATER YEARS CAME A FRENCH RENAULT, A BUICK "TOWN-CAR" AND FINALLY TWO PIERCE-ARROWS, ONE DONE IN STUNNING LAVENDER AND GOLD.

THE RENAULT GAVE CONTINUAL TROUBLE. MRS. WINCHESTER CALLED IN A SAN FRANCISCO MECHANIC, FRED LARSEN, TO DIAGNOSE THE PROBLEMS. HE DID THIS SO QUICKLY AND EFFICIENTLY SHE ASKED HIM TO STAY ON. FRED VERY FIRMLY REFUSED. SARAH COULD MATCH ANY STUBBORNESS. SHE PERSISTED, FINALLY ASKING HIM TO NAME HIS OWN SALARY. HERE WAS AN OUT AND FRED NAMED A FABULOUS FIGURE. SHE IMMEDIATELY ACCEPTED AND FRED STAYED WITH HER TO THE END.

MRS. WINCHESTER HAD A REMARKABLE MEMORY AND KNEW LOCATION OF EVERY PIECE OF MATERIAL IN THE MANSION, EVEN IN THE VAST STORE-ROOMS. THE STORY IS TOLD THAT SHE ASKED FRED TO FIX A GATE. HE FOUND SIX BRASS-COLORED SCREWS IN A STORE ROOM DRAWER. LATER SARAH ASKED, "FRED, THERE ARE SIX SCREWS MISSING FROM THE STORE-ROOM. DID YOU TAKE THEM?" FRED HESITATED AND THEN REPLIED, "YES, MAM. I TOOK THEM TO FIX THAT GATE". TO WHICH SARAH GENTLY SAID, "FRED, THOSE SCREWS WERE SOLID GOLD! I WAS SAVING THEM FOR SOMETHING SPECIAL; LET'S USE SOMETHING CHEAPER".

LEO SULLIVAN, OUR VALLEY'S MOST POPULAR ORCHESTRA LEADER WITH THE JOSÉ AND VICTORY THEATERS IN EARLIER DAYS FURNISHES AN INTERESTING ANECDOTE. MRS. WINCHESTER HAD A FAVORITE FRENCH MAID WHO, ON HER NIGHTS OFF, ATTENDED THE CURRENT PERFORMANCES, USUALLY A PRODUCTION OR A "PLAY" BY A LOCAL STOCK COMPANY. THE MAID UPON HER RETURN, DELIGHTED IN REGALING HER MISTRESS WITH THE EVENING'S HIGHLIGHTS. IF THESE HAD APPEAL, MRS. WINCHESTER WOULD ASK THE PLAYERS TO STAGE EXCERPTS OR SKITS, OFTEN AFTER MIDNIGHT, IN HER SPACIOUS BALL ROOM. IN VIEW OF HER

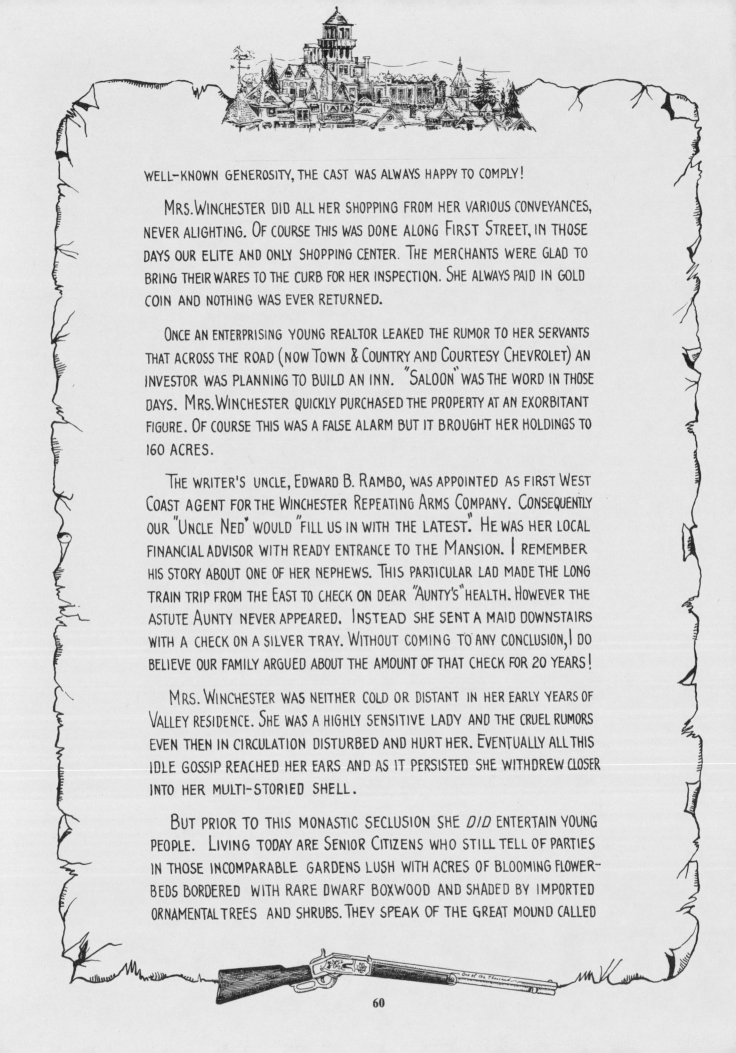

WELL-KNOWN GENEROSITY, THE CAST WAS ALWAYS HAPPY TO COMPLY!

MRS. WINCHESTER DID ALL HER SHOPPING FROM HER VARIOUS CONVEYANCES, NEVER ALIGHTING. OF COURSE THIS WAS DONE ALONG FIRST STREET, IN THOSE DAYS OUR ELITE AND ONLY SHOPPING CENTER. THE MERCHANTS WERE GLAD TO BRING THEIR WARES TO THE CURB FOR HER INSPECTION. SHE ALWAYS PAID IN GOLD COIN AND NOTHING WAS EVER RETURNED.

ONCE AN ENTERPRISING YOUNG REALTOR LEAKED THE RUMOR TO HER SERVANTS THAT ACROSS THE ROAD (NOW TOWN & COUNTRY AND COURTESY CHEVROLET) AN INVESTOR WAS PLANNING TO BUILD AN INN. "SALOON" WAS THE WORD IN THOSE DAYS. MRS. WINCHESTER QUICKLY PURCHASED THE PROPERTY AT AN EXORBITANT FIGURE. OF COURSE THIS WAS A FALSE ALARM BUT IT BROUGHT HER HOLDINGS TO 160 ACRES.

THE WRITER'S UNCLE, EDWARD B. RAMBO, WAS APPOINTED AS FIRST WEST COAST AGENT FOR THE WINCHESTER REPEATING ARMS COMPANY. CONSEQUENTLY OUR "UNCLE NED" WOULD "FILL US IN WITH THE LATEST." HE WAS HER LOCAL FINANCIAL ADVISOR WITH READY ENTRANCE TO THE MANSION. I REMEMBER HIS STORY ABOUT ONE OF HER NEPHEWS. THIS PARTICULAR LAD MADE THE LONG TRAIN TRIP FROM THE EAST TO CHECK ON DEAR "AUNTY'S" HEALTH. HOWEVER THE ASTUTE AUNTY NEVER APPEARED. INSTEAD SHE SENT A MAID DOWNSTAIRS WITH A CHECK ON A SILVER TRAY. WITHOUT COMING TO ANY CONCLUSION, I DO BELIEVE OUR FAMILY ARGUED ABOUT THE AMOUNT OF THAT CHECK FOR 20 YEARS!

MRS. WINCHESTER WAS NEITHER COLD OR DISTANT IN HER EARLY YEARS OF VALLEY RESIDENCE. SHE WAS A HIGHLY SENSITIVE LADY AND THE CRUEL RUMORS EVEN THEN IN CIRCULATION DISTURBED AND HURT HER. EVENTUALLY ALL THIS IDLE GOSSIP REACHED HER EARS AND AS IT PERSISTED SHE WITHDREW CLOSER INTO HER MULTI-STORIED SHELL.

BUT PRIOR TO THIS MONASTIC SECLUSION SHE *DID* ENTERTAIN YOUNG PEOPLE. LIVING TODAY ARE SENIOR CITIZENS WHO STILL TELL OF PARTIES IN THOSE INCOMPARABLE GARDENS LUSH WITH ACRES OF BLOOMING FLOWER-BEDS BORDERED WITH RARE DWARF BOXWOOD AND SHADED BY IMPORTED ORNAMENTAL TREES AND SHRUBS. THEY SPEAK OF THE GREAT MOUND CALLED

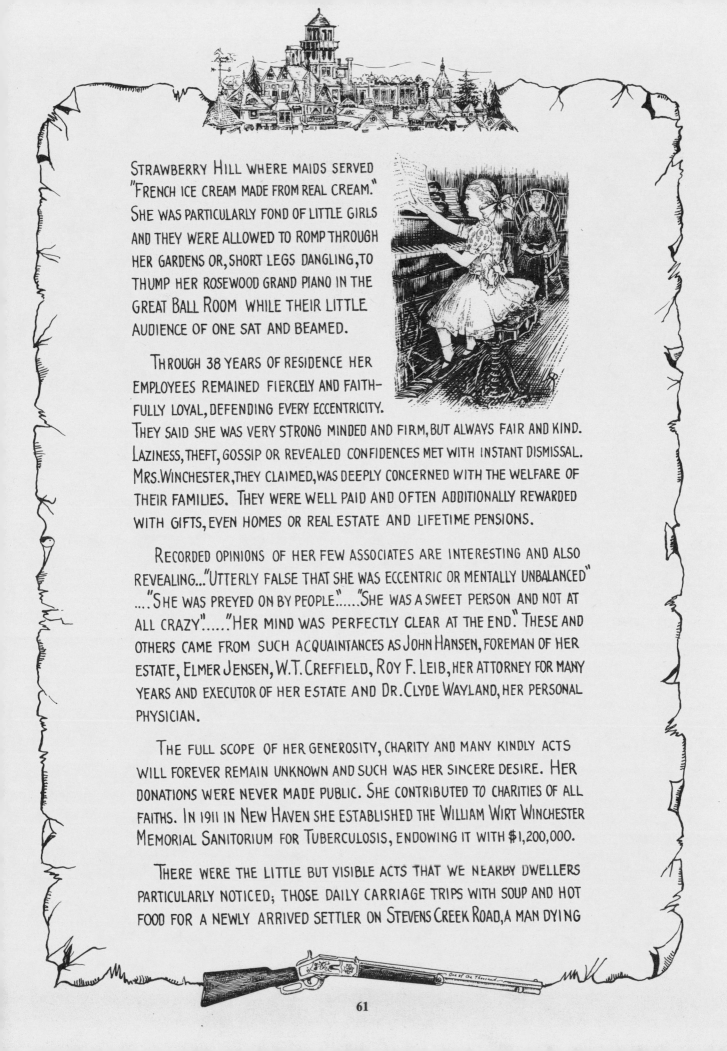

Strawberry Hill where maids served "French ice cream made from real cream." She was particularly fond of little girls and they were allowed to romp through her gardens or, short legs dangling, to thump her rosewood grand piano in the Great Ball Room while their little audience of one sat and beamed.

Through 38 years of residence her employees remained fiercely and faithfully loyal, defending every eccentricity. They said she was very strong minded and firm, but always fair and kind. Laziness, theft, gossip or revealed confidences met with instant dismissal. Mrs. Winchester, they claimed, was deeply concerned with the welfare of their families. They were well paid and often additionally rewarded with gifts, even homes or real estate and lifetime pensions.

Recorded opinions of her few associates are interesting and also revealing..."Utterly false that she was eccentric or mentally unbalanced"...."She was preyed on by people"......"She was a sweet person and not at all crazy"......"Her mind was perfectly clear at the end". These and others came from such acquaintances as John Hansen, foreman of her estate, Elmer Jensen, W. T. Creffield, Roy F. Leib, her attorney for many years and executor of her estate and Dr. Clyde Wayland, her personal physician.

The full scope of her generosity, charity and many kindly acts will forever remain unknown and such was her sincere desire. Her donations were never made public. She contributed to charities of all faiths. In 1911 in New Haven she established the William Wirt Winchester Memorial Sanitorium for Tuberculosis, endowing it with $1,200,000.

There were the little but visible acts that we nearby dwellers particularly noticed; those daily carriage trips with soup and hot food for a newly arrived settler on Stevens Creek Road, a man dying

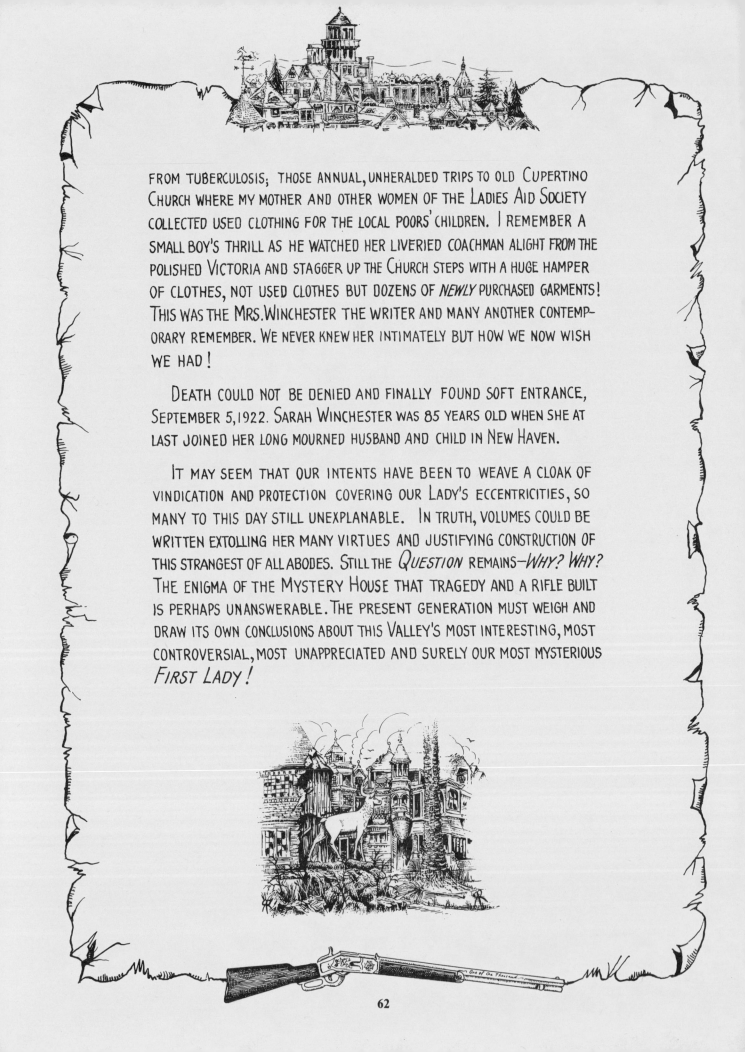

FROM TUBERCULOSIS; THOSE ANNUAL, UNHERALDED TRIPS TO OLD CUPERTINO
CHURCH WHERE MY MOTHER AND OTHER WOMEN OF THE LADIES AID SOCIETY
COLLECTED USED CLOTHING FOR THE LOCAL POORS' CHILDREN. I REMEMBER A
SMALL BOY'S THRILL AS HE WATCHED HER LIVERIED COACHMAN ALIGHT FROM THE
POLISHED VICTORIA AND STAGGER UP THE CHURCH STEPS WITH A HUGE HAMPER
OF CLOTHES, NOT USED CLOTHES BUT DOZENS OF *NEWLY* PURCHASED GARMENTS!
THIS WAS THE MRS. WINCHESTER THE WRITER AND MANY ANOTHER CONTEMP-
ORARY REMEMBER. WE NEVER KNEW HER INTIMATELY BUT HOW WE NOW WISH
WE HAD!

DEATH COULD NOT BE DENIED AND FINALLY FOUND SOFT ENTRANCE,
SEPTEMBER 5, 1922. SARAH WINCHESTER WAS 85 YEARS OLD WHEN SHE AT
LAST JOINED HER LONG MOURNED HUSBAND AND CHILD IN NEW HAVEN.

IT MAY SEEM THAT OUR INTENTS HAVE BEEN TO WEAVE A CLOAK OF
VINDICATION AND PROTECTION COVERING OUR LADY'S ECCENTRICITIES, SO
MANY TO THIS DAY STILL UNEXPLANABLE. IN TRUTH, VOLUMES COULD BE
WRITTEN EXTOLLING HER MANY VIRTUES AND JUSTIFYING CONSTRUCTION OF
THIS STRANGEST OF ALL ABODES. STILL THE *QUESTION* REMAINS—*WHY? WHY?*
THE ENIGMA OF THE MYSTERY HOUSE THAT TRAGEDY AND A RIFLE BUILT
IS PERHAPS UNANSWERABLE. THE PRESENT GENERATION MUST WEIGH AND
DRAW ITS OWN CONCLUSIONS ABOUT THIS VALLEY'S MOST INTERESTING, MOST
CONTROVERSIAL, MOST UNAPPRECIATED AND SURELY OUR MOST MYSTERIOUS
FIRST LADY!

SIERRA SANTA

BY RALPH RAMBO

Dear Reader,

This book's a sleeper. It is generally overlooked because of two mistakes, the title and the original cover design. These give it the appearance of a holiday book or a children's book. It *is* a holiday book and it *is* a children's book (ages 9 to 90). Readers write, assuring me that it has become a custom for their Christmas Eve family gatherings to read this simple tale.

Here again, like *Me & Cy,* this is a homely fiction built around actual fact, real characters, and a still existent stage setting.

Mariposa is well known to any local tourist. It's the terminal of Highway 49. The Sierra Santa character was inspired by my wife's Uncle Charley who was a legendary old Mariposa gold prospector we often visited. He lived in a 49er cabin close to Mariposa and the fact that he never struck any gold vein or gold larger than "skeeter eyes" failed to discourage him. He was known to Mariposans as "Dull Pick Charley". The story is fictional but firmly researched as regards the Mt. Ophir Mint and the $50 slugs or double-eagles, worth from $2,000 to $5,000 apiece now. Even the possibility of that hidden cache is still alive!

Read it. Be a child again. It *almost* happened!

Yours Truly
Ralph Rambo

ONCE UPON A TIME THERE LIVED AN OLD MAN ON A HILLTOP IN THE LOWER SIERRAS. STRANGE TO SAY, HIS NAME WAS CLAUS. STRANGE BECAUSE HE WAS SHORT, FAT, HAD A LONG WHITE BEARD AND DRESSED IN A RED FLANNEL SHIRT WITH LEVI PANTS STUFFED IN HEAVY BOOTS. ABOVE HIS RED NOSE, BUSHY WHITE EYEBROWS ALMOST COVERED HIS FRIENDLY, TWINKLING EYES. HE ALWAYS WORE A BROAD SMILE AND WAS BELOVED BY EVERY CHILD THAT MET HIM. NOW WITH THAT DESCRIPTION WOULDN'T YOU EXPECT TO SEE A HERD OF REINDEER IN HIS CORRAL? AND MAYBE A SLEIGH PARKED IN THE SHED? BUT HE OWNED NARY A REINDEER; ONLY ONE SLEEPY LITTLE BURRO. OF COURSE THE CHILDREN NAMED THE BURRO RUDOLPH OR ROODY FOR SHORT. EVERY CHRISTMAS, ROODY PATIENTLY WORE A PAIR OF DEERHORNS STRAPPED BETWEEN HIS EARS—SO THAT HE LOOKED LIKE A REINDEER. ANYHOW, THE CHILDREN THOUGHT THAT HE DID WHICH IS ALL THAT MATTERS.

FOR A FEW HOURS OF UTTERLY SAFE RELIEF, A GENERATION OF TIRED MOTHERS HAD SENT A GENERATION OF RESTLESS YOUNGSTERS UP THE WELL WORN PATH LEADING TO THIS OLD MAN'S CABIN. "WHY DON'T YOU VISIT GRAMPA SANTA TODAY?" AND SO THEY DID, JOYOUSLY. THEY COULD EXPECT A WARM WELCOME, A CANDY BAR, MAYBE A THRILLING STORY, A RIDE ON ROODY OR A SHORT "PROSPECTIN' TRIP" DOWN IN THE CANYON BELOW.

FOR TINY, FIRST-TIME VISITORS WHO EXPECTED TO SEE A "REAL" SANTA CLAUS THERE WAS A STOCK EXPLANATION. "NO, HONEY, I AINT 'ZACTLY THE REAL SANTA CLAUS. ACTUAL, MY NAME IS HIRAM CLAUS." THEN IF THEY LOOKED DISAPPOINTED HE WOULD BRIGHTLY CONTINUE, "BUT I COULD BE SANTA CLAUS'S BROTHER!" 'COUNT OF MY RHEUMATICS AND ARTHURITIS, I HAD TO MOVE DOWN FROM THE NORTH POLE TO A WARMER CLIMATE. RECKON I DO LOOK LIKE MY BROTHER SOMEWHAT. SO JIST GO AHEAD AND CALL ME GRAMPA SANTA."

AND SO TO THE CHILDREN OF THE PIONEER MINING TOWN OF MARIPOSA AND SURROUNDING HILLS, HIRAM CLAUS BECAME "GRAMPA SANTA." AMONGST THE GROWNUPS HE WAS FONDLY KNOWN AS "OUR OLD PROSPECTOR". THE DIGNIFIED MARIPOSA CHAMBER OF COMMERCE PROUDLY REFERRED TO HIM AS "OUR SIERRA SANTA".

ONE TIME AN ILL-MANNERED, SMART-ALECK TOURIST DARED CALL HIRAM "OLD PARENTHESIS" BECAUSE HIRAM WAS SLIGHTLY BOWLEGGED. THE INSULT SPREAD LIKE WILDFIRE. HIS INDIGNANT YOUNGSTER FRIENDS QUIETLY LET THE AIR OUT OF THE INSULTER'S TIRES AND NEARLY DRAINED HIS GAS TANK. WHEN THE CULPRIT CLUMPED DOWN TO THE GAS STATION, THE ATTENDANT, A HIRAM FAN, MOST POLITELY INFLATED HIS TIRES TO TEN POUNDS PRESSURE AND ALMOST FILLED HIS GAS TANK. THEN WITH REVENGEFUL HUMOR HE ADDED A LIBERAL DASH OF PURE MOUNTAIN WATER TO THE GASOLINE. TOWNSPEOPLE AND HILL FOLK WERE ALL HIRAM LOYALISTS AND AS WE SAID, CHILDREN LOVED HIM. TO ANY NATIVE, HIRAM WAS THEIR REMAINING SYMBOL OF "THE DAYS OF OLD, THE DAYS OF GOLD".

HIRAM REGISTERED AS A PROSPECTOR BY PROFESSION. AND INDEED HE WAS — AT LEAST TO ALL APPEARANCES AND SPECIALLY FOR BENEFIT OF VACATIONING MOTORISTS ALONG MOTHER LODE HIGHWAYS. MANY A ROMANTIC TOURIST VISIONED HIRAM AS ONE OF THE ORIGINAL 49'RS AND NO NATIVE HASTENED TO CORRECT THEIR HAZY IMPRESSION OR THEIR VAGUE HISTORICAL ARITHMETIC. HIRAM WAS NOT 150 YEARS OLD BUT HE COULD HAVE BEEN 75.

HIS GRANDFATHER WAS A COVERED-WAGON PIONEER OF THE 1850'S ARRIVING FROM MISSOURI AND SETTLING AT MORMON BAR. HIRAM'S FATHER WORKED IN THE MOUNT BULLION MINE. BOTH MEN PROSPECTED FITFULLY BUT WITH LITTLE SUCCESS. HIRAM INHERITED HIS FOREFATHERS' "GOLD FEVER" WITH THE SAME DRAB RESULTS BUT WITH THEIR SAME HOPEFUL PERSEVERANCE.

HIRAM'S SCHOOLING HAD BEEN LIMITED. HE HAD NEVER MARRIED AND FOR MANY YEARS FOLLOWED

A SET ROUTINE OF LIVING. SPRING AND SUMMER HE HAD EMIGRATED TO THE GREAT SAN JOAQUIN VALLEY BELOW. THERE HE HAD WORKED IN THE GRAINFIELDS TO ACCUMULATE HIS FALL AND WINTER GRUBSTAKE. ALWAYS HE RETURNED WITH REFRESHED HOPES OF A LUCKY STRIKE.

TIME PASSED. THE WEIGHT OF YEARS INTERRUPTED HIRAM'S ANNUAL SCHEDULE. BLESSED WITH ABUNDANT HEALTH FOR A MAN PAST THE THREE SCORE AND TEN MARK, HIRAM NOW LIVED YEAR ROUND IN HIS PATCHED-UP CABIN ON ROAD RUNNER HILL. HE STILL PROSPECTED IN A CASUAL AND UNUSUAL MANNER. HIRAM MAY HAVE LACKED EDUCATION BUT HE WAS SMART ENOUGH TO REVISE HIS OLD WAYS OF LIFE. HIRAM HAD FITTED HIMSELF INTO MODERN TIMES; SUDDENLY TRANSFORMED HERE IN HIS MOUNTAINS BY HIGHWAYS, AUTOMOBILES AND ACCOMPANYING TOURISTS. YET FOR REASONS TO BE DISCLOSED, HIRAM DID NOT RESENT TOURISTS.

ON THIS DECEMBER DAY, HIRAM STOOD IN THE DOOR OF HIS HOME ON ROAD RUNNER HILL. HIS ONE-ROOM CABIN DATED BACK A HUNDRED YEARS, STILL RETAINING THE ORIGINAL NATIVE ROCK WALLS AND RECONSTRUCTED FIREPLACE. A RUSTY TIN ROOF HAD REPLACED THE HAND-SPLIT SHINGLES. ROODY SWITCHED HIS TAIL CONTENTEDLY IN A CRUDELY BUILT LEAN-TO ATTACHED TO THE CABIN. A CROOKED PIPE LEADING FROM A HILLSIDE SPRING DRIPPED INTO A DOORSIDE BARREL. ONE IMMENSE LAUREL TREE MODESTLY HID THE PRIVY. A SINGLE COPPER AERIAL WIRE STRETCHED FROM THE CABIN TO A TALL PINE TREE AND GAVE THE ONLY MODERN LOOK. HIRAM HAD AN ATWATER KENT BATTERY RADIO. SOMETIMES HE USED EAR-PHONES BECAUSE HE WENT TO BED AT SUNDOWN. IF HE DIDN'T FALL ASLEEP, HE TUNED IN THE EVENING NEWS FROM MERCED AND THE WEATHER REPORT. GOOD WEATHER MEANT TOURISTS AND AS WE HINTED, TOURISTS WERE IMPORTANT TO HIRAM. BUT NOT AT THIS MOMENT. ─ HIRAM STEPPED FROM HIS DOOR AND SHADED HIS EYES SO THAT HE COULD VIEW THE QUIET SCENE BELOW. HERE AND THERE HE GLIMPSED THE NARROW PAVED ROAD LEADING FROM MARIPOSA TO BEAR VALLEY AND

HORNITOS, WINDING ITS WAY THROUGH THE PINE-COVERED CANYON. ABOVE THE PINE TREES THE WHITE SPIRE OF MARIPOSA'S COUNTY COURT HOUSE GLEAMED IN THE AFTERNOON SUN. IN THE EASTERN DISTANCE A SKY'S CANOPY OF AZURE BLUE DIPPED TO MEET ROWS OF SNOW-COVERED PEAKS IN THE HIGH SIERRAS. A COLD WINTER WIND SIGHED THROUGH THE PINES ON ROAD RUNNER HILL.

HIRAM TUGGED AT A POCKET IN HIS FADED BLUE LEVIS AND EXTRACTED A SILVER WATCH THE SIZE OF A TURNIP. HE COULD EASILY HAVE LOOKED AT THE SOLID GOLD WRIST WATCH HIDDEN BY THE SLEEVE OF HIS RED FLANNEL SHIRT—BUT HE DIDN'T. HIRAM WAS A MAN OF HABIT—AND MODESTY. THE GOLD WATCH WAS A GIFT FROM THE MARIPOSA CHAMBER OF COMMERCE.

"SCHOOL BUS MUSTA COME BY NOW," HE MUTTERED ANXIOUSLY. "I HOPE BIG BERTHA HAS GONE TO MEET HER." A BLUEJAY SQUAWKED AND DROPPED AN ACORN. "YEP, HERE THEY COME."

TO ANY BUT THE EYES OF HIRAM, A STRANGE LOOKING PAIR APPROACHED. HARDLY TO BE CALLED A ROAD, A STEEP TRAIL, APPARENTLY ALMOST ABANDONED YET SHOWING TIRE MARKS, LED FROM THE CANYON'S DEPTHS PAST HIRAM'S CABIN. UP THIS TRAIL, BENT TO CLIMB THE ASCENT, CAME A FRECKLED-FACED LITTLE GIRL PERHAPS SEVEN YEARS OLD. HER CLOTHES WERE NEAT AND CLEAN BUT UNMISTAKABLY HOMEMADE. DESPITE THE SEASON, PERCHED UPON HER PIGTAILED HEAD WAS A TINY STRAW HAT HELD UNDER HER CHIN BY A RUBBER BAND. SHE WORE ALMOST-WHITE TENNIS SHOES.

AND HER COMPANION! WAS ANYONE EVER BETTER ESCORTED OR GUARDED? A DOG SO LARGE THAT THE LITTLE GIRL WAS DWARFED. HIRAM NEVER CEASED TO MARVEL AT THE SIZE OF BIG BERTHA. HE TOOK GREAT JOY IN DESCRIBING HER IN DETAIL TO MRS. PEEBLES WHO OWNED MARIPOSA'S BONANZA ANTIQUE AND CURIO SHOP.

"I SWEAR, MIZ PEEBLES, BIG BERTHA'S BIG AS A DANG CALF! WEIGHS MORE THAN 150 POUNDS. WHAT BREED? ONE OF THEM SAINT BERNARDS FOR SURE; KIND THAT RESCUES FOLKS AND LOVES CHILDERN. EVER TIME I LOOK AT THAT HOOGE ANIMAL I THINK OF THAT FEEROSHUS DOG IN THAT SHEERLOCK HOMES STORY; SEEMS I RECOLLECK IT WAS CALLED THE HOUND OF THE BASTARDVILLES. ONLY, LORDY, BIG BERTHA AINT FIERCE. SURE SHE'S BIG AS ALL

OUTDOORS AND LOOKS AWFUL SAD BUT SHE'S GENTLE AS A KITTEN, LEASTWISE LONG AS NO ONE HARMS DORY."

"DORY," HIRAM CALLED HER BUT HER REAL NAME WAS DORA. HIRAM HAD ONLY KNOWN HER FOR A FEW WEEKS. SHE AND HER WIDOWED MOTHER WERE NEW-COMERS TO THE HILLS AND LIVED AT THE DEAD-END OF THE TRAIL-ROAD PASSING HIRAM'S CABIN.

HIRAM HAD INTIMATELY KNOWN MANY CHILDREN BUT NONE TO MATCH DORA. SOMEHOW THE OLD MAN WAS UTTERLY CHARMED BY THIS LITTLE CHARACTER. PERHAPS IT WAS HER WARM AFFECTION, HER TALKATIVE FRANKNESS AND HER CONSTANT CURIOSITY ABOUT THIS STRANGE COUNTRY, SO NEW TO HER, SO OLD TO HIRAM.

THE LITTLE GIRL AND THE BIG DOG TOILED SLOWLY UP THE HILL. HUNG AROUND BIG BERTHA'S NECK WAS THEIR AMPLE TIN LUNCH BUCKET. AT SIGHT OF HIRAM DORA SMILED. IF A DOG CAN SMILE, SO DID BERTHA.

"COME IN AND SET AND WARM YERSELF, DORY, YOU LOOK PLUMB TUCKERED OUT," GRAMPA GREETED, "I DIDN'T SEE BIG BERTHA GO DOWN THE HILL TO MEET YOU."

"SHE DIDN'T, GRAMPA SANTA," DORA REPLIED, "SHE WENT TO SCHOOL WITH ME TODAY!"

"MEAN THAT ELYPHUNT OF A DOG RODE ON THE SCHOOL BUS? AND SET WITH YOU IN SCHOOL? HOW COME, DORY? WHY?"

DORA HESITATED. "OH, JUST BECAUSE —."

"BECAUSE WHY?"

"I FEEL BETTER WITH HER I GUESS."

"BUT WHY TAKE HER TO SCHOOL?"

"MAYBE BECAUSE I'M NEW OR MAYBE BECAUSE MY CLOTHES ARE KINDA FUNNY AND DIFFERENT. BUT I DON'T THINK THE KIDS WILL CALL ME HUNKY DOREY ANYMORE. NOT AFTER THEY SAW BIG BERTHA!"

HIRAM NODDED, FROWNED, MUTTERED AND CHANGED THE SUBJECT.

"TIME FOR YOUR MOM TO GET HOME FROM WORK AINT IT, DORY?"

"SOMETIMES SHE WORKS A LITTLE LATER," DORA REPLIED, "MAMA'S GOT TWO JOBS NOW. MORNINGS SHE DOES HOUSEKEEPING AT THE MARIPOSA AUTO COURT AND AT LUNCHTIME SHE WAITS ON TABLES AT THE BUTTERFLY RESTAURANT. MAMA SAYS CHRISTMAS IS ALMOST HERE AND BESIDES, WE NEED THREE NEW TIRES AND A NEW BATTERY FOR OUR MODEL A FORD. WE'RE NOT GOING TO MOVE AWAY, GRAMPA. WE LOVE IT HERE AND MAMA SAYS SHE'S SURE SHE CAN FINISH PAYING FOR OUR CABIN AND THE TWO ACRES."

"COURSE SHE CAN AND WILL," HIRAM SAID WITH ASSURANCE, "DON'T YOU EVER WORRY ONE DURN MINUTE."

THEN THE CONVERSATION BRIGHTENED. GRINDING GEARS BROKE THE HILLSIDE STILLNESS. "THERE'S MAMA NOW, GRAMPA. I MUST GO. KNOW WHAT DAY TOMORROW IS? SATURDAY! ARE WE GONNA PROSPECT FOR GOLD AND HUNT FOR OLD MINERS' BOTTLES AND OLD 49'R THINGS? YOU SAID WE MIGHT. YOU PROMISED A WEEK AGO. REMEMBER?"

"I DID, HUH?" HIRAM MUSED, "WELL, LET'S SEE? RECKON I COULD FIGGER OUT MY SPARE TIME SOME HOW." AS A HIDDEN MATTER OF FACT HE HAD BEEN CAREFULLY "FIGGERIN" ON NOTHING ELSE BUT JUST SUCH A JAUNT FOR THE PAST SIX DAYS, CAREFULLY PLANNED IN EVERY DETAIL.

"GOODBYE, DORY, I'LL SEE YOU TOMORROW," AND THE OLD PROSPECTOR RECEIVED A HUG FROM THE LITTLE GIRL WHILE HE GRAVELY SHOOK HANDS WITH BIG BERTHA. THEN HE CALLED TO DORA:

"BY THE WAY, DORY, WHAT YOU BEEN FEEDIN' BIG BERTHA LATELY? SHE LOOKS FATTER THAN A HOG."

"IT'S NOT WHAT SHE EATS, GRAMPA," DORA CALLED, "SHE EATS SAME AS US. MAMA SAYS SHE'S GOING TO HAVE A FAMILY REAL SOON. PUPPIES!"

"OH," SAID AN ASTONISHED HIRAM, "I RECKON THAT 'SPLAINS THE SITCHIASHUN."

AND SO, NEXT DAY, AT THE CRACK OF DAWN, THE QUARTET ASSEMBLED; GRAMPA SANTA,

DORA, BIG BERTHA AND ROODY. TO AN INNOCENT OBSERVER, ROODY MIGHT APPEAR CRUELLY OVERLOADED. FROM HIS FAT SIDES HUNG TWO HUGE CANVAS-COVERED PACKS; PICK, SHOVEL, AND GOLD PAN ARTISTICALLY ARRANGED THEREON. BUT RUDOLPH WAS FAR FROM BEING ABUSED. FOR LOOKS, THE PACKS WERE STUFFED WITH STRAW. TRUE, THE STRAW CONCEALED A FEW NECESSITIES; TWO BOX LUNCHES FROM THE BUTTERFLY RESTAURANT, A CANTEEN OF LEMONADE, A CARTON OF CORNFLAKES FOR ROODY'S LUNCH, TWO POUNDS OF BOLONEY FOR BERTHA, A TIN BOX OF NABISCO SUGAR WAFERS AND A BOTTLE OF SLOAN'S LINIMENT.

"LET'S WORK UP THE CRICK AND HILLSIDES TOWARD BEAR VALLEY AND HORNITOS", GRAMPA SUGGESTED, "PAST MOUNT BULLION, RUINS OF TRABUCCO STORE AND THE OLD PRINCETON MINE. WE GOTTA HIT NEW TERRITORY, DORY. THEM JAYHAWKER TOURISTS WITH THEIR NEW FANGLED 'LECTRIC METAL DETECTIVES JIST ABOUT CLEANED OUT THE BEST PLACES TO HUNT."

"BUT YOU'RE GOING TO PROSPECT FOR GOLD TOO, AREN'T YOU, GRAMPA?" DORA ASKED ANXIOUSLY.

"SURE, SURE, IN SORT OF A QUEER WAY, DORY, AS I JIST MIGHT SHOW OFF PURTY SOON. YOU KNOW WELL AS I DO THERE'S NUTHIN WORTH WHILE IN GOLD LEFT IN THE CRICK 'CEPT SKEETER-EYES."

"WHAT'S SKEETER-EYES, GRAMPA?"

"JIST WHAT THE OLD PROSPECTORS CALLED 'EM DORY, LITTLE SPECKS OF GOLD NO BIGGER THAN A MUSKEETER'S EYE. SELDOM MORE THAN A THIN DIME'S WORTH IN A PAN WASHIN'. SARTIN THERE'S STILL MILLIONS DOWN DEEP BELOW BUT PRICE OF GOLD AINT KEPT PACE WITH COST OF DIGGIN'. BESIDES, PICK AND SHOVEL WORK HAS LONG GONE OUT OF STYLE. ACTUAL, NOW THERE'S MORE MONEY PROSPECTIN FOR ANTEEKS AND MINERS' RELISHS."

"BUT WHAT'S A MINER'S RELISH, GRAMPA?" DORA ASKED.

"RELISH OR RELIK, I FERGIT WHICH MIZ PEEBLES CALLS 'EM, BUT MEANS ABOUT SAME AS ANTEEKS. A MINER'S RELISH IS SOMETHIN' OLD AND NO 'COUNT, A PLUMB WORE OUT 49'R ARTICLE THAT MIZ PEEBLES CUSTOMERS WILL PAY MOST ANY FANCY PRICE FER."

"MIZ PEEBLES MY SALES AGENT", GRAMPA CONTINUED PROUDLY, "AWFUL NICE, REFINED LADY

AND KNOWS THE HISTORY OF THIS COUNTRY. I TAKE EVERYTHIN' I FIND TO HER, OLD OX SHOES, OLD FRUIT JARS, OLD BOTTLES, BUSTED WAGON WHEELS, BOB-WIRE, GLASS INSULATORS, EVEN CRACKED CHINY CHAMBER POTS—STYLISH TO PLANT FLOWERS IN. SHE GIVES ME 80% OF WHAT SHE SELLS AND KEEPS 20%. AINT NO WONDER I TURNED DOWN A COUNTY PENSION AND GOTTA PUT MONEY IN THE BANK EVER MONTH."

ARRIVING AT THE CANYON'S SHADED CREEK, OUR PARTY RESTED, FIRST PUTTING THE CANTEEN OF LEMONADE IN THE CREEK WATER TO COOL. FROM THE ROAD ABOVE THEM A SPORTY LITTLE CONVERTIBLE WITH TWO JAZZY OCCUPANTS HALTED AND HONKED THEIR HORN.

"HEY THERE, GRAMPS", ONE OF THE YOUNGSTERS SHOUTED, "HOW LONG HAS THIS LOUSY OLD COUNTRY BEEN DEAD?"

QUICK AS A FLASH HIRAM REPLIED, "I RECKON NOT LONG, BUB. YOU'RE THE FIRST TWO BUZZARDS WE'VE SEEN." ⌒ THE CAR DEPARTED.

"I HEAR ANOTHER CAR COMIN', DORY," HIRAM SAID HOPEFULLY, "MEBBE NOW I CAN PUT ON A QUEER KIND OF A HOLD-UP SHOW FOR YOU. PLAY LIKE I'M SORT OF A BLACK BART, THE BANDIT, ONLY WITH WHITE WHISKERS. YOU JIST GET OVER CROSS THE CRICK AND SET UNDER THAT PINE TREE. PUT YOUR ARMS AROUND BIG BERTHA. LOOK SAD AND DEJECTIPATED. MIGHT AS WELL TAKE OFF YOUR SHOES AND STOCKIN'S AND HIDE 'EM. THEN WATCH ME GO TO WORK." DORA WONDERED, BUT OBEYED ORDERS.

MEANWHILE SIERRA SANTA SET HIS STAGE. ROODY NEEDED NO REHEARSAL AND PRESENTED HIS USUAL SAD PICTURE, AN APPARENTLY OVERBURDENED LITTLE BURRO, EYES CLOSED, FLOPPING EARS, YELLOW TEETH EXPOSED. HIRAM PRODUCED A SMALL MEDICINE BOTTLE FROM HIS POCKET AND SPRINKLED SOME SHINY GRAINS INTO THE BLACK SAND THAT HE HAD SCOOPED FROM THE CREEK INTO HIS RUSTY GOLD PAN. THEN SIERRA SANTA CAREFULLY COMBED HIS LONG, CLEAN, WHITE BEARD, PULLED HIS SHIRT SLEEVE OVER HIS GOLD WRIST WATCH AND BENT OVER THE STREAM.

WITHOUT TURNING HIS HEAD HE LOUDLY WHISPERED, "IT'S A BIG FANCY CADILLAC, DORY! TRY TO LOOK SADDER BUT NOT QUITE TO THE BAWLIN' STAGE."

ON THE ROAD ABOVE THEM, THE BRAKES OF A LUXURIOUS CAR SCREECHED TO A SUDDEN HALT. WHAT FOLLOWED COULD HAVE APPEARED TO ANYONE, INCLUDING DORA, A PURE PANTOMIME, A SILENT MOVIE OR A PICTURE WITHOUT WORDS.

A STYLISHLY DRESSED *LADY* ALMOST PUT OUT HER HUSBAND'S EYE AS SHE POINTED TO THE ROMANTIC SCENE BELOW. EVEN DORA COULD HEAR HER SCREAM, "LOOK, JOHN, JUST WHAT WE'VE ALWAYS HUNTED FOR! THE REAL THING! OUR CHANCE OF A LIFETIME!"

OUT PILED THE *MAN*, HUNG WITH EXPENSIVE STILL AND MOVIE CAMERAS, FILM BOXES, LIGHT METERS, EVEN A HEAVY TRIPOD. HE STUMBLED AWKWARDLY DOWN TO THE CREEK. DORA STRAINED BUT COULD NOT HEAR THE CONVERSATION. SHE SAW GRAMPA DISPLAY THE GOLD PAN AND SADLY SHAKE HIS HEAD. WHILE SHE TRIED TO MAINTAIN HER SAD EXPRESSION AND STAY AWAKE, SHE SLEEPILY WATCHED CAMERAS CLICK AND BULBS FLASH FOR IT SEEMED THIRTY MINUTES. SHE FINALLY SAW THE *MAN* SOMEWHAT APOLOGETICALLY PRESS A GREEN BILL INTO GRAMPA'S HAND, THEN WATCHED THE *MAN'S* OVERLOADED RETREAT TO THE CAR. BUT THE CAR REMAINED PARKED AND DORA SENSED AN ARGUMENT IN PROGRESS BETWEEN THE *MAN* AND *LADY*. FINALLY THE *LADY* MAJESTICALLY DESCENDED FROM THE CAR AND UNMAJESTICALLY SLID DOWN THE CREEK BANK. SHE ENGAGED HIRAM IN ANIMATED, WHISPERED CONVERSATION NOW AND THEN POINTING HER FINGER AT DORA'S FORLORN FIGURE. BIG BERTHA HAD LONG AGO GONE TO SLEEP, LEANING AGAINST THE DOZING LITTLE GIRL.

GRAMPA APPEARED TO BE EXPLAINING SOMETHING IN A RELUCTANT MANNER. AT THIS POINT THE *LADY* OPENED HER ELEGANTLY ORNAMENTED HAND BAG AND HANDED GRAMPA ANOTHER GREEN BILL. THEN INELEGANTLY, THE *LADY* SCRAMBLED UP TO THE CAR TO SMUGLY RESUME HER THRONE. AT LAST THE CAR SLOWLY ROLLED AWAY, STILL IN A CLOUD OF ARGUMENT AND UNDEVELOPED FILM. AND SO THE EPISODE ENDED? NOT YET.

AT LAST DORA AND GRAMPA RELAXED AS THEY HUNGRILY OPENED THEIR BOX-LUNCHES. "TELL ME EXACTLY WHAT HAPPENED, GRAMPA," SAID DORA, NOW FULLY AWAKENED AND NATURALLY CURIOUS.

"HOLD MY HAM SANDRICH A MINUTE, DORY, I DO BELIEVE BIG BERTHA'S GOT A WOOD TICK IN HER LEFT EAR," GRAMPA VAGUELY REMARKED, PUTTING ON HIS STEEL RIMMED SPECTACLES. "LATE IN THE SEASON FER TICKS. SIGN OF A DRY WINTER."

"I SAID, TELL ME EXACTLY WHAT HAPPENED, GRAMPA," DORA FIRMLY INSISTED.

HIRAM CONTINUED TO STALL FOR AN ANSWER. "WELL, I RECKON I MIGHT AS WELL TELL YOU. THIS TIME MY FOOL SCHEME WORKED OUT JIST AS SLICK AS GREASED LIGHTENIN' AND SMOOTH AS FROG'S HAIR. I SOLEM PROMISE I'LL NEVER DO IT AGAIN! I MEAN LEASTWISE WITH YOU SETTIN' IN THE PITCHER."

"GRAMPA, YOU STILL HAVEN'T TOLD ME!"

"WELL, YOU AST FER IT," HIRAM SURRENDERED, "ANYWAY PARTLY YOUR FAULT—YOU SHOULDN'T HAVE ACTED SO GOOD. AS YOU PLAIN SEEN, THE DUDE TOORIST CAME TEARIN' DOWN AND AST ME PERLITE LIKE, COULD HE TAKE MY PITCHER? AND AS YOU SEEN, HE DID TAKE MY PITCHER IN EVER POSITION EXCEP' STANDIN' ON MY HEAD. THEN HE HANDS ME A DOLLAR BILL WHICH ACCORDIN' TO MY RECORDS IS STINKIN' CHEAP AND STINGY FER A CADILLAC, WAY BELOW AVERAGE. THEN YOU SEEN HIM GO BACK TO THE CAR AND START ARGYFYING WITH HIS WIFE. THEN SHE COMES SLIDIN' DOWN AND REAL DEMANDIN' LIKE, SHE ASKS ALL ABOUT YOU."

"DORY, IT WAS ALL SO KINDA SUDDEN I GOT PLUMB FLABBERGASTED FER A MINUTE. REMEMBER, DORY, I JIST MIGHT BE GETTIN' SOMEWHAT OLD AND SOMETIMES MIXED-UP AND FORGETFUL."

"KEEP TALKING, GRAMPA," DORA ENCOURAGED, "THEN WHAT DID YOU TELL THE *LADY* ABOUT ME?"

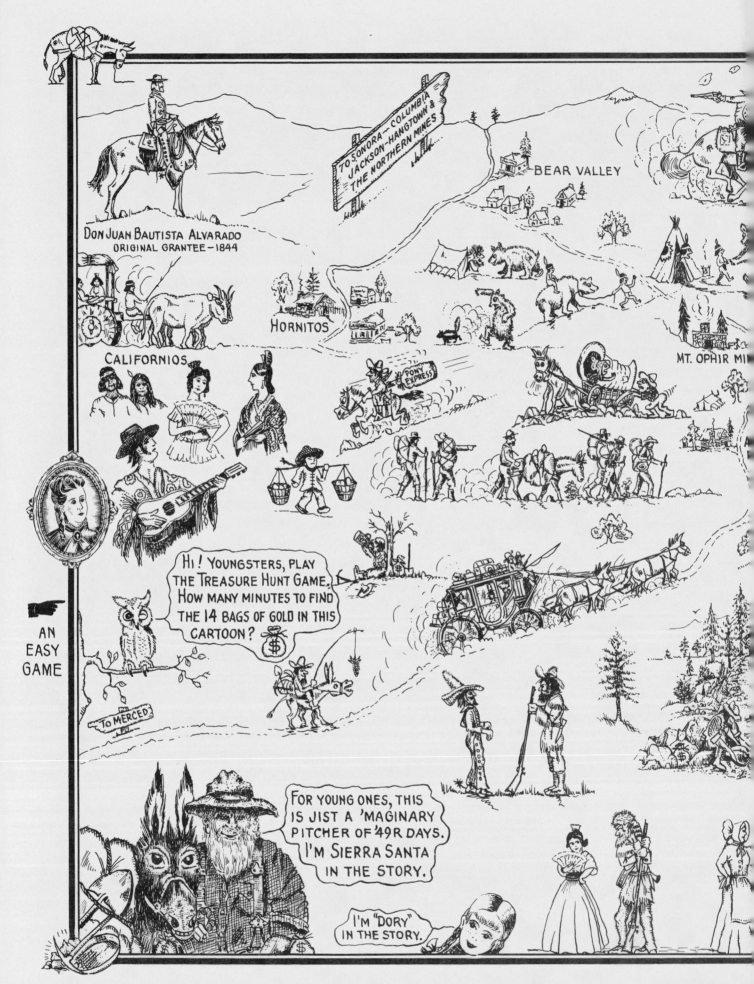

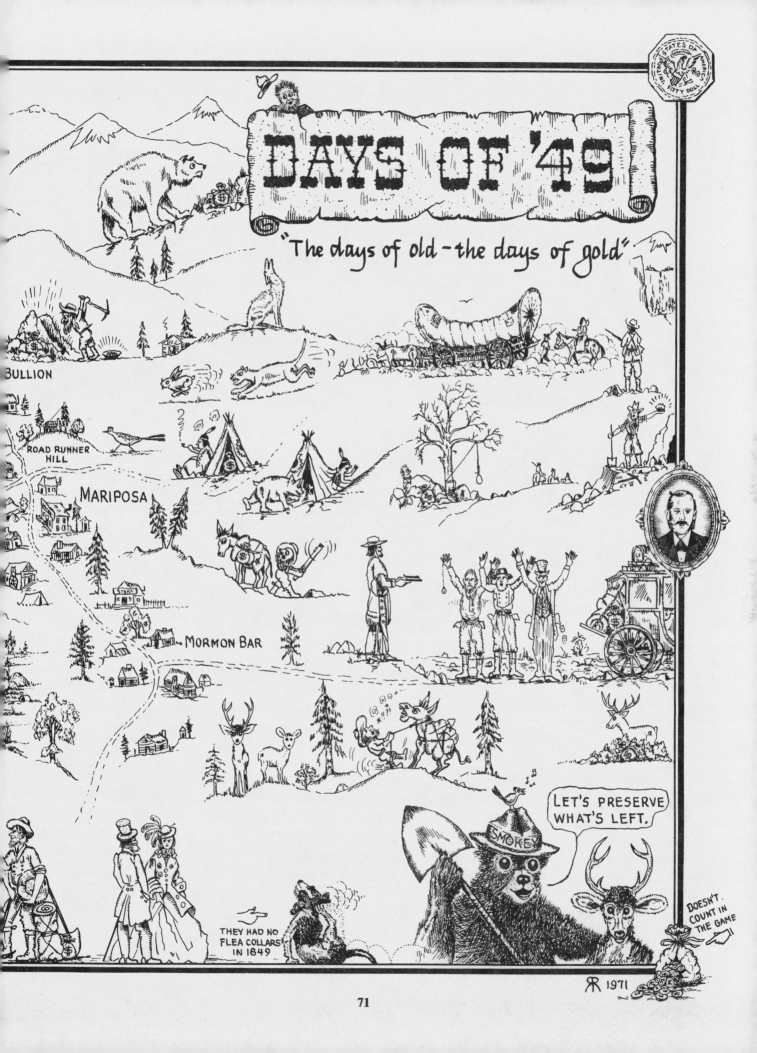

"Well, Dory, here it comes," Grampa finally confessed, "I don't know why but I just busted out by tellin' her you was my pore lil orphan grand-daughter, what lived alone with me in my cabin!"

Dora was between tears and laughter, "Oh! Grampa!" as she hugged the old man, "It wasn't the truth but second best I can't think of any-thing nicer".

Hiram breathed easier. "But that aint all, Dory, not quite." Extracting his tattered but fat wallet, he produced a crisp twenty dollar bill and handed it to Dora. "The *LADY* fished in her bag and handed this to me and pointed to you. Take it and buy your Mom some Chrismus presents". Then Grampa chuckled, "I almost fergot, *LADY* said to buy you some shoes and stockin's."

The joyful day progressed rapidly. Sierra Santa, with Dora carefully excluded, posed for only two more tourists. As Hiram reported, "Slimmer day than usual; jist a dinky four bits from a jeep and a dollar from a old Buick camper".

Otherwise the journey was another one of Hiram's priceless tours. The old prospector could name any flower, tree, rock, bird or historical ruin. With his constant flow of conversation, and Dora's lively imagination, the little girl could relive the golden days of '49.

"Time to call it a day, Dory," said Grampa at last, "Big Bertha's plumb tuckered out, look at her tongue hangin' out a foot. She's packin' more of a load than Roody. We did purty good today. Let's see, my toorist trade, special that Cadillac rumpus. And you found some real promisin' old bottles, that old Chinese opium jar, three mule shoes and four arrowheads. I'll take 'em down to Miz Peebles on Monday. Hurry, Dory, the sun's settin'. Jist got time to cut your Chrismus tree."

"Can't we go again next Saturday, Grampa?" Dora asked anxiously.

"Well, reckon I jist might arrange it some how," Hiram allowed. Actually he had never had anything else in mind. How often can the pleasures of youth and old age be so joyously mutual?

But the next Saturday dawned a cold and rainy day. Disconsolate over abandoned plans, Hiram dozed before a roaring fire of pine cones in the stone fireplace. He was lonesome. From his outdoor lean-to, Rudolph the burro poked his head through a plainly man-made hole in the stone wall. It was a hole for companionship and feed-ing convenience. Roody chose the moment to give out with a sudden loud bray that start-led the drowsy prospector. Hiram arose with a groan, broke open a carton of corn-flakes and dumped the contents into a specially built trough below the hole. He added half a loaf of stale French bread and four equally stale doughnuts.

"There, you spoiled, pint-size jackass!" Hiram fumed, "Eat that and hush up! You plumb fergot the meanin' of hay and oats. You don't seem to 'preciate the fak that I gotta leave a standin' order at the Mariposa Bakery fer them two-day old donuts and stale French bread. No, I aint even gonna slice the bread fer you this time."

Hardly had Hiram resumed his easy chair when there came a gentle knock on the door. He opened it to greet a muddy-footed little Dora. She was almost completely concealed by a huge, dripping umbrella. Big Bertha sloshed behind, only her head protruding from her overcoat of old canvas.

"We both got sad and lonesome, Grampa," Dora said, "Mama's working and no trip today on account of the rain. I was wondering if you would tell me stories about these hills when they were full of gold and miners?"

"YOU'RE WELCOME AS THE FLOWERS IN MAY, DORY," HIRAM SAID WITH CONCEALED JOY, "HOPE YOU HAVEN'T ET LUNCH YET. JIST FIXEN ME A RAINY-DAY LIGHT SNACK. THAT IRON POT ON BACK OF STOVE IS SIMMERIN' WITH PINK BEANS AND CHUNKS OF HAM. PAN OF CORN BREAD IN THE OVEN WITH A FRESH PAT OF BUTTER AND A SQUARE OF HONEYCOMB TO TOP IT OFF. I SAVED THE HAM BONE FER BIG BERTHA." HEARING HER NAME AND LIFTING HER GREAT HEAD TO SNIFF DELICIOUS ODORS, BERTHA APPLAUDED BY THUMPING HER TAIL LOUDLY AGAINST A CONVENIENT TIN WASHTUB.

"NOW WHAT KIND OF STORIES YOU WANT, DORY, TRUTH OR FRICTION? I CAN TELL EITHER KIND."

"WHAT'S FRICTION, GRAMPA?" DORA ASKED AS SHE PERCHED ON THE ARM OF HIS CHAIR. BIG BERTHA HAD SETTLED ON HER CHOICE SPOT, A MOTH-EATEN BEAR RUG.

"FRICTION, OR MEBBE IT'S PERNOUNCED FICTION, IS JUST OPPOSITE OF TRUTH," GRAMPA REPLIED, "MEANS STORIES THAT AINT TRUE BUT STILL INTERESTIN' AND HARMLESS AND WHAT MOST PEOPLE NOWDAYS WANT TO HEAR OR READ. WHAT KIND YOU WANT, DORY? I'M PARTICKLER GOOD ON FRICTION."

"I'D RATHER HEAR THE TRUTH", DORA QUICKLY REPLIED, "ABOUT WHERE WE ARE RIGHT NOW AND HOW IT WAS LIKE A HUNDRED YEARS AGO."

"SO BE IT," HIRAM AGREED, "STRAIGHT FROM WHAT MY PA TOLD ME AND WHAT HIS PA TOLD HIM. PLUS SOME THINGS MIZ PEEBLES TOLD ME OUT OF HER HISTRY BOOKS AND COURT HOUSE RECORDS."

"AND I BET YOU DIDN'T KNOW MARIPOSA'S GOT THE OLDEST COUNTY COURT HOUSE IN CALIFORNIA, BUILT IN 1854 AND STILL USED. THE CLOCK IN THE TOWER'S BEEN RUNNIN' STEADY SINCE 1866. MARIPOSA WAS THE BIGGEST COUNTY IN THE UNITED STATES, RAN ALL THE WAY TO LOS ANGELES. NOW IT'S CUT UP INTO TEN COUNTIES. THE WORD MARIPOSA MEANS BUTTERFLIES IN SPANISH, 'COUNT OF ALL THE BUTTERFLIES SEEN HERE BY THE SPANISH EXPLORER, GABRIEL MORAGA IN 1806."

"BUT FACKS AND FIGGERS CAN BE KINDA DULL, CAN'T THEY, DORY? LET'S STICK TO JIST WHAT YOU AST FER — 'BOUT RIGHT WHERE WE ARE, MARIPOSA, MOUNT BULLION AND I CAN'T LEAVE OUT THE MOUNT OPHIR MINT."

"WHAT'S A MINT, GRAMPA?" DORA ASKED.

"MEMBER I POINTED OUT THE 30 BY 30 FOOT MOUNT OPHIR MINT RUINS ON OUR LAST TRIP? I'LL GET TO IT LATER AND THE EXCITIN' MYSTERY THAT GOES WITH IT."

GRAMPA WAS HERE INTERRUPTED BY A SERIES OF LOUD SNEEZES FROM ROODY WHO EVIDENTLY CRAVED NOTICE AND ATTENTION.

"HE'S CATCHING COLD, GRAMPA," DORA SAID ANXIOUSLY, "WHY DON'T YOU BRING HIM IN? HE'S SO LITTLE. BIG BERTHA SLEEPS NEXT TO MY BED IN AN OLD PIANO BOX EVERY NIGHT."

"DON'T WORRY, DORY," GRAMPA CONFIDED, "I LET HIM SLEEP INDOORS EVER COLD NIGHT. BUT I SHORE DON'T ADMIT IT TO NOBODY! SOME FOLKS THINK THAT I'M QUEER 'NUFF AS 'TIS. BUT ROODY'S NEAT AS A PIN. HE'S PROPER HOUSE-BROKE. HE GETS UP AND GOES OUTDOORS WITH ME TWICET A NIGHT."

GRAMPA CHUCKLED, "LET'S HOPE THAT WE WONT BE SO ROODYLY INTERRUPTIPATED AGIN. I WAS SPLAININ' ABOUT THE MINT. IN THESE PARTS IN 1849 AND '50'S GOLD WAS THICKER THAN FLEAS ON A DOG'S BACK. COME OUT IN CHUNKS OR NUGGETS OF GOLD, SOME RIGHT ON TOP OF THE GROUND, SOME IN QUARTZ ROCK, SOME JIST GOLD PARTICKLES IN THE CRICK'S SAND. IT WAS WORTH ABOUT $16 A OUNCE WEIGHED OUT BY GUESS AND BY GOSH."

"I COULD TELL YOU A BOOKFUL OF GOLD STORIES ABOUT THE MOTHER LODE, CALLED THE 'GOLDEN BACKBONE OF CALIFORNIA' WITH MARIPOSA AS THE SOUTHERN END. HOW ONE TIME A MAN DOWN TOWN FOUND A BIG DIRTY PIECE OF QUARTZ IN HIS

BACKYARD; CRACKED IT UP AND TUK OUT $600; OR HOW A KENTUCKY DOCTOR IN 1850 GRUBSTAKED AND OUTFITTED TWO OF HIS BLACK SLAVES AND SENT 'EM TO CALIFORNIA TO WORK OUT THEIR PRICE OF FREEDOM. THEY WORKED ONLY TWO OR THREE MONTHS AND SENT THE DOCTOR THE RIGHT SUM, $800, AND THEN LATER, SENT ENOUGH MORE TO ALSO FREE THEIR SISTER SO THAT SHE COULD JOIN THEM."

"NEAR ANGELS CAMP IS THE FAMUS CARSON HILL COUNTRY. IN 1849, UP THERE A MINER DIED AND THEY WAS HAVIN' HIS FUNERAL ON A HILL, COFFIN SETTIN' ON THE GROUND WHILE THEY FINISHED DIGGIN' THE GRAVE. PREACHER SUDDEN LIKE NOTICED SOME GOLD SPARKLES IN THE FRESH GRAVE DIRT. PREACHER SAYS, 'MEN, WHAT'S THAT MIXED WITH THE DIRT? LOOKS LIKE GOLD! IT IS GOLD! FUNERAL POSTPONED AND CONGREGATION DISMISSED!' SO THEY LEFT THE DEAD MAN IN HIS COFFIN AND RIGHT THEN AND THERE WENT TO WORK STAKIN' OUT THEIR CLAIMS AND ALL DIGGIN' FER GOLD. THAT SPOT BECOME THE MORGAN MINE WHICH STARTED OUT WITH A HOLE TWENTY FEET LONG, SIX FEET WIDE AND NINE FEET DEEP ON A HILL HOLDIN' OVER THREE MILLION DOLLARS"

"MORE IMPORTANT, GRAMPA," DORA ASKED, "WHAT BECAME OF THE POOR DEAD MAN IN THE COFFIN?"

"I'VE AST MYSELF THE VERY SAME QUESTION MANY A TIME, DORY. NEVER RIGHTLY HEERD. BUT MINERS WERE KIND MEN. LET'S JIST ALLOW THEY TUK OUT A FEW THOUSAND DOLLARS FROM THE GRAVE DIRT AND SENT IT BACK EAST TO THE DEAD MINER'S WIDDER AND HER TEN CHILDERN. THEN BURIED HIM PROPER LIKE."

"NOW WE GOT HIM SETTLED DOWN, LET'S GET BACK TO HOME TERRYTORY. THIS WAS ALL GENERAL FREMONT COUNTRY. FREMONT HAD A 'NORMOUS LAND GRANT DOWN AROUND MODESTO. KNOW WHAT HE DID? SOON AS GOLD WAS DISCOVERED HE PULLED POLOTIK STRINGS IN WASHINGTON AND HAD HIS GRANT MOVED UP HERE IN GOLD COUNTRY! 'PATHFINDER OF THE WEST' YOUR HISTRY BOOKS CALL HIM," GRAMPA SNORTED, "GIVE ME MEN LIKE KIT CARSON, JIM BRIDGER AND ELISHA STEVENS. THEY MADE THE PATHS FREMONT FOLLERED. BUT HERE I'M STRAYIN' OFF THE SUBJICK AGIN, DORY, AND I'M ITCHIN' TO GET BACK TO MOUNT OPHIR MINT."

"YOU STILL HAVEN'T TOLD ME WHAT A MINT IS, GRAMPA," SAID DORA A TRIFLE IMPATIENTLY.

"SO I HAVEN'T, DORY," SAID HIRAM, "GIMME TIME. LIKE I SAID, HERE IN '49 AND '50'S, MILLIONS IN GOLD DUST, NUGGETS AND QUARTZ GOLD WAS BEIN' TUK OUTEN THESE HILLS. BEIN' MONTHS AWAY FROM THE EAST, MINERS HAD NO COINS. THEY JIST USED THE NUGGETS OR GOLD DUST FER MONEY WEIGHED ON SCALES CARELESS LIKE TO BUY THINGS AND LOST A LOT BY CHEATERS. MY FATHER SAID THEY TORE DOWN A OLD SALOON NEAR MOUNT BULLION ABOUT 1870. AND UNDER THE FLOOR, JIST IN GOLD DUST THAT OVER THE YEARS HAD BEEN SWEPT THROUGH THE CRACKS, TWO SMALL BOYS PANNED OUT $300."

"YOU CAN SEE HOW THEY NEEDED REAL MONEY, HARD MONEY, COINS LIKE NICKELS, DIMES AND DOLLARS, ONLY MADE OF GOLD. SO IN 1850 A MAN NAMED JOHN L. MOFFAT CAME WEST TO SAN FRANCISCO. HE KNEW PLENTY ABOUT MININ' 'CAUSE HE WAS IN A GOLD STRIKE WAY BACK EAST MOST PEOPLE NEVER HEERD ABOUT; HAPPENED IN GEORGIA AND THE CAROLINAS IN THE 1830'S AND '40'S. ANYWAY IT SO HAPPENED THAT MOFFAT WAS A UNITED STATES ASSAYER WHICH MEANT THAT HE COULD, OFFISHUL LIKE, HANDLE GOLD OR SET UP A MINT TO MAKE COIN MONEY."

"NOW AT LAST ANSWERIN' YOUR QUESTION, DORY. A MINT IS A PLACE WHERE THEY MELT UP RAW GOLD OR SILVER, THEN POUR IT INTO MOLDS AND MAKE COINS INTO DIFFRUNT SIZES AND DEZINES

"GOLD EAGLES"

LIKE FIVE, TEN AND TWENTY DOLLAR GOLD-PIECES. MOFFAT STARTED A MINT IN SAN FRANCISCO AND A LITTLE ONE HERE AT MOUNT OPHIR. HERE IN 1851 THEY MINTED JIST A FEW BIG FIFTY DOLLAR GOLD PIECES WITH EIGHT SIDES. I CAN SHOW YOU A PITCHER OF ONE, EAGLE AND ALL. MINERS WAS GLAD TO GET

THESE COINS INSTEAD OF CARRYIN' LOOSE NUGGETS AND GOLD DUST IN BUCKSKIN BAGS. THE FIFTY DOLLAR GOLD PIECES WERE CALLED SLUGS OR FIVE EAGLES, AN EAGLE BEIN' TEN DOLLARS."

"NOW COMES THE EXCITIN' PART BEEN ON MY MIND FER YEARS, DORY. SOME OF IT'S IN COUNTY RECORDS, PART MIZ PEEBLES VERTIFIED OUT OF HER BOOKS AND SOME I REMEMBER PA TOLD ME. BACK IN THE 1850'S OR '60'S THERE WAS A MAN, SEEMS THAT HIS NAME WAS JOSEPH MARRE OR JOE FARR, WHO WAS COUNTY TAX COLLECTOR. HE DIDN'T BELIEVE IN BANKS AND BESIDES, ALL HE HAD TO KEEP THE TAX MONEY IN WAS A FLIMSY OLD DESK WHICH YOU COULD KICK A HOLE THROUGH WITH YOUR STOCKIN' FOOT. FARR BEIN' SOMEWHAT PEECOOLYER, TOOK PRIDE IN HIDIN' THE MONEY IN QUEER PLACES; FACT HE BRAGGED ABOUT HIS HIDIN' SPOTS; SAID THEY WAS CLOSE BY AND JIST AS SAFE AS A BANK. COME TAX COLLECTIN' TIME ONE YEAR AND JOE FARR HAD A BAG OF THESE MOSTLY NEW GOLD COINS AMOUNTIN' TO $15,000. JOE MADE A HORSE-BACK TRIP TO STOCKTON ONE WINTER DAY AND GOT CAUGHT IN A FLASH FLOOD, BELIEVE IT WAS IN THE MERCED RIVER. HE AND HIS HORSE WAS FOUND DEAD BUT NO MONEY ON HIM. HE HAD HID IT SOMEWHAR CLOSE BY AND MIGHTY CLEVER. SO SOMEWHAR, DORY, TUCKED AWAY AND NEAR HERE, THERE'S $15,000 ALL IN GOLD COINS!"

DORA WAS RATHER YOUNG TO APPRECIATE THE VALUE OR PICTURE $15,000 IN GOLD COINS. ONE DOLLAR OR EVEN FIVE DOLLARS WAS UNDERSTAND-ABLE BUT SHE NEEDED COMPARISON OR EXPLANA-TION OF THIS, TO HER, LARGE AMOUNT.

"YOU MEAN, GRAMPA," SHE ASKED, "IF SOMEONE FOUND ALL THIS $15,000, THAT THEY WOULD BE RICH, LIKE A BANK OR THOSE CADILLAC PEOPLE?"

HIRAM SNORTED. "DORY, IT'S BEEN MORE THAN A HUNDERD YEARS SINCE JOE FARR HID THAT MONEY! LISTEN CAREFUL; I'LL TRY TO 'SPLAIN. TODAY THAT MONEY'S SO OLD THAT IT'S ANTEEK. NOWADAYS THERE'S A TRIBE OF FOLKS SPRUNG UP CALLED COIN COLLECTORS. THERE AINT A HANDFUL OF THEM COINS TO BE HAD, NO WHERE, NO HOW. THEY'RE JIST SIMPLE, PRACTICAL, EXSTINK. TO A COIN COLLECTOR THEY'RE WORTH MAYBE TEN OR TWENTY TIMES $15,000. WHY ONE HISTRY BOOK MIZ PEEBLES GOT SAYS IN THESE VERY WORDS THAT I TOOK PARTICKLER

PAINS TO MEMYRIZE 'BY HEART — 'TODAY ONE OF THESE ($50) SLUGS, IF IT COULD BE FOUND, MIGHT BE VALUED AT $10,000.'" *

THE SMALL GIRL'S EYES WIDENED. WITH HER CHILDISH IMAGINATION, THE STORY WAS NOW BEING CLOAKED WITH REALITY. "YOU MEAN, GRAMPA, THAT IF WE EVER FOUND THIS JOE FARR'S OLD GOLD MONEY, WE COULD BUY MAMA FOUR NEW TIRES INSTEAD OF THREE AND A NEW BATTERY, MAYBE HAVE 'LECTRICITY AND A BATHROOM IN OUR HOUSE AND I COULD BUY BRAND NEW CLOTHES ALL READY-MADE AND A PAIR OF COWBOY BOOTS AND BUY BIG BERTHA A FANCY NEW DOG COLLAR?"

DORA'S ENTHUSIASM WAS CONTAGIOUS. NOW HIRAM WAS REALLY FIRED UP! AT LAST HE HAD SOMEONE TO SHARE THE POSSIBILITIES OF HIS LONG SLUMBERING DREAM. "LORDY MERCY, HONEY," HE EXCLAIMED, "YOU AINT SCRATCHED THE SURFACE! FOUR NEW TIRES? HA! YOUR MOM COULD RUN THAT OLD MODEL A FORD OFF THE CLIFF AT LOVER'S LEAP INTO THE AUTO-DUMP AND BUY THE FINEST CAR THEY GOT IN THE CITY OF MERCED. SHE COULD PAY OFF THE MORGAGE AND FIX UP YOUR HOUSE WITH EVER 'LECTRIC, LABOR-SAVIN' GADGET THAT MODERN MAN HAS INVENTED. WHY SHE COULD BUY THE AUTO COURT AND RESTAURANT WHERE SHE WORKS. AND CLOTHES FER YOU? HELL'S BELLS, DORY, YOU COULD DRESS IN WILD WEST DUDS THAT'D MAKE HOOT GIBSON AND TOM MIX LOOK LIKE TRAMPS! BIG BERTHA? DOG FOOD IN GALLON CANS, DIFFRUNT FLAVOR EVER MEAL AND A NEW THREE INCH DOG-COLLAR SET WITH GOLD NUGGETS."

DORA WIGGLED IN SILENT ECSTASY. THEN SHE SOBERED. "IT'S LIKE A BEAUTIFUL FAIRY STORY, GRAMPA, A BEAUTIFUL STORY WITH THE LAST PAGE MISSING. BUT LET'S DREAM ANYWAY, GRAMPA, JUST YOU AND ME?"

THE OLD MAN SIGHED. "HONEY, I'VE BEEN DREAMIN' JIST SUCH DREAMS ALL MY LIFE. BUT IT'S JIST SUCH DREAMS THAT MAKES LIFE WORTH LIVIN'."

AS PROMISED, THE NEXT SATURDAY, THE DAY BEFORE CHRISTMAS, HIRAM HAD ROODY PROPERLY PACKED AND AWAITED DORA. IT WAS LONG PAST THEIR PLANNED STARTING TIME. A DOZEN TIMES HE HAD CONSULTED THE

* "Historic Spots in California" — HOOVER, RENSCH & ABELOE.

TURNIP-SIZE TIME PIECE, EVEN NERVOUSLY LOOKED AT HIS CONCEALED WRIST WATCH. AT LAST HE DECIDED TO HUNT UP HIS YOUNG COMPANION. AS HE NEARED HER HOME A FRANTIC LITTLE FIGURE RAN TO MEET HIM.

"OH! GRAMPA, I KNOW I'M LATE. MAMA'S GONE TO WORK AND I'M SO WORRIED!"

"WHAT IN THE WORLD'S THE MATTER, DORY?"

"I CAN'T FIND BIG BERTHA! I'VE CALLED HER AND CALLED HER."

"BEEN ALL THE PLACES THAT SHE MIGHT PROWL?"

"EVERYWHERE!"

"CALM DOWN, HONEY. THINK WHERE WE MIGHT STILL LOOK."

"SHE COULDN'T BE THERE!"

"COULDN'T BE WHERE?"

"COULDN'T BE IN SKUNK CAVE."

"NEVER HEERD OF IT. 'SPLAIN YOURSELF, DORY."

"I NAMED IT SKUNK CAVE. NO ONE KNOWS ABOUT IT. IT'S ON A HILL BACK OF OUR HOUSE, A LITTLE CAVE, WHERE TWO ROCKS COME TOGETHER. MAMA WONT LET ME CRAWL BACK INTO IT 'COUNT OF SNAKES AND THINGS."

"WHAT WE WAITIN' FER?" SAID HIRAM, "JIST ABOUT TIME BIG BERTHA MIGHT HAVE A GOOD REASON TO HUNT UP A CAVE."

PAST THE HOUSE AND THROUGH DENSE PINES, DORA LED THE OLD PROSPECTOR UP A NARROW, ROCKY CANYON. COMPLETELY HIDDEN AMIDST THICK CHAPARRAL, HUGE GRANITE ROCKS HAD FALLEN TO FORM A SMALL CAVE. APPARENTLY THE ONLY ENTRANCE WAS A TRIANGULAR OPENING LESS THAN THREE FEET WIDE.

"I NAMED THIS SKUNK CAVE", SAID DORA, "ONE DAY I SAW BERTHA GO INTO IT TWICE, ONCE AFTER A CHIPMUNK AND ONCE CHASING A PACK-RAT."

"NUTHIN' TO DO BUT 'VESTIGATE, DORY," HIRAM SAID, "WAIT A DERN MINUTE. I GOT A FLASHLIGHT IN MY PACK. NO USE FER ME TO GET MY FAT BELLY STUCK IN THAT LIL HOLE. TAKE THE FLASHLIGHT AND CRAWL IN AWFUL SLOW AND CAREFUL. DON'T BE AFEERD OF SNAKES. THEY'RE HIBERNATIN' THIS

TIME OF YEAR. MEANS THEY'RE ASLEEP. I'LL TIE A ROPE AROUND YOU. I JIST GOT A HUNCH THAT BIG BERTHA'S HAD THIS CAVE IN MIND FER SOME TIME."

WITH ONLY A QUESTIONING LOOK, DORA PREPARED HERSELF. HIRAM SQUATTED DOWN, ROPE IN HAND, TENSELY WAITING. DORA CRAWLED INTO THE CAVE.

"SEE ANYTHIN', DORY?" HIRAM SHOUTED.

"NOT YET, GRAMPA", CAME A FAINT VOICE, "IT'S SO DARK AND COBWEBBY AND SMELLS AWFUL SCARY. UGGH! A SNAKE-SKIN!"

"SHINE THE LIGHT WAY AHEAD, DORY, KEEP GOIN'."

A LONG SILENCE. THEN A SCREAM!

"TWO SHINING EYES, GRAMPA! IT'S BIG BERTHA!"

"'COURSE IT IS, DORY," GRAMPA SAID WITH A SIGH OF RELIEF, "WHAT'S GOIN' ON WITH HER?"

ANOTHER LONG SILENCE. ANOTHER SCREAM!

"PUPPIES, GRAMPA! OODLES OF THEM! BERTHA'S DUG A HOLE IN THE SAND AND MADE A NEST. THEY'RE SUCKING MY FINGERS AND BERTHA'S LICKING MY FACE."

"HOW MANY, DORY?"

"I CAN'T COUNT THEM, GRAMPA. THEY SQUIRM SO!"

"OH, LORDY," HIRAM GROANED, "WELL, PASS 'EM OUT. HERE, I'LL SLING MY GOLD PAN IN TO YOU AND YOU CAN LOAD IT UP. I SHORE NEVER FIGGERED ON EVER PANNIN' OUT A MESS OF PUPS!"

FINALLY THE SMALL FIGURE EMERGED PUSHING THE LOADED GOLD PAN AHEAD OF HER; HER FACE, COVERED WITH SAND AND COBWEBS, FAIRLY BEAMED.

"AREN'T THEY JUST BEAUTIFUL, GRAMPA?"

"I RECKON SO," HIRAM ALLOWED, "I MUST ADMIT THAT BIG BERTHA SHORE GOES IN FER COLOR AND QUANTITY. LET'S SEE, TEN, NEAR AS I CAN COUNT THE WIGGLERS, LONG HAIR, SHORT HAIR, WHITE, BROWN, YALLER, SPOTTED—I CANT RECALL MEETIN' THE FATHER. TOO BAD THEY DIDN'T HATCH OUT ALREADY WEANED. ONE PUP WOULD JIST ABOUT FIT INTO A CHRISMUS STOCKIN'."

WITH A PROUD BIG BERTHA BESIDE THEM, THE TRIO SAT IN SILENT ADMIRATION.

FINALLY GRAMPA BROKE THE SILENCE.

"WELL, DORY," HIRAM SAID, "RECKON YOU CAN UNLAX. YOUR LOST DOG'S FOUND AND YOU GOT TEN MORE. RUN UP TO THE HOUSE AND GET A WASHTUB. THEY'RE SPILLIN' OUT OF MY GOLD PAN".

WHILE SHE WAS GONE, HIRAM SAT IN THOUGHTFUL CONTEMPLATION. THEN WITH THE SOUND OF A PISTOL SHOT HE SLAPPED HIS LEG. HE HAD BEEN STRUCK BY A DAZZLING, HAIR-RAISING POSSIBILITY!

"DORY," WHEN SHE RETURNED, "WHAT ELSE DID YOU SEE WAY BACK IN THAT CAVE?"

"NOTHING, GRAMPA," DORA REPLIED, BUSILY LOADING THE TUB WITH FLUFFY, SQUIRMING PUPS, "NOTHING BUT A BROKEN WHISKEY BOTTLE AND A PACK-RAT'S NEST."

"ARE YOU SURE, DORY?" GRAMPA PERSISTED.

"WELL," AS DORA PAUSED IN HER HAPPY LABOR, "I TOLD YOU THAT BERTHA DUG A HOLE IN THE SAND TO LAY HER PUPPIES. NOT VERY DEEP BECAUSE SHE CAME TO A COUPLE OF OLD GLASS FRUIT JARS AND SHE COULDN'T DIG ANY FARTHER. ONLY THE TOPS WERE STICKING OUT."

THE OLD PROSPECTOR VALIANTLY TRIED TO CONTROL HIMSELF. "LISTEN, CHILD, DROP THEM PUPPIES! YOU STILL GOT WORK TO DO! NEVER MIND THAT MESS OF BABY DOGS! DUMP 'EM OUT OF THE TUB UNDER THE SHADE OF THAT BUSH AND LET BIG BERTHA TAKE OVER".

WITH TREMBLING HANDS HIRAM FISHED IN HIS PANTS' POCKETS AND UNCLASPED THE BLADE OF A KNIFE LARGE ENOUGH TO SKIN A BUFFALO. "TAKE THIS TOAD-STABBER, DORY, AND MY GOLD PAN AND THE FLASHLIGHT. I'LL STILL TIE A ROPE AROUND YOU. CRAWL BACK IN THERE AND KNIFE OUT THEM TWO JARS REAL GENTLE LIKE."

GRAMPA WAS SO NERVOUS, SO SERIOUS, SO INSISTENT THAT WITH ONLY A QUESTIONING LOOK AND WITHOUT A WORD, DORA OBEYED. STILL TREMBLING, STILL CROUCHED ON HIS KNEES AT CAVE'S MOUTH, HIRAM WAITED.

FINALLY CAME A FAINT VOICE, "GRAMPA, I'M DIGGING OUT THE OLD DIRTY JARS. BUT THE SAND'S SO HARD."

"KEEP ON, DORY, NICE AND STEADY," HIRAM SHOUTED, "DON'T CUT YER FINGERS."

MINUTES PASSED. THEN A FAINT CALL FROM THE INTERIOR DARKNESS, "GRAMPA, I GOT BOTH OLD JARS LOOSE. BUT THEY'RE SO HEAVY. I CAN HARDLY LIFT THEM."

"THAT'S JIST WHAT I WANTED TO HEAR, DORY!" HIRAM FAIRLY BELLOWED, "SLIDE 'EM BOTH INTO THE GOLD PAN, PUT THE ROPE 'ROUND IT AND THEN I'LL SNAKE 'EM OUT."

FINALLY OUTSIDE, THE PAN LAY BEFORE THEM. IT HELD TWO ANCIENT GLASS FRUIT JARS ENCRUSTED WITH DIRT AND SAND. THE STROKES OF HIRAM'S KNIFE HAD EXPOSED AZURE BLUE GLASS FLECKED HERE AND THERE WITH BUBBLES. ON THE SIDES, IN THE CLEAN SPOTS, THEY COULD FAINTLY SEE THE EMBOSSED LETTERS M-A-S—AND 185—.

"GIMME A BIG ROCK, DORY," SAID THE EXCITED HIRAM," I'M GONNA BUST 'EM."

"BUT THOSE OLD JARS, GRAMPA! MRS. PEEBLES MIGHT SELL THEM?"

"SELL HELL!" HIRAM REPLIED, FORGETTING HIS MANNERS, "THE HECK WITH THE JARS! IT'S WHAT MIGHT BE INSIDE 'EM. STAND BACK, DORY!"

WITH TREMBLING BUT MIGHTY BLOWS, HIRAM SHATTERED THE CONTAINERS. AND AS HE DID SO, *A YELLOW FLOOD OF STILL SHINY GOLD PIECES OF ALL SIZES DRAMATICALLY SLOSHED ACROSS THE GOLD PAN FILLING IT TO THE BRIM!*

FOR A MOMENT—COMPLETE SILENCE. THEN HIRAM GASPED, "LORDY MERCY, DORY, LOOK AT THEM FIVE AND TEN AND TWENTY DOLLAR EAGLES. AND LOOK!—AT LEAST A DOZEN OF THEM BIG, EIGHT-SIDED FIFTY DOLLAR GOLD PIECES, ALMOST AS FRESH AS THE DAY THEY WAS MINTED!"

REALIZATION CAME SLOWLY TO DORA BUT WHEN IT DID IT CAME WITH A RUSH, "OH, GRAMPA!", SHE SCREAMED, "THIS MUST BE JOE FARR'S $15,000!"

"NUTHIN' ELSE BUT," HIRAM WHEEZED, "HID SAFE AND SOUND AND CLOSE BY JIST LIKE HE BRAGGED; BURIED FER OVER A HUNDERD YEARS AND NOW MULTIPIDE MORE THAN TEN TIMES OVER!"

DORA'S EYES WIDENED, "THEN DOES THIS

REALLY MEAN THAT SORT OF A FAIRY STORY YOU TOLD ME COULD COME TRUE, GRAMPA, NEW AUTOMOBILE, ELECTRICITY, COWBOY BOOTS AND EVERYTHING?"

TEARS CAME EASILY TO HIRAM. "YES, HONEY, ALL COME TRUE AND MORE TOO." HE WIPED HIS EYES AND LOUDLY BLEW HIS NOSE.

THE LITTLE GIRL HUGGED AND PLANTED A DAMP KISS ON THE OLD PROSPECTOR'S ALREADY WET CHEEK. "TO THINK", SHE WHISPERED, "THAT THIS COULD ALL HAPPEN ON THE DAY BEFORE CHRISTMAS! I JUST CAN'T WAIT TO TELL MAMA!"

SEEING SUCH AN EXCITING AND AFFECTIONATE DEMONSTRATION, THE DIGNIFIED BIG BERTHA AROSE FROM HER BROOD AND WITH HER LONG TONGUE TENDERLY SLURPED HIRAM'S FACE. EVEN ROODY TURNED HIS HEAD, OPENED ONE EYE AND KICKED VICIOUSLY AT A HORSEFLY.

HIRAM WAS DEEPLY AFFECTED BUT HE TRIED TO HIDE HIS FEELINGS. "COME, LET'S GET BACK TO EARTH, DORY. SCOOP UP THE PUPS AND GET 'EM SETTLED IN YOUR HOUSE IN BERTHA'S PIANER BOX. YOU AND ME GOTTA TAKE ALL THIS LOOT DOWN TO THE BANK AND THEN YOUR MOM—INCLUDIN' MIZ PEEBLES. I CAN JIST SEE MIZ PEEBLES! LORDY, SHE'S GONNA FLIP A FIT! I'LL BET SHE WILL TELEPHOME NEWSPAPERS, RADIO STATION AND PROBABLE MAKE A TRIP TO SAN FRANCISCO. YOU AND ME MAY HAFTA MAKE OURSELVES MIGHTY SCARCE FER A SPELL. SOON AS NEWS GETS OUT, THESE HILLS GONNA BE CRAWLIN' WITH GREEN-HORN TOORISTS AND JAYHAWKERS HUNTIN' FER HIDDEN TREASURE. FER THE NEXT MONTH WE——"

BUT GRAMPA NEVER FINISHED. NOW WILD WITH JOY, DORA INTERRUPTED, "LET'S HAVE A MERRY CHRISTMAS PARADE, GRAMPA! JUST YOU AND ME AND ROODY. POOR BERTHA WAS THE HERO BUT SHE HASTA STAY HOME AND BABY-SIT. FIRST, WE'LL STOP AT YOUR HOUSE AND YOU CAN STRAP THE DEER HORNS ON ROODY AND MAKE A WREATH TO HANG AROUND HIS NECK. THEN WE'LL MARCH DOWN THE MAIN STREET OF MARIPOSA TO THE BANK AND MAMA AND MRS. PEEBLES. BUT WAIT A MINUTE, GRAMPA, I ALMOST FORGOT SOMETHING. I WANT TO GET MAMA'S LIPSTICK."

"WHAT IN ALL THE TARNATION WORLD DO YOU WANT RIGHT NOW WITH A LIPSTICK, DORY?" HIRAM PUZZLED.

"BECAUSE I WANT TO PAINT ROODY'S NOSE BRIGHT RED", DORA DECLARED, "THEN WHILE WE MARCH, I CAN SING THAT SONG, 'RUDOLPH THE RED-NOSED REINDEER'. GRAMPA! DON'T YOU REMEMBER? TONIGHT'S CHRISTMAS EVE!"

THE LITTLE HOUSE

BY A PIONEER OCCUPANT · ꓤꓤ ·

Dear Reader,

This book has proved extremely popular. Out of many thousands sold, there has been no reader criticism—with one exception, a Burlingame millionairess, one of my reader clients. She sharply complained that I was "writing and illustrating beneath the dignity of the craft." She can probably be excused because of her total lack of ever contacting our subject matter!

Chic Sale wrote his famous *The Specialist* (on the subject of outhouses) in 1926. I will never equal him in volume of editions produced, but modern freedom in writing on delicate subjects gave me opportunity to discuss this antique landmark even more fully and frankly than Chic Sale. While he surpassed me in sales, today's freedom of expression gives our *The Little House* the edge? (I think.)

Some conservationists may be unduly concerned with the thought that our precious old antique privies may be an "endangered species". They need not be concerned. It has been roughly estimated that a million of such still remain in our U.S.A. They shyly stand in subdued, isolated locations, either retired or in intermittent occupation.

Enjoy these exaggerated memoirs of a native son, once a regular occupant of "little houses" before the turn-of-the-century.

Yours Truly
Ralph Rambo

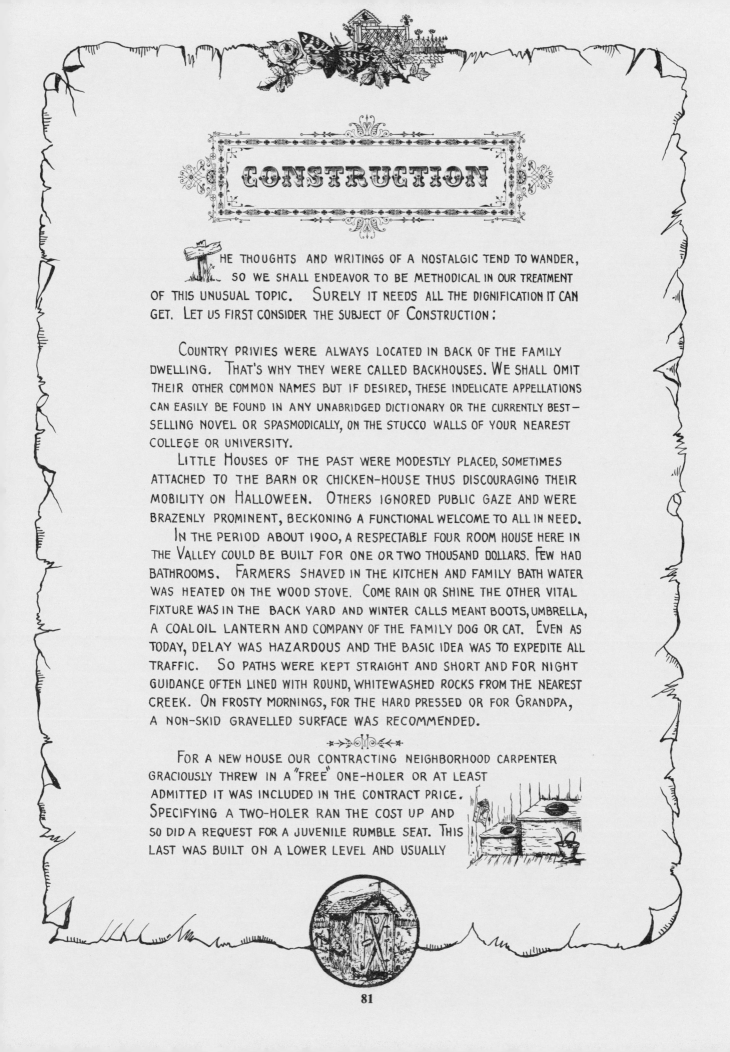

CONSTRUCTION

HE THOUGHTS AND WRITINGS OF A NOSTALGIC TEND TO WANDER, SO WE SHALL ENDEAVOR TO BE METHODICAL IN OUR TREATMENT OF THIS UNUSUAL TOPIC. SURELY IT NEEDS ALL THE DIGNIFICATION IT CAN GET. LET US FIRST CONSIDER THE SUBJECT OF CONSTRUCTION:

COUNTRY PRIVIES WERE ALWAYS LOCATED IN BACK OF THE FAMILY DWELLING. THAT'S WHY THEY WERE CALLED BACKHOUSES. WE SHALL OMIT THEIR OTHER COMMON NAMES BUT IF DESIRED, THESE INDELICATE APPELLATIONS CAN EASILY BE FOUND IN ANY UNABRIDGED DICTIONARY OR THE CURRENTLY BEST-SELLING NOVEL OR SPASMODICALLY, ON THE STUCCO WALLS OF YOUR NEAREST COLLEGE OR UNIVERSITY.

LITTLE HOUSES OF THE PAST WERE MODESTLY PLACED, SOMETIMES ATTACHED TO THE BARN OR CHICKEN-HOUSE THUS DISCOURAGING THEIR MOBILITY ON HALLOWEEN. OTHERS IGNORED PUBLIC GAZE AND WERE BRAZENLY PROMINENT, BECKONING A FUNCTIONAL WELCOME TO ALL IN NEED.

IN THE PERIOD ABOUT 1900, A RESPECTABLE FOUR ROOM HOUSE HERE IN THE VALLEY COULD BE BUILT FOR ONE OR TWO THOUSAND DOLLARS. FEW HAD BATHROOMS. FARMERS SHAVED IN THE KITCHEN AND FAMILY BATH WATER WAS HEATED ON THE WOOD STOVE. COME RAIN OR SHINE THE OTHER VITAL FIXTURE WAS IN THE BACK YARD AND WINTER CALLS MEANT BOOTS, UMBRELLA, A COAL OIL LANTERN AND COMPANY OF THE FAMILY DOG OR CAT. EVEN AS TODAY, DELAY WAS HAZARDOUS AND THE BASIC IDEA WAS TO EXPEDITE ALL TRAFFIC. SO PATHS WERE KEPT STRAIGHT AND SHORT AND FOR NIGHT GUIDANCE OFTEN LINED WITH ROUND, WHITEWASHED ROCKS FROM THE NEAREST CREEK. ON FROSTY MORNINGS, FOR THE HARD PRESSED OR FOR GRANDPA, A NON-SKID GRAVELLED SURFACE WAS RECOMMENDED.

FOR A NEW HOUSE OUR CONTRACTING NEIGHBORHOOD CARPENTER GRACIOUSLY THREW IN A "FREE" ONE-HOLER OR AT LEAST ADMITTED IT WAS INCLUDED IN THE CONTRACT PRICE. SPECIFYING A TWO-HOLER RAN THE COST UP AND SO DID A REQUEST FOR A JUVENILE RUMBLE SEAT. THIS LAST WAS BUILT ON A LOWER LEVEL AND USUALLY

CAUSED LENGTHY DEBATE BETWEEN CARPENTER AND OWNER REGARDING GROWING RATE OF CHILDREN, NECESSARY ALLOWANCE FOR THE PROPER AMOUNT OF LEG-DANGLE AND THE HOLE SIZE.

WITH QUIET ADMIRATION WE YOUNGSTERS WATCHED OUR CARPENTER DEFTLY WIELD AUGER, KEY-HOLE SAW, WOOD-RASP AND SANDPAPER. I MEAN WHEN HE TACKLED THE BIG SEAT-BOARD AND CUT OUT THE HOLES. CUTTING SEAT-HOLES WAS CONSIDERED QUITE A PRIDEFUL ART AND REQUIRED EXPERT CRAFTMANSHIP. THE CUT-OUT PIECES WERE CAREFULLY SAVED. HOPEFULLY TO BE USED AS LID-COVERS BUT INVARIABLY THEY "FELL IN", TO BE FOREVER LOST. SEAT-HOLES VARIED IN SIZE AND SHAPE DEPENDING ON THE AVERAGE SPREAD OF FAMILY BOTTOMS. IT WAS THE CARPENTER'S PROBLEM TO STRIKE AN ACCEPTABLE AND COMFORTABLE MEDIUM. CERTAIN SCHOOLS OF THOUGHT ARGUED FOR PLAIN ROUND APERTURES, OTHER PREFERRED THE OVAL SHAPED WHILE A FEW ESTHETICS CLAIMED THAT THE HEART-SHAPED WAS NOT ONLY FORM-FITTING BUT GAVE AN ADDED TOUCH OF ROMANTIC ARTISTRY.*

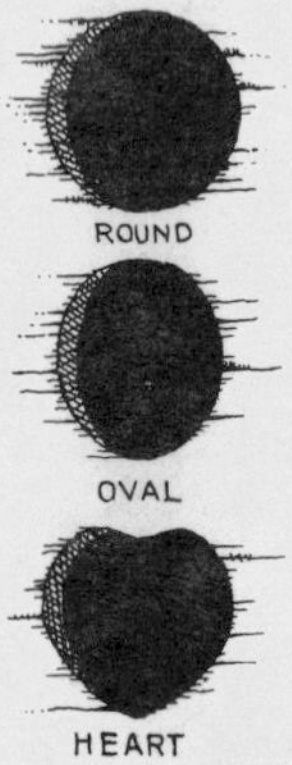

ROUND

OVAL

HEART

SETH BELSHAZER, THE EXPERIENCED PRIVY-CARPENTER WHO BUILT OUR OUTHOUSE, INSISTED ON HINGING THE ENTIRE TWO-HOLER SEAT INCLUDING MY UNDERSLUNG RUMBLE JOB. "BEFORE YOU SET," SETH GRAVELY WARNED, "RAISE UP THE WHOLE SEAT AND LET'R BANG DOWN LOUD. NEVER CAN TELL WHAT UNDER-SIDE OF SEAT IS HARBORIN' — BUGS GALORE MEBBE, WASPS, LIZARDS, EVEN A BLACK-SPIDER!" THEN HE LAUNCHED INTO A LONG, HORRIFYING STORY ABOUT HIS UNCLE IN THE SAN JOAQUIN VALLEY WHO EVIDENTLY FORGOT TO "BANG DOWN LOUD;" WAS BITTEN BY A BLACK SPIDER AND "PLUMB PARALYZED IN HIS HIND LEGS, DRUG HIS SELF HALF A MILE TO A NEIGHBORS FER HELP." WE NEVER FORGOT TO BANG OUR SEATS.

QUALITY AND STYLE OF LITTLE HOUSE CONSTRUCTION WAS GOVERNED BY FAMILY DISPOSITION AND CIRCUMSTANCES. TAKING A SUNDAY DRIVE IN THE ONE-HORSE SHAY DOWN OLD STEVENS CREEK ROAD OR ANY COUNTRY ROAD IN THE OLD VALLEY, A FAMILY'S COMMUNITY STANDING, BOTH SOCIAL AND FINANCIAL, COULD BE ESTIMATED BY SURVEYING THEIR BACKHOUSE.

* IN HIS BOOK, CHIC SALE SUGGESTS — SQUARE HOLES TO DISCOURAGE LONG VISITS.

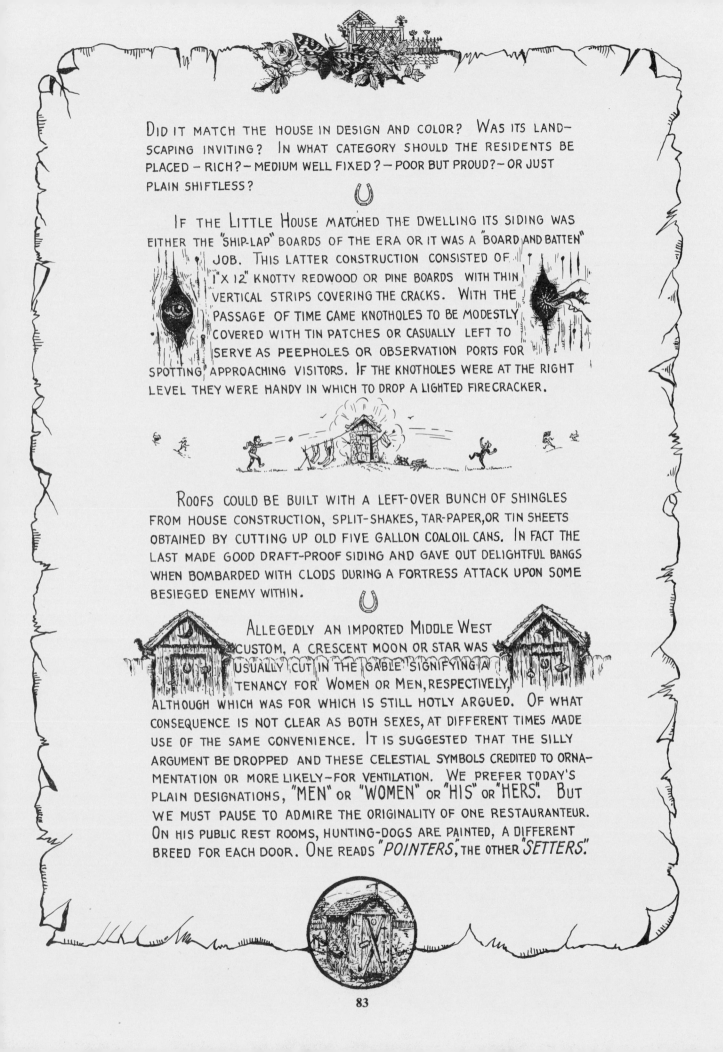

DID IT MATCH THE HOUSE IN DESIGN AND COLOR? WAS ITS LAND-SCAPING INVITING? IN WHAT CATEGORY SHOULD THE RESIDENTS BE PLACED – RICH? – MEDIUM WELL FIXED? – POOR BUT PROUD? – OR JUST PLAIN SHIFTLESS?

IF THE LITTLE HOUSE MATCHED THE DWELLING ITS SIDING WAS EITHER THE "SHIP-LAP" BOARDS OF THE ERA OR IT WAS A "BOARD AND BATTEN" JOB. THIS LATTER CONSTRUCTION CONSISTED OF 1"X 12" KNOTTY REDWOOD OR PINE BOARDS WITH THIN VERTICAL STRIPS COVERING THE CRACKS. WITH THE PASSAGE OF TIME CAME KNOTHOLES TO BE MODESTLY COVERED WITH TIN PATCHES OR CASUALLY LEFT TO SERVE AS PEEPHOLES OR OBSERVATION PORTS FOR SPOTTING APPROACHING VISITORS. IF THE KNOTHOLES WERE AT THE RIGHT LEVEL THEY WERE HANDY IN WHICH TO DROP A LIGHTED FIRECRACKER.

ROOFS COULD BE BUILT WITH A LEFT-OVER BUNCH OF SHINGLES FROM HOUSE CONSTRUCTION, SPLIT-SHAKES, TAR-PAPER, OR TIN SHEETS OBTAINED BY CUTTING UP OLD FIVE GALLON COALOIL CANS. IN FACT THE LAST MADE GOOD DRAFT-PROOF SIDING AND GAVE OUT DELIGHTFUL BANGS WHEN BOMBARDED WITH CLODS DURING A FORTRESS ATTACK UPON SOME BESIEGED ENEMY WITHIN.

ALLEGEDLY AN IMPORTED MIDDLE WEST CUSTOM, A CRESCENT MOON OR STAR WAS USUALLY CUT IN THE GABLE SIGNIFYING A TENANCY FOR WOMEN OR MEN, RESPECTIVELY, ALTHOUGH WHICH WAS FOR WHICH IS STILL HOTLY ARGUED. OF WHAT CONSEQUENCE IS NOT CLEAR AS BOTH SEXES, AT DIFFERENT TIMES MADE USE OF THE SAME CONVENIENCE. IT IS SUGGESTED THAT THE SILLY ARGUMENT BE DROPPED AND THESE CELESTIAL SYMBOLS CREDITED TO ORNA-MENTATION OR MORE LIKELY—FOR VENTILATION. WE PREFER TODAY'S PLAIN DESIGNATIONS, "MEN" OR "WOMEN" OR "HIS" OR "HERS". BUT WE MUST PAUSE TO ADMIRE THE ORIGINALITY OF ONE RESTAURANTEUR. ON HIS PUBLIC REST ROOMS, HUNTING-DOGS ARE PAINTED, A DIFFERENT BREED FOR EACH DOOR. ONE READS "POINTERS", THE OTHER "SETTERS".

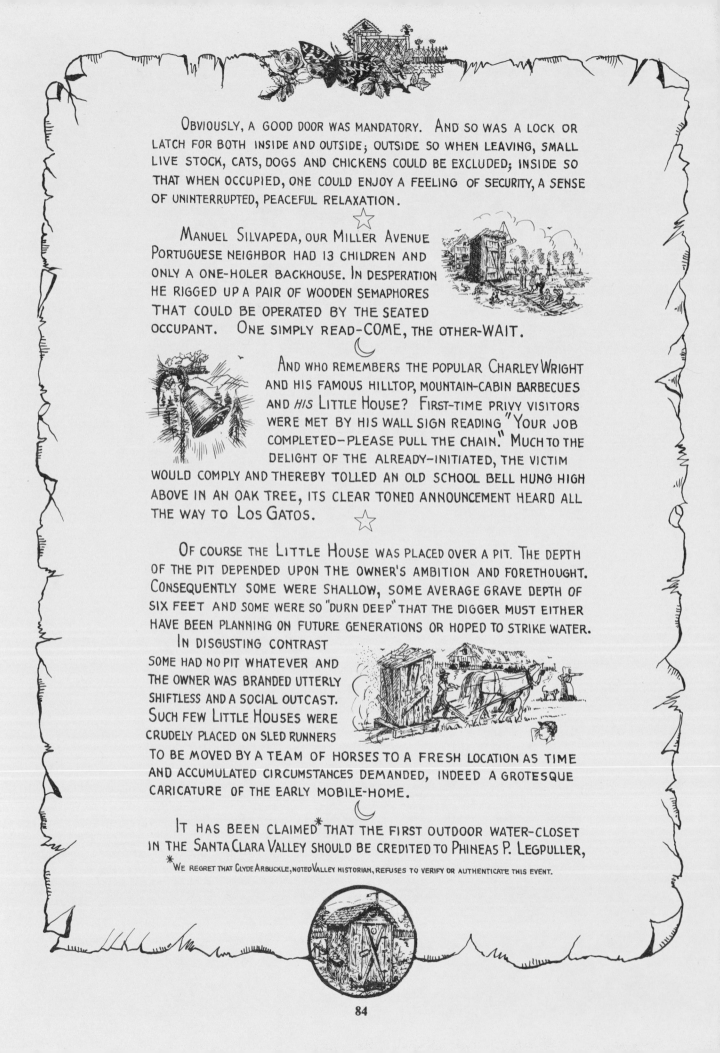

OBVIOUSLY, A GOOD DOOR WAS MANDATORY. AND SO WAS A LOCK OR LATCH FOR BOTH INSIDE AND OUTSIDE; OUTSIDE SO WHEN LEAVING, SMALL LIVE STOCK, CATS, DOGS AND CHICKENS COULD BE EXCLUDED; INSIDE SO THAT WHEN OCCUPIED, ONE COULD ENJOY A FEELING OF SECURITY, A SENSE OF UNINTERRUPTED, PEACEFUL RELAXATION.

MANUEL SILVAPEDA, OUR MILLER AVENUE PORTUGUESE NEIGHBOR HAD 13 CHILDREN AND ONLY A ONE-HOLER BACKHOUSE. IN DESPERATION HE RIGGED UP A PAIR OF WOODEN SEMAPHORES THAT COULD BE OPERATED BY THE SEATED OCCUPANT. ONE SIMPLY READ-COME, THE OTHER-WAIT.

AND WHO REMEMBERS THE POPULAR CHARLEY WRIGHT AND HIS FAMOUS HILLTOP, MOUNTAIN-CABIN BARBECUES AND *HIS* LITTLE HOUSE? FIRST-TIME PRIVY VISITORS WERE MET BY HIS WALL SIGN READING "YOUR JOB COMPLETED-PLEASE PULL THE CHAIN." MUCH TO THE DELIGHT OF THE ALREADY-INITIATED, THE VICTIM WOULD COMPLY AND THEREBY TOLLED AN OLD SCHOOL BELL HUNG HIGH ABOVE IN AN OAK TREE, ITS CLEAR TONED ANNOUNCEMENT HEARD ALL THE WAY TO LOS GATOS.

OF COURSE THE LITTLE HOUSE WAS PLACED OVER A PIT. THE DEPTH OF THE PIT DEPENDED UPON THE OWNER'S AMBITION AND FORETHOUGHT. CONSEQUENTLY SOME WERE SHALLOW, SOME AVERAGE GRAVE DEPTH OF SIX FEET AND SOME WERE SO "DURN DEEP" THAT THE DIGGER MUST EITHER HAVE BEEN PLANNING ON FUTURE GENERATIONS OR HOPED TO STRIKE WATER.

IN DISGUSTING CONTRAST SOME HAD NO PIT WHATEVER AND THE OWNER WAS BRANDED UTTERLY SHIFTLESS AND A SOCIAL OUTCAST. SUCH FEW LITTLE HOUSES WERE CRUDELY PLACED ON SLED RUNNERS TO BE MOVED BY A TEAM OF HORSES TO A FRESH LOCATION AS TIME AND ACCUMULATED CIRCUMSTANCES DEMANDED, INDEED A GROTESQUE CARICATURE OF THE EARLY MOBILE-HOME.

IT HAS BEEN CLAIMED* THAT THE FIRST OUTDOOR WATER-CLOSET IN THE SANTA CLARA VALLEY SHOULD BE CREDITED TO PHINEAS P. LEGPULLER,

*WE REGRET THAT CLYDE ARBUCKLE, NOTED VALLEY HISTORIAN, REFUSES TO VERIFY OR AUTHENTICATE THIS EVENT.

A PIONEER SETTLER ON THE NORTHERN EXTREMITY OF THE ALVISO ROAD.
IN HIS ERA THIS COUNTRY NEAR TIDEWATER WAS CALLED THE "LOWLANDS."
ARRIVING FROM KOKOMO, INDIANA IN MAY, 1872 PHINEAS BOUGHT 159.46
ACRES ADJOINING THE BAY, BUILT A MODEST HOUSE AND STARTED EXCA-
VATIONS FOR HIS PRIVY PIT. HE WAS TOTALLY UNAWARE THAT HE HAD
SETTLED IN THE HEART OF THE *ARTESIAN* BELT. BEFORE HE HAD
REACHED A DEPTH OF SEVEN FEET PHINEAS STRUCK A TREMENDOUS
GUSH OF ARTESIAN WATER. UNDISMAYED, OVER THIS FOUNTAIN HE
ELEVATED HIS PRIVY ON STILTS, DUG A LONG CANAL TO TIDEWATER
AND LATER PLANTED HIS ACREAGE TO PEAR TREES. THUS OUR HARDY
PIONEER MADE TRIPLE USE OF MOTHER NATURE'S BOUNTIFUL GIFT.
HE SOLVED HIS ORCHARD IRRIGATION PROBLEM, ENJOYED AN EVER-
FLOWING HOUSE-WELL AND WAS THE FIRST MAN IN THE VALLEY TO
POSSESS AN OUTDOOR, SELF-FLUSHING WATER-CLOSET.

WHILE WE ARE STILL ENGAGED WITH THE PIT DIVISION OF PRIVY-
CONSTRUCTION PERHAPS WE SHOULD CONCLUDE WITH ANOTHER ALLEGEDLY
TRUE STORY.

HECTOR O. BRIGHTSTONE, Ph.D., WE SHALL CALL HIM. HE IS A COMFORT-
ABLY RETIRED GEOLOGY PROFESSOR AND AUTHOR, (STANFORD UNIVERSITY,
CLASS OF 1919.) HECTOR NOW ENJOYS PLEASURABLE SEARCH FOR REMOTE
WESTERN MINES AND GHOST TOWNS. ON THIS PARTICULAR TRIP HE WAS
SEARCHING THE MOTHER LODE COUNTRY BETWEEN MARIPOSA AND SONORA.
NORTH OF MOUNT BULLION HE TURNED HIS JEEP INTO AN APPARENTLY
DESERTED SIDE ROAD BUT TO HIS SURPRISE HE SAW FAINT SIGNS OF
FRESH TIRE TRACKS. HE FINALLY LEFT THE JEEP AND CONTINUED THE
TORTUOUS CLIMB ON FOOT. ANOTHER MILE AND HE DESCENDED INTO A
DEAD-END CANYON. HIS PERSISTENCE WAS REWARDED FOR ON THE MOUNTAIN-
SIDE HE SAW AN ABANDONED MINE MARKED ONLY BY ITS SKELETAL RUINS
AND RUSTY MACHINERY. IN THE CANYON BELOW WERE THE WEATHERED
REMAINS OF MINERS' SHACKS. SHADED BY AN AGED FIG TREE ONE
COTTAGE STOOD FAIRLY INTACT. AGAIN TO THE PROFESSOR'S SURPRISE

A MONGREL DOG BARKED AN ALARM AND A SMALL BOY APPEARED. THE LAD THREW A PIECE OF QUARTZ AT THE ANIMAL AND SHYLY APPROACHED HIS UNEXPECTED VISITOR.

THE PROFESSOR WAS A KINDLY MAN AND HAD A WAY WITH CHILDREN. AFTER AN EXCHANGE OF FRIENDLY GREETINGS CAME THE FOLLOWING CONVERSATION:

"FOLKS HOME, SON?"
"ONLY MA. PA WORKS IN SONORA DRIVIN' A LUMBER TRUCK."
"I'M VERY INTERESTED IN OLD MINES."
"THAT'S WHY WE LIVE HERE. PA EXPLORES THE MINE ON WEEK ENDS."
"COULD THIS BE THE RUINS OF THE BUZZARD HILL GOLD MINE?"
"THAT'S WHAT PA SAYS. BUT HOW'D YOU KNOW?"
"I FOUND IT ON AN OLD MAP. I'M WRITING A BOOK ABOUT LOST MINES."
"ABOUT THIS ONE? MAYBE 'BOUT PA?—AND MA?—EVEN ME?"
"OF COURSE I WILL. BUT I'LL NEED YOUR HELP."
"YOU BET, MISTER! JIST ASK ME *ANYTHING!*"
"FIRST, TELL ME THE *ONE* MOST INTERESTING THING ABOUT THE OLD MINE THAT WE CAN STILL SEE."

THE SMALL BOY FROWNED AS HE PONDERED THIS *ONE* MOST INTERESTING QUESTION. FINALLY THE SUN BROKE THROUGH HIS CLOUD OF THOUGHT. HIS FACE BRIGHTENED—AND THEN

"NOW I KNOW, MISTER! SEE THAT KINDA LEANIN' LITTLE HOUSE UP ON THAT LOW HILL IN FRONT OF THE MINE? THAT'S OUR PRIVY! IT'S SETTIN' ON AN OLE MINE SHAFT 297 FEET DEEP! MY PA SAYS IT'S *'THE DEEPEST DAMN PRIVY HOLE IN THE WHOLE WORLD!'*"

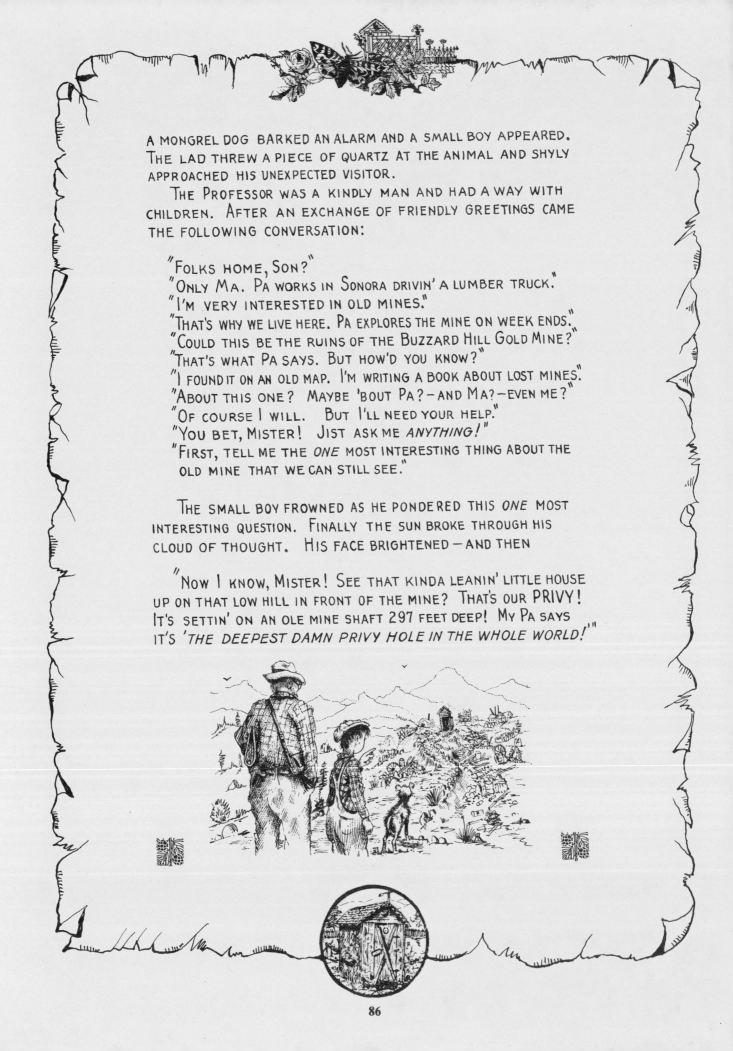

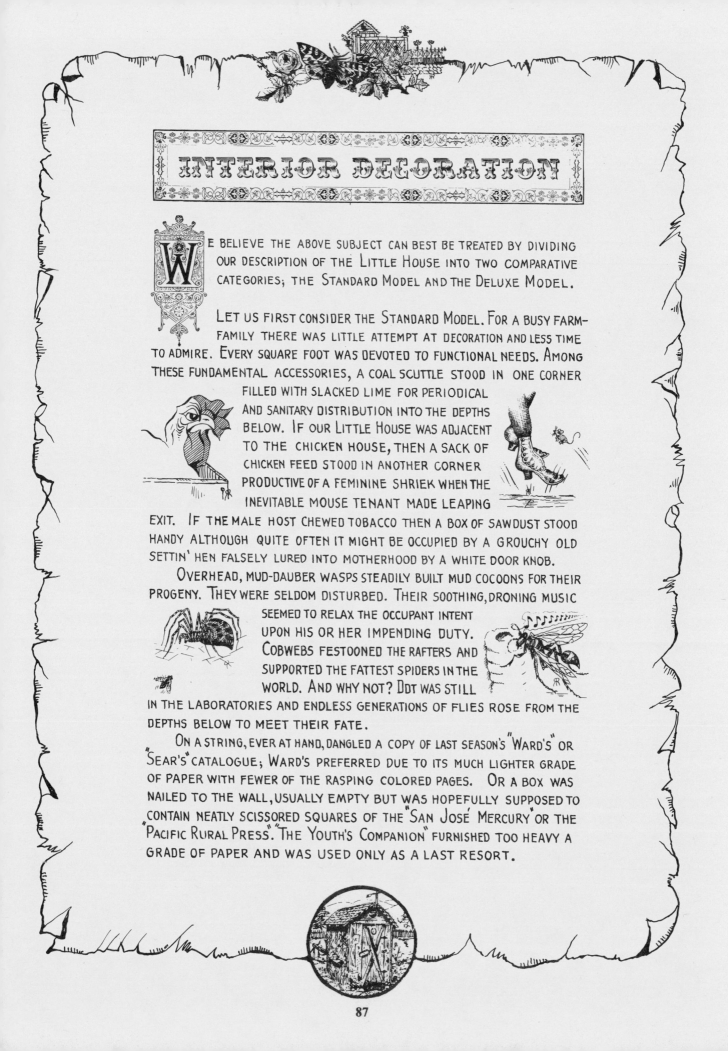

INTERIOR DECORATION

WE BELIEVE THE ABOVE SUBJECT CAN BEST BE TREATED BY DIVIDING OUR DESCRIPTION OF THE LITTLE HOUSE INTO TWO COMPARATIVE CATEGORIES; THE STANDARD MODEL AND THE DELUXE MODEL.

LET US FIRST CONSIDER THE STANDARD MODEL. FOR A BUSY FARM-FAMILY THERE WAS LITTLE ATTEMPT AT DECORATION AND LESS TIME TO ADMIRE. EVERY SQUARE FOOT WAS DEVOTED TO FUNCTIONAL NEEDS. AMONG THESE FUNDAMENTAL ACCESSORIES, A COAL SCUTTLE STOOD IN ONE CORNER FILLED WITH SLACKED LIME FOR PERIODICAL AND SANITARY DISTRIBUTION INTO THE DEPTHS BELOW. IF OUR LITTLE HOUSE WAS ADJACENT TO THE CHICKEN HOUSE, THEN A SACK OF CHICKEN FEED STOOD IN ANOTHER CORNER PRODUCTIVE OF A FEMININE SHRIEK WHEN THE INEVITABLE MOUSE TENANT MADE LEAPING EXIT. IF THE MALE HOST CHEWED TOBACCO THEN A BOX OF SAWDUST STOOD HANDY ALTHOUGH QUITE OFTEN IT MIGHT BE OCCUPIED BY A GROUCHY OLD SETTIN' HEN FALSELY LURED INTO MOTHERHOOD BY A WHITE DOOR KNOB.

OVERHEAD, MUD-DAUBER WASPS STEADILY BUILT MUD COCOONS FOR THEIR PROGENY. THEY WERE SELDOM DISTURBED. THEIR SOOTHING, DRONING MUSIC SEEMED TO RELAX THE OCCUPANT INTENT UPON HIS OR HER IMPENDING DUTY. COBWEBS FESTOONED THE RAFTERS AND SUPPORTED THE FATTEST SPIDERS IN THE WORLD. AND WHY NOT? DDT WAS STILL IN THE LABORATORIES AND ENDLESS GENERATIONS OF FLIES ROSE FROM THE DEPTHS BELOW TO MEET THEIR FATE.

ON A STRING, EVER AT HAND, DANGLED A COPY OF LAST SEASON'S "WARD'S" OR "SEAR'S" CATALOGUE; WARD'S PREFERRED DUE TO ITS MUCH LIGHTER GRADE OF PAPER WITH FEWER OF THE RASPING COLORED PAGES. OR A BOX WAS NAILED TO THE WALL, USUALLY EMPTY BUT WAS HOPEFULLY SUPPOSED TO CONTAIN NEATLY SCISSORED SQUARES OF THE "SAN JOSÉ MERCURY" OR THE "PACIFIC RURAL PRESS." THE YOUTH'S COMPANION" FURNISHED TOO HEAVY A GRADE OF PAPER AND WAS USED ONLY AS A LAST RESORT.

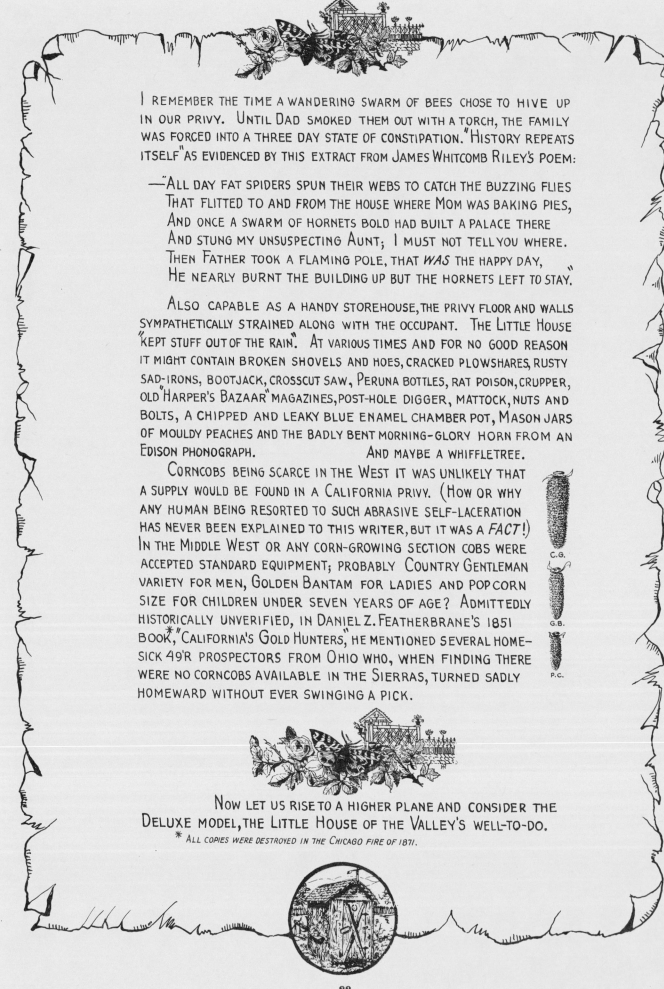

I remember the time a wandering swarm of bees chose to hive up in our privy. Until Dad smoked them out with a torch, the family was forced into a three day state of constipation. "History repeats itself" as evidenced by this extract from James Whitcomb Riley's poem:

—"All day fat spiders spun their webs to catch the buzzing flies
That flitted to and from the house where Mom was baking pies,
And once a swarm of hornets bold had built a palace there
And stung my unsuspecting Aunt; I must not tell you where.
Then Father took a flaming pole, that *was* the happy day,
He nearly burnt the building up but the hornets left to stay."

Also capable as a handy storehouse, the privy floor and walls sympathetically strained along with the occupant. The Little House "kept stuff out of the rain". At various times and for no good reason it might contain broken shovels and hoes, cracked plowshares, rusty sad-irons, bootjack, crosscut saw, Peruna bottles, rat poison, crupper, old "Harper's Bazaar" magazines, post-hole digger, mattock, nuts and bolts, a chipped and leaky blue enamel chamber pot, Mason jars of mouldy peaches and the badly bent morning-glory horn from an Edison phonograph. And maybe a whiffletree.

Corncobs being scarce in the West it was unlikely that a supply would be found in a California privy. (How or why any human being resorted to such abrasive self-laceration has never been explained to this writer, but it was a *fact!*) In the Middle West or any corn-growing section cobs were accepted standard equipment; probably Country Gentleman variety for men, Golden Bantam for ladies and popcorn size for children under seven years of age? Admittedly historically unverified, in Daniel Z. Featherbrane's 1851 book,*"California's Gold Hunters," he mentioned several home-sick 49'r prospectors from Ohio who, when finding there were no corncobs available in the Sierras, turned sadly homeward without ever swinging a pick.

C.G.

G.B.

P.C.

Now let us rise to a higher plane and consider the Deluxe model, the Little House of the Valley's well-to-do.

* All copies were destroyed in the Chicago fire of 1871.

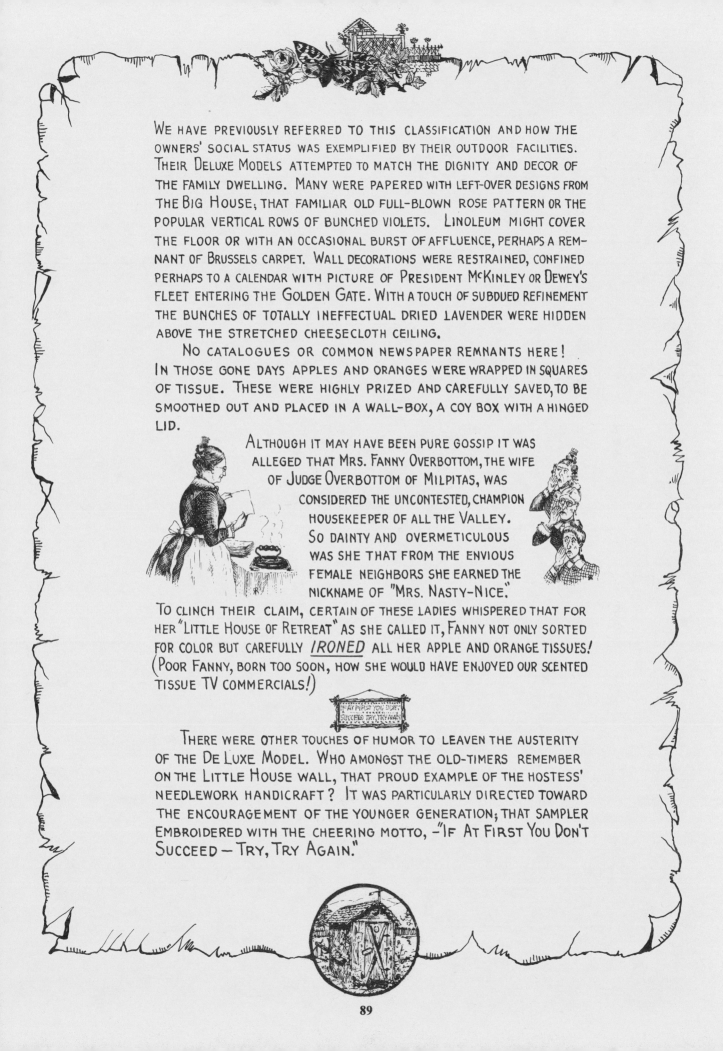

WE HAVE PREVIOUSLY REFERRED TO THIS CLASSIFICATION AND HOW THE OWNERS' SOCIAL STATUS WAS EXEMPLIFIED BY THEIR OUTDOOR FACILITIES. THEIR DELUXE MODELS ATTEMPTED TO MATCH THE DIGNITY AND DECOR OF THE FAMILY DWELLING. MANY WERE PAPERED WITH LEFT-OVER DESIGNS FROM THE BIG HOUSE; THAT FAMILIAR OLD FULL-BLOWN ROSE PATTERN OR THE POPULAR VERTICAL ROWS OF BUNCHED VIOLETS. LINOLEUM MIGHT COVER THE FLOOR OR WITH AN OCCASIONAL BURST OF AFFLUENCE, PERHAPS A REMNANT OF BRUSSELS CARPET. WALL DECORATIONS WERE RESTRAINED, CONFINED PERHAPS TO A CALENDAR WITH PICTURE OF PRESIDENT McKINLEY OR DEWEY'S FLEET ENTERING THE GOLDEN GATE. WITH A TOUCH OF SUBDUED REFINEMENT THE BUNCHES OF TOTALLY INEFFECTUAL DRIED LAVENDER WERE HIDDEN ABOVE THE STRETCHED CHEESECLOTH CEILING.

NO CATALOGUES OR COMMON NEWSPAPER REMNANTS HERE! IN THOSE GONE DAYS APPLES AND ORANGES WERE WRAPPED IN SQUARES OF TISSUE. THESE WERE HIGHLY PRIZED AND CAREFULLY SAVED, TO BE SMOOTHED OUT AND PLACED IN A WALL-BOX, A COY BOX WITH A HINGED LID.

ALTHOUGH IT MAY HAVE BEEN PURE GOSSIP IT WAS ALLEGED THAT MRS. FANNY OVERBOTTOM, THE WIFE OF JUDGE OVERBOTTOM OF MILPITAS, WAS CONSIDERED THE UNCONTESTED, CHAMPION HOUSEKEEPER OF ALL THE VALLEY. SO DAINTY AND OVERMETICULOUS WAS SHE THAT FROM THE ENVIOUS FEMALE NEIGHBORS SHE EARNED THE NICKNAME OF "MRS. NASTY-NICE."

TO CLINCH THEIR CLAIM, CERTAIN OF THESE LADIES WHISPERED THAT FOR HER "LITTLE HOUSE OF RETREAT" AS SHE CALLED IT, FANNY NOT ONLY SORTED FOR COLOR BUT CAREFULLY *IRONED* ALL HER APPLE AND ORANGE TISSUES! (POOR FANNY, BORN TOO SOON, HOW SHE WOULD HAVE ENJOYED OUR SCENTED TISSUE TV COMMERCIALS!)

THERE WERE OTHER TOUCHES OF HUMOR TO LEAVEN THE AUSTERITY OF THE DE LUXE MODEL. WHO AMONGST THE OLD-TIMERS REMEMBER ON THE LITTLE HOUSE WALL, THAT PROUD EXAMPLE OF THE HOSTESS' NEEDLEWORK HANDICRAFT? IT WAS PARTICULARLY DIRECTED TOWARD THE ENCOURAGEMENT OF THE YOUNGER GENERATION; THAT SAMPLER EMBROIDERED WITH THE CHEERING MOTTO, -"IF AT FIRST YOU DON'T SUCCEED — TRY, TRY AGAIN."

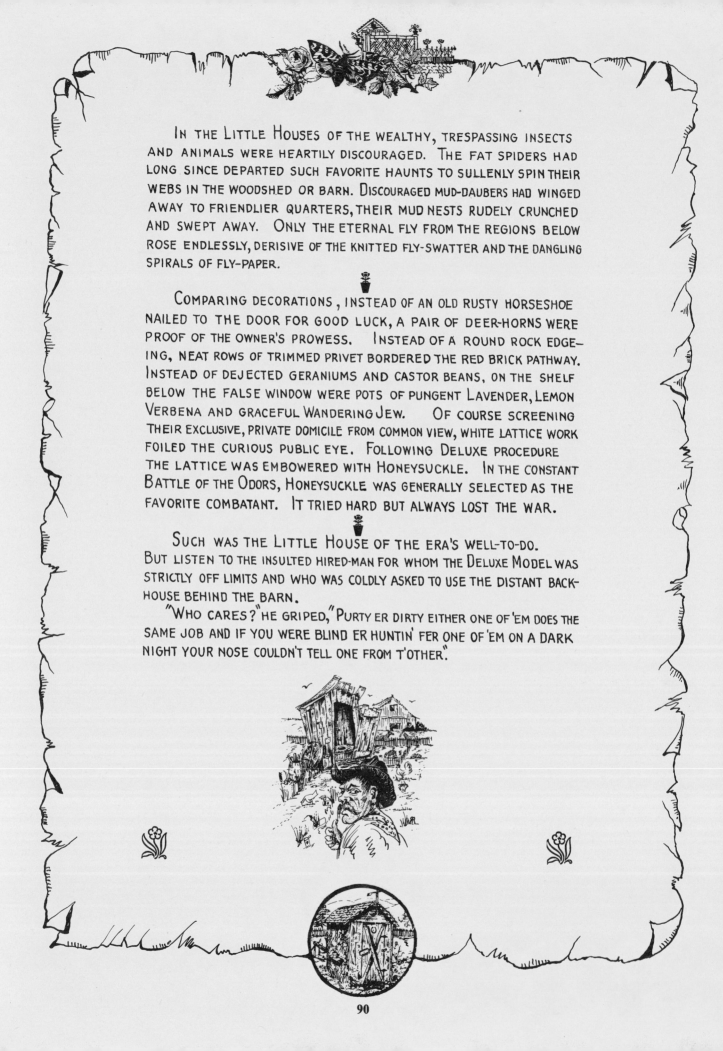

IN THE LITTLE HOUSES OF THE WEALTHY, TRESPASSING INSECTS AND ANIMALS WERE HEARTILY DISCOURAGED. THE FAT SPIDERS HAD LONG SINCE DEPARTED SUCH FAVORITE HAUNTS TO SULLENLY SPIN THEIR WEBS IN THE WOODSHED OR BARN. DISCOURAGED MUD-DAUBERS HAD WINGED AWAY TO FRIENDLIER QUARTERS, THEIR MUD NESTS RUDELY CRUNCHED AND SWEPT AWAY. ONLY THE ETERNAL FLY FROM THE REGIONS BELOW ROSE ENDLESSLY, DERISIVE OF THE KNITTED FLY-SWATTER AND THE DANGLING SPIRALS OF FLY-PAPER.

COMPARING DECORATIONS, INSTEAD OF AN OLD RUSTY HORSESHOE NAILED TO THE DOOR FOR GOOD LUCK, A PAIR OF DEER-HORNS WERE PROOF OF THE OWNER'S PROWESS. INSTEAD OF A ROUND ROCK EDGE-ING, NEAT ROWS OF TRIMMED PRIVET BORDERED THE RED BRICK PATHWAY. INSTEAD OF DEJECTED GERANIUMS AND CASTOR BEANS, ON THE SHELF BELOW THE FALSE WINDOW WERE POTS OF PUNGENT LAVENDER, LEMON VERBENA AND GRACEFUL WANDERING JEW. OF COURSE SCREENING THEIR EXCLUSIVE, PRIVATE DOMICILE FROM COMMON VIEW, WHITE LATTICE WORK FOILED THE CURIOUS PUBLIC EYE. FOLLOWING DELUXE PROCEDURE THE LATTICE WAS EMBOWERED WITH HONEYSUCKLE. IN THE CONSTANT BATTLE OF THE ODORS, HONEYSUCKLE WAS GENERALLY SELECTED AS THE FAVORITE COMBATANT. IT TRIED HARD BUT ALWAYS LOST THE WAR.

SUCH WAS THE LITTLE HOUSE OF THE ERA'S WELL-TO-DO. BUT LISTEN TO THE INSULTED HIRED-MAN FOR WHOM THE DELUXE MODEL WAS STRICTLY OFF LIMITS AND WHO WAS COLDLY ASKED TO USE THE DISTANT BACK-HOUSE BEHIND THE BARN.

"WHO CARES?" HE GRIPED, "PURTY ER DIRTY EITHER ONE OF 'EM DOES THE SAME JOB AND IF YOU WERE BLIND ER HUNTIN' FER ONE OF 'EM ON A DARK NIGHT YOUR NOSE COULDN'T TELL ONE FROM T'OTHER."

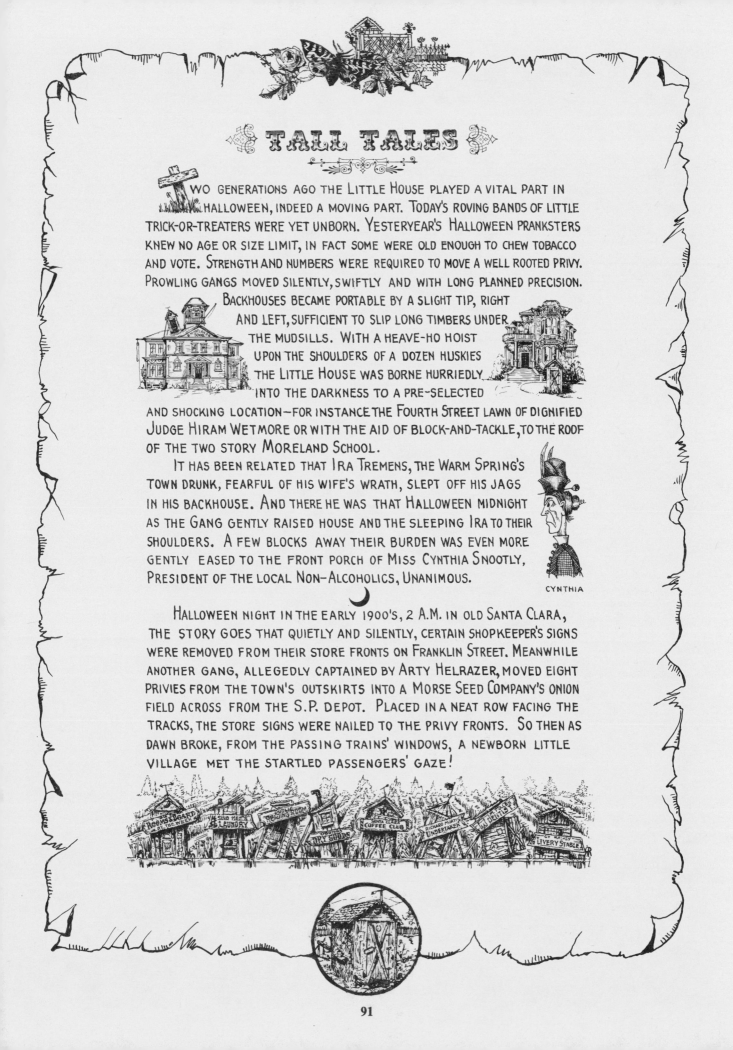

TALL TALES

TWO GENERATIONS AGO THE LITTLE HOUSE PLAYED A VITAL PART IN HALLOWEEN, INDEED A MOVING PART. TODAY'S ROVING BANDS OF LITTLE TRICK-OR-TREATERS WERE YET UNBORN. YESTERYEAR'S HALLOWEEN PRANKSTERS KNEW NO AGE OR SIZE LIMIT, IN FACT SOME WERE OLD ENOUGH TO CHEW TOBACCO AND VOTE. STRENGTH AND NUMBERS WERE REQUIRED TO MOVE A WELL ROOTED PRIVY. PROWLING GANGS MOVED SILENTLY, SWIFTLY AND WITH LONG PLANNED PRECISION. BACKHOUSES BECAME PORTABLE BY A SLIGHT TIP, RIGHT AND LEFT, SUFFICIENT TO SLIP LONG TIMBERS UNDER THE MUDSILLS. WITH A HEAVE-HO HOIST UPON THE SHOULDERS OF A DOZEN HUSKIES THE LITTLE HOUSE WAS BORNE HURRIEDLY INTO THE DARKNESS TO A PRE-SELECTED AND SHOCKING LOCATION—FOR INSTANCE THE FOURTH STREET LAWN OF DIGNIFIED JUDGE HIRAM WETMORE OR WITH THE AID OF BLOCK-AND-TACKLE, TO THE ROOF OF THE TWO STORY MORELAND SCHOOL.

IT HAS BEEN RELATED THAT IRA TREMENS, THE WARM SPRING'S TOWN DRUNK, FEARFUL OF HIS WIFE'S WRATH, SLEPT OFF HIS JAGS IN HIS BACKHOUSE. AND THERE HE WAS THAT HALLOWEEN MIDNIGHT AS THE GANG GENTLY RAISED HOUSE AND THE SLEEPING IRA TO THEIR SHOULDERS. A FEW BLOCKS AWAY THEIR BURDEN WAS EVEN MORE GENTLY EASED TO THE FRONT PORCH OF MISS CYNTHIA SNOOTLY, PRESIDENT OF THE LOCAL NON-ALCOHOLICS, UNANIMOUS.

CYNTHIA

HALLOWEEN NIGHT IN THE EARLY 1900'S, 2 A.M. IN OLD SANTA CLARA, THE STORY GOES THAT QUIETLY AND SILENTLY, CERTAIN SHOPKEEPER'S SIGNS WERE REMOVED FROM THEIR STORE FRONTS ON FRANKLIN STREET. MEANWHILE ANOTHER GANG, ALLEGEDLY CAPTAINED BY ARTY HELRAZER, MOVED EIGHT PRIVIES FROM THE TOWN'S OUTSKIRTS INTO A MORSE SEED COMPANY'S ONION FIELD ACROSS FROM THE S.P. DEPOT. PLACED IN A NEAT ROW FACING THE TRACKS, THE STORE SIGNS WERE NAILED TO THE PRIVY FRONTS. SO THEN AS DAWN BROKE, FROM THE PASSING TRAINS' WINDOWS, A NEWBORN LITTLE VILLAGE MET THE STARTLED PASSENGERS' GAZE!

IN THAT ALMOST FORGOTTEN ERA THERE WERE FLAGPOLE SITTERS AND ON A LOWER LEVEL, PRIVY SETTERS, BOTH SET TO BREAK RECORDS. WATCHFUL NEIGHBORS CLAIMED THAT URIAH BULHORN OF CAMPBELL HELD THE WORLD'S DURATION RECORD FOR "SETTIN". (YOU WILL RECALL THAT THE AGED URIAH WAS PART INDIAN.) FOR YEARS, SO EXTENDED WERE HIS PRIVY VISITS THAT HIS FAITHFUL WIFE, LILYANA, ON COLD WINTER DAYS WAS OFTEN SEEN TAKING HIM A SWEATER, OR THE COALOIL STOVE OR PERHAPS A CUP OF COFFEE AND A SANDWICH. THEN TIME TOOK ITS TOLL AND FROM OLD AGE AND WEATHER EXPOSURE, LILYANA PASSED AWAY. IT WAS THEN THAT THE GRIEVING URIAH BEGAN SPENDING MORE AND MORE TIME IN HIS LITTLE HOUSE. AFTER HE HAD NOT BEEN SEEN FOR FOUR DAYS, ANXIOUS NEIGHBORS INVESTIGATED AND FOUND HIM IN HIS USUAL HAUNT, COLD, STIFF—AND DEAD. OF COURSE UNCOUTH NEIGHBORS OFFERED GHOULISH SUGGESTIONS FOR HIS FUNERAL BUT THE UNDERTAKER, RICHARD MORTIS, WAS EQUAL TO THE OCCASION. HE SAW THAT URIAH'S LAST WISH WAS DIGNIFIEDLY EXECUTED. YOU MUST KNOW THAT IN HIS WILL, URIAH HAD FIRMLY REQUESTED THAT HE BE BURIED INDIAN STYLE — IN A SITTING POSITION.

THEN THERE WAS THE LEGEND OF THE HENPECKED TITUS BAKSTOP AND HIS WIFE SERAPHIM. THEY OWNED AN ISOLATED ELEVEN ACRE PRUNE ORCHARD NORTH OF SARATOGA ON THE BANKS OF THE CALABAZAS CREEK. THIS WAS IN 1911 AND SERAPHIM WAS THE PROUD OWNER OF A NEW INDOOR WATER-CLOSET WITH PULL-CHAIN. AH! BUT POOR TITUS WOULD NEVER USE IT. HE PARTLY ESCAPED HER CONSTANT NAGGING BY BUILDING AN OUTDOOR JOB. HIS BACKHOUSE SAT ON SORT OF A RICKETY WHARF SUPPORTED BY REDWOOD POLES AND EXTENDING HALF WAY OVER THE CREEK BED. FORTUNATELY IN THOSE DAYS THE CREEK RAN YEAR-ROUND (EXCEPT FROM JUNE TO NOVEMBER.) YOU NO DOUBT WILL PROMPTLY RECALL THAT 1911 WAS A YEAR OF FLOODS (SEASON RAIN-FALL-31.65 INCHES) IT WAS 4:59 A.M. JUST BEFORE DAWN ON THAT RECORD STORMY NIGHT OF JANUARY 7, 1911 WHEN TITUS HAD AN URGENT CALL OF NATURE. BLEARY-EYED AND FORGETTING TO LIGHT HIS LANTERN, TITUS STUMBLED OUT THROUGH THE RAIN TO HIS PRIVY. AS ALWAYS, HIS HOUND FOLLOWED HIM. HE FAILED TO NOTICE THAT THE FLOOD WATERS OF THE CALABAZAS WERE EVEN THEN LAPPING HIS TIPSY LITTLE BUILDING. WHAT HAPPENED

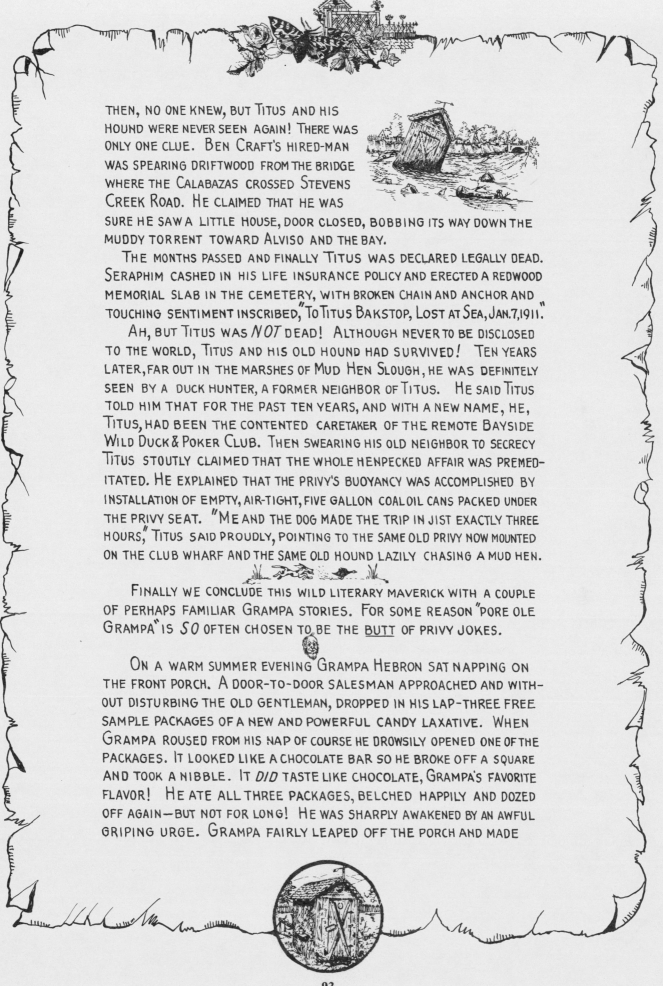

THEN, NO ONE KNEW, BUT TITUS AND HIS HOUND WERE NEVER SEEN AGAIN! THERE WAS ONLY ONE CLUE. BEN CRAFT'S HIRED-MAN WAS SPEARING DRIFTWOOD FROM THE BRIDGE WHERE THE CALABAZAS CROSSED STEVENS CREEK ROAD. HE CLAIMED THAT HE WAS SURE HE SAW A LITTLE HOUSE, DOOR CLOSED, BOBBING ITS WAY DOWN THE MUDDY TORRENT TOWARD ALVISO AND THE BAY.

THE MONTHS PASSED AND FINALLY TITUS WAS DECLARED LEGALLY DEAD. SERAPHIM CASHED IN HIS LIFE INSURANCE POLICY AND ERECTED A REDWOOD MEMORIAL SLAB IN THE CEMETERY, WITH BROKEN CHAIN AND ANCHOR AND TOUCHING SENTIMENT INSCRIBED, "TO TITUS BAKSTOP, LOST AT SEA, JAN.7, 1911."

AH, BUT TITUS WAS *NOT* DEAD! ALTHOUGH NEVER TO BE DISCLOSED TO THE WORLD, TITUS AND HIS OLD HOUND HAD SURVIVED! TEN YEARS LATER, FAR OUT IN THE MARSHES OF MUD HEN SLOUGH, HE WAS DEFINITELY SEEN BY A DUCK HUNTER, A FORMER NEIGHBOR OF TITUS. HE SAID TITUS TOLD HIM THAT FOR THE PAST TEN YEARS, AND WITH A NEW NAME, HE, TITUS, HAD BEEN THE CONTENTED CARETAKER OF THE REMOTE BAYSIDE WILD DUCK & POKER CLUB. THEN SWEARING HIS OLD NEIGHBOR TO SECRECY TITUS STOUTLY CLAIMED THAT THE WHOLE HENPECKED AFFAIR WAS PREMEDITATED. HE EXPLAINED THAT THE PRIVY'S BUOYANCY WAS ACCOMPLISHED BY INSTALLATION OF EMPTY, AIR-TIGHT, FIVE GALLON COAL OIL CANS PACKED UNDER THE PRIVY SEAT. "ME AND THE DOG MADE THE TRIP IN JIST EXACTLY THREE HOURS," TITUS SAID PROUDLY, POINTING TO THE SAME OLD PRIVY NOW MOUNTED ON THE CLUB WHARF AND THE SAME OLD HOUND LAZILY CHASING A MUD HEN.

FINALLY WE CONCLUDE THIS WILD LITERARY MAVERICK WITH A COUPLE OF PERHAPS FAMILIAR GRAMPA STORIES. FOR SOME REASON "PORE OLE GRAMPA" IS *SO* OFTEN CHOSEN TO BE THE <u>BUTT</u> OF PRIVY JOKES.

ON A WARM SUMMER EVENING GRAMPA HEBRON SAT NAPPING ON THE FRONT PORCH. A DOOR-TO-DOOR SALESMAN APPROACHED AND WITHOUT DISTURBING THE OLD GENTLEMAN, DROPPED IN HIS LAP THREE FREE SAMPLE PACKAGES OF A NEW AND POWERFUL CANDY LAXATIVE. WHEN GRAMPA ROUSED FROM HIS NAP OF COURSE HE DROWSILY OPENED ONE OF THE PACKAGES. IT LOOKED LIKE A CHOCOLATE BAR SO HE BROKE OFF A SQUARE AND TOOK A NIBBLE. IT *DID* TASTE LIKE CHOCOLATE, GRAMPA'S FAVORITE FLAVOR! HE ATE ALL THREE PACKAGES, BELCHED HAPPILY AND DOZED OFF AGAIN—BUT NOT FOR LONG! HE WAS SHARPLY AWAKENED BY AN AWFUL GRIPING URGE. GRAMPA FAIRLY LEAPED OFF THE PORCH AND MADE

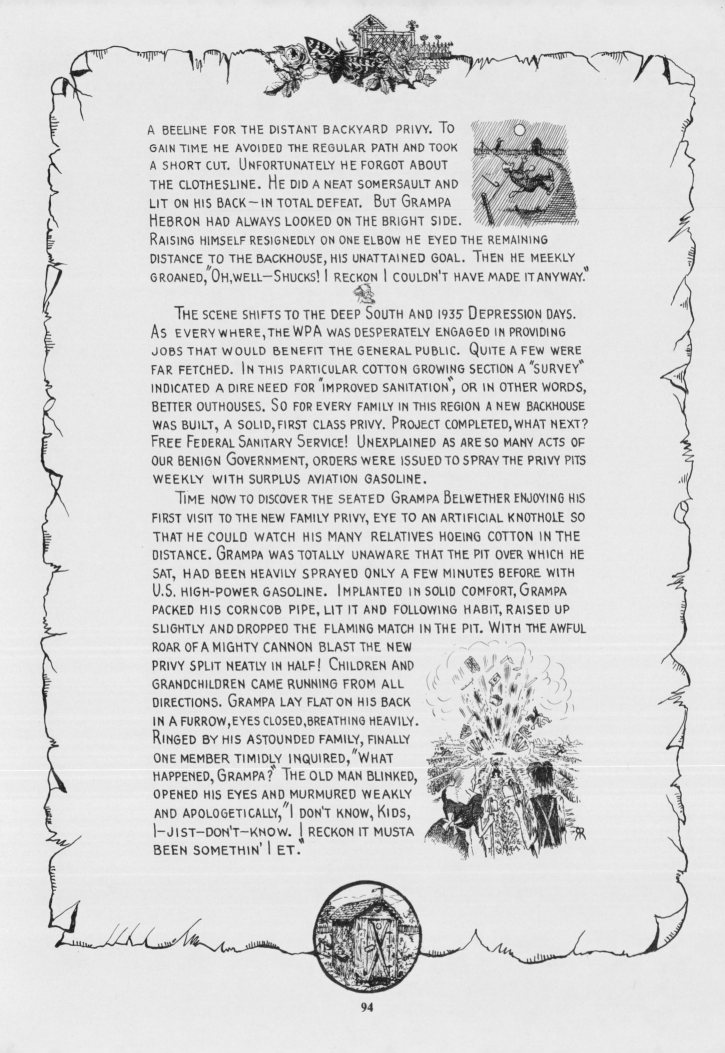

A BEELINE FOR THE DISTANT BACKYARD PRIVY. TO GAIN TIME HE AVOIDED THE REGULAR PATH AND TOOK A SHORT CUT. UNFORTUNATELY HE FORGOT ABOUT THE CLOTHESLINE. HE DID A NEAT SOMERSAULT AND LIT ON HIS BACK — IN TOTAL DEFEAT. BUT GRAMPA HEBRON HAD ALWAYS LOOKED ON THE BRIGHT SIDE. RAISING HIMSELF RESIGNEDLY ON ONE ELBOW HE EYED THE REMAINING DISTANCE TO THE BACKHOUSE, HIS UNATTAINED GOAL. THEN HE MEEKLY GROANED, "OH, WELL — SHUCKS! I RECKON I COULDN'T HAVE MADE IT ANYWAY."

THE SCENE SHIFTS TO THE DEEP SOUTH AND 1935 DEPRESSION DAYS. AS EVERYWHERE, THE WPA WAS DESPERATELY ENGAGED IN PROVIDING JOBS THAT WOULD BENEFIT THE GENERAL PUBLIC. QUITE A FEW WERE FAR FETCHED. IN THIS PARTICULAR COTTON GROWING SECTION A "SURVEY" INDICATED A DIRE NEED FOR "IMPROVED SANITATION", OR IN OTHER WORDS, BETTER OUTHOUSES. SO FOR EVERY FAMILY IN THIS REGION A NEW BACKHOUSE WAS BUILT, A SOLID, FIRST CLASS PRIVY. PROJECT COMPLETED, WHAT NEXT? FREE FEDERAL SANITARY SERVICE! UNEXPLAINED AS ARE SO MANY ACTS OF OUR BENIGN GOVERNMENT, ORDERS WERE ISSUED TO SPRAY THE PRIVY PITS WEEKLY WITH SURPLUS AVIATION GASOLINE.

TIME NOW TO DISCOVER THE SEATED GRAMPA BELWETHER ENJOYING HIS FIRST VISIT TO THE NEW FAMILY PRIVY, EYE TO AN ARTIFICIAL KNOTHOLE SO THAT HE COULD WATCH HIS MANY RELATIVES HOEING COTTON IN THE DISTANCE. GRAMPA WAS TOTALLY UNAWARE THAT THE PIT OVER WHICH HE SAT, HAD BEEN HEAVILY SPRAYED ONLY A FEW MINUTES BEFORE WITH U.S. HIGH-POWER GASOLINE. IMPLANTED IN SOLID COMFORT, GRAMPA PACKED HIS CORNCOB PIPE, LIT IT AND FOLLOWING HABIT, RAISED UP SLIGHTLY AND DROPPED THE FLAMING MATCH IN THE PIT. WITH THE AWFUL ROAR OF A MIGHTY CANNON BLAST THE NEW PRIVY SPLIT NEATLY IN HALF! CHILDREN AND GRANDCHILDREN CAME RUNNING FROM ALL DIRECTIONS. GRAMPA LAY FLAT ON HIS BACK IN A FURROW, EYES CLOSED, BREATHING HEAVILY. RINGED BY HIS ASTOUNDED FAMILY, FINALLY ONE MEMBER TIMIDLY INQUIRED, "WHAT HAPPENED, GRAMPA?" THE OLD MAN BLINKED, OPENED HIS EYES AND MURMURED WEAKLY AND APOLOGETICALLY, "I DON'T KNOW, KIDS, I — JIST — DON'T — KNOW. I RECKON IT MUSTA BEEN SOMETHIN' I ET."

ALMOST FORGOTTEN

Cartoon
Pen and Inklings
of the
Old Santa Clara Valley

by a native

Dear Reader,

"Flushed with pride" and inspired by the reception of *Looking Backward 1900* (My first homemade book, written in 1963), I determined to write a book to sell. I had no idea whatever about writing or publishing, but I could learn from experience and with the help of my kind professional friends—top historians, authors, and publishers.

I did decide to include some simple history in *Almost Forgotten.* "Why the Name?" is a summary of biographies and/or descriptions with illustrations and briefs on certain pioneers, places or events. They answer many common questions asked by Valley newcomers. There are also "word pictures" on subjects such as Transportation, The Alameda, Country Schools, and the 1900 Parlor.

Although it was my first book, *Almost Forgotten* continues to be an enduring top seller. One reason? Our busy inhabitant of the New Valley "looks at the pictures" before ever reading! The original *Almost Forgotten* has more pen and ink drawings than any of my other books.

Yours Truly
Ralph Rambo

P.S.   For any obvious errors in our "Why the Name?" definitions, I ask the reader's tolerance. Please remember that these descriptions were hand-lettered *twenty* years ago and we are not disturbing what time and progress has changed or eliminated.

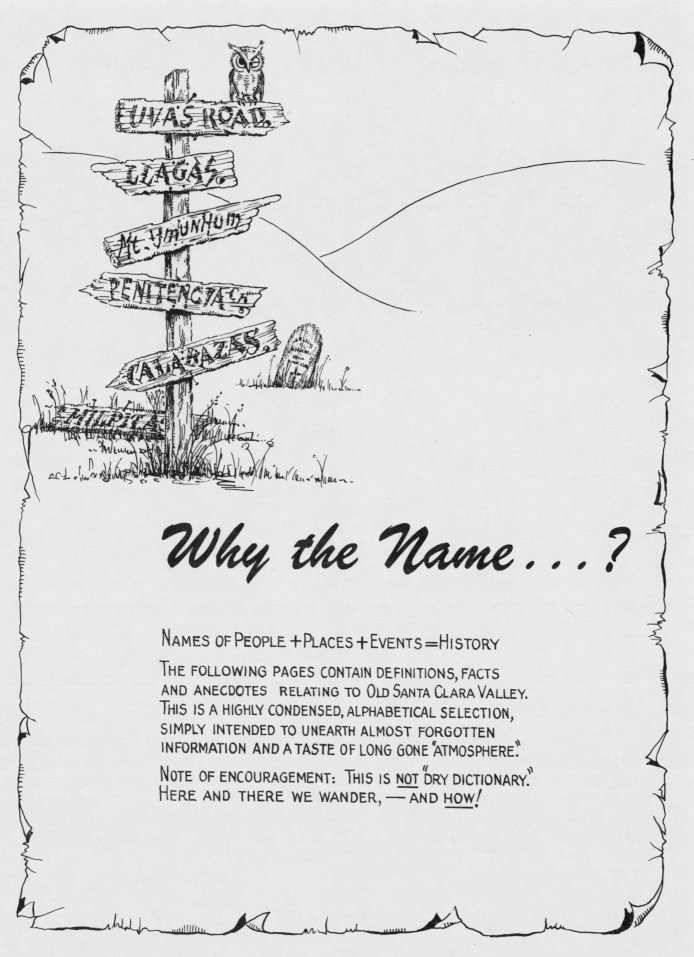

Why the Name...?

NAMES OF PEOPLE + PLACES + EVENTS = HISTORY

THE FOLLOWING PAGES CONTAIN DEFINITIONS, FACTS AND ANECDOTES RELATING TO OLD SANTA CLARA VALLEY. THIS IS A HIGHLY CONDENSED, ALPHABETICAL SELECTION, SIMPLY INTENDED TO UNEARTH ALMOST FORGOTTEN INFORMATION AND A TASTE OF LONG GONE "ATMOSPHERE."

NOTE OF ENCOURAGEMENT: THIS IS NOT "DRY DICTIONARY." HERE AND THERE WE WANDER, — AND HOW!

Why the Name...?

AGNEW: "AGNEWS" COMMONLY USED BUT ABRAM AGNEW SETTLED IN THIS TERRITORY NORTH OF SANTA CLARA ABOUT 1873. THE ORIGINAL "AGNEWS INSANE ASYLUM" SHOWN ABOVE (1894) WAS PRACTICALLY DESTROYED BY 1906 QUAKE AND OVER 125 KILLED.

ALMADEN: (SEE SPECIAL PAGE) MEANS "THE MINE". NEW ALMADEN IS PROPER, BEING NAMED FOR THE OLD ORIGINAL IN SPAIN, RICHEST QUICKSILVER MINE IN THE WORLD, PRODUCING 200 LBS. OF QUICKSILVER PER TON OF ORE TO NEW ALMADEN'S 20 LBS. VALLEY INDIANS FIRST USED THE VERMILION CINNABAR AS FACE AND BODY PAINT DESPITE SEVERE SALIVATING. ORE DISCOVERY IN 1822. WORKED FOR GOLD AND SILVER BY DON SUÑOL IN 1824. NO RESULTS. QUICKSILVER RECOGNIZED BY DON CASTILLERO AT SANTA CLARA MISSION IN 1845.

ALMA: (AND LEXINGTON) CHARMING LITTLE MOUNTAIN TOWNS 3 MILES ABOVE LOS GATOS ON THE SAN JOSE-SANTA CRUZ RAILROAD. NOW BURIED BENEATH LEXINGTON DAM. BOTH ON STAGE LINE. SHIPPING POINTS FOR MOUNTAIN FRUIT AND LUMBER. 8 SAWMILLS, POST OFFICES, STORES, BLACKSMITHS.

ALVISO: 8 MILES N. OF SAN JOSE. ONCE CALLED EMBARCADERO DE SANTA CLARA. EARLIEST LANDING POINT FOR FIRST SEA-FARING SETTLERS. EXTENSIVE SHIPPING POINT FOR OLD VALLEY HIDES, TALLOW GRAIN, LUMBER AND QUICKSILVER. SITE OF A HOPEFUL "NEW CHICAGO", A MARSHY SUBDIVISION, SO WET, MAIL-ORDER BUYERS FOUND THEIR LOTS BY ROW-BOAT. NAMED FOR DON IGNACIO ALVISO WHO ARRIVED WITH DE ANZA IN 1776. SETTLED HERE IN 1838. ONCE THE SITE OF LARGE SHIPPING WAREHOUSES, CANNERIES, OYSTER BEDS PLANTED WITH EASTERN OYSTERS, ASPARAGUS FIELDS, POULTRY SHELL PLANT. HEART OF THE ARTESIAN WELL SECTION. FIRST PLANTING OF VALLEY PEAR ORCHARDS.

AGRICULTURAL PARK OR FAIR GROUNDS ON THE ALAMEDA WEST OF RACE STREET TURN. 76 ACRES BOUGHT IN 1859 FROM GEN. NAGLEE FOR $6000. BICYCLE RACES, BALLOON ASCENSIONS, BUFFALO BILL. GEN. GRANT WATCHED LELAND STANFORD'S HORSE RACE HERE. AND THROUGH A KNOT HOLE THE WRITER AT A TENDER AGE WATCHED BARNEY OLDFIELD BREAK THE WORLD'S AUTO SPEED RECORD AT A HAIR-RAISING 60 MILES PER HOUR.

ALUM ROCK: CITY PARK NAMED FOR CLIFF AT CANYON ENTRANCE CONTAINING ALUM MINERAL. FOUNDED 1872. SERVED AT VARIOUS TIMES BY OMNIBUS, STEAM TRAIN AND ELECTRIC CARS. AT ONE SIDE OF THE PARK ROAD WAS A TON SIZE METEOR. DURING WORLD WAR I "PATRIOTICALLY" DESTROYED FOR ITS METAL! ONLY A FEW OF THE MANY MINERAL SPRINGS NOW FLOW, ONCE HIGHLY REGARDED AS CURES FOR PIONEER ACHES AND PAINS.

AMUSEMENTS: HOW? WITHOUT CARS, RADIO OR TV? FINE UNCROWDED TROUT FISHING IN EVERY CREEK. SWARMS OF GEESE AND DUCKS, GAME IN THE HILLS. SMALL FOLKS—MARBLES, KITES, TOPS. STATE LEAGUE BASE BALL AT LUNA PARK. BABE RUTH VISITS HAL CHASE OUR GREATEST. SODALITY PARK, SCHEUTZEN PARK, GARDEN CITY WHEELMEN, RIFLE CLUBS. PICNICS AT ALUM ROCK, CONGRESS SPRINGS, SODA ROCK. THEATERS: LIBERTY, UNIQUE, LYRIC, VICTORY, EMPIRE, RINGLING BROS. SELLS-FLOTO, BARNUM & BAILEY. MEDICINE SHOWS LIKE FERDON OR KAMAMA. SARATOGA BLOSSOM FESTIVALS AND ROSE CARNIVALS. A SALUTE TO THE ONLY SURVIVOR,—PORTUGUESE FIESTAS!

ANTIMACASSAR: INTERESTING OLD WORD, STILL ALIVE. PIONEER MEN PLASTERED DOWN THEIR HAIR WITH MACASSAR OIL IMPORTED FROM MACASSAR —IN THE CELEBES. IN DESPERATION, LADIES MADE ANTI-MACASSARS TO PROTECT CHAIRS. STILL IN USE, NOW TO COMBAT THAT "GREASY KID STUFF."

Why the Name...?

ARTESIAN: The Valley's early settlers depended on shallow surface wells, springs and creeks for water supply. But in 1854 on 5th. Street, the Merrit brothers tried for a lower stratum. At 50 feet struck a gusher. Some 6" wells spouted 16 feet. Most famous well in history,—G.A. Dabney's on San Fernando St. Flooded the town. City council imposed $50 a day fine for every day it ran. Had no effect on well, or Dabney. Other wells gradually decreased its flow. More and more wells and the artesian period ends.

ARTESIAN
ALVISO ROAD
1894

AZULE: Springs and mountain section near Saratoga; Mt. Eden district. AZULE means "blue". Could have been named for blue waters of springs or heavy growth of wild lilac or ceanothus in that locality.

BACON: Frank Bacon, the actor, received much of his early experience locally before his great success in the title role of LIGHTNIN' which ran three years on Broadway. He enjoyed a vacation orchard home near Mountain View.

LIGHTNIN'

BALDWIN: In 1892 Rear Admiral Charles S. Baldwin purchased 137 acres between Cupertino and Monta Vista. Besides residence, guest house and stone winery, he built Le Petit Trianon. This was a replica of a miniature Versailles Palace Louis XVI presented to Marie Antoinette. He called his place Beaulieu (good earth) and had one of the first swimming pools, polo fields and a French automobile, importing a French chauffeur to run it, which it did,—occasionally. Now, this estate is site for new De Anza College with possible Trianon preservation.

BASCOM: Dr. and Mrs. Bascom owned 135 acres on the west side of the present avenue near Santa Clara and built home in 1852. "Grandma Bascom" conducted a high class boarding house in 1849, the year that State Legislature met for the first

SUPPER!

time in San Jose, the new State Capitol. Some of her guests were Fremont, Pico, Suñol, Reeds and Murphys.

BEE: Harry Bee,—one of early San Jose's best known. Was sheriff in 1849 and White was Alcalde. White got the gold fever and left for the mines, telling Bee to do as he pleased with ten Indian prisoners, some murderers. Harry turned them loose, taking the gang to the mines to work for him. All went well for 3 months. Then Harry scented rebellion. He slipped back to San Jose with a fortune. The Indians worked just one day afterward, got drunk, fought and conveniently and practically, exterminated themselves.

ARRIVED 1830
1896

BERNAL: Joaquin Bernal held a grant of 9,647 acres 8 miles south of San Jose as a reward from the King of Spain for investigating California's mineral wealth in 1795. He was the typical Don. Large hacienda, swimming pool antedating Baldwin's by a century. Arena for "bull and grizzly" fights. Lived to age 97, his wife, 110 and left seventy-eight children and grandchildren.

BERRYESSA: Named for the earliest settler in this district east of San Jose, Nicolás Antonio Berryessa member of the De Anza 1769 expedition. For decades this then "remote spot" was marked only by store, church, post office blacksmith and vast, quiet acres.

GROCERIES JW SHAW PROVISION
SHAW'S GROCERY 1896

BRET HARTE: Made several trips to San Jose while editor of Overland Monthly and lectured here. Described by Sawyer: "Small, dapper, elegantly clothed, black mustachios, burnsides, pock-marked".

BUNTLINE: Ned Buntline (Col. E.C. Judson) was the originator of the dime novel. Discovered Wm. Cody (Buffalo Bill) and with his pen alone, made this little known hunter for the army the most famous man in America. Buntline was a reformed drunkard. Gave prohibition lectures in S.J. 1858.

Why the Name...?

CALABAZAS: Means gourds, pumpkin or squash. Could have been so named because the Indians camped along this little west side creek raised these vegetables. Gourds used for drinking vessels. Pioneers remember encampments of natives on Stevens Creek Road Craft Ranch who were clearing brush for settlers and sold them pumpkins.

CALAVERAS: Means "skulls", probably so named by early Spaniards because of large quantities of human bones and skulls found in this northeastern area. Possibly a battle ground.

CALIFORNIA: No one knows exact origin. First shown on Spanish map, 1562. Senator Phelan's Saratoga estate is named Montalvo which might hold a clue. In the early sixteenth century, a Montalvo wrote a romance called Las Sergas de Esplandian dealing with a fantastic land of Amazons, gold and silver plus a queen named Calafía. Writing said to have inspired Cortez west coast expedition. On the other hand "calida fornax(L) means "hot furnace". From the Greek,- "kala phor neia"="new country". From the Spanish "colofonia" = "resin" and California Indians used "kali forno" meaning "mountains or hills." So,- quien sabe?

CAMPBELL: William Campbell, veteran of War of 1812, travelled part way west with Donner Party in 1846. Had a saw mill above Saratoga. His son, Benjamin for whom city is named, subdivided in 1885. Each deed contained proviso that should liquor ever be sold on the premises the land would be forfeit. In 1903 Pres. Theodore Roosevelt planted the much disputed redwood tree, at this writing, struggling for survival.

CARRETA: Most primitive of vehicles, painfully simple and simply painful for riders. The two wheels were sections of a log; axle attached with wood pegs kept wheels from falling off. Another pole attached to axle became the tongue. Upon this was built either a plain or elaborate wickerwork frame tied with strips of hide. Pulled by slow oxen prodded with a sharp stick squeaks could be heard for a mile. Senoritas screamed for little Indian boy to dose the axles with tallow.

CATALÁ: Franciscan priest of Santa Clara Mission 1794. A most devout ascetic considered by his congregation to be saintly. In 1795 with 200 Indian neophytes (converts) he layed out and planted the almost impassable Alameda to 3 rows of willows, joining pueblos of Santa Clara and San Jose. Made barefoot missionary trips to all parts of Valley. No pictures of him exist.

CHINESE: San Jose once had the second largest Chinatown in the United States numbering over 4000. They flocked to S.F. and this area after the gold rush and colonized for protection against persecution by Mexicans and Americans. We had four of such Chinatowns but the largest and last was in the area of Seventh and Taylor. All are gone and this is now an international settlement. For fifty years one could step into another world, a little China with "hatchet men", slave girls, opium dens and lottery parlors. Tongs were formed, either for protection from criminals or for highbinder tribute like Eastern gangsters. In 1867 the Hip Sing Tong was formed with rival, the Hop Sing Tong. As late as 1923 a gun battle was fought on the one main street. Gradually the Americanization of the youngsters and laws against gambling led to Chinatown's downfall. All that remained was the brick headquarters of the Hop Sing Tongs and where they worshipped their gods, the old Joss House. These were (unfortunately) dismantled in 1949. Burial societies insured return of ashes to homeland. Deceased, delinquent with dues?, were paraded in style to Oak Hill's Chinese cemetery headed by Will Lake's Municipal Band. Paid professional mourners wept and wailed. Then sacrifices on brick altar, roast duck or pork, closely observed by hungry hoboes,- even small boys might..... (skip it.) We hired coolies to pick our prunes. Our gang was camped next to a chicken house subject to nightly raids by a skunk. One night we were awakened by the explosions of firecrackers. Dad stuck his head through the screen and received this Oriental explanation, "So solly Mr. Lambo, juss fli-klackas, litty black pussy cat,- too stink!"

* Translation = "Scat!"

100

COFFEE CLUB:

A CO-OPERATIVE, NON-PROFIT PROJECT CONDUCTED BY EARLY SANJOSEANS ON SOUTH SECOND STREET. A MOST POPULAR EATING AND MEETING PLACE FOR COUNTRY FOLKS ON THEIR INFREQUENT "TOWN" TRIPS. THE 5 & 10 CENT PRICES OF COFFEE, PIE, BAKED BEANS, ETC., INDICATED A "GREASY SPOON" TYPE OF RESTAURANT. IT WAS *NOT*. NICE PEOPLE ATE THERE INCLUDING THE WRITER. READING AND RECREATION ROOMS FOR MEN AND WOMEN. AS A SMALL BOY, WRITER WAS FASCINATED BY A GROUP OF VERY OLD CHARACTERS FOREVER PLAYING CHECKERS. THEY WERE SO SLOW BETWEEN MOVES, ANY ONE OF THEM COULD HAVE PASSED AWAY AND RIGOR MORTIS SET IN WITHOUT ATTRACTING PUBLIC NOTICE.

CONGRESS SPRINGS:

OR PACIFIC CONGRESS SPRINGS, - NAMED FOR EASTERN COUNTERPART IN SARATOGA, N.Y. ONE MILE ABOVE SARATOGA. DISCOVERED 1862 BY JERD CALDWELL. ELEGANT RESORT HOTEL BUILT ON 720 ACRES. MINERAL SPRING WATER SUPPLIED TO ALL WESTERN CITIES. PENINSULA R.R. EXTENDED LINE IN 1925 AND THIS BECAME EVEN MORE A POPULAR VALLEY PICNIC GROUNDS. DIFFICULT NOW TO PICTURE OR EVEN LOCATE.

COOKS POND:

A SMALL, FORGOTTEN LAKE NEAR THE PRATT-LOW WATER TOWER, SOUTHERN S.C. CITY LIMITS. ORIGINALLY, THIS LONG GONE LAKE WAS FED BY BROOKS FROM THE STOCKTON AVENUE AND THE ALAMEDA SECTIONS. A CANAL DUG FROM IT, IRRIGATED THE MISSION'S GARDENS AND ORCHARD IN THE 1770'S. LATER BECAME A RECREATION PARK. ONE OF THE TWO REDWOODS AT ENTRANCE ON THE ALAMEDA CAN STILL BE SEEN.

COOPER:

A.D.M. COOPER WAS ONE OF THE OLD VALLEY'S MOST POPULAR ARTISTS. HE SPECIALIZED IN ALLEGORICAL SUBJECTS AND UNLIKE MAJORITY OF TODAY'S PAINTERS, FEARLESSLY PORTRAYED THE HUMAN FIGURE, USUALLY SHOWN LIFE SIZE. WITH HIS SCENES SET IN MILD CLIMATES, HIS FEMALE FIGURES REQUIRED LITTLE DRAPERY. HIS ADMIRERS WERE LEGION.

HIS ENORMOUS WORKS OF ART CAN STILL BE VIEWED IN SEVERAL PUBLIC PLACES. OTHER ARTISTS OF GREAT TALENT AND POPULARITY WERE CHARLES HARMON, ANDREW P. HILL; PAINTING EARLY PIONEER SCENES AND VALLEY'S BEAUTY.

CORY:

DR. BENJAMIN CORY WAS THE VALLEY'S FIRST "HORSE AND BUGGY" DOCTOR, ARRIVING IN 1847 AND HIS SERVICES WERE AVAILABLE FOR 47 YEARS. POPULAR, KIND HEARTED AND GENEROUS TO A FAULT WITH HIS BILL COLLECTIONS. ONLY ONCE DID THE GOOD DOCTOR GENTLY REMONSTRATE WITH A PATIENT WHO NOT ONLY REFUSED PAYMENT BUT CONSIDERED HIMSELF INSULTED! HE CHALLENGED DR. CORY TO A DUEL! THE DOCTOR ACCEPTED AND WHEN GIVEN CHOICE OF WEAPONS, PROMPTLY SAID, "SHOT GUNS AT 10 PACES". NO DUEL. BILL PAID.

COYOTE:

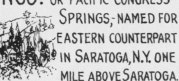

12 MILES SOUTH OF S.J. FROM THE MEXICAN-AZTEC WORD "COYOTL" PERTAINING TO THE WESTERN WOLF. THE ARROYO DE COYOTE WAS NAMED BY 1776 EXPEDITION OF DE ANZA.

CUPERTINO:

(SEE PICTURE ON BLACKSMITH PAGE) HERE WAS THE WRITER'S BOYHOOD TERRITORY. THIS WEST SECTION WAS NAMED CUPERTINO FOR AN ITALIAN SAINT JOSEPH OF COPERTINO BY PADRE FONT OF THE DE ANZA EXPEDITION. THESE EXPLORERS MADE CAMP NEAR THE PRESENT BLACKBERRY FARM (MONTA VISTA). THIS WAS MARCH 1776. THEY CALLED THE STREAM ARROYO DE SAN JOSE CUPERTINO. THIS LATER WAS CALLED STEVENS CREEK. (SEE "STEVENS CREEK"). A POST OFFICE WAS ESTABLISHED IN 1882 ON McCLELLAN ROAD CALLED CUPERTINO, CHANGED TO WEST SIDE IN 1895 AND BACK TO CUPERTINO IN 1900 AT INTERSECTION LOCATION ON HIGHWAY 9. OF COURSE ELISHA STEVENS (ACTUALLY "STEPHENS") WAS ONE OF THE FIRST PIONEERS ARRIVING IN EARLY '50'S AND SETTLING NEAR BLACKBERRY FARM. PETER BALL SETTLED ON 350 ACRES; 1850 AND W.L. BLABON IN 1860 PAID ABOUT $10 AN ACRE FOR 350 A. ON HWY 9. OTHER EARLY CUPERTINO PIONEERS, SUTHERLAND GRIMES, MONTGOMERY, DOYLE, SELINGER, WILLIAMS, REGNART. AN INTERESTING SETTLEMENT SIDELIGHT, - ABOUT 1880 AN UNUSUAL GROUP ARRIVED TO POPULATE THIS SECTION. THEY WERE ALL RETIRED SEA CAPTAINS WITH FAMILIES. EACH BOUGHT ABOUT 50 ACRES, ALL BUILT GOOD (CAPE COD) HOMES, ALL PLANTED VINEYARDS, ALL PROSPERED; AS WOOD, CROSSLEY BLAKE, ROSS, DUNBAR, PORTER, MERITHEW, HARRIMAN, GIBSON.

Why the Name...?

DÁVILA: AGUSTÍN DÁVILA, ARTIST, DECORATED THE 5TH. SANTA CLARA MISSION CHURCH WITH MURALS AIDED BY INDIAN NEOPHYTES. PIGMENTS, INCLUDING ALMADEN CINNABAR VERMILION, WERE MIXED WITH *MAGUEY*, OR CACTUS JUICE AND PAINTED ON ADZED SLABS OF REDWOOD, 1825. RETAINED INTACT AS LATE AS 1860 BUT 1926 FIRE ENTIRELY DESTROYED. DÁVILA'S NAME BRIEFLY SHOWN IN MISSION RECORDS. BACKGROUND A MYSTERY. IT IS KNOWN IN 1845 HE WAS GRANTEE OF "3 LEAGUES" IN SANTA BARBARA COUNTY OF 13,332 ACRES (WORTH A FEW CENTS AN ACRE THEN)

DAWSON: DR. JAMES M. DAWSON IN 1871 NOTICED THE EVER INCREASING ACREAGE AND HEAVY CROPS OF PERISHABLE FRUIT IN THE VALLEY, MUCH OF IT GOING TO WASTE. IN THE BACK YARD OF HIS HOME ON THE ALAMEDA, OVER A COOKING STOVE IN A 12 X 16 SHED, HE SUCCESSFULLY PRESERVED THE FIRST FRUIT IN TIN CONTAINERS. THE FIRST SEASONS PACK—350 CASES. THUS STARTED AN INDUSTRY THAT WOULD ESTABLISH THE SANTA CLARA VALLEY AS THE FRUIT CANNING CENTER OF THE WORLD.

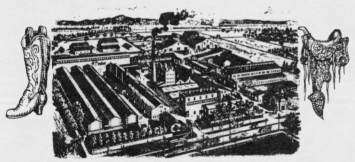

EBERHARD TANNING CO., THE OLDEST INDUSTRIAL PLANT IN THE VALLEY. LOCATED ON EL CAMINO REAL ACROSS FROM SANTA CLARA MISSION. NEW ENGINEERING AND LIBRARY NOW OCCUPY EXACT OLD SITE. REMNANTS DEMOLISHED TEN YEARS AGO. UNOFFICIAL INFORMATION PLACES ITS EXISTENCE EARLY AS 1847, BELONGING TO A DON RAMÓN. THE EBERHARDS ACQUIRED IN 1861 AND FOR 85 YEARS WAS WORLD FAMOUS AS PRODUCERS OF HIGHEST QUALITY LEATHERS, SPECIALLY FOR SADDLES. MOST FAMOUS WAS THE $10,000 PRODUCTION FOR J.C. MILLER, THE WILD WEST SHOW PRODUCER. THE ANNUAL INCOME WAS A MILLION DOLLARS AND 29,000 HIDES, 3000 CALF SKINS AND 10,000 SHEEP SKINS WERE PROCESSED YEARLY. ADVENT OF AUTO, DECLINE OF THE HORSE AND STOCK INDUSTRY PLUS A DISASTROUS FIRE SET BY A REVENGEFUL BAND OF GYPSIES SPELLED DOOM FOR THIS PIONEER FACTORY. IMMIGRANT GERMANS WERE MAINLY EMPLOYED. I REMEMBER THEIR "BEER BREAK" AND THAT STEADY PROCESSION ACROSS THE ALAMEDA TO A CAFE, NO! I MEAN A SALOON! LOWER RIGHT, SITE OF OUR FOOTBALL FIELD COVERED WITH A "TURF" OF SHAVINGS FROM GROUND UP BARK OF OAK AND LAUREL USED IN TANNING.

EDENVALE: SIX MILES SOUTH OF SAN JOSE MARKED BY THE PALATIAL GROUNDS OF E.A. AND J.O. HAYES, EARLY SAN JOSE MERCURY PUBLISHERS AND PROMINENT VALLEY POLITICIANS. MADE THEIR FORTUNES IN MICHIGAN IRON MINES. BUILT FAMOUS MANSION, PLANTING PARK IN 1887. MANSION NOW IN REAR *NOT* THE ORIGINAL WHICH BURNED. GROUNDS WERE OPEN TO THE PUBLIC. ALL THIS 40 ACRES OF PARK NOW THE FRONTIER VILLAGE, A VERY HIGH CLASS OLD WEST PLAYGROUND. HAYES' ORIGINAL PLANTING CLEVERLY SPARED AND PRESERVED.

EL QUITO: SPANISH FOR "QUITS"! NEVER MIND,— TO CHEER PRESENT SQUATTERS, IN EARLY DAYS, VALLEY INDIANS CALLED IT "TITO". RANCHO QUITO WAS GRANTED BY GOV. ALVARADO TO JOSÉ MORIEGA AND FERNÁNDEZ IN 1841. DON JOSE ARGÜELLO PLANTED AN OLIVE GROVE IN THIS SECTION ABOUT 1860. SOME OF THE TREES WERE MOVED TO WORLDS FAIR GROUNDS IN 1939. THIS 81 ACRES OF OLIVES LATER OWNED BY GOODRICH, PRODUCED A GRADE OF OIL FAR SUPERIOR TO THE ITALIAN, WINNING WORLD PRIZES. THE PUBLIC DEMAND NEVER COULD BE SUPPLIED. ALAS, MAN'S LONGEST LIVED, PRODUCTIVE TREES FINALLY SUCCUMBED TO PROGRESS, A LA "BELLE ACRES" OR "BEDSIDE MANOR", ETC......

EL CAMINO REAL: PREFERABLY THE "ROYAL ROAD", AND *NOT* THE "KING'S HIGHWAY." ROUTE ALONG COAST (101) LITTLE CHANGED SINCE FIRST "PATHFOUND" BY THE PADRES.

ESCHSCHOLTZIA CALIFORNICA, A HEFTY NAME FOR OUR VALLEY POPPY! THE EARLY SPANIARDS HAD MUCH NICER NAMES,—"AMAPOLA" AND COPA DE ORA (CUP OF GOLD), BUT THEIR MOST CHARMING WAS "DORMIDERA",—(THE SLEEPY ONE.)

Why the Name . . . ?

FISHER:
In 1820 a New England lad boarded a clipper ship bound for California and cargo of hides and tallow. Anchored in Monterey Bay this young cabin boy saw and admired a new land. In 1845 he returned and fell in love with Santa Clara Valley. An auction was in progress; the vast Rancho Laguna Seca, 4 square leagues or 23,040 acres. Fisher bid $1000, then $2000. Finally after bids of 3 and 4 he reached $6000. His competitor Americans and Mexicans turned away in utter disgust at such "insanity." The rest is historical success. Now subdivided, William Fischer's descendents long enjoyed this man's courage and foresight in acquiring such an early Valley empire. Located 12 miles south of San Jose. Give a pause. How many acres TODAY for $6000? Right! Maybe ONE.

FLICKINGER:
Few will remember this trademark, world famous for quality canned fruit. The J.H. Flickinger family owned 500 acres of orchard near Berryessa and pioneered this early cannery around 1900. Resin was used in can sealing, followed later by hand soldering each can. Other turn of the century canners; the Wool family, J.F. Pyle and Sorosis Fruit.

FORBES MILL:
James Forbes in 1854 built a stone flour mill powered by Los Gatos Creek to serve the then great acreage of Valley wheat. Later became a power house, ice plant, storehouse. Lower story still visible directly next Santa Cruz freeway in L.G.

FREDRICKSBURG BREWERY SINCE 1869.

ORIGINAL BEFORE QUAKE

Falstaff now occupies site and original brick frame still intact except for German style castle towers and turrets that fell in 1906 quake. Once two artesian wells on property. Original capacity 10,200 barrels YEARLY. Present output, 2000 barrels DAILY!

FREMONT:
Histories thoroughly cover this "Pathfinder of the West." He crossed and recrossed this Valley many times as evidenced by perpetuation of his name on streets, cities, schools, mountain peaks, and brand names. Most interesting, the bitter dispute amongst historians regarding Fremont's REAL fame. Only study can form one's opinion; great or near great?

GILROY
John Gilroy, "scurvy ridden", some claim, jumped ship at Monterey in 1814 and became the Valley's first white settler although later became a naturalized Mexican citizen. Married an Ortega senorita whose family owned the huge San Ysidro (ĒĒ-SĒĒ-DRŌ) grant covering the southern end of Valley. City of Gilroy named for this Scot who, despite his native reputation, lived in idle contentment, squandered his wealth and died destitute, 1869.

GILROY HOT SPRINGS
Discovered in 1865 by a Mexican sheep herder named Francisco Cantau, but some historical accounts claim that De Anza camped there and mentions in his 1776 trip diary. At one time a highly developed health resort and hotel area.

GOAT:
1875
C.P. Bailey raised Angora goats for over 30 years for mohair, fleece, gloves, etc. Took all Worlds Fair prizes. Kept a herd of 10,000 and raised more mohair than all other goat raisers in U.S. (I agree! So what?)

GOODRICH
Stone quarry. Only hillside scars off the Almaden road mark spots where the light brown stone was quarried for St. Mary's church, Hall of Justice, Library (once Post Office) and Stanford University.

GUBSERVILLE:
A forgotten 1880 stage stop & P.O., Saratoga-S.C. road. Lost beneath a shopping center.

GUADALUPE
creek, mines. Named by De Anza, 1776. Means "wolf river". Guada, "river", lupus, "wolf". Why "wolf"? I dunno.

Why the Name...?

HECKER PASS: HIGHWAY CONNECTING GILROY AND WATSONVILLE. ONCE CALLED THE LAST LINK OF "YOSEMITE TO THE SEA" HIGHWAY. NAMED FOR HENRY HECKER, SUPERVISOR, UPON COMPLETION IN 1928.

LAWRENCE: ROAD AND STATION. FOR 50 YEARS "FAR OUT IN THE STICKS", A FLAG-STOP ON THE S.P. WITH ONLY A TINY DEPOT AND WAREHOUSE. ☞ SEE PHOTO SKETCH.

LICK: GAVE $400,000 ENDOWMENT FOR LICK'S OBSERVATORY. TO THE VALLEY HE WAS A GENEROUS PHILANTHROPIST AND BENEFACTOR. BY HIS FEW ACQUAINTANCES HE WAS CONSIDERED, CRABBED, COLD, A SOLITARY ECCENTRIC. LICK MADE HIS MILLIONS ABOUT 1847, BUYING SAN FRANCISCO SAND HILLS, SELLING AT FABULOUS PROFITS. TO HIS CREDIT, HE STARTED GIVING IT AWAY IN 1873. FAILURE OF A MAGNIFICENT, ORNATELY FURNISHED FLOUR MILL HE BUILT NEAR ALVISO MADE LITTLE DENT IN HIS FORTUNE, IN FACT SERVED A CERTAIN PURPOSE, SATISFYING A SLUMBERING SPITE; AT LEAST HE SENT A PICTURE OF THE MILL EAST TO A YOUNG LADY (AND HER FATHER) WHO ONCE CONSIDERED LICK A "POOR BOY WITH NO FUTURE" AND SPURNED HIS PROPOSALS. HE WAS A PENNSYLVANIA GERMAN (1796-1876). JAMES LICK'S TOMB IS BELOW THE OBSERVATORY DOME.

LINCOLN TO ABRAHAM LINCOLN, SANTA CLARA VALLEY MUST HAVE BEEN A REMOTE CORNER WITH OUR FEW PROBLEMS INSIGNIFICANT COMPARED TO A RAGING CIVIL WAR. (SEE ALMADEN FULL PAGE FOR ONE OF HIS ACTS.) IN 1865, JUST A MONTH BEFORE HIS ASSASSINATION, HE SIGNED A DEED RETURNING 20 ACRES OF SANTA CLARA MISSION CHURCH LAND, LOST IN SECULARIZATION.

LLAGAS (PRONOUNCED YAH-GUS), CREEK & SOUTHERN VALLEY DISTRICT. MEANS "WOUNDS". SPANISH NAMED FOR WOUNDS IN HANDS AND FEET OF ST. FRANCIS SIMILAR TO THOSE OF JESUS. REASON FOR NAMING UNKNOWN (TO ME.)

LOMA-PRIETA (MTN.) FAMILIAR, PROMINENT PEAK IN SOUTHERN RANGE. ORIGINAL NAME MT. BACHE. MEANS "BLACK HILL". ALTITUDE 3,790 FEET. A MORE EXTENSIVE VIEW FROM THIS HEIGHT THAN FROM MT. HAMILTON. IN VIEW, — SALINAS AND SANTA CLARA VALLEYS, SANTA CRUZ, SAN FRANCISCO AND MONTEREY BAY COAST LINE.

LONDON: JACK LONDON WAS WELL ACQUAINTED WITH THIS VALLEY. HE ENJOYED FREQUENT VISITS WITH LITERARY FRIENDS, ALSO BICYCLING DOWN FROM OAKLAND ON WEEK ENDS TO MEET A CERTAIN YOUNG LADY. LONDON'S SUCCESS CAUGHT ON FIRE WITH HIS CALL OF THE WILD. IT SOLD A MILLION AND A HALF COPIES AND FROM A STRUGGLING EXISTENCE, DEMAND FOR MORE OF THE SAME, GAVE HIM A $75,000 A YEAR INCOME. REMEMBER BUCK, HERO DOG OF CALL OF THE WILD, HALF SHEPHERD, HALF ST. BERNARD? BUCK WAS BORN ON JUDGE BOND'S ESTATE, THEN ON PRESENT SITE OF CARMELITE MONASTERY IN SANTA CLARA. IT IS ALLEGED LONDON AND/OR ACCOMPLICE, SPIRITED BUCK AWAY ONE MOONLIT NIGHT, PUTTING HIM ABOARD A TRAIN AT THE LITTLE OLD COLLEGE PARK DEPOT ON STOCKTON AVENUE. AS A MATTER OF FACT LONDON PRACTICALLY ADMITS IT.

LOS ALTOS MEANS "THE HEIGHTS". COMPARATIVELY A "NEW SETTLEMENT". POST OFFICE ESTABLISHED 1908.

LOS GATOS: A MEXICAN GRANT NAMED RINCONADO DE LOS GATOS, 1840. MEANS "THE ENCLOSED ANGLE (OR CORNER) OF THE CATS." FIRST, FORBES MILL, 1880'S THEN FORBESTOWN, FINALLY LOS GATOS AND FULL LIFE WITH COMING OF THE RAILROAD IN 1877. SCREAMS OF MOUNTAIN LIONS INFESTING THE HILLS, PROMPTED SPANISH WORD GATOS OR "CATS". HOWEVER, LEO AND LEONA, THE TWO DIGNIFIED AND MAJESTIC SCULPTURED WORKS OF ROBERT PAINE ARE *NOT* MOUNTAIN LIONS. THEY ARE CALIFORNIA WILD CATS, BOBCATS OR LYNX (SHORT TAILED.) THEIR KIND STILL INHABIT THE LOS GATOS MOUNTAINS. "REASONABLE FACSIMILES" ABOVE EXCEPT FOR EXPRESSIONS.

LYNDON HOTEL, GONE BUT STILL FRESH IN MOST MEMORIES. JOHN W. LYNDON ARRIVED IN 1859. A BANKER STOREKEEPER, LUMBERMAN. SUBDIVIDED LOS GATOS AND BUILT MANY MAIN (OLD) BUILDINGS, INCLUDING HIS HOTEL.

MADRONE TOWN 8 MILES S. OF S.J. THE TREE HAS RED BARK, RED SEED; ONE OF OUR BEAUTIFUL MOUNTAIN NATIVES, 20 TO 100 FEET HEIGHT. SPANISH NAMED IT MADROÑO, "STRAWBERRY" TREE.

Why the Name . . . ?

MANLY: MAN OF TWO VALLEYS, DEATH AND SANTA CLARA. HIS LIFE WOULD FILL AN EXCITING BOOK. FORTUNATELY ONE EXISTS, QUITE A RARITY BUT AVAILABLE IN MOST LIBRARIES. IN THIS BOOK, "DEATH VALLEY IN '49", JAMES MANLY MODESTLY BUT TRUTHFULLY RELATES HIS HEROIC RESCUE OF THE BENNETT PARTY IN DEATH VALLEY, WELCOME MEETING WITH KINDLY SPANISH CALIFORNIANS, HIS ADVENTURES IN THE GOLD COUNTRY AND OF LOCAL INTEREST, HIS OBSERVANCE OF THIS VALLEY IN '49. HE PAUSED LONG ENOUGH TO CLIMB BOTH EASTERN AND WESTERN HILLS FOR A LONG LOOK,- GRIZZLY BEAR, WILD CATTLE IN DENSE WILLOW JUNGLES (OF WILLOW GLEN), "WILD MUSTARD HIGH AND STRONG ENOUGH TO SUPPORT CHATTERING SQUIRRELS." AFTER THE GOLD RUSH HE RETURNED TO THIS VALLEY. THOMPSON & WEST'S 1876 ATLAS CLEARLY SHOWS HIS 250 ACRE FARM (JUST SOUTH OF OAK HILL CEMETERY) FOR WHICH HE PAID $16 AN ACRE. SITE OF HIS TOWN RESIDENCE ON STOCKTON AVENUE IS PRESENTLY DESIGNATED BY A DILAPIDATED HISTORICAL MARKER.

MANZANITA: A REDDISH BARK, EVERGREEN SHRUB VERY COMMON IN OUR LOCAL MOUNTAINS. THE SPANISH NAME IS DIMINUTIVE OF MANZANA OR "APPLE" BECAUSE ITS TINY SEEDS RESEMBLE THAT FRUIT.

MARCELLO: THE FAMOUS SANTA CLARA MISSION INDIAN. RESEARCH ONLY REVEALS EACH HISTORIAN TRYING TO OUTDO THE OTHER WITH LEGENDARY STORIES ABOUT THIS CHARACTER. MAJORITY CLAIM HE LIVED TO 125 BUT S.C. MISSION ARCHIVES (BAPTISMAL RECORDS) SHOW HE DID

1875 DRESSED FOR FIRST & LAST PHOTO

NOT REACH 100. HIS ORIGIN WAS RATHER MYSTERIOUS BECAUSE HE WAS 6 FEET 2 INCHES, WEIGHING 250, ABOUT DOUBLE SIZE OF AVERAGE VALLEY INDIAN. ON HIS FIRST MISSION VISIT WITH TWO COMPANIONS, HE MET FR. VIADER, QUITE A MAN HIMSELF. FOR SOME REASON THEY DECIDED TO ATTACK THIS PADRE WHO PROMPTLY THRASHED THE TRIO, BUMPED THEIR HEADS TOGETHER AND AS PROMPTLY FORGAVE THEM! THIS SO SURPRISED MARCELLO THAT EVER AFTER HE WAS MISSION'S BEST WORKER, BUILDING FOREMAN AND SERVED AS AN ALCALDE (JUDGE). PIO PICO, LAST MEXICAN GOVERNOR OF CALIFORNIA, IN 1845 GRANTED *RANCHO ULISTAC* TO THREE SANTA-CLARA INDIANS, PIO, CRISTOBAL AND MARCELLO, (A 2127 ACRE TRACT OF AGNEWS-ALVISO LOWLAND.) MEETING THE FATE OF ALL LAND OWNERS AFTER THE *GRINGOS* CAME, MARCELLO

ALLEGEDLY SOLD HIS SHARE TO JACOB HOPPE, SAN JOSE'S FIRST POSTMASTER FOR $500. HE STILL CLAIMED AND LIVED ON THE LAND HE ONCE OWNED SWEARING THAT HE WAS DRUNK WHEN HE SOLD IT TO HOPPE. TWICE A YEAR THIS OLD GIANT HOBBLED FROM ALVISO TO SANTA CLARA TO SAY HIS PRAYERS AT THE MISSION CHURCH. TO THE LAST HE CLAIMED TO BE 125 YEARS OLD. MARCELLO'S FOE AND FRIEND, CHIEF YÑIGO DID REACH 103 YEARS.

MARK TWAIN: FRESH FROM HIS TRIP TO THE HAWAIIAN ISLANDS, MADE HIS FIRST "TRYOUT" LECTURE IN SAN JOSE IN 1866. IN THE GOLD COUNTRY TWAIN HAD MET A CHARACTER NAMED STEWART WHO HAD A SALOON ON FOUNTAIN ALLEY IN S.J. STEWART WAS KNOWN AS THE "EARTHQUAKE MAN" CLAIMING HE WAS A RELIABLE FORECASTER. HE WAS ALSO A LOYAL ADMIRER OF TWAIN AND COLLECTED EVERY WORD MARK WROTE. CONSEQUENTLY AND PROUDLY HE WAS TWAIN'S HOST AND HELPED PROMOTE A MOST SUCCESSFUL FINANCIAL LECTURE HERE. BUT FOR SOME THOUGHTLESS, ORNERY REASON, WHEN TWAIN RETURNED EAST, HE WROTE A CRUEL, SARCASTIC ARTICLE PICKING POOR STEWART AS VICTIM OF HIS RIDICULE! MONTHS PASSED AND FINALLY STEWART'S EYE FELL ON THIS ARTICLE! HE WAS SURPRISED, HURT, THEN FURIOUSLY ANGRY. HE WROTE A LETTER THAT MUST HAVE BEEN A CLASSIC OF *PURE LITERARY VENOM!* IT ACTUALLY PIERCED THE TOUGH HIDE OF MARK TWAIN WHO IMMEDIATELY DISPATCHED A LONG LETTER OF HUMBLE, ABJECT APOLOGY; EVEN OFFERING TO PROMOTE A BOOK OF "POEMS" STEWART HAD "COMPOSED". ALL WAS FORGIVEN.

MAYFIELD: NOW SOUTH PALO ALTO ONCE CALLED THE MAYFIELD FARM OF E.O. CROSBY. POST OFFICE CALLED MAYFIELD AND TOWN SURVEYED IN 1876.

McGUFFY READER: THE BEST KNOWN OLD ELEMENTARY SCHOOL BOOK. DURING THE WINTER OF 1846, MRS. OLIVE MANN ISBELL, NIECE OF HORACE MANN, THE EDUCATOR, OPENED THE FIRST ENGLISH LANGUAGE SCHOOL IN CALIFORNIA. IT WAS LOCATED ON THE SANTA CLARA MISSION GROUNDS IN AN ADOBE ONCE A STABLE. SHE HAD BROUGHT ACROSS THE PLAINS, THREE SLATES, SEVEN McGUFFY READERS, TWO ATLASES AND A FEW PENCILS.

Why the Name...?

McKIERNAN (MOUNTAIN CHARLEY) 1812-1902

AS NAMED BY THE ZAYANTE INDIANS OF THE SANTA CRUZ MOUNTAINS. ALSO KNOWN AS SILVER SKULL CHARLEY OR HAIR-BRAIN CHARLEY DUE TO THAT FAMOUS ENCOUNTER WITH A BEAR. BORN IN IRELAND, 1812. WORKED WAY BY SHIP TO SAN FRANCISCO IN 1848. AFTER GOLD MINING, MADE HIS WAY TO THIS VALLEY. FOUND ALL HOMESTEAD LAND TAKEN SO SETTLED CLOSE TO SUMMIT OF SAN JOSE—SANTA CRUZ SUMMIT NEAR CLOUD'S REST. MARTIN SCHULTHEIS AND McKIERNAN WERE VERY FIRST SETTLERS IN THESE MOUNTAINS. RAISED SHEEP BUT PLAGUED BY LIONS AND BEAR. HUNTED DEER FOR THE S.F. MARKET. ON ONE OF THESE HUNTS IN 1854, A MOTHER BEAR WITH CUB ATTACKED HIM, CRUSHING HIS SKULL. TERRIBLY WOUNDED, HIS PARTNER, TAYLOR AND MARTIN SCHULTHEIS RESCUED HIM. DRS. BELL & INGERSOLL, WITHOUT ANESTHETIC, CLOSED HOLE IN HIS SKULL WITH A PLATE MADE FROM TWO SILVER MEXICAN HALF DOLLARS. A YEAR LATER, SUFFERING TORTURING HEADACHES, A DR. SPENCER OPENED OLD WOUND AND REMOVED A WAD OF HAIR! HENCE ABOVE NICKNAMES. McKIERNAN LIVED ANOTHER HEARTY 48 YEARS. THESE MOUNTAINS WERE THEN HAUNTS AND HIDE-OUTS FOR FUGITIVES AND OUTLAWS. WHILE LAWMEN WATCH-ED, CHARLEY STAGED A RIP-ROARING, _REAL_ OLD WESTERN SHOOTOUT WITH A PAIR OF BANDITS, CAPTURING BOTH. HIS CABIN MARKED, A GIANT REDWOOD AND TOLL ROAD HE BUILT WITH HORSE-SCRAPER, ALL STILL BEAR HIS NAME.

MILLER: (OF MILLER & LUX)

OWNED THE RICHEST LAND EMPIRE ON THE FACE OF THE EARTH. CONCERNING EXTENT OF HIS SANTA CLARA VALLEY HOLDINGS HE TESTI-FIED IN COURT, "IT WAS AN EXTENT OF TWENTY FOUR MILES NORTH AND SOUTH AND ABOUT SEVEN OR EIGHT MILES EAST AND WEST." PART OF THIS WILL BE RECALL-ED AS THE OLD BLOOMFIELD RANCH SOUTH OF GILROY. MILLER'S TOTAL HOLDINGS IN OREGON AND CALIFORNIA WERE POPULARLY ACCEPTED AS 14,520,000 ACRES BUT SAWYER CLAIMS 3,000,000 ACRES A CONSERVATIVE FIGURE. HIS LIFE STORY READS LIKE A FAIRY TALE. BORN IN 1827 IN GERMANY, A FARMER BOY, HERDED GEESE. CAME TO CALIFORNIA WITH GOLD RUSH, BUTCHER SHOP IN S.F., PARTNER WITH CHARLES LUX IN CATTLE RAISING. MILLER PURCHASED LAND BY THE SQUARE MILE, OFTEN FOR A FEW CENTS AN ACRE. HE WAS HIGHLY REGARDED BY RICH AND POOR FOR HIS HONESTY AND GENEROSITY AND HIS TREMENDOUS AID IN CALIFORNIA LAND DEVELOPMENTS. HENRY MILLER LIVED TO AGE 90. IN APPEARANCE HE WAS GENERAL GRANT'S DOUBLE.

MILPITAS:

DIMINUTIVE OF MILPAS, OR "CORN," HENCE "LITTLE CORNFIELDS." MILPITAS VILLAGE IS SHOWN ON PLAT OF RINCON DE LOS ESTEROS GRANT OF 1858. FOR 75 YEARS A VERY "RURAL" DISTRICT. BUTT OF MANY VAUDEVILLE JOKES SUCH AS ELECTION TIME PUN, "AS MILPITAS GOES, SO GOES THE NATION." BUT MILPITAS HAS HAD THE LAST LAUGH. NOW THE NATION _DOES_ "GO" ON THE ONCE "LITTLE CORNFIELD'S" PRODUCTS,—FORD AND NEIGHBORING GENERAL MOTORS.

MISSION CREEK:

A ONCE IMPORTANT LITTLE WATER-WAY, NOW COMPLETELY LOST AND FORGOTTEN. MUCH OF THE LAND NORTH OF SANTA CLARA-SAN CARLOS STREETS TO ALVISO WAS SATURATED WITH MARSHES, SPRINGS AND LITTLE LAKES AS SHOWN ON ALL OLD MAPS, CIRCA 1860. MISSION CREEK HEADED FROM A LARGE SPRING IN HANCHETT PARK AREA, FLOWED ACROSS THE ALAMEDA PAST PRESENT BREWERY, PICKING UP A BROOK FROM STOCKTON AVENUE. IT FOLLOWED EAST SIDE OF THE ALAMEDA WATERING FR. CATALA'S WILLOWS, FED COOK'S POND, MEANDERED PAST PRESENT PRATT-LOW CAN-NERY, REFRESHED THE OLD ORIGINAL S.C. MISSION PEAR ORCHARD AND FINALLY JOINED THE GUADALUPE.

MONTA VISTA:

MEANS "MOUNTAIN VIEW". ANOTHER COMPARITIVELY NEW SETTLEMENT, A TURN OF THE CENTURY SUBDIVISION. IN VALLEY HISTORY, KNOWN AS DE ANZA'S 1776 CAMP GROUND THUS RESPONSIBLE FOR NAMING THE PROPOSED DE ANZA COLLEGE.

MONTEBELLO:

WESTERN FOOTHILL DISTRICT MEANING "BEAUTIFUL MOUNTAIN".

MONTGOMERY

JOHN MONTGOMERY PERFECTED A GLIDER THAT MADE FIRST _CONTROLLED_ FLIGHT IN THE U.S. DAN MALONEY, HIS TEST PILOT, WAS LIFTED 4000 FT. BY A HOT AIR BALLOON, CUT LOOSE AND EXECUTED EVERY FREE FLIGHT MANEUVER. 1905 FLIGHT WAS FROM SANTA CLARA COLLEGE GROUNDS, (MONUMENT), LANDING AT PREDESTINED SPOT, POPLAR AND ALVISO STS. MONTGOMERY MADE 50 SUCCESSFUL FLIGHTS. FINALLY KILLED AT EVERGREEN, 1911.

SMITHSONIAN PHOTO

Why the Name...?

MOODY GULCH: ABOVE LOS GATOS TO RIGHT OF HIGHWAY IN A CANYON. OIL DISCOVERED IN 1873 BY R.C. McPHERSON. AS LATE AS 1922 THE OIL WAS SOLD IN SAN JOSE IN SMALL QUANTITIES. WHILE UNDEVELOPED, AN OIL BELT IS APPARENT FROM HERE THROUGH ALMADEN TO BREA FIELDS OF SARGENTS AND CHITTENDEN.

MORGAN HILL: NOT AS A NEWCOMER MIGHT THINK, THE NAME OF HILL OVERSHADOWING THE TOWN. OWNING THE ORIGINAL TOWNSITE AND SURROUNDING TERRITORY, MARTIN MURPHY (1844) WILLED THIS TO DAUGHTER DIANA WHO MARRIED A MORGAN HILL. SOME HISTORIANS CLAIM PORTOLA HAD FIRST VIEW OF S.C. VALLEY FROM THIS HEIGHT.

MT. HAMILTON: 28 MILES FROM S.J. ALT. 4,200 FT. NAMED FOR A SAN JOSE PREACHER, REV. L. HAMILTON WHO HAD ACCOMPANIED BREWER AND HOFFMAN IN 1861 ON A SURVEYING EXPEDITION. HE WAS FIRST TO REACH THE SUMMIT. THEY WERE UNAWARE IT WAS ALREADY NAMED MT. ISABEL OR THAT IT LACKED 14 FEET OF BEING THE HIGHEST PEAK. AND SO,— THE OBSERVATORY IS ACTUALLY ON MT. ISABEL PEAK! HOWEVER THE U.S. GEODETIC SURVEY HAS ALLOWED THE ENTIRE MOUNTAIN ELEVATION TO BE CALLED MT. HAMILTON.

MT. MADONNA: WEST OF GILROY. ALT. 1897 FT. HENRY MILLER, THE CATTLE KING, BUILT A MANSION ON THIS HEIGHT WHERE HE VACATIONED AND FROM WHERE, AS FAR AS EYE COULD REACH, HE MIGHT SURVEY HIS KINGDOM. HIS ENTIRE HOLDINGS WERE TWICE THE AREA OF BELGIUM.

MT. UMUNHUM: DIRECTLY SOUTH OF S.J. WITH THAT REVOLVING RADAR GUARDING US. PRONOUNCED "OOMOONOON". UNCERTAIN BUT COMMONLY ACCEPTED,— AN INDIAN WORD MEANING "HUMMING BIRD." IN THEIR MYTHOLOGY, (LOCAL COSTANOAN TRIBE), THE EAGLE, COYOTE AND HUMMING BIRD CREATED THE WORLD.

MT. VIEW: ONCE A STAGE STOP ON ROAD TO S.F. 1864 COMING OF SOUTHERN PACIFIC MOVED TOWN ONE MILE NORTH, LEAVING "OLD MT. VIEW." POP. 1898–900.

MURPHY: MARTIN MURPHY, SENIOR AND JUNIOR, LEFT ST. JOSEPH MISSOURI WITH 100 WAGONS AND REACHED CALIFORNIA IN 1844, TWO YEARS AHEAD OF THE DONNER PARTY. IN FACT THIS ILL FATED BAND USED CABINS IN THE SIERRAS BUILT BY THE MURPHYS. THE SENIOR MURPHY SETTLED ON A GRAND ESTATE NEAR THE MONTEREY ROAD'S OLD 21 MILE HOUSE. JUNIOR MURPHY BOUGHT AN ENORMOUS TRACT EMBRACING THE ENTIRE SUNNYVALE TERRITORY. THEIR HOUSE WAS CUT AND FRAMED IN BOSTON AND SHIPPED AROUND THE HORN IN '49. FAMOUS FOR THEIR ENTERTAINMENT OF EVERY PROMINENT PUBLIC FIGURE VISITING THIS VALLEY INCLUDING BAYARD TAYLOR, SUBJECT OF LATER COMMENT. NEEDLESS TO SAY THE HOUSE WAS RECENTLY "REMOVED."

NOTRE DAME: CATHOLIC COLLEGE FOR YOUNG LADIES ON SANTA CLARA STREET WHERE NOW DE ANZA HOTEL STANDS. ORGANIZED 1851. COVERED 10 ACRES.

NOVITIATE: TRAINING SCHOOL FOR JESUIT PRIESTS. ORGANIZED 1866. TWO HUNDRED ACRES, VISIBLE HIGH ABOVE LOS GATOS ON A MOUNTAIN BENCH. SURROUNDED BY HILLSIDE VINEYARDS PRODUCING THE HIGH QUALITY NOVITIATE BRAND TABLE WINES.

NOSTALGIA: MEANING A LONGING TO RETURN. WE HOPE THIS BOOK HAS NOT GIVEN SUCH AN IMPRESSION! A NOSTALGIC OLDSTER CAN BE AN AWFUL BORE, SPECIALLY TO THE YOUNGER GENERATION. HE HARPS ONLY ON THE GOOD IN THE "GOOD OLD DAYS" AND IGNORES THE BAD. TRY A BALANCE SHEET OF PROS AND CONS. TRUE, THE OLD VALLEY WAS QUIET, PEACEFUL, WITH NO TRAFFIC OR SMOG PROBLEMS. FOLKS SEEMED MORE FRIENDLY. PUBLIC TRANSPORTATION WAS FAR SUPERIOR TO TODAY'S. PRICES WERE LOW. SO WERE WAGES. ON THE OTHER SIDE OF THE LEDGER, OVERWORKED MEN, WOMEN AND CHILDREN, FORTUNATELY WITH NO IDEA OF CONVENIENCES TO COME, LUXURIES WE ACCEPT TODAY WITH VERY LITTLE APPRECIATION. WE FORGET THAT LACK OF SANITATION AND REFRIGERATION. WE FORGET PEOPLE, PERHAPS OLD RELATIVES, WHO, IN THEIR PRIME, SUFFERED DISEASES AND TORTURES THAT MODERN SURGERY OR DRUGS COULD NOW CURE OR RELIEVE. THIS BOOK WAS SIMPLY AIMED TO BE *INFORMATIVE*. HOWEVER, SHOULD SOME SENIOR CITIZEN READER BE NOSTALGICALLY AFFECTED,....... GOOD!

Why the Name...?

OAK HILL CEMETERY CONTAINS ONE OF THE BEST PIONEER SECTIONS IN THE STATE. IT HAD BEEN USED AS A PUBLIC BURYING GROUND (SPANISH AND INDIAN) SINCE 1839. BUT THE OLDEST HEADSTONE IS 1850. HERE LIE THE REEDS, DONNERS, DR. CORY, OUR FIRST DOCTOR AND PIERRE PELLIER, TO WHOM WE OWE OUR MULTI-MILLION DOLLAR PRUNE INDUSTRY. IN TOTAL THERE ARE NOW OVER 60,000 INTERMENTS. MORBIDLY, OFTEN OUR STEPS LEAD TO THE DRAMATIC DUNHAM MURDER VICTIMS' LAST RESTING PLACE; DRAB STORY PREVIOUSLY RELATED.

MARY DONNER HOUGHTON 1828-1860

O'CONNOR'S SANITARIUM WAS SITUATED WHERE NOW SEARS IS LOCATED. OUR OLD HISTORIAN, EUGENE SAWYER, MENTIONS ITS AREA AS "14 ACRES SURROUNDING AND FOREVER PROTECTING."...LITTLE DID THIS GOOD MAN FORSEE "PROGRESS". IT WAS A BEAUTIFULLY LANDSCAPED INSTITUTION ENDOWED BY THE HON. M.P. O'CONNOR, IRISHMAN, A HIGHLY SUCCESSFUL '49 MINER, ATTORNEY AND STATE LEGISLATOR. ERECTED 1887 AND ADMINISTERED BY THE DAUGHTERS OF CHARITY OF ST. VINCENT DE PAUL. WELL KNOWN RELOCATION.

PACHECO PASS: LINKING SAN JOAQUIN AND SANTA CLARA VALLEYS. FRANCISCO PÉREZ PACHECO CAME TO CALIFORNIA FROM MEXICO IN 1819. THE FATHERS OF SAN JUAN BAUTISTA GAVE HIM PERMISSION TO SETTLE ON CHURCH LANDS EXTENDING UP INTO THE PASS. HE RECEIVED FINAL GRANT IN 1833 AND HIS BROTHER JUAN IN 1843 TO THE RANCHOS SAN LUIS GONZAGA AND ALISAYMAS y SAN FELIPE. THESE PROPERTIES EXTENDED ACROSS THE MOUNTAIN PASS INTO MERCED COUNTY, THOUSANDS OF UNSURVEYED ACRES. DON JUAN, IN HIS HACIENDA ON THAT FIRST CROSSING OF THE CREEK, 9 MILES NORTH OF HOLLISTER, ALWAYS WORE A MEXICAN SERAPE WITH A HOLE TO PUT HIS HEAD THROUGH. THIS TYPICAL DON KEPT $9000 OR $10,000 IN GOLD COIN IN A BARREL, A COMMON PRACTICE AMONGST WEALTHY SPANISH-CALIFORNIANS. THE BARRELS WERE SELDOM TAPPED UNTIL WE AMERICANS CAME.

PALO ALTO: MEANS "HIGH TREE", THE LONE REDWOOD AT CITY'S CREEK AND RAILROAD CROSSING. MENTIONED IN DIARIES OF FRS. FONT, PALOU AND DE ANZA. TOWN LAID OUT IN 1891 FOR BENEFIT OF THE NEWLY FOUNDED STANFORD UNIVERSITY.

PELLIER: LOUIS PELLIER, VINE AND FRUIT GROWER IN FRANCE, CAME TO SAN JOSE IN 1849. AFTER A MINING STINT, ESTABLISHED A NURSERY ON SAN PEDRO STREET CALLED PELLIER'S GARDENS. IN 1850 HIS BROTHER PIERRE BROUGHT THE FIRST PRUNE CUTTINGS FROM FRANCE. NOT ACCEPTED AT FIRST, IT WAS LATER POPULARIZED BY JOHN ROCK, PIONEER NURSERYMAN. NEVER WAS OR WILL BE POPULAR WITH WRITER, SHOWN ABOVE, 1901.

PENITENCIA CREEK FLOWING FROM ALUM ROCK PARK TOWARD BERRYESSA. SO NAMED BECAUSE THE PADRES IN MISSION DAYS HEARD PENITENTS MAKE CONFESSIONS IN A SMALL ADOBE NEAR MOUTH OF THE CANYON.

PENINSULAR RAILWAY: FOR THIRTY YEARS, SWIFT, CONVENIENT ELECTRIFIED TRANSIT TO ALL PARTS OF THIS VALLEY. TO DATE, WE HAVE NOTHING TO COMPARE. THE LONG RED CARS WERE CALLED "BIG RED'S" AND TRAVELLED 60 MI. AN HOUR TO CAMPBELL, LOS GATOS, SARATOGA, CUPERTINO AND PALO ALTO. LIFE SPAN—1904-1934 ENDED BY AUTOS.

PERMANENTE CREEK AND CANYON. SPANIARDS USED THE WORD TO DESIGNATE A WATER COURSE FLOWING YEAR ROUND. NAME DATES BACK TO 1839 WHEN CREEK WAS DIVIDING LINE BETWEEN GRANTS OF MARTIN MURPHY JR. AND MARIANO CASTRO, EACH OWNING 4000 ACRES. THE WORD MAY SOON BE AN "ALMOST FORGOTTEN" AS CEMENT COMPANY USING THE NAME HAVE DROPPED IT. BUT THE STEEP LITTLE CREEK CLIMBED UP AND DOWN BY WRITER 60 YEARS AGO FISHING FOR "BLACK RAINBOWS", STILL FLOWS SEAWARD,...... THROUGH A CORRUGATED, GALVANIZED PIPE.

PLUMBING: (OUTDOOR) WITH APOLOGIES TO ANY PRUDISH READER, WE INCLUDE THIS LITTLE REST ROOM, NECESSARY OUTHOUSE FOR THOUSANDS OF OLD VALLEY COUNTRY HOMES. AN UNABASHED WEBSTER STILL CALLS IT A PRIVY. IT MIGHT BE SAID THEY WERE ANCESTORS OF TODAYS PORTABLE HOUSES, AT LEAST EVERY HALLOWEEN. THEY CAME IN ALL MODELS; ONE SEATERS, TWO SEATERS, SOME WITH AN UNDERSLUNG RUMBLE SEAT FOR SMALL JUVENILES. STANDARD READING ROOM EQUIPMENT,—SEARS OR WARD CATALOGUES.

Why the Name...?

PLUMBING

(INDOOR) NO, FEW OLD VALLEY FARMERS "SHOWERED" EVERY MORNING. MOST 1900 COUNTRY FARMHOUSES HAD NO BATH ROOM AND BATHING COULD BE QUITE A CHORE. DID ANY OLDSTER READER EVER STEP OUT OF ONE OF THOSE GALVANIZED WASHTUB SQUARELY UPON A CAKE OF IVORY SOAP? AND HAVE MAMA PICK PINE SPLINTERS FROM YOUR TENDER WHITE BOTTOM? HERE'S ONE LITTLE KNIGHT OF THE BATH DID! SATURDAY NIGHT, THAT IS.

PORTAL

: A ONCE PROMINENT ESTATE ON STEVENS CREEK ROAD, MANSION NOW "REMOVED". LOUIS PORTAL, A WEALTHY FRENCHMAN, ARRIVED IN 1850. HE PURCHASED 400 ACRES AND PLANTED LARGE VINEYARDS IN 1860. USED CAPTAIN'S-WALK AROUND ORNATE CUPOLA OF HOUSE AND A POWERFULL TELESCOPE TO DETECT SLOW VINEYARD WORKERS. REFUSED RIGHT-OF-WAY TO A RAILROAD BECAUSE IT MIGHT DISTURB AGEING OF HIS WINES. AFTER DEVASTATING VINEYARD BLIGHT OF 1910-15 RETURNED TO FRANCE. PROMINENT RELATIVES REMAINED.

QUAKERS:

INSERTED BECAUSE WRITER SO RAISED. AS YOU DRIVE ACROSS OVERPASS TOWARD SANTA CLARA ON THE ALAMEDA YOU CAN SEE THIS LITTLE CHURCH ON THE NORTH BANK. IT IS THE FRIEND'S MEETING HOUSE, A QUAKER CHURCH IN CONTINUOUS USE SINCE 1885. THIS WAS THE CONSERVATIVE OR ORTHODOX BRANCH, NO MUSIC, NO PASTOR, ONE SQUIRMED UPON HARD BENCHES UNTIL SOME ELDER "GOT THE POWER." THEY WERE NO DOUBT ELOQUENT BUT WRITER WAS TOO YOUNG TO APPRECIATE MUCH BUT THE "SEMI-ANNUAL" DINNERS, QUAKER COOKING SUPREME. A YOUNG MAN ATTENDING STANFORD, WAS TAKEN ILL AND CARED FOR BY QUAKER JOEL BEAN. THE YOUNG MAN, ALSO A QUAKER, ATTENDED THIS CHURCH. HIS NAME,- HERBERT HOOVER.

QUICKSILVER

(ADDENDA TO THE ALMADEN PAGE.) CAST IRON FLASKS SHOWN BEING FILLED, WEIGHED 76 POUNDS EACH. ONE LAYER OF THESE CYLINDERS ON THE BED OF A HAY WAGON WAS A FULL LOAD FOR FOUR HORSE TEAM TRANSPORTING THIS MERCURY FROM MINES TO ALVISO OR RAILROAD. THAT'S WHY WE KIDS CALLED MR. WELCH, ONE OF THESE TEAMSTERS, "THAT MAN WHO (APPARENTLY TO US) ALWAYS DRIVES AN EMPTY WAGON."

RENGA:

ANOTHER NAME ALSO INSERTED ENTIRELY FOR WRITER'S PERSONAL SATISFACTION. NEXT DOOR TO THE OLD TOWER SALOON ON MARKET ST. WAS RENGA'S, A TINY HOLE-IN-THE-WALL CANDY STORE, MY BOYHOOD HANGOUT. THERE WERE NICER CANDY STORES,-OBRIEN'S, MRS. RUDOLPH'S, THE CHOCOLATE SHOP, YES, SHORTY HIND'S. BUT RENGA'S PRICES WERE FLEXIBLE, A THREE SIZE CHOICE OF ICE CREAM "SODYS", 5, 10 AND 15¢. WHILE MR. RENGA NO DOUBT WAS RESPONSIBLE FOR AN EARLY SET OF FULL DENTURES, HIS GENEROUS, STRIPED BAGS OF HAND PULLED PINK TAFFY ARE STILL REMEMBERED, DESPITE THEIR TENDENCY TO TRIGGER OFF ONE WHALE OF A FIVE-CENT-BELLYACHE.

RICARD:

FATHER RICARD OF SANTA CLARA COLLEGE, A RESPECTED AND EMINENT METEOROLOGIST. HIS WEATHER PREDICTIONS WERE BASED ON VARIATION INTENSITIES OF SUN SPOTS. THIS WAS PERIOD 1907-30. HIS DEDUCTIONS WERE GIVEN WIDE SPREAD AND SERIOUS ACCEPTANCE BY OLD VALLEY ORCHARDISTS AND FARMERS. HE HAD A SANTA CLARA RIVAL IN WEATHER PROGNOSTICATION (OK,-FORECASTING) AND HIS NAME WAS SING KEE. WE SHALL ARRIVE AT SING KEE'S LAUNDRY AT THE PROPER ALPHABETICAL SEQUENCE.

SAN FELIPE:

VALLEY NEAR GILROY NAMED FOR THE ORIGINAL GRANT. OF PASSING INTEREST BECAUSE IN 1898 TOBACCO WAS GROWN THERE, PRODUCING 1200 POUNDS PER ACRE. THERE WAS A CIGAR FACTORY IN GILROY.

SAN JOSE:

NAMED FOR SAINT JOSEPH BY LT. MORAGA OF THE DE ANZA PARTY, 1777, "PUEBLO DE SAN JOSE DE GUADALUPE". THIS MEANS "THE TOWN OF SAN JOSE ON THE WOLF RIVER". HISTORICAL MATERIAL AVAILABLE IN ALL LOCAL LIBRARIES.

SAN JOSE, MISSION:

FOUNDED 1779 POST OFFICE IN TOWN ESTABLISHED 1850. COMPARATIVELY, THE MISSION IS OF LESSER TOURIST ATTRACTION BUT ITS EARLY HISTORY IS INTERESTING AND EXCITING.

Why the Name...?

SANTA CLARA
SAINT CLEAR, SAINT BRIGHT. A NAME HONORING SAINT CLARE OF ASSISI, THE FIRST FRANCISCAN NUN (ORDER OF POOR CLARES). THE MISSION WAS NAMED MISSION SANTA CLARA DE ASSIS, JAN. 12, 1777. BOTH TOWN AND COUNTY FELL HEIR TO NAME ABOUT 1850.

SARATOGA
MARTIN McCARTHY, ONE OF THE EARLIEST SETTLERS, TOOK UP A QUARTER SECTION HERE IN 1849. FIRST POST OFFICE 1855. TOWN PLANNED 1863. NAMED SARATOGA BECAUSE THE SPRINGS ABOVE TOWN HAD SAME "FLAVOR" AS THE FAMOUS CONGRESS SPRINGS OF SARATOGA, N.Y.

SARGENT.
MOST SOUTHERN OF COUNTY'S EARLY SETTLEMENTS. BOTH MILLER AND J.P. SARGENT OWNED GREAT RANCHOS HERE, SARGENT'S COVERING A "MERE" 10,000 ACRES. WHEN S.P. ARRIVED IN 1869 THIS WAS A MOST IMPORTANT SHIPPING POINT FOR ALL THE SURROUNDING TERRITORY.

ST. JAMES PARK:
LITTLE KNOWN FACT THAT THIS PARK WAS PLANNED IN 1848 BY THE THEN RULING MEXICAN GOVERNMENT WHO GAVE C.S. LYMAN ORDERS TO SURVEY. NOW BISECTED BY A STREET, IT BEARS LITTLE RESEMBLANCE TO ORIGINAL OLD FASHIONED, FLOWERED LANDSCAPE WITH STATUES, GAS LAMPS, FOUNTAINS, LAZY FAT GOLD FISH AND SPOUTING DOLPHINS.

ST. JOHN THE BAPTIST HILLS:
OR SAN JUAN BAUTISTA HILLS, AN ALMOST FORGOTTEN NAME OF ROLLING HILLS JUST SOUTH OF OAK HILL CEMETERY. A LARGE WOODEN CROSS STOOD ON SUMMIT MARKING A NOW COMPLETELY LOST 1870 GRAVEYARD. GRAVE OF LOUIS PELLIER, BROTHER OF PIERRE, IS SOMEWHERE IN THIS FORGOTTEN 12 ACRES.

SAN TOMAS AQUINAS:
CREEK AND DISTRICT. NAMED BY SPANIARDS FOR ST. TOMAS AQUINAS. WHO ELSE PRAY TELL?!

SAN MARTIN:
MARTIN MURPHY, EARLIEST SETTLER NAMED TOWN FOR HIS PATRON SAINT. ENOUGH OF THESE OBVIOUS FILLERS!

SILK
DON LOUIS PREVOST, NURSERYMAN IN EARLY '50'S HAD DREAMS OF A NEW INDUSTRY. WHILE BACKED BY STATE FUNDS TO RAISE SILKWORMS, A DRY CYCLE KILLED LARGE PLANTINGS OF MULBERRY TREES.

BATTLE OF SANTA CLARA:

IF YOU SEARCH YOU CAN FIND THIS 1847 EVENT WELL COVERED IN CALIF. HISTORIES. BUT HERE IS A SHORT SCENARIO. THIS BRIEF CONFLICT, BORDERING THE COMIC OPERA LEVEL, TOOK PLACE JUST PREVIOUS TO TERMINATION OF MEXICO'S HOLD ON CALIFORNIA. MEXICAN LEADERS WERE ALARMED AT TIDE OF AMERICAN SETTLERS, TOO MANY OF WHOM FELT MIGHT MEANT RIGHT, (INCLUDING GEN. FREMONT.) BATTLEFIELD WAS AREA NORTHWEST OF SANTA CLARA, BOUNDED BY KIFER AND LAWRENCE ROADS, SCOTTS BLVD. AND HWY. 101. THE 250 MEXICANS LEAD BY FRANCISCO SANCHEZ WERE RECRUITED FROM LOCAL RANCHOS. THE 101 AMERICANS WERE COMMANDED BY CAPTAIN WEBER AND LT. MURPHY. SANTA CLARA MISSION WAS FORTIFIED, WOMEN AND CHILDREN BROUGHT WITHIN. ROADS WERE BLOCKED WITH TREES CUT FROM THE ALAMEDA. THE POPULACE OF SANTA CLARA WATCHED FROM HOUSETOPS AS "BATTLE WAS JOINED." AMERICANS HAD ADVANTAGE OF ARTILLERY, A TINY HAND-DRAWN CANNON FIRING A 6 POUND BALL. IT ONLY FRIGHTENED THE HORSES. WITH A THIRD SHOT, BARREL KICKED OFF AND ARTILLERY SHYLY BURIED ITSELF IN DEEP ADOBE MUD. THROUGH ACRES OF HEAD HIGH WILD MUSTARD, THE BATTLE "RAGED" AT A CAREFUL AND CAUTIOUS LONG RANGE. SANCHEZ WAS FINALLY DRIVEN INTO THE LOS GATOS MOUNTAINS AND SURRENDERED. THE CONFLICT MOVED TO OTHER FIELDS, AS THE BEAR FLAG INCIDENT. WITHIN A FEW WEEKS ALL STRIFE WAS FORGOTTEN AND SOLDIERS FROM BOTH SIDES WERE BACK TOGETHER ON THEIR RANCHOS ON BEST OF FRIENDLY, NEIGHBORLY TERMS. CASUALTIES,- FOUR MEXICANS KILLED, ONE AMERICAN WOUNDED, ONE CANNON LOST.

SING KEE:
SANTA CLARA'S FAMOUS LAUNDRYMAN AND WEATHER PROPHET ABOUT 1905-1915. BASED HIS PREDICTIONS ON ATTITUDE OR REACTIONS OF A PET TOAD KEPT IN HIS BACK ROOM! HERE, 'TWAS SAID, ONE MIGHT ALSO MARK A LOTTERY TICKET. HIS PREDICTIONS WERE SO REMARKABLY ACCURATE, SING WAS DAILY FEATURED IN S.J. AND S.F. NEWSPAPERS. IF IN DOUBT, HIS FAVORITE REMARK,- "MEBBE LITTY LAIN, MEBBE LITTY SUN. SO FATHER RICARD AND SING KEE HAD THEIR FOLLOWERS WHO SOWED AND REAPED ACCORDING TO SUN OR TOAD. MEANWHILE THE OLD U.S. WEATHER BUREAU FINISHED A POOR THIRD.

Why the Name...?

SKINNER: A TIP FOR NEWCOMERS AND THEIR BACK YARD FAMILY-ORCHARDS. SANTA CLARA VALLEY IS NOT AN "APPLE VALLEY" BUT THERE IS <u>ONE</u> IDEAL VARIETY, BOTH FOR EATING OR COOKING. THIS IS THE SKINNER SEEDLING, THE SEEDS BROUGHT ACROSS THE PLAINS BY JUDGE HENRY SKINNER IN 1850. STOCK SCARCE, <u>MIGHT</u> BE LOCATED IN LARGE NURSERIES.

STANFORD UNIVERSITY ESTABLISHED IN 1885 BY LELAND STANFORD (1824-1893), BUILDER OF RAILROADS, GOVERNOR OF CALIFORNIA AND U.S. SENATOR. THE NAME LELAND STANFORD JUNIOR UNIVERSITY IS IN MEMORY OF MR. AND MRS. STANFORDS' SON WHO DIED IN 1884.

STEVENS CAPTAIN ELISHA STEVENS, 1801-1884, OF THE STEVENS-MURPHY-TOWNSEND OVERLAND PARTY OF 1844 SETTLED ON THE CREEK OF HIS NAME IN THE 1850'S ON THE PRESENT BLACKBERRY FARM SITE. HIS FOUR ACRES OF MISSION GRAPES CONSIDERED FIRST VINEYARD PLANTED IN THIS REGION. ELISHA, A TRUE FRONTIERSMAN, ONCE TREATING HIS NEIGHBOR CAPTAIN GRANT (GRANT ROAD) TO RATTLESNAKE MEAT "GOOD AS CHICKEN". WITH FEELINGS A HUNDRED YEARS IN ADVANCE OF HIS TIME, ABOUT 1860, ELISHA COMPLAINED THE COUNTRY "TOO DURN CIVILIZED" AND MOVED TO WILDER ENVIRONMENTS. COULD HE NOT TODAY GATHER DISCIPLES WITH THE SAME URGE? IN THE COPY ABOVE OF A RARE OLD PHOTOGRAPH, HE CLUTCHES A HUGE BOWIE KNIFE. GRIZZLY FLAT, A FEW MILES ABOVE, ON HIS CREEK, WAS NOT FALSELY OR IDLY NAMED.

STEVENS CREEK ROAD: ("BOULEVARD")
STILL <u>ROAD</u> TO THE FEW WHO REMEMBER WHEN A RUNAWAY WAS THE ONLY EXCITEMENT ON THIS OLD GRAVELLED THOROUGHFARE. IF IT WAS WIDE IN SPOTS IT WAS BY NECESSITY OF MAKING NEW WAGON TRACKS AROUND MUD HOLES. FOR THIS SAME REASON, PIONEERS CLAIMED "THE ROAD TO SAN FRANCISCO WAS THREE MILES WIDE." EXCEPT FOR A FEW UNBROKEN TRACTS OF ORCHARD, THE PRESENT "BOULEVARD" BEARS NO RESEMBLANCE TO THE ONE WRITER DROVE BY HORSE-AND-BUGGY OVER 60 YEARS AGO. GONE,-THE REDWOOD PICKET FENCES BORDERING EVERY ORCHARD, GRAINFIELD AND VINEYARD. GONE,-THE WATER TANKS WHERE SPRINKLING-WAGONS FILLED TO SUBDUE THE CHOKING DUST. GONE,-THE WATERING-TROUGHS WHERE OUR SWEATY OLD HORSE COULD BURY HIS MUZZLE IN THE COOL WATER SWIMMING WITH LONG GREEN MOSS; NOISY FROGS HIDING IN THE CATTAILS AND DAMP DARKNESS BELOW ALWAYS LEAKING TANKS, DARTING DRAGONFLIES, RED-WING BLACKBIRDS, DIVING SWALLOWS AND THOSE SAD CRIES OF DISTANT KILLDEER. GONE,- THE ONE ROOM COUNTRY SCHOOLS, PORTAL'S MANSION, BLACKMAR'S AND SAM STORM SALOONS AT THE "CORNERS", TURKEY-SHOOTS UNDER THE OAK GROVES, JESS BOLLINGER AND BAER'S BLACKSMITH SHOPS. GONE,- GOOD ALEX MONTGOMERY, "MAYOR" OF CUPERTINO AND HIS SCREAMING PEACOCKS. ON AND UP INTO THE MOUNTAINS ABOVE SODA ROCK AND GRIZZLY FLAT, GONE INJUN JOE WITH HIS SECRET GOLD MINE AND LITTLE DAVE, THE SHINGLE-SPLITTER AND CHARCOAL-BURNER, MEN OF DELIGHTFUL MYSTERY. GONE THE MUSICAL HAME BELLS OF THE PICCHETTI AND BORDI WOOD-WAGONS WARNING THAT NERVOUS HORSE-AND-BUGGY PICNICKER. ONLY DEEP CLIFF AND THE SOFT CONTOURS OF THE HAZY BLUE MOUNTAINS, STILL UNCHANGED. REGRETS? NO, LUCKY. WE SAW IT <u>WHEN</u>.

STEVENS CREEK
DE ANZA CAMPED ON THIS CREEK MARCH 25, 1776, NOT FAR FROM THE SITE OF ELISHA STEVENS HOME. THIS HAS BEEN PROVEN BY A LEAD PLAQUE FOUND NEAR THE MONTA VISTA WINERY IN 1906 SHORTLY AFTER THE EARTHQUAKE. THERE ARE LIVING PIONEERS WHO SAW THIS PLAQUE AND CAN FURNISH PROOF OF ITS EXISTENCE. DE ANZA NAMED CREEK ARROYO DE SAN JOSE DE COPERTINO. COPERTINO WAS HOME TOWN OF ST. JOSEPH IN ITALY BUT MOST REFERENCES USE LATIN "CUPERTINO."

Why the Name...?

STRICKLETT: Inserted solely for baseball fans. Elmer Stricklett was the inventor of the spitball pitch and used for three seasons with Brooklyn Dodgers, 1905 through 1907. He pitched for San Jose in the old State League during 1908 and 1909; finally a Valley orchardist. His wet pitch outlawed but slyly lingers.

SUNNYVALE once "Murphy's Station." A 1900 subdivision by W.F. Crossman with slogan "The City of Destiny." Slumbered for years. Now the dream is fulfilled and only occasionally disturbed by traffic nightmares.

SUÑOL We can be proud of this noble citizen. Don Antonio Suñol came to San Jose in 1818. He was owner of ranchos in Alameda County and married Dolores Bernal, heiress to the vast Santa Teresa estate south of S.J. Although he did not discover mercury ore, he was first to work Almaden Mines in 1824. He was San Jose's first postmaster, 1846, and an Alcalde. Gave site for St. Joseph Church. Unlike so many of our Spanish-California Dons in dealing with and always losing to Americans, Don Suñol could out-trade the sharpest gringo, INCLUDING Sutter! He died a very wealthy man.

TAYLOR: It seems no historical writing on this Valley is complete without quoting Bayard Taylor, world famous poet and writer, a visitor to Santa Clara Valley in the 1850's......... He loved it! His expressions are flowery, impassioned word paintings, typical of that era. And remember, below was written over 100 years ago when this man saw Santa Clara Valley at the very peak of its natural unspoiled beauty. Read these sample lines. Then let your reactions simmer. Examples: "How shall I describe a landscape so unlike anything else in the world?.....Giant sycamores, trunks gleaming like silver.......Park-like groves of oaks....... In the distance, redwoods rising like towers....... A mountain chain, full lighted by the sun, rose colored, touched with violet shadows........... I indulge in another dream.........I may live to see it before my prime is over.....San Jose but five days distant from New York ....Cars which will speed on unknown rail from the Mississippi to the Pacific......Then let me build a cottage..... Embowered in acacia, eucalyptus and tall spires of Italian cypress......There shall my nightingale sing.... My orange blossoms sweeten the air....I had ANOTHER grander dream........ONE HUNDRED years had now passed and I saw the Valley humming with human life....Mansions fair as temples.....Statues peeping from the bloom of laurel bowers......I saw a more beautiful race.....Symmetry and grace of the Greek restored.....Milder manners.....Keener appreciation of all the arts which enrichen and embellish life. Was it only a dream?" (Our reader will have his or her private opinion.)

TOWER: San Jose Electric Tower was a most conspicuous landmark. Built in 1881. It stood 10 stories high, its iron tubing structure tapering from four corners of Market and Santa Clara streets. For a life of 36 years it helped to illuminate the business section until rust and a wind storm caused its downfall. The 24000 candle power lamps at peak of tower gave most brilliant light at that time in the U.S.A. Its fame spread abroad and citizens were proud to see it written up in Harpers Weekly. Christmas time its giant tree shape was strung with colored lights and Fourth of July its top platform served as a launching pad for fireworks. Ducks? Story goes, when Tower first erected, ducks, then in dense morning flights, would strike the tower during a heavy fog. One had but to pick up a mess of duck for dinner! Writer believes it.

TRUCKEE: Chief Truckee considered San Jose a WINTER RESORT! He had guided the Quivey family across Sierras in '49. Gratefully, he was invited to be a guest in their 4th St. home. Unexpectedly, he accepted! For many winters, Truckee & family made FOOT-TREK to a wickiup built in Quivey's backyard!

Why the Name . . . ?

UVAS: CREEK AND SOUTHERN VALLEY DISTRICT. MEANS "GRAPE". PRONOUNCED OO-VAS. SPANIARDS PROBABLY NAMED BECAUSE OF THE WILD GRAPES GROWING ALONG THIS STREAM.

VENDOME HOTEL WAS A HOSTELRY OF WHICH EARLY SAN JOSEANS MIGHT WELL BE PROUD. BUILT 1888, IT WAS SET IN PARK-LIKE LANDSCAPED ACRES ON NORTH FIRST STREET. THE FOUR STORIES WERE "QUEEN ANNE" DESIGN IN KEEPING WITH THE ORNATE STYLE OF THAT PERIOD. HOSTED ALL THE NOTABLE OLD VALLEY VISITORS, HIGHLIGHTED BY A RECEPTION FOR PRESIDENT WILLIAM McKINLEY AND HIS CABINET, 1904. EARTHQUAKE OF 1906 INFLICTED SEVERE DAMAGE AND THE AREA LATER BECAME A RESIDENTIAL SECTION.

VILLA MARIA: LOCATED AT MOUTH OF STEVENS CREEK CANYON BELOW THE DAM. 320 ACRES PURCHASED BY SANTA CLARA COLLEGE IN 1870. DEVELOPED 75 ACRES OF GRAPES AND OLIVES, A  WINERY, WORKERS' HOMES, CHAPEL AND RETREAT FOR JESUIT FACULTY. THOSE PINE TREES BY ROADSIDE WERE PLANTED BY VINCENT PICCHETTI ALMOST A HUNDRED YEARS AGO. ORIGINALLY GOVERNMENT LAND, THE FIRST DEEDS WERE SIGNED BY PRESIDENT GRANT IN 1869. NATIVES ALWAYS REFER TO IT AS THE "FATHERS' VILLA".

VICTORY THEATER ERECTED BY SENATOR JAMES D. PHELAN IN 1899. STILL OPERATING. NEXT FEW DECADES SAW ON STAGE SUCH THESPIANS AS MAUDE ADAMS, BILLIE BURKE, E.A. SOTHERN, ROBERT MANTEL, ANNA HELD, GEO. M. COHAN, ETHEL BARRYMORE, JULIA MARLOWE, NAT GOODWIN; SCORES MORE INCLUDING SEVERAL OPERA COMPANIES. ALL THE BEST TOURING ROAD SHOWS WERE HERE AND HIGH CLASS VAUDEVILLE. STAGE WAS ONE OF FEW ON COAST LARGE ENOUGH TO PRESENT WITH TEAMS OF HORSES, THE BEN HUR CHARIOT RACE. STILL OPEN IS THE JOSE BUILT IN 1904 WITH ED REDMOND 10-20-30¢ STOCK COMPANY, NEW PLAY EACH WEEK. CAN BE PLEASANTLY REMEMBERED. CORNY? YES, BUT WE DIDN'T KNOW IT. MANY OTHER OLD THEATERS; EMPIRE, HIPPODROME, GARDEN, T&D, UNIQUE, LYRIC, ALL GONE.

WOOLEN MILLS: THE SAN JOSE WOOLEN MILLS OPERATED 1870, WHEN SHEEP RAISING WAS AN IMPORTANT OLD VALLEY INDUSTRY. LOCATED IN NORTHERN PART OF EARLY SAN JOSE. WITH 43 EMPLOYEES, YEARLY PRODUCED 144,000 YARDS OF CASHMERE, 64,000 YARDS OF FLANNEL AND 5000 PAIRS OF BLANKETS.

WRIGHTS: S.P. MOUNTAIN STATION ON ABANDONED S.J.-SANTA CRUZ RAILROAD. NAMED FOR JAS. WRIGHT, EARLY SETTLER. SURPRISINGLY, AN EARLY DAYS SHIPPING POINT, TWO CARS OF FRESH FRUIT SHIPPED DAILY. 3200 ACRES OF ORCHARDS IN THIS VICINITY. MANY R.R. TUNNELS ON THIS SCENIC LINE WERE BLASTED BY THE ARMY FOR "PRACTICE" DURING WORLD WAR I. (PASSING THOUGHT. COULD THIS LOW LEVEL TRAIN ROUTE HAVE BEEN CONVERTED INTO ANOTHER ROAD TO SANTA CRUZ?) HERE IS AN INTERESTING WRIGHT'S SIDELIGHT: AMBROSE BIERCE, NOTED SATIRIST AND SHORT-STORY WRITER LIVED NEAR WRIGHTS FOR SOME YEARS. HE OFTEN BICYCLED TO SAN JOSE. THEN CAME HIS MYSTERIOUS, UNSOLVED DISAPPEARANCE. SAWYER, OLD HISTORIAN, CLAIMED TO HAVE ANSWER. BIERCE WENT TO MEXICO IN 1913, JOINING THE CARRANZA SIDE. VILLA FORCES CAPTURED HIM AND IN 1915 HE FACED A FIRING SQUAD. A PHOTO FURNISHED PROOF.

ZITHER  END OF ALPHABET REACHED AND NO OLD VALLEY Z'S! SO ALLOW US TO IMPROVISE WITH A "PERSONAL". WHEN WRITER WAS A LITTLE BOY, A ZITHER SALESMAN CAME TO OUR RANCH HOME. ZITHERS WERE POPULAR THEN AND HOW THIS KID LONGED FOR ONE. AND THESE ZITHERS WERE EXTRA-SUPER! SIMPLY SLIP A SHEET OF NOTES UNDER THE STRINGS AND "LEARN TO PLAY IN 10 EASY LESSONS". THIS SALESMAN DEMONSTRATED ABLY WITH A MOST HEART RENDING ANNIE LAURIE. DAD WAS AFFECTED BUT NOT TOUCHED TO TUNE OF $14.99, EVEN WITH 10 EASY LESSONS THROWN IN! WITH MUSICAL CAREER SO HALTED, I RECALL WEEPING. SOMETIME AFTERWARD, I HEARD MY AGED QUAKER GRANDMOTHER QUAVERINGLY ASK MY MOTHER, "DORA, THE GOOD BOOK SAYS IN HEAVEN WE SHALL PLAY ON HARPS. NOW THEE KNOWS I AM NOT MUSICAL. DOES THEE THINK I COULD EVER LEARN TO PLAY ON A HARP?".........
SHUCKS, I THOUGHT, OF COURSE GRANDMA COULD, AND, ACCORDING TO THAT ZITHER SALESMAN, IN ONLY TEN EASY LESSONS, TOO! ON THAT SAD MUSICAL NOTE, WE *END*.

1900 PARLOR

WITH THE EARLY SETTLERS IN SANTA CLARA VALLEY CAME THEIR MIDWESTERN PARLOR. FOR OUR YOUNGER GENERATION THE BEST DEFINITION OF A PARLOR IS TO SAY IT WAS EXACT OPPOSITE OF TODAY'S RUMPUS ROOM. IT WAS A PLACE OF DIGNITY WITH BLINDS PULLED DURING THE WEEK, RAISED ONLY TO BROOM-SWEEP OR FEATHER DUST. THIS OPERATION SIMPLY MOVED DUST FROM ONE LOCATION TO ANOTHER AND LEFT A STRANGE, SOLEMN, FUNEREAL ODOR, (AND FOR SUCH OCCASIONS OUR PARLOR WAS SO USED)......ON THE OTHER HAND, THE ROOM HELD JOYOUS SCENES SUCH AS WEDDINGS, RELATIVE REUNIONS, SUNDAY VISITORS AND CHRISTMAS CELEBRATIONS.......IT WAS THE FAMILY MUSEUM, "WHATNOT" AS CENTERPIECE ..... THIS MIGHT DISPLAY AN OSTRICH EGG, BABY SHOE, SHARK'S TOOTH, SEA SHELL CONTAINING ALLEGED OCEAN ROAR, STUFFED BIRD, TINTYPES OF BUG-EYED RELATIVES AND GLASS DOMED CASE WITH A LOCK OF AUNT MARY'S CURLS. ALWAYS A PAIR OF EITHER KINDLY OR CRITICAL ANCESTORS LOOKED DOWN UPON US FROM THEIR ENORMOUS FRAMES. A VISIT COULD BE LIGHTENED BY A ROUND WITH THE STEREOSCOPE AND LATEST SLIDES OF DEWEY'S FLEET OR THE RUSSO-JAPANESE WAR. THE FAMILY ALBUM WAS LAST RESORT AND ABOUT AS EXCITING AS LAST YEAR'S ALMANAC. WE YOUNGSTERS AVOIDED THE LEATHER FURNITURE WITH STABBING HORSE HAIR. YET SOMEHOW I BELIEVE OUR ANCESTORS WOULD ENJOY A MODERN LIVING ROOM, EVEN A FEW WHO WOULD GO FOR THE RUMPUS ROOM!

1900 KITCHEN

FOR MAMA OR GRANDMA, HERE THEIR THEME SONG COULD BE "HOME ON THE RANGE". COMPARATIVELY SPEAKING IT WAS A HOT, INCONVENIENT PLACE OF DRUDGERY. FORTUNATELY TODAY'S DREAM KITCHEN COULD NOT THEN BE EVEN IMAGINED. WHY HERE DESCRIBE THOSE OLD FAMILIAR DISHES OR THE UNBELIEVABLE BAKERY AND CANNERY PRODUCTION THIS SMALL ROOM PRODUCED? WHY NOT MAKE A 60 YEAR LAPSE COMPARISON; FOR INSTANCE, PREPARATION OF A CHICKEN DINNER FOR FOUR? START THE FILM AND CRANK RAPIDLY: FIRST, DAD CHASED DOWN A "LIKELY LOOKIN'" RHODE ISLAND RED OR PLYMOUTH ROCK. (NO, YOUNGSTER, NO PILGRIMS INVOLVED). MEANWHILE THE RANGE WAS STOKED UP TO HEAT SCALDING WATER FOR PLUCKING AFTER THE CHOPPING BLOCK TRAGEDY. THEN CAME CLEANING, DISJOINTING, WASHING, FLOURING AND SKILLET FRYING IN DEEP FAT. POTATOES WERE DUG, WASHED, PEELED, BOILED, MASHED.

GARDEN PEAS WERE PICKED, SHELLED AND STEWED. FOR PIE APPLES WERE PICKED, WASHED, PEELED, CORED AND SLICED. FOR PIE CRUST, FLOUR SIFTED, SHORTENING ADDED, MIXED, ROLLED, PLACED IN PIE TIN FILLED WITH SEASONED APPLES AND ARTISTIC LATTICE TOP ADDED. RANGE AGAIN STOKED AND PIES SHOVED IN TO BAKE AT A BY-GUESS AND BY-GOSH TEMPERATURE, — ELAPSED TIME, 3 OR 4 HOURS AND EXPENDITURE OF ABOUT FOUR BITS FOR STORE STAPLES. CHANGE THE FILM AND PRESS THE BUTTON FOR TODAY. SO AS NOT TO MISS THAT RE-RUN OF GUNSMOKE OR WAGON TRAIN, WE CRAWL INTO OUR UNPAID-FOR CAR AND RACE THREE BLOCKS TO THE NEAREST SAFEWAY. WE GRAB FOUR GRANDMA JONES TV FROZEN CHICKEN DINNERS, A PACKAGE OF AUNTY MARY'S FROZEN PEAS AND A MOTHER McKREE'S FROZEN APPLE PIE. THEN ELECTRIC OVEN FOR 30 MIN. @ 400°. SIMPLE. AND NOTE GRANDMA, AUNTY AND MAMA ARE STILL AVAILABLE!

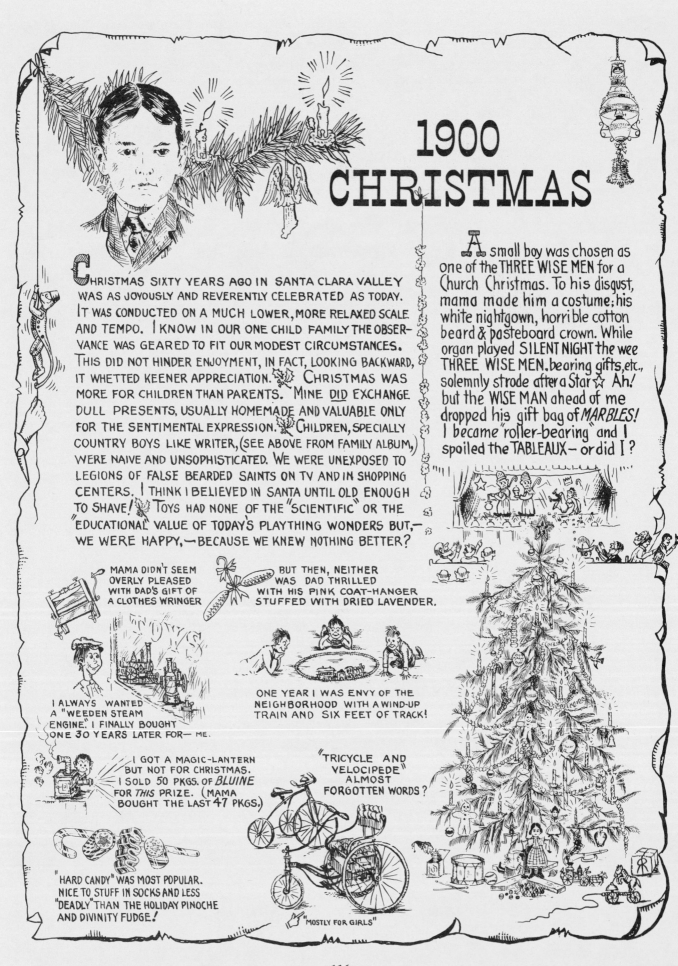

1900 CHRISTMAS

CHRISTMAS SIXTY YEARS AGO IN SANTA CLARA VALLEY WAS AS JOYOUSLY AND REVERENTLY CELEBRATED AS TODAY. IT WAS CONDUCTED ON A MUCH LOWER, MORE RELAXED SCALE AND TEMPO. I KNOW IN OUR ONE CHILD FAMILY THE OBSERVANCE WAS GEARED TO FIT OUR MODEST CIRCUMSTANCES. THIS DID NOT HINDER ENJOYMENT, IN FACT, LOOKING BACKWARD, IT WHETTED KEENER APPRECIATION. CHRISTMAS WAS MORE FOR CHILDREN THAN PARENTS. MINE DID EXCHANGE DULL PRESENTS, USUALLY HOMEMADE AND VALUABLE ONLY FOR THE SENTIMENTAL EXPRESSION. CHILDREN, SPECIALLY COUNTRY BOYS LIKE WRITER, (SEE ABOVE FROM FAMILY ALBUM,) WERE NAIVE AND UNSOPHISTICATED. WE WERE UNEXPOSED TO LEGIONS OF FALSE BEARDED SAINTS ON TV AND IN SHOPPING CENTERS. I THINK I BELIEVED IN SANTA UNTIL OLD ENOUGH TO SHAVE! TOYS HAD NONE OF THE "SCIENTIFIC" OR THE "EDUCATIONAL" VALUE OF TODAY'S PLAYTHING WONDERS BUT,— WE WERE HAPPY,— BECAUSE WE KNEW NOTHING BETTER?

A small boy was chosen as one of the THREE WISE MEN for a Church Christmas. To his disgust, mama made him a costume; his white nightgown, horrible cotton beard & pasteboard crown. While organ played SILENT NIGHT the wee THREE WISE MEN, bearing gifts, etc., solemnly strode after a Star ☆ Ah! but the WISE MAN ahead of me dropped his gift bag of MARBLES! I became "roller-bearing" and I spoiled the TABLEAUX — or did I ?

MAMA DIDN'T SEEM OVERLY PLEASED WITH DAD'S GIFT OF A CLOTHES WRINGER

BUT THEN, NEITHER WAS DAD THRILLED WITH HIS PINK COAT-HANGER STUFFED WITH DRIED LAVENDER.

I ALWAYS WANTED A "WEEDEN STEAM ENGINE". I FINALLY BOUGHT ONE 30 YEARS LATER FOR— ME.

ONE YEAR I WAS ENVY OF THE NEIGHBORHOOD WITH A WIND-UP TRAIN AND SIX FEET OF TRACK!

I GOT A MAGIC-LANTERN BUT NOT FOR CHRISTMAS. I SOLD 50 PKGS. OF BLUINE FOR THIS PRIZE. (MAMA BOUGHT THE LAST 47 PKGS.)

"TRICYCLE AND VELOCIPEDE" ALMOST FORGOTTEN WORDS ?

"HARD CANDY" WAS MOST POPULAR. NICE TO STUFF IN SOCKS AND LESS "DEADLY" THAN THE HOLIDAY PINOCHE AND DIVINITY FUDGE!

"MOSTLY FOR GIRLS"

1900
Country Store

Out in the country about 1900 B.C. (before cars) getting dressed, maybe even taking a bath, hitching up a slow horse and driving to San Jose might consume an entire day. Consequently, convenient little one room "shopping centers" sprang up at cross road corners and were called Country Groceries. They were not cash-and-carry. One could run a bill for six months or a year and pay when crops were in. Cash was scarce and folks traded butter, eggs and fruit for groceries. Store stock was amazingly diversified, much of it now obsolete and unfamiliar to new generations. Our grocery man could provide lamp wicks, button hooks, collar-buttons, sulphur matches, celluloid collars (cleaned with a damp rag) flower pots, bean pots and chamber pots, whipple-trees, kicking straps, cruppers, coffee grinders and do-it-yourself shoe-maker kits. He would gladly snip off a yard of gingham from the variegated bolts on his shelves. The edibles were as good in quality and flavor as todays but lacked the variety and convenience. We saw no gaudy labelled containers or pesky cellophane. All was open for inspection including the soda crackers and dill pickles for the local pot-bellied stove club. (Grocer quietly added samplings to their bills.) No, I never saw that proverbial cat asleep in a box of dried prunes. We live today in a wonder age of "pre-washed, pre-peeled, pre-cooked, and pre-wrapped, everything but prepaid."

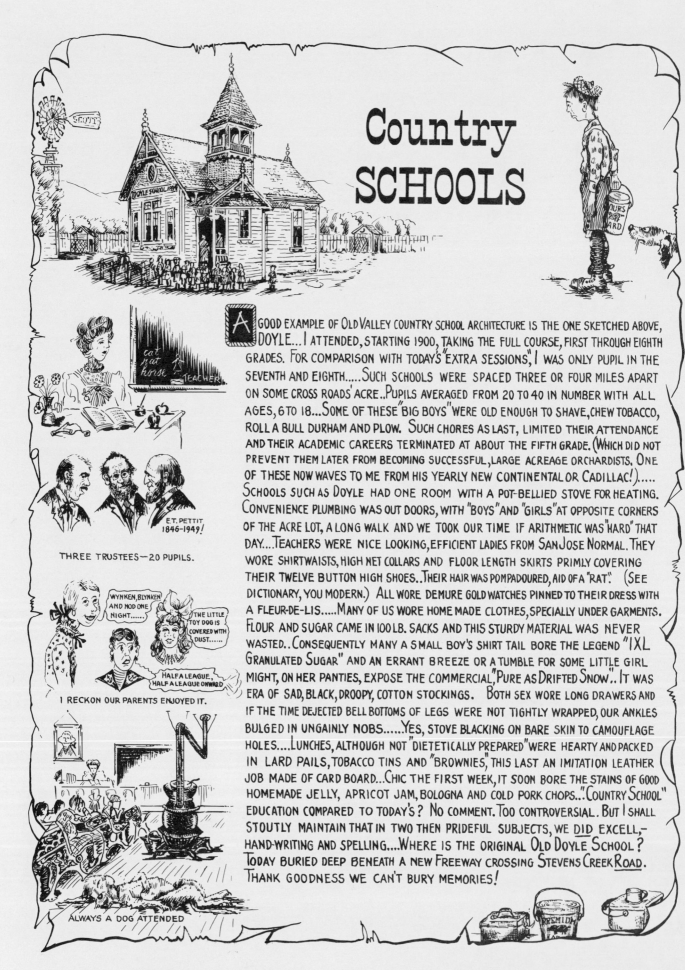

Country SCHOOLS

A GOOD EXAMPLE OF OLD VALLEY COUNTRY SCHOOL ARCHITECTURE IS THE ONE SKETCHED ABOVE, DOYLE...I ATTENDED, STARTING 1900, TAKING THE FULL COURSE, FIRST THROUGH EIGHTH GRADES. FOR COMPARISON WITH TODAY'S "EXTRA SESSIONS", I WAS ONLY PUPIL IN THE SEVENTH AND EIGHTH.....SUCH SCHOOLS WERE SPACED THREE OR FOUR MILES APART ON SOME CROSS ROADS' ACRE..PUPILS AVERAGED FROM 20 TO 40 IN NUMBER WITH ALL AGES, 6 TO 18...SOME OF THESE "BIG BOYS" WERE OLD ENOUGH TO SHAVE, CHEW TOBACCO, ROLL A BULL DURHAM AND PLOW. SUCH CHORES AS LAST, LIMITED THEIR ATTENDANCE AND THEIR ACADEMIC CAREERS TERMINATED AT ABOUT THE FIFTH GRADE. (WHICH DID NOT PREVENT THEM LATER FROM BECOMING SUCCESSFUL, LARGE ACREAGE ORCHARDISTS. ONE OF THESE NOW WAVES TO ME FROM HIS YEARLY NEW CONTINENTAL OR CADILLAC!).....SCHOOLS SUCH AS DOYLE HAD ONE ROOM WITH A POT-BELLIED STOVE FOR HEATING. CONVENIENCE PLUMBING WAS OUT DOORS, WITH "BOYS" AND "GIRLS" AT OPPOSITE CORNERS OF THE ACRE LOT, A LONG WALK AND WE TOOK OUR TIME IF ARITHMETIC WAS "HARD" THAT DAY...TEACHERS WERE NICE LOOKING, EFFICIENT LADIES FROM SAN JOSE NORMAL. THEY WORE SHIRTWAISTS, HIGH NET COLLARS AND FLOOR LENGTH SKIRTS PRIMLY COVERING THEIR TWELVE BUTTON HIGH SHOES..THEIR HAIR WAS POMPADOURED, AID OF A "RAT". (SEE DICTIONARY, YOU MODERN.) ALL WORE DEMURE GOLD WATCHES PINNED TO THEIR DRESS WITH A FLEUR-DE-LIS.....MANY OF US WORE HOME MADE CLOTHES, SPECIALLY UNDER GARMENTS. FLOUR AND SUGAR CAME IN 100 LB. SACKS AND THIS STURDY MATERIAL WAS NEVER WASTED..CONSEQUENTLY MANY A SMALL BOY'S SHIRT TAIL BORE THE LEGEND "IXL GRANULATED SUGAR" AND AN ERRANT BREEZE OR A TUMBLE FOR SOME LITTLE GIRL MIGHT, ON HER PANTIES, EXPOSE THE COMMERCIAL, "PURE AS DRIFTED SNOW".. IT WAS ERA OF SAD, BLACK, DROOPY, COTTON STOCKINGS. BOTH SEX WORE LONG DRAWERS AND IF THE TIME DEJECTED BELL BOTTOMS OF LEGS WERE NOT TIGHTLY WRAPPED, OUR ANKLES BULGED IN UNGAINLY NOBS......YES, STOVE BLACKING ON BARE SKIN TO CAMOUFLAGE HOLES....LUNCHES, ALTHOUGH NOT "DIETETICALLY PREPARED" WERE HEARTY AND PACKED IN LARD PAILS, TOBACCO TINS AND "BROWNIES", THIS LAST AN IMITATION LEATHER JOB MADE OF CARD BOARD...CHIC THE FIRST WEEK, IT SOON BORE THE STAINS OF GOOD HOMEMADE JELLY, APRICOT JAM, BOLOGNA AND COLD PORK CHOPS..."COUNTRY SCHOOL" EDUCATION COMPARED TO TODAY'S? NO COMMENT. TOO CONTROVERSIAL. BUT I SHALL STOUTLY MAINTAIN THAT IN TWO THEN PRIDEFUL SUBJECTS, WE DID EXCELL,- HAND-WRITING AND SPELLING....WHERE IS THE ORIGINAL OLD DOYLE SCHOOL? TODAY BURIED DEEP BENEATH A NEW FREEWAY CROSSING STEVENS CREEK ROAD. THANK GOODNESS WE CAN'T BURY MEMORIES!

THREE TRUSTEES — 20 PUPILS.

E.T. PETTIT 1846-1949!

WYNKEN, BLYNKEN AND NOD ONE NIGHT......

THE LITTLE TOY DOG IS COVERED WITH DUST......

HALF A LEAGUE, HALF A LEAGUE ONWARD

I RECKON OUR PARENTS ENJOYED IT.

ALWAYS A DOG ATTENDED

Last of the Village Blacksmiths

"Under the spreading chestnut tree". The tree was missing but otherwise stage setting and leading character were duplicate perfection for Longfellow's immortal poem. William Baer was one of Valley's last typical country blacksmiths. I never grew tired of watching this friendly, powerful man at work. Usually begrimed in a clean sort of way, he had muscles equal to Mr. America's. Always he would pause to answer this small boy's endless queries. What better blacksmith shop "atmosphere" than a brief description of "gettin' our old nag shod"? Unhitched from our spring wagon or buggy, Prince was led into the smokey, dirt floored smithy. Turning his back to horse's rear end, our smith would pick up a hind foot and hold it between his (Mr. Baer's) legs, placing it on his heavy leather apron. Old shoes were pried off, old nails snipped clean and hoof bottom pared down smooth and white. Then Mr. Baer would select a new horseshoe from the stack of size numbered little kegs...Then toss one in the forge and start pumping the huge wooden and leather hand-made bellows. Slumbering charcoal embers would awaken to emit little spiral curls of pleasant smelling smoke. Finally small tongues of darting flame enveloped the iron blue horse shoe buried in the coals. When white hot, with his long tongs, Mr. Baer withdrew the shoe and planted it firmly against the bare hoof. (No, pain, gentle reader.) Sizzling, acrid smoke curled up with an unforgettable smell....Mr. Baer would then critically examine the scorched surface. By burned and unburned areas he could exactly see how shoe fit contour of hoof. With sledge and anvil he would deliver a few mighty corrective blows. This operation was repeated until by trial and error Mr. B. was satisfied and after tub water tempering, nailed on the shoe. Yes, he made a nail "ring" for me, as naturally expected as butcher-wagon free bologna. End of act. Dad painfully opened his long leather purse and doled out six bits or a silver dollar. I forget which. Good men,—my Dad and William Baer. Both worked a sixty hour week at honest manual labor. Went to church on Sunday, still very tired. And the Rev. Coleman's sermons were sometimes long and dry. Consequently it took many a wifely nudge to head off a snoring duet, Mr. Baer, deep bass, Dad, high tenor.....Long gone the pungent odors of burnt horse hoof, sweat, charcoal, stale tobacco smoke, the musical clank and clang of anvil and wheezing bellows. Came the Auto Age and Last of the Village Blacksmiths.

Pictured at right, the village corners of West Side, now Cupertino. This was and is the intersection of Stevens Creek Road and Sunnyvale-Saratoga Road. (Hwy. 9) Baer Blacksmith shop far right. Sketched from 1898 photo loaned by Mrs. Arch Wilson, my Doyle School teacher.

1906
EARTHQUAKE

THIS CLOCK SKETCHED FROM PHOTO OF ACTUAL AGNEWS ASYLUM CLOCK, SHOWING MONTH, DAY, HOUR AND MINUTE IT WAS STOPPED BY QUAKE!

Hundreds of Santa Clara Valley clocks stopped at exactly 13½ minutes past 5 on morning of April 18, 1906, stopped by a destructive earthquake unequalled in recorded American history. With indescribable grinding roar, the earth rocked for 45 seconds, paused for 10, followed by an after wave of 25 seconds. Minor tremors continued for weeks. Again the San Andreas Fault had been aroused. (See map at right). Originating somewhere in the Pacific off Cape Mendocino it crept like a serpent of destruction 600 miles southward. This weakness in earth's crust has caused our coastal quakes for centuries. Spaniards called the big ones *TERRAMOTOS* and the minor shudders, *TEMBLORS* ～ Mercifully, this calamity occurred at an early hour, sparing thousands. Great crevices and landslides developed all along this fault line. Redwoods hundreds of years old in the Santa Cruz Mountains were shifted across canyons or whipped to splinters. 16 were killed in San Jose with 8000 left homeless. The Agnews Insane Asylum's main building collapsed killing over 100. Stanford University, only 15 years old, suffered 5 million dollars damage in fallen stone and mosaic. Hardly a brick chimney in the Valley survived and many public buildings damaged or destroyed. Artesian wells started flowing. The Loma Prieta lumber mill was engulfed, burying nine men. Literally in fear and trembling, hundreds of valley inhabitants cooked and slept outdoors for weeks after.

In our orchard home on the West side, our small family needed no alarm clock THAT morning! I was at the impressionable age of 12. The three of us, scantily clad, shiveringly emerged to view our new windmill and tank, a mass of twisted ruin. Dad and I whipped up horse and buggy townward, urged by morbid curiosity and mother's frantic order for sacks of sugar and flour. Everyone hoarded food. (Will history repeat?)

Valley earthquakes that ruined missions and once "destroyed every (adobe) house in the Valley," occurred in 1800, 1818, 1865 & 1868. Our David Starr Jordan of Stanford suggested a cycle of 30-40 years but in finality said, "We can expect minor shakes at intervals and a *TERRAMOTO* once in a generation. ～

EUREKA
CAPE MENDOCINO
UKIAH
POINT ARENA
FORT ROSS
TOMALES BAY
S.F. OAKLAND
WOODSIDE
PALO ALTO
SAN JOSE
WRIGHTS
SANTA CRUZ
MONTEREY

THE SAN ANDREAS
•••FAULT LINE•••

MERCURY-HERALD.
SAN JOSE, CALIFORNIA, APRIL 18, 1906.
SAN FRANCISCO REPORTED DESTROY
EXTRA! EXTRA!
PROCLAMATION!

Old Valley Transportation

ALPHA

In 1899, in all these United States, there were less than 8000 autos and only 134 miles of paved roads. The New York Times warned, "Man loves the horse and he is not likely to ever love an automobile!..... Nor will he get used, in this generation, to speeding along the road behind 'NOTHING!'" (Would that this scribe could have envisioned Stevens Creek Blvd. at 5 p.m.!)

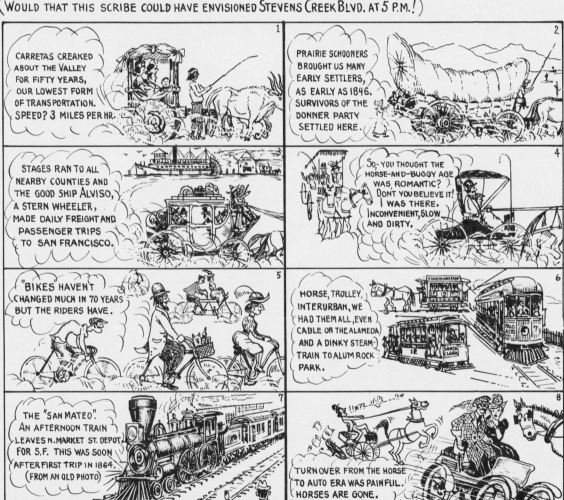

1. Carretas creaked about the Valley for fifty years, our lowest form of transportation. Speed? 3 miles per hr.

2. Prairie schooners brought us many early settlers, as early as 1846. Survivors of the Donner Party settled here.

3. Stages ran to all nearby counties and the good ship Alviso, a stern wheeler, made daily freight and passenger trips to San Francisco.

4. So - you thought the horse-and-buggy age was romantic? Don't you believe it! I was there. Inconvenient, slow and dirty.

5. "Bikes haven't changed much in 70 years but the riders have."

6. Horse, trolley, interurban, we had them all, even cable on the Alameda and a dinky steam-train to Alum Rock Park.

7. The "San Mateo". An afternoon train leaves N. Market St. depot for S.F. This was soon after first trip in 1864. (From an old photo)

8. Turn over from the horse to auto era was painful. Horses are gone. — It's still painful.

Once upon a time, 5¢ street car service was available on all San Jose streets and in the early 1900's, big, fast, low fare inter-urbans ran to Campbell, Los Gatos, Saratoga, Cupertino and Stanford. We had reached the per capita peak of good public transportation.

OMEGA

 # The Alameda

BETWEEN MISSION SANTA CLARA AND THE PUEBLO OF SAN JOSE TRAVEL WAS DIFFICULT, EVEN DANGEROUS. NUMEROUS LITTLE BROOKS, MARSHES AND SMALL LAKES HINDERED THE PEDESTRIAN OR HORSEMAN AND BOGGED DOWN THE HEAVY CARRETA WHEELS. ADDED HAZARDS WERE THE BANDS OF WILD CATTLE THAT ROAMED THIS UNFENCED TERRITORY, AT TIMES A FOREST OF YELLOW MUSTARD 10 TO 12 FEET HIGH. IN WINTER A DETOUR OF 6 MILES TO THE WEST WAS NECESSARY. SO WAS BORN THE PLAN OF FATHER MAGIN CATALA, "HOLY MAN OF THE SANTA CLARA MISSION." FROM THE BANKS OF THE GUADALUPE HE TOOK BLACK WILLOW CUTTINGS AND STARTED A NURSERY OF THOUSANDS. FOR TWO YEARS HE TENDED THEIR GROWTH. THEN, 18 YEARS AFTER MISSION FOUNDING, IN 1795, WITH TWO HUNDRED INDIAN NEOPHYTE HELPERS, HE STAKED OUT AND PLANTED THE ENTIRE 3 MILES OF OUR ALAMEDA. (MEANING: A GROVE OF SHADE TREES.) IRRIGATED BY DITCH DUG FROM THE GUADALUPE, THEY FLOURISHED, THEIR TOP BOUGHS EVENTUALLY MEETING TO FORM A NATURAL CANOPY. FOR 75 YEARS THEY REMAINED UNDESPOILED. "MANY PASSED, THE NAKED RED MAN, THE DARK, SLOW MOVING DON AND THE BLUE EYED GRINGO." BENEATH THEIR SHELTER PASSED THE SAINTLY FATHER SERRA AND THE BANDIT SINNER, VASQUEZ; BEAUTIFUL SENORITAS, CABALLEROS, PIONEERS, GOLD HUNTERS, WEDDINGS, FUNERALS, PARADES OF EVERY DESCRIPTION, FROM THE PRANCING, VICTORIOUS JUAN PRADO WITH THE HEAD OF THE RENEGADE INDIAN YOSCOLO ON A POLE, DOWN TO OUR ALMOST FORGOTTEN BUT LOVELY FIESTA de las ROSAS SPECTACLES.... AS TRAFFIC INCREASED, RAIN MADE TRAVEL ALMOST IMPOSSIBLE. IN 1856, CRANDALL BROS. STARTED AN OMNIBUS LINE. FROM 1868 TO 1878 THE SAN JOSE & SANTA CLARA HORSE RAILWAY CO. MADE ITS SLOW BUT SURE WAY AND IN 1870 WAS GRANTED RIGHT TO USE "STEAM, PONY, OR PNEUMATIC POWER". AN ATTEMPTED UNDERGROUND TROLLEY SYSTEM HAD BEEN SOON FLOODED OUT IN 1886. WITH ADVENT OF ELECTRIC STREET CARS IN 1887 CAME DESTRUCTION OF THE CENTER ROW OF TREES. (DUE TO PUBLIC INDIGNATION, DONE DURING NIGHT.) GRADUALLY THESE AGED SENTINELS MARKING OUR MOST HISTORIC AND ROMANTIC HIGHWAY HAVE FALLEN BEFORE THE MARCH OF TIME OR PROGRESS. TODAY, 1964, I SEE ONLY ONE BRAVE AND HEALTHY SPROUT STILL SPARED FRONTING THE SAN JOSE INN.

THE PEN AND INK DRAWING ABOVE WAS SKETCHED FROM AN ORIGINAL PHOTO TAKEN BETWEEN 1868-78. THE CAR IS ON EAST SIDE OF THE ALAMEDA RETURNING TO SAN JOSE. SHOWN WERE REMAINING CATALA WILLOWS.

remember when...

A boy's-eye view
of an
OLD VALLEY

by
F. RALPH RAMBO

Sequel to "Almost Forgotten"

Dear Reader,

Again, pleasantly surprised with my first book *Almost Forgotten,* I determined to produce a sequel, *Remember When.* It would lean heavily on "atmosphere", way of life, and nostalgia of the Old Valley around the turn-of-the-century. As a matter of fact, many sections and impressions would be simply recollections from my own boyhood days. All these would be well-provided with appropriate cartoons.

Among the many subjects that I selected were Stevens Creek Road, descriptions of the Valley's particularly quaint characters, public amusements, and some ridiculous but true comedy skits. I admit that *Remember When* is certainly no contribution to our valued historical heritage. It is just an attempt to retain, or rather reveal, pictures of an Old Valley whose "way of life" is gone forever.

To help paint this picture in the reader's mind, I devoted the epilogue section to straight cartooning. You will find several of these cartoons in the "Art" section of this book.

I'll pat myself on the back in retrospect. In 1964-65, to supply public demand for my first two books, it was necessary to run off three separate editions in about three consecutive months of both *Almost Forgotten* and *Remember When.*

Yours Truly
Ralph Rambo

Saga of the Old Road

How leisurely were our trips to and from old San Jose sixty years ago as Dad and I drove down the rural Stevens Creek Road with our horse-and-buggy. This road, the "grass roots of my childhood" had a beauty not only of the land but in the happy associations with the people we met along the way.

We knew every neighbor, every orchard, every tree and windmill on the route. Sometimes we halted and passed the time of day whenever we met friends. A routine trip would follow this pattern:

Dad would draw up the reins and visit for about fifteen minutes. This time it was Bill Craft leaning over the picket fence with a string of gopher traps dangling from his shoulders. Conversation centered around subjects such as unusual weather, sticky adobe and the miserable price of dried prunes.

Today if one stopped for fifteen minutes at this same spot, there would be four miles of honking, bumper-to-bumper, irate motorists. We would probably receive a "ticket" from some shiny booted "marble top" highway officer. Time marches on. Not only here but Main Street, Anywhere, U.S.A.

Sometimes we would see the fragile, elderly Mrs. Scantlebury cutting sweet pea blossoms from vines higher than her head. It was an old fashioned garden fronting a tiny frame cottage and a creaking wooden windmill. If Dad stopped to ask about status of her sciatica she always picked a bouquet of flowers for Mom.

Continuing another few miles Dad would pull off the road to let Emil Bordi pass with his four horse wagon load of manzanita root chunks and a few barrels of foothill Muscatel.

Then not too many years ago came "progressive man" who took inventory of our Valley's charm and growth potential. Stevens Creek Road was widened into a six lane highway replacing the narrow gravelled road. The name was changed to Stevens Creek Boulevard. Orchards were the primary victims of expansion and the first to go.

The word "boulevard" means a wide avenue lined with tall shade trees carrying an "air of dignity." This suits the former name better as it was once heavily bordered with oaks, sycamores and eucalyptus. Gone was the "air of dignity" when these trees were cut down.

This highway is now lined with shopping centers ranging from the miniature to the monumental, stores of every kind from the hurdy gurdy operation to the exclusive; subdivisions of tract homes, endless tiers of mushroom apartments, bowling alleys, super-markets, restaurants and acres of used car lots. A maze of gaudy signs confuse instead of beckon.

Small wonder I feel a twist at my heart whenever I drive down this "boulevard"; now so many missing leaves in my boyhood memory album.

I'm not complaining. "It ain't like it usta be" conversations bore me, specially the gripe variety. I can offer no solution for this ever changing skyline. Personally, I think it rather interesting, at least to watch. I haven't missed anything and Valley newcomers don't know what they have missed. I saw it "WHEN." After all it isn't so much when or where we live that counts BUT how much we enjoy the living.

The following narrative is my boyhood impressions of this road or "Boulevard", once a vein of travel, now a pulsating artery of business.

Coming from San Jose by wagon, or later, on the Peninsular Railway Interurban street cars, we always felt Stevens Creek Road started at O'Connor Sanitarium. This hospital then occupied the entire block at Race and San Carlos, now Sears Roebuck.

This old fashioned 1888 red brick edifice complete with gingerbread cupolos, cornices, windmills and tanks held a sentimental place in many a pioneer's heart. It did in mine. Here close members of my family saw either their first light of Day or approaching Night.

Mrs. O'Connor designed the home and landscaped gardens and later donated the estate to Daughters of Charity of St. Vincent de Paul for a hospital.

Sometimes we glimpsed the nuns strolling around the gardens in billowing blue dress with expansive starched headgear remindful of bobbing white cyclamen blossoms.

ORIGINAL
O'CONNOR
SANITARIUM
FOUNDED 1888

Geometrically designed beds of annuals blossomed the year round, rare flowering trees,

Giant locusts and magnolias brightened many a convalescence.

Continuing west we saw the first orchards, grain fields and berry patches for a mile followed by a cluster of houses and a row of small stores. This was called Rose Lawn now known as Burbank District. Luther Burbank, this state's noted horticulturist, had a school here dedicated with his name.

The intersection at Bascom Avenue and Stevens Creek Road was end of the street car line and marked the beginning of open country. Here the conductor switched his trolley and often in the fall slyly crossed the road to fill his pockets with almonds from the old Bradley orchard.

Jogging along one could see more orchards, hayfields and everywhere clusters of great oaks. Settlers farmed around these oak trees using them for shade and homesite protection.

The Santa-Clara-Saratoga road crossing was called Meridian Corners (map meridian.) How clearly I remember one Sunday when we were driving home from church and we saw a Turkey Shoot in progress. My parents were SO shocked! Only the turkey's head was exposed and for four bits one could shoot at this target. My parents explained this constituted both cruelty and gambling. From a small boy's standpoint, it wasn't much of a gamble, at least for the bird. Sooner or later the turkey would get it in the neck.

After I married we built a home under these same oak trees at scene of Turkey Shoot. Here we raised our two sons, enjoyed country living and spent the happiest years of our lives.

Meridian Corners had a store, Bollinger's blacksmith shop and two saloons, Blackmar's and Sam Storm's, both typical Old Valley tap rooms. Looking backward, the Blackmars and the Storms were GOOD people but not according to MY puritanical parents! They sold liquor, mostly beer and were open on Sundays! I recall my parents utter horror one Sunday when they recognized our local "Dude" and his rubber-tired buggy parked at Blackmar's hitching rack. In his "rig" sat a pretty young

LADY IN HER OSTRICH PLUMED HAT. UNFORTUNATELY WE PASSED JUST AS HER MALE ESCORT EMERGED FROM THE "FAMILY ENTRANCE" CARRYING A TRAY WITH TWO SMALL GLASSES OF BEER! FROM OUR DISTANCE IT MIGHT HAVE BEEN SARSAPARILLA. MY PARENTS ARGUED THE POINT BUT DAD POINTED OUT SAGELY THAT THE LIQUID WAS FOAMY, OR, AS HE EXPRESSED IT, "HAD A HEAD ON IT." THEY BOTH SEEMED PLEASED WITH THIS DAMNING AND CONCLUSIVE EVIDENCE. THEN MY MOTHER SUDDENLY REHEATED THE ARGUMENT BY ASKING DAD HOW <u>HE</u> WAS SO FAMILIAR WITH THE BEVERAGE!

CONTINUING A SHORT DISTANCE WE MET A DOYLE SCHOOLMATE OF MINE ON HIS REGULAR SUNDAY ERRAND TO BLACKMARS' FOR "REFRESHMENTS". I WAVED BUT DAD WHIPPED UP THE HORSE AND MOTHER MURMURED, "MERCY!" MY SCHOOLMATE WAS HAVING HIS TROUBLES. HE WAS TRYING TO BALANCE A GALLON LARD PAIL OF UNMISTAKABLE, FOAMY, SLOSHING OLD JOE'S STEAM BEER ON HIS HANDLEBARS!

NEXT WE PASSED DOYLE SCHOOL DWELT ON IN VARIED DETAIL ELSEWHERE. NOW THE OLD SITE IS BURIED UNDER A FREEWAY. EVAN T. PETTIT, SCHOOL TRUSTEE AND PROMINENT DOYLE ROAD RESIDENT, PLANTED ONE OF THE FIRST LARGE APRICOT ORCHARDS IN THE VALLEY IN 1881, DIED IN 1949 AT THE AGE OF 102.

FROM DOYLE SCHOOL TO MILLER AVENUE WAS THE MOST FAMILIAR STRETCH OF THE ROAD AND SCENE FOR MAJORITY OF MY BOYHOOD ADVENTURES.

FARTHER ALONG ON THE NORTH SIDE OF THE ROAD WAS THE FAMOUS PORTAL ESTATE, A SHOW PLACE OF THE VALLEY AND FORTUNATELY, FOR PRESERVATION'S SAKE, SUBJECT OF MANY AN ARTIST'S PAINTING OR PHOTOGRAPHER'S REPRODUCTION. IN RECENT YEARS THIS OLD

LANDMARK WAS BULLDOZED INTO OBLIVION FOR THE USUAL SUBDIVISION DEVELOPMENT.

J.B.J. PORTAL, A NATIVE OF FRANCE, ARRIVED IN THE VALLEY IN 1860 AND PURCHASED 400 ACRES OF LAND. THIS WAS PLANTED IN VINEYARDS WITH CUTTINGS BROUGHT FROM HIS NATIVE FRANCE.

HIS ESTATE INCLUDED HUGE BARNS, A COMPLETE BLACKSMITH SHOP, WINERY, COOPERAGE AND THE VALLEY'S FIRST PUMPING STEAM ENGINE FOR A FAR-AHEAD-OF-ITS-TIME UNDERGROUND IRRIGATION SYSTEM.

A HIGHLY ORNATE, EIGHTEEN ROOM, STAINED GLASS WINDOWED MANSION CENTERED THE 400 ACRES. IT WAS TOPPED WITH A PROMINENT TOWER WHERE THE OWNER COULD SURVEY THE ESTATE FROM AN ENCIRCLING PORCH CALLED A "CAPTAIN'S WALK". THIS IS JUST WHAT MR. PORTAL DID DURING HARVEST SEASON WITH AID OF A SPY-GLASS TELESCOPE. NAPPING GRAPE-PICKERS WERE SURPRISED AND PAID OFF BY THE FOREMAN.

ONE TIME A RAILROAD APPLIED FOR A RIGHT OF WAY THROUGH J.B.J'S VINEYARDS. THEY WERE STERNLY REFUSED ON GROUNDS THAT NOISY TRAINS WOULD DISTURB THE AGEING WINES IN HIS CELLARS.

IN 1910, AS THROUGHOUT THE VALLEY, PHYLLOXERA, (LOUSE) STRUCK HIS VINEYARD AND PORTAL RETURNED TO FRANCE. SEVERAL FAMILY MEMBERS REMAINED, BECOMING PROMINENT CITIZENS. IN SEVENTY YEARS WE HAVE WITNESSED AMAZING SUCCESSIVE PLANTINGS ON THIS ACREAGE, FROM WHEAT TO VINEYARD, PRUNES, CHERRIES, STRAWBERRIES AND NOW TO ROWS OF TRACT HOMES.

EVERY MILE OR TWO, THE COUNTY BUILT ELEVATED ROADSIDE TANKS, SOME WITH THEIR OWN WELL AND WINDMILL. EACH HAD A WATERING TROUGH WHERE THIRSTY HORSES BURIED NOSES IN COOL, FLOATING GREEN MOSS. THE TANKS HAD OVER-HANGING SPOUTS WITH A CANVAS HOSE FOR FILLING THE COUNTY WATER WAGONS. DURING THE SUMMER, THICK DUST WOULD HAVE BEEN INTOLERABLE WITHOUT THIS DAILY SPRINKLING.

HOW THE CHILDREN LOVED THESE WATER TANKS, SPECIALLY WHEN WALKING TO AND FROM SCHOOL. LEAKS AND OVERFLOW IN THE DRY SUMMERTIME MADE SUCH REFRESHING LANDMARKS INTO GREEN OASES. THIS ATTRACTED REDWING BLACKBIRDS AND KILLDEER, SPROUTED LUSH GRASS, REEDS, CAT-TAILS, WILD ROSES, AND POOLS OF GREEN WATER WITH POLLYWOGS, FROGS

TOADS AND SALAMANDERS. SWALLOWS AND FLY-CATCHERS BUILT THEIR MUD NESTS UNDER THE TANKS' STOUT FRAMES.

CUPERTINO, NOW ONE OF THE VALLEY'S FASTEST GROWING CITIES, FOR DECADES WAS ONLY A TYPICAL COUNTRY CROSS ROADS (SEE SKETCH). ONCE WITH A POST OFFICE CALLED WEST SIDE, FOR YEARS IT WAS SIMPLY MARKED BY THE MONTGOMERY-WILSON STORE AND BAER'S SMITHY. AS LATE AS 1922, EUGENE T. SAWYER, ONE OF OUR EARLY LOCAL HISTORIANS, IN HIS HISTORY OF SANTA CLARA VALLEY, GIVES CUPERTINO A SCANT <u>ONE</u> LINE, "..... LITTLE MORE THAN A STOP ON THE PENINSULAR RAILWAY."

ABOVE CUPERTINO, AFTER ASCENDING A GRADE SO GRADUAL IT WAS NOTICEABLE ONLY TO THE SMALL BOY PUMPING A BIKE LOADED WITH LUNCH AND FISHING GEAR, WE ARRIVED AT MONTA VISTA. WE HAD JUST PASSED LE PETIT TRIANON, THE "YELLOW DEVIL'S" HOME (DEALT WITH ELSEWHERE.) MONTA VISTA, LATER TO BECOME THE VALLEY'S EARLIEST FOOTHILL SUBDIVISON, BEARS HIDDEN FAME AS ONE OF DE ANZA'S CAMP GROUNDS. THE ROUTE PLUNGED INTO A RAVINE OR LITTLE VALLEY AND IT WAS HERE THAT THIS ROAD RECEIVED ITS NAME, STEVENS CREEK. TO THE NORTH AND ALONG THE STREAM WAS NATHAN HALL'S 1853 PIONEER HOME AND VINEYARD, ORIGINALLY PART OF THE SAN ANTONIO GRANT. THIS LAND ONCE SOLD FOR $1.25 AN ACRE.

BLACKBERRY FARM WAS FIRST LOCATION FOR CAPTAIN ELISHA STEVENS, RESPONSIBLE FOR THE ROAD'S NAME. CAPTAIN STEVENS (1801-1884) WAS FAMED LEADER OF THE 1844 STEVENS-MURPHY OVERLAND PARTY. HE WAS ANOTHER ONE OF THOSE <u>REAL</u> PIONEERS, BLAZING A CLEAR TRAIL FOR THE SO CALLED, "PATHFINDER OF THE WEST,"

ELISHA STEVENS
(FROM HIS ONLY PHOTO)

GENERAL FREMONT. AS "MOUNTAIN CHARLEY" McKIERNON WAS CONSIDERED THE FIRST SETTLER IN THE LOS GATOS MOUNTAIN AREA, CAPTAIN ELISHA STEVENS WAS THE ORIGINAL PIONEER OF OUR WESTERN FOOTHILLS. IT IS TO BE SINCERELY HOPED THAT SOME HISTORIOGRAPHER WILL EVENTUALLY PAY THIS LITTLE KNOWN OLD VALLEY CHARACTER LONG OVERDUE TRIBUTE.

STRETCHING WESTWARD ABOVE MONTA VISTA WAS A PLATEAU PLANTED TO VINEYARDS. INSTEAD OF CONTINUING STRAIGHT AHEAD INTO PERMENENTE COUNTRY, WE MADE A SHARP LEFT TURN TO ENTER STEVENS CREEK CANYON. OFF TO OUR LEFT WE COULD SEE (THEN STILL INTACT) A LUXURIOUS ESTATE CALLED "DEEP CLIFF." IN THE 70'S THIS BELONGED TO L. SELINGER AND AROUND 1905 BECAME THE PROPERTY OF DE LAVEAGA. THE MASSIVE AND SHEER LANDSLIDE AT SHARP TURN OF THE CREEK GAVE THE NAME "DEEP CLIFF." AS THIS IS WRITTEN, THE BULL-DOZERS HAVE REMOVED ALL TRACES, EXCEPT THE CLIFF! AND BY THE WAY,- IT WAS "<u>CLIFF</u>", NOT "<u>CLIFFE</u>", AS PRETENTIOUS REALTY SIGNS NOW PROCLAIM.

STEVENS CREEK ROAD CROSSING SUNNYVALE-SARATOGA ROAD AT WEST SIDE (CUPERTINO). FROM 1895 PHOTO

128

BEFORE ASCENDING CREEK CANYON PROPER AND PASSING THE PRESENT DAM SITE, ON THE LEFT WAS VILLA MARIE OR "FATHERS' VILLA", 320 ACRES PURCHASED IN 1873 BY SANTA CLARA COLLEGE FOR A JESUIT RETREAT. THE FLATS AND HILLSIDES WERE PLANTED TO MANY FINE WINE GRAPE VARIETIES.

FORTUNATELY THE VINES WERE CONVENIENTLY CLOSE TO THE ROAD, BEYOND THE PADRES' VIEW AND WE BOYS USUALLY FOUND A LOOSE PICKET IN THE FENCE. WE ALWAYS CHECKED FOR A GOOD VINTAGE YEAR AND HERE WERE THE BEST MUSCATS AND "SWEET WATERS" I EVER TASTED.

NOW OUR ROUTE NARROWED TO A STEEPER, ONE-WAY ROAD AND A FEW MILES REACHED SODA ROCK. HERE THE CREEK WOUND AROUND AN OVERHANGING ROCK FORMATION AND FROM ITS MOSSY CREVICES TRICKLED MANY STREAMS OF EFFERVESCENT MINERAL WATER HEAVILY CHARGED WITH SODA. THIS WAS A MOST POPULAR SUNDAY SCHOOL AND FAMILY PICNIC GROUND. WOE BETIDE THE PERSON WHO FORGOT TO INCLUDE LEMONS AND SUGAR IN THE LUNCH BOX! WITH WRY FACES, OUR PARENTS SMACKED THEIR LIPS AND SAID IT WAS "GOOD FOR WHAT AILED YOU". MOST OF US KIDS THOUGHT IT A NASTY WASTE OF LEMONS AND SUGAR.

TIME HAS NOT GREATLY CHANGED THIS FINAL STRETCH OF OLD STEVENS CREEK ROAD. SOME BRIDGES HAVE REPLACED THE SHALLOW FORDS WHERE WE STOPPED OUR OVER HEATED OLD HORSE OR LATER, OUR EQUALLY OVER HEATED MODEL T, IN EITHER CASE TO FILL THEM UP WITH AT LEAST A TEMPORARY SUPPLY OF COLD CREEK WATER.

IF YOU WERE REAL ADVENTURESOME AND SOUGHT THE ULTIMATE IN REMOTENESS, YOU CONTINUED ON A MILE OR SO TO GRIZZLY FLAT, NAMED AFTER A FORMER FOUR FOOTED INHABITANT OF THAT AREA.

HOW WELL I REMEMBER CAMPING TWO WEEKS ON THIS GRIZZLY FLAT WITH ANOTHER NEIGHBOR FAMILY ABOUT 1905. IT IS DIFFICULT TO BELIEVE BUT SUCH A JOURNEY TRUELY REQUIRED MORE PLANNING AND PREPARATION THAN A PRESENT DAY WEEK-END JAUNT TO TAHOE OR YOSEMITE! ACTUALLY WE WERE ONLY FIFTEEN MILES FROM HOME, HIGH ABOVE THE VALLEY FLOOR YET WITHOUT AUTO, PHONE, RADIO OR MAIL WE FELT THAT WE HAD SEVERED ALL TIES WITH CIVILIZATION.

MODERN CAMPING EQUIPMENT SUCH AS SLEEPING BAGS, AND GASOLINE COOKING STOVES WERE UNKNOWN. WE MADE "SPRINGY BEDS OF PINE-SCENTED BOUGHS AND BRANCHES" WHICH QUICKLY PROCEEDED TO LOSE THEIR SPRING THE FIRST NIGHT. GRIZZLY FLAT WAS FLAT BUT NOT SOFT!

WE SAW "LITTLE DAVE" ASTRIDE HIS GAUNT MULE, THE LONE INHABITANT OF THE CANYON. HE CAREFULLY AVOIDED US. (READERS SHALL MAKE HIS INTIMATE ACQUAINTANCE LATER.)

MEN AND BOYS SPENT THE DAYS CATCHING UNLIMITED SMALL TROUT AND LARGE DOSES OF POISON OAK. WOMEN FUSSED OVER SMOKY CAMPFIRES FRYING HUGE PANS OF FISH AND TRYING TO BAKE BREAD IN DUTCH OVENS. FOR RECREATION THESE LADIES DUG THE ABUNDANT MAIDEN-HAIR AND FIVE-FINGER FERNS, TRANSPLANTING THEM TEMPORARILY INTO OLD WASHTUBS BROUGHT ALONG FOR THAT PURPOSE. IT SEEMED TO ME A LADY'S SOCIAL STATUS IN THOSE DAYS WAS DETERMINED BY THE NUMBER OF STEVENS CREEK FERNS DECORATING HER SCREEN PORCH.

A CAMPING TRIP WAS A DELIGHTFUL ESCAPE FOR THE SMALL BOY, THANKS TO THAT "TOO COLD CRICK" BATH WATER. CAME BEDTIME, WE SIMPLY TOOK OFF OUR SHOES AND HATS BEFORE CRAWLING UNDER THE QUILTS WITH OUR FAMILY DOG AND HIS WOOD TICKS. SLEEP WAS IMMEDIATE AND OUR DREAMS ONLY OCCASIONALLY DISTURBED BY A GRIZZLY BEAR NIGHTMARE.

PURE HAPPINESS IS SOMETHING WE CAN'T EXPLAIN BUT SUCH CHILDHOOD ADVENTURE IS OUR CLOSEST APPROACH.

THESE WERE A SMALL BOY'S IMPRESSIONS OF RURAL STEVENS CREEK ROAD WHEN IT WAS A ROAD, —NOT A "BOULEVARD"! I HAVE NO DESIRE TO LOWER ITS PRESENT STATUS NOR DO I CRAVE "RETURN". YET IF WE COULD ONLY BE GRANTED ONE REQUEST!

IF, BY SOME SUPERNATURAL POWER, WE COULD BRING BACK A GROUP OF LONG DEPARTED WEST SIDE PIONEERS AND LEAD THEM, BLINDFOLDED TO THE CORNER OF WINCHESTER AND STEVENS CREEK BOULEVARDS AT THE HOUR OF 5 P.M.! THEN REMOVE THEIR BLINDFOLDS AND LISTEN. WHAT WOULD THEY SAY?

Memory Lane

STROLL WITH ME DOWN MEMORY LANE. FOR THE NOSTALGIC READER THESE BOYISH RECOLLECTIONS MAY HAVE A FAMILIAR RING. FOR THE YOUNGER GENERATION THEY COULD FURNISH A GLIMPSE OR A SNIFF OF TRUE OLD VALLEY "ATMOSPHERE".

I REMEMBER MOTHER'S ENTHUSIASM SHARED BY HER HOT-KITCHEN-STOVE FRIENDS OVER PURCHASE OF A "FIRELESS COOKER". THEN THERE WAS THE "EGG LAYIN' SEASON", WHEN WE BROUGHT UP THE POTTERY CROCKS AND "WATER GLASS" FROM THE BASEMENT TO PRESERVE THE "HEN FRUIT". I THOUGHT THE RESULTING EMBALMED EGGS WERE FOUL BUT MOTHER MAINTAINED IT WAS JUST MY IMAGINATION. YOU COULDN'T BEAT THOSE FRESH, BROWNISH EGGS FROM RHODE ISLAND REDS OR PLYMOUTH ROCKS. THEY WERE "RICHER" TASTING THAN THOSE "INSIPID" WHITE EGGS FROM WHITE LEGHORNS, OR SO ARGUED THE TWO POULTRY-WISE SCHOOLS OF THOUGHT.

MOTHER HAD A SPECIAL TALENT FOR IMPROVISING FOOD, NECESSITATED BY DOMESTIC EMERGENCIES. WHEN UNEXPECTED MEAL TIME GUESTS HOVE IN SIGHT SHE COULD ESTIMATE THE EXACT AMOUNT REQUIRED AND QUICKLY ADD MORE CARROTS, POTATOES AND ONIONS TO THE SIMMERING STEW. SHE RESLICED THE APPLE PIE OR CAKE TO FIT THE CROWD, PUNCHED OUT THE BISCUIT DOUGH WITH A SMALLER JELLY GLASS OR OPENED ANOTHER MASON JAR OF TOMATOES OR PICCALILLI.

I CAN STILL REMEMBER THE TANTALIZING AROMA OF HER POUNDED ROUND STEAK AND COUNTRY GRAVY! BUTCHER-WAGON STEAK WAS NOT "CORN FED" OR "TENDERIZED". IT WAS *TOUGH*. IT PROBABLY CAME FROM SOME QUITE AGED, NON-PRODUCTIVE FAMILY COW. BUT MOTHER, WITH KITCHEN MAGIC, PRODUCED GOURMET DELIGHTS. SHE WOULD SLAP THE STEAK ON A BREAD-BOARD, BEAT IT SAVAGELY WITH A CARPENTER'S HAMMER AND THEN CUT IT INTO BITE SIZE CHUNKS. SEASONING IT WITH SALT AND PEPPER, THE MEAT WAS FRIED IN DEEP FAT IN A HEAVY BLACK IRON FRYING PAN UNTIL CRISP AND BROWN. LATER THE FLOUR AND SWEET MILK WERE ADDED TO THE DRIPPINGS STIRRING THEM IN WITH NEVER A LUMP. THIS THICK, REAL COUNTRY GRAVY FLOATING WITH DELICIOUS CUBES OF MEAT ON HOME MADE BREAD! FOR THE VEGETARIAN READER I COULD ELABORATE ON HER FRESH MUSTARD GREENS BUT I STILL HATE MUSTARD GREENS.

MOTHER WAS PRESIDENT OF THE WEST SIDE (CUPERTINO) LADIES AID SOCIETY. EACH YEAR THEY HAD A CLOTHING DRIVE FOR THE NEEDY, SPECIALLY CHILDREN. AS A VERY SMALL BOY, I REMEMBER SARAH WINCHESTER (YES, OF THE MYSTERY HOUSE) DRIVING UP TO OUR CHURCH STEPS IN HER CARRIAGE WITH LIVERIED COACHMAN. HE WOULD CARRY A LARGE HAMPER INTO THE CHURCH HALL AND THEN QUICKLY LEAVE.

THIS HAMPER WAS ALWAYS FILLED WITH A HUGE ASSORTMENT OF BRAND NEW CHILDRENS' CLOTHING SPECIALLY PURCHASED FOR THIS DRIVE! MRS. WINCHESTER CONTINUED SUCH ANNUAL DISTRIBUTION OF CLOTHES (TO ALL DENOMINATIONS) DURING ALL HER THIRTY YEARS IN THE VALLEY. THIS WAS ONLY ONE OF HER MANY UNKNOWN CHARITIES. YES, SHE WAS PECULIAR, SHY AND RETIRING, BUT THIS WRITER CLAIMS SHE WAS ONE OF THE OLD VALLEY'S FINEST LADIES.

MANY YEARS LATER THE NAME WINCHESTER CAME INTO MY LIFE AGAIN. MY UNCLE EDWARD, THE FIRST WEST COAST AGENT FOR WINCHESTER REPEATING ARMS CO., WAS ONE OF THE FEW PEOPLE WHO REALLY <u>KNEW</u> THE "MYSTERIOUS" SARAH WINCHESTER AND, AS HER BUSINESS AGENT, ALWAYS ENJOYED ENTRANCE TO HER PALATIAL MONSTROSITY. (AT LEAST IT MUST HAVE BEEN ENJOYABLE SUPPLYING THAT FREE-SPENDING, GENEROUS DOWAGER WITH STEADY INCOME OF $1000 PER DAY!)

IN 1873 THE WINCHESTER COMPANY MADE ONE THOUSAND SUPERLATIVE, PERFECT 44 CALIBER RIFLES EACH WITH *"One of One Thousand"* ENGRAVED ON THE BARREL. THESE FAMOUS GUNS WERE GIVEN TO EXECUTIVES AND NOTABLES. UNCLE EDWARD GAVE DAD ONE OF THESE. WHY, I DON'T KNOW BECAUSE DAD NOW HUNTED NOTHING LARGER THAN A GOPHER. I DON'T BELIEVE HE EVER KNEW THE SIGNIFICANCE OF THE BARREL INSCRIPTION. FOR 50 YEARS IT GATHERED DUST AND RUST.

AROUND 1950, LONG AFTER DAD WAS GONE, JIMMY STEWART STARRED IN A POPULAR MOVIE, "WINCHESTER 73." ABOUT THE SAME TIME THE WINCHESTER COMPANY CONDUCTED A NATIONAL SEARCH TRYING TO DISCOVER HOW MANY OF THOSE *"One of One Thousands"* WERE STILL IN EXISTENCE. IMMEDIATELY ANTIQUE GUN COLLECTORS BEGAN FRANTIC SEARCH FOR THIS PARTICULARLY RARE ITEM.

REMEMBERING THE RIFLE UNCLE ED GAVE TO DAD, AFTER SEEING ABOVE MOVIE, I HURRIED HOME AND FOUND THE OLD WEAPON. WITH TREMBLING HANDS I BRUSHED AND SCRUBBED THE BARREL. THAT LINE OF FINE ENGRAVED SCRIPT SLOWLY CAME TO LIGHT, *One of One Thousand"*! ABOUT THIRTY OF THESE RIFLES WERE FOUND IN THE UNITED STATES. PHOTO AND SERIAL NUMBER OF MINE WAS AUTHENTICATED BY THE WINCHESTER COMPANY.

DURING A FINANCIAL CRISIS IN 1952 AND WITH REGRET SINCE, I SOLD THE RIFLE. THE PRICE, NEARING FOUR FIGURES, SATISFIED MY EMERGENCY AS WELL AS FULFILLING THE CHERISHED DREAM OF A LOCAL COLLECTOR.

DAD'S DRAMATIC PRODUCTION OF HIS SEMI-ANNUAL LETTER TO HIS SISTER "WAY-BACK-EAST" ENTERTAINED MOTHER AND ME THROUGHOUT THE YEARS. IT WAS SUCH A STRUGGLE FOR HIM

AND YET HE NEVER DEVIATED FROM THIS RITUAL.

FIRST HE METHODICALLY ASSEMBLED HIS TOOLS. NEXT HE STIRRED THE INK BOTTLE, SCRAPED THE RUSTY, CORRODED PEN POINT CAREFULLY AND FINALLY TURNED UP THE COAL-OIL LAMP WICK FOR ACTION. HIS BROWS, GATHERED IN SEVERE LINES, SUGGESTED AN ATTITUDE OF DEEP THOUGHT. HIS ARM BEGAN LONG FLOURISHING MOVEMENTS ACCOMPANIED BY AN OCCASIONAL LOW, HEART RENDING GROAN. HE DID WRITE A BEAUTIFUL ELABORATE SCRIPT, A QUITE COMMON ACCOMPLISHMENT IN THOSE DAYS.

YES, THE LETTER INVARIABLY STARTED WITH THE "I TAKE MY PEN IN HAND TO LET YOU KNOW"; JUST WHAT, WE NEVER <u>COULD</u> FIGURE. AND AS YOU MIGHT SUSPECT, BE WE WELL, SICK OR DYING, THE EPISTLE ALWAYS WOUND UP WITH THAT "WE ARE ALL WELL AND HOPE YOU ARE THE SAME".

AN ENTIRE EVENING PRODUCED ONLY ONE PAGE SIGNED WITH A GRAND FINALE FLOURISH AND A LOUD GROAN OF RELIEF. DAD HAD JUST COMPLETED HIS LABORIOUS SEMI-ANNUAL DUTY. NOW HE COULD RELAX AGAIN FOR ANOTHER SIX MONTHS.

RURAL LIFE ALSO HAD ITS DRAMA! HOW WELL I STILL REMEMBER THE DAY THAT DAD DECIDED TO SHOOT PRINCE, OUR HORSE, BECAUSE "HE WAS SO CONFOUNDED OLD AND NO ACCOUNT." MOM AND I HAD SHARED THAT OPINION FOR YEARS BUT WE BALKED AT THIS PRE-MEDITATED BARN YARD MURDER. FOR ONCE DAD PREVAILED.

DAD DUG A GRAVE BIG ENOUGH TO BURY AN ELEPHANT. IT REQUIRED TWO DAYS DIGGING IN OUR STICKY, BLUE ADOBE. I RECALL HE HAD TO USE A PICK.

WITH THE PRELIMINARIES COMPLETED HE GOT OUT THAT RUSTY OLD WINCHESTER 44 RIFLE,

"THE GUN THAT WON THE WEST." THEN HE FOUND SOME VERY ANCIENT AMMUNITION. THE BRASS CARTRIDGES WERE SO OLD THEY WERE COVERED WITH GREEN CORROSION. I DON'T KNOW WHY BUT MOM AND I FOLLOWED TO THE GRAVE.

DAD MADE QUITE A CEREMONY OF THIS TRAGIC AFFAIR. HE EVEN BLINDFOLDED PRINCE WITH HIS RED BANDANA. MOM COVERED HER FACE WITH HER APRON. I TURNED MY HEAD. WE HEARD A CLICK, FOLLOWED BY MORE FAST CLICKS AND THEN SEVERAL SHORT BLASPHEMOUS WORDS WE DIDN'T KNOW DAD HAD IN HIS VOCABULARY! FINALLY WE UNCOVERED OUR EYES. DAD WAS LEADING PRINCE BACK TO THE BARN! PRINCE LIVED FOR MORE YEARS THAN I CARE TO REMEMBER.

WE NEVER OWNED AN AUTOMOBILE OR A TRACTOR. MOM ARGUED THAT AT LEAST "THEY DIDN'T STAND IN THE BARN EATING THEIR HEADS OFF WHEN THEY WEREN'T WORKING." DAD'S REBUTTAL TO THIS ARGUMENT WAS THE POPULAR RETORT OF THE DAY, "NEITHER OF THESE MACHINES WOULD EVER BE PERFECTED." AS A CLINCHER, HE ADDED, "WHEN A HORSE WASN'T WORKING, AT LEAST HE WAS PRODUCING GOOD ORCHARD FERTILIZER, AND LET A TRACTOR OR AUTOMOBILE MATCH THAT"!

TWENTY TO THIRTY INCH RAINFALL IN WINTER WERE NOT UNCOMMON FIFTY YEARS AGO. CREEKS RAN HIGH AND SWIFT BENEATH NARROW WOODEN BRIDGES. WE YOUNGSTERS STOOD ON THE BRIDGE RAILINGS WITH SHARPENED IRON SPEARS, "SPEARIN' WINTER WOOD FOR OUR FOLKS." WE WERE UTTERLY UNAWARE OF DANGER. UNAPPRECIATIVE PARENTS OFTEN "TANNED OUR HIDES" FOR THIS DARING SPORT BUT IT WAS GREAT FUN THANKS TO THAT GUARDIAN ANGEL OF SMALL BOYS! WE SPEARED OLD LUMBER, LOGS, BARRELS, FIVE GALLON OIL CANS, CHICKEN COOPS, ANYTHING SMALLER THAN AN ERRANT BOBBING "BACKHOUSE" OR HOG PEN; IN FACT EVERYTHING BUT WINTER FIREWOOD FOR OUR FOLKS.

AS MY THOUGHTS WANDER BACK I CAN STILL SEE MR. PARRISH, COUNTRY BUTCHER AND HIS TEAM OF HORSES PULLING THE CANVAS COVERED WAGON WITH A HIGHLY APPROPRIATE BULL'S HEAD PAINTED ON THE SIDE. HE CALLED ONCE A WEEK AND WAS OUR ONLY SOURCE OF FRESH MEAT, — WELL, FAIRLY FRESH MEAT. STEPPING DOWN, HE WOULD WALK TO THE BACK END OF THE WAGON AND IN HIS USUAL CORDIAL MANNER TOOK OUR ORDER. THERE WAS SUCH A DRAMATIC IMPORTANCE ATTACHED TO THE MEAT CUTTING. HE SLICED THE ROUND STEAK FROM A HUGE LEG OF BEEF (OR COW), SLAPPED IT ON THE SWINGING SCALES AND MURMURED IN AN APOLOGETIC VOICE, "ABOUT TWO BITS WORTH."

← CAT TAILS

MOTHER, MYSELF, CATS, DOGS AND FLIES WOULD GATHER ROUND HIS PORTABLE MEAT MARKET. OF COURSE HE STOPPED SLICING HALFWAY AND SAWED THROUGH THE ROUND CENTER BONE, ONE WITH RICH MARROW IN THE CENTER, REAL TASTY WHEN FRIED. BOLOGNA AND WEENIES WERE HANDED OUT GRATIS TO SMALL BOYS. SOMETIMES LIVER WAS FREE BUT I HATED LIVER. STILL DO.

THEN THERE WAS THE FISH PEDDLER, OLD JOE, A LITTLE ROTUND MAN WITH FACE AS RUDDY AS A WINTER APPLE. HE DROVE WHAT WE TODAY WOULD TERM A "COMPACT", A SMALL, BOX-LIKE CONVEYANCE DRAWN BY A PONY SIZE, PATHETIC HORSE. HIS TRADEMARK, A BLOATED LEVIATHAN, WAS PAINTED ON SIDES OF HIS WAGON. AS HE APPROACHED OUR HOUSE HE WOULD GIVE OUT WITH A SERIES OF GABRIEL BLASTS ON HIS LONG TIN TRUMPET. ONE TOOT WOULD HAVE BEEN SUFFICIENT. ON HOT SUMMER DAYS THAT BIG CAKE OF ICE MELTED EARLY IN THE MORNING. WE COULD SMELL HIM COMING. SO COULD OUR CATS.

NICKEL BASEBALLS LOOKED, WHEN NEW, EXACTLY SAME AS THE PROFESSIONAL "DOLLAR AND A QUARTER." HOWEVER, ONE GOOD SWAT AND WE HAD AN EGG-SHAPED BALL LEAKING SAWDUST. SO MOST OF OUR BASEBALLS WERE HOMEMADE. BY STARTING WITH A ROUND ROCK THE

SIZE OF A GOLF BALL, YOU WRAPPED AND WRAPPED OLD SALVAGED STRING UNTIL YOU REACHED THE "BIG LEAGUE" SIZE. THIS WAS FINISHED OFF BY COVERING IT WITH A FIVE CENT ROLL OF BICYCLE TAPE. THIS BALL LASTED INDEFINITELY. THEY WERE HEAVY, HARD AS A ROCK AND PRACTICALLY A LETHAL WEAPON.

I RECALL ONE CRUCIAL MOMENT IN A COW PASTURE BALL GAME. SOME NEIGHBOR'S GENTLE OLD BOSSY WAS GRAZING IN SHORT CENTER FIELD. I WAS AT BAT AND CONNECTED SOLIDLY WITH ONE OF THESE HOME MADE BASEBALLS. BOSSY CAUGHT IT SQUARELY BETWEEN THE EYES AND TOOK IT FOR A KNOCKOUT. OTHERWISE I'M SURE THE SWAT WOULD HAVE BEEN GOOD FOR A HOME RUN. INSTEAD I SETTLED FOR A RUN HOME!

I WANTED TO BE A CARTOONIST AS LONG AS I CAN REMEMBER. I LIKED TO DRAW AND WAS INTRIGUED WITH THE ENTICING CORRESPONDENCE COURSES ADVERTISED IN THOSE DAYS. THIS WAS A TYPICAL HEADING:

YOU MAY HAVE TALENT!
DRAW ME AND SEE | CARTOONISTS MAKE $50.00 PER WEEK!

I ENROLLED IN A CORRESPONDENCE CARTOON COURSE AS A TEENAGER. THE "SCHOOL" WAS ACTUALLY ONE MAN, A RETIRED, FAMOUS CARTOONIST. WITH EACH DRAWING LESSON, HE RETURNED IT WITH HIS PERSONAL CRITICISMS. IN ADDITION HE DREW COUNTLESS LITTLE BORDER ILLUSTRATIONS FOR FURTHER GUIDANCE. THE TOTAL COST OF THE COURSE WAS $25 FOR 25 LESSONS. THAT WAS FIFTY-FIVE YEARS AGO. COMPARE THAT TUITION COST WITH TODAYS AND REMEMBER THAT MY TUTOR WAS CONSIDERED TOPS IN HIS PROFESSION.

I SUPPOSE MANY OF US YOUNGSTERS VERGED ON THE DELINQUENT. AS MY MOTHER TERMED IT, WE WERE "JUST PLAIN ORNERY." WE SMOKED DRY PRUNE OR WALNUT LEAF CIGARETTES OR, WITH MANLY PUFFS, VAINLY TRIED TO KEEP A STALK OF DRIED SWEET ANISE AGLOW. (WHAT READER REMEMBERS "CUBEBS"?)

DURING THE PRUNE HARVEST, USUALLY ON DARK NIGHTS, WE BOYS GANGED UP AND THREW ADOBE CLODS AT CHINESE COOLIE PRUNE-PICKER CAMPS. THEY LIVED IN MAKESHIFT SHELTERS OF UPRIGHT, WOODEN DRYING TRAYS. A WELL DIRECTED HIT RESULTED IN A SATISFYING CRASH.

THIS WOULD BE FOLLOWED BY AN EXCITED CHORUS OF MAD CHINESE WORDS SO BITTERLY VITUPERATIVE THEY NEEDED NO TRANSLATION!

ON VALENTINE'S DAY WE BOUGHT THOSE HIDEOUS COLORED ONE SHEET CARTOONS CALLED "PENNY AWFULS" WITH AN INSULTING VERSE. WE INTENDED THEM TO MATCH OUR VICTIM'S PERSONALITY. LOOKING BACK, I REALIZE WHAT A THOUGHTLESS, CRUEL PRANK IT WAS. YOUNGSTERS NOWADAYS HAVE MORE SENSE, I TRUST.

WE SHOT BIRDS, CHICKENS, CATS AND GENTLE FAMILY COWS WITH OUR SLING SHOTS AND DAISY AIR RIFLES. IF WE COULD AFFORD A 22 RIFLE WE SHOT HOLES IN THE REDWOOD STAVED WATER WAGON SUPPLY TANKS SPACED ALONG STEVENS CREEK ROAD. THERE WERE FEW UNBROKEN (OBSOLETE) GREEN GLASS INSULATORS ON THE TELEPHONE POLE CROSS PIECES.

WE HAD NO SUPERVISED "PLANNED ACTIVITIES." AND YET THE LONG SUMMER DAYS WERE ALL TOO SHORT FOR OUR NUMEROUS PROJECTS OR, AS MY MOTHER MIGHT HAVE APTLY EXPRESSED IT, "PURE DEVILMENT"!

WE DUG PIRATE CAVES IN THE CLAY BANKS OF THE DRY CREEKS AND BURIED OUR "TREASURE." IF POOLS REMAINED IN THE CREEKS AFTER THE WINTER RUN OFF, WE SCOOPED UP BARLEY SACKS OF STRANDED SUCKERS AND TROUT, PRESENTING THEM PROUDLY TO OUR DISTRACTED MOTHERS. WE MADE POP-GUNS AND WHISTLES FROM ELDERBERRY OR WILLOW. WE MADE BOLAS, SORT OF A DAVID & GOLIATH SLING WITH A ROCK ATTACHED TO EACH END OF A LONG CORD. IT COULD DELIGHTFULLY COIL AROUND TELEPHONE WIRES, WINDMILL FANS AND COWS' LEGS.

BOYS AND GIRL PARTIES WERE TO BE AVOIDED.

THEY JUST WEREN'T WORTH THE TROUBLE! SUCH AS TAKING AN OFF-SCHEDULE BATH IN MIDDLE OF THE WEEK

AND DRESSING IN STIFF STARCHED CLOTHES! OUR SHORT PANTS NEVER MET THOSE LONG BLACK RIBBED STOCKINGS. JUST IMAGINE US ON A HORSEHAIR SOFA, DISH BALANCED ON OUR KNEES, TRYING TO SPOON HARD ICECREAM AND TUGGING AT THOSE SHORT PANTS TO HIDE OUR CREEPING WHITE DRAWERS! THEN "SURE AS SHOOTIN", ALONG ABOUT THE SHANK OF THE EVENING (9:30 P.M.) SOME ROMANTIC 'BABY DOLL' WOULD WANT US ALL TO PLAY "POST OFFICE"! (QUICK, BOYS, OUT THE BACKDOOR!)

LIZARD LASSOING, ONCE A POPULAR SPORT, WAS ONE OF MY FAVORITE RECREATIONS. LIZARDS ARE STILL ABUNDANT IN THE VALLEY TODAY JUST AS THEY WERE FIFTY YEARS AGO YET THIS EXCITING PASTIME IS ALMOST FORGOTTEN.

FIRST, YOU STRIP THE GREEN (OR DRY) GRAIN KERNELS PODS FROM A LONG STEM OF WILD OATS OR BARLEY. THIS LEAVES ONE TOUGH, TAPERED, HAIR-LIKE STRAND ON THE END OF THE STALK. TIE AN OLD-FASHIONED SLIP-KNOT NOOSE ON THE DELICATE END AND BE SURE IT SLIPS EASILY.

NOW YOU ARE READY FOR ACTION. CAMOUFLAGED BY NATURE, THE LIZARD LIES MOTIONLESS, SUNNING HIMSELF ON SOME FENCE OR ROCK. IN INDIAN FASHION, SNEAK UP ON HIM SLOWLY AND SILENTLY. CAUTIOUSLY AND STILL SLOWLY, REACH OUT AND GENTLY SLIP NOOSE OVER LIZARD'S HEAD FOLLOWED BY A QUICK JERK. YOU WILL HAVE A DELIGHTFULLY WRIGGLING "BLUE BELLY" ON YOUR "POLE." WHILE OUR VALLEY LIZARDS ARE DRAB IN APPEARANCE NATURE HAS COMPENSATED THEM WITH A BRILLIANT BLUE BELLY. YOU WILL NEED TO PRACTICE STEALTH BUT IT CAN BE A SURPRISING "ACCOMPLISHMENT."

OF COURSE WE EVENTUALLY FREED THE OFTEN SLIGHTLY "SHOP WORN" LIZARD. BUT WE HAD BEEN AMPLY REPAID WITH SCREAMS OF LITTLE GIRLS OR CONSTERNATION OF TEACHER IN FINDING A "BLUE BELLY" IN HER DESK!

NOW EMPLOYING ONE OF MY "GAME" GRAND DAUGHTERS AS AN EXCUSE, I STILL INDULGE IN "LIZARD CATCHIN"! SHE REACTS WITH SAME ENTHUSIASM I DID OVER SIXTY YEARS AGO.

TRY IT SOMETIME AND YOU WILL FIND THE YEARS WILL LIFT WITH THE LIZARD!

TIME PLAYS TRICKS WITH AN OLDSTER'S MEMORIES. WE CAN FORGET WHAT WE SAID OR DID A WEEK AGO! WE CAN STUMBLE THROUGH THE TWENTY THIRD PSALM. WE MUFF A WORD IN ALLEGIANCE TO OUR FLAG. WE OFTEN FUMBLE A LINE OF THE STAR SPANGLED BANNER. AND YET ONE OF US MIGHT REMEMBER EVERY WORD OF THAT OVERWORKED LITTLE POEM WE RECITED IN THE SECOND GRADE OVER SIXTY YEARS AGO. REMEMBER WHEN.....? LAST DAY OF SCHOOL, DOYLE SCHOOL, NOW BURIED UNDER AN EIGHT LANE FREEWAY.

BEFORE PROUD BUT NERVOUS PARENTS, FIDGETY, SWEATY, BUG-EYED, WE, (AND HOW MANY OTHERS?) BLURTED THIS OUT:

"YOU'D SCARCE EXPECT ONE OF MY AGE
TO SPEAK IN PUBLIC ON THE STAGE,
BUT IF I CHANCE TO FALL BELOW
DEMOSTHENES OR CICERO, (WE ALWAYS MESSED THIS LINE)
DON'T VIEW ME WITH A CRITIC'S EYE,
BUT PASS MY IMPERFECTIONS BY,
LARGE STREAMS FROM LITTLE FOUNTAINS FLOW,
TALL OAKS FROM LITTLE ACORNS GROW,
AND THOUGH I AM NOW SMALL AND YOUNG,
YET ALL GREAT LEARNED MEN, — LIKE ME,
ONCE LEARNED TO READ THEIR A, B, C's."

AND SO CAN END ONE OF OUR SHORT EXCURSIONS DOWN MEMORY LANE. FORTUNATE ARE WE WHO CAN RETRACE OUR CHILDHOOD STEPS WITH PLEASURE AND YET RETURN TO ENJOY THE AMAZING SURPRISES OF THIS PRESENT DAY.

TODAY'S GENERATION MAY WONDER WHAT AMUSE-MENTS ENTERTAINED THE OLD VALLEY ADULTS AND YOUNGSTERS. WE HAD NO RADIO, TELEVISION, MOTION PICTURES OR DRIVE-INS. AUTOMOBILES WERE FEW AND ONLY THE ORCHARDIST WITH A BUMPER CROP OF PRUNES AND A SPIRIT OF ADVENTURE WOULD SPORT A REO, FRANKLIN, MOON, DORT, OR HUPMOBILE. ONLY BANKERS' SONS AND OUR RICH SAN FRANCISCO RELATIVES WERE SEEN IN THOMAS FLYERS, POPE-TOLEDOS, PACKARDS, STEVENS-DURYEAS, WINTONS, MARMONS OR PIERCE ARROWS.

DESPITE THIS SO CALLED LACK OF LUXURIES WE FOUND SATISFYING ENTERTAINMENT AND AMUSEMENTS. PERHAPS WE HAD A GOOD TIME BECAUSE WE KNEW NOTHING BETTER. RECREATION APPRECIATION IS MEASURED ON A BASIS OF COMPARISON. OUR HOMELY PURSUIT OF PLEASURE COULD NOT COMPARE WITH THE MODERN DAY'S PASTIMES.

JUST AS TODAY OUR CHILDREN FEEL SUPERIOR WITH THEIR ADVANTAGES, WE TOO, HAD A FEELING OF SUPERIOR-ITY OVER OUR PRECEEDING GENERATION'S IDEA OF RECRE-ATION. TO US THE ANTIQUATED DIVERSIONS OF OUR PARENTS WERE A BORE AS THEY TOLD, RETOLD AND RELIVED THE TAFFY-PULLS, CHURCH-SUPPER-BOX LUNCHES, HAY-RIDES, MAY-POLES AND SHIVAREES. THEY COULDN'T UNDERSTAND OUR LAGGING INTEREST IN CROKINOLE, SPIN-THE-PLATTER, PARCHEESI, SHINNY, BEAN-BAG, OLD MAID, AUTHORS, PIT OR FLINCH. IF WE MUST HAVE EXCITEMENT, – GO THE LIMIT, – PLAY POST OFFICE.

ONE AMUSEMENT PROBLEM, SPECIALLY FOR MOTHERS, WAS A SMALL COUNTRY BOY, ISOLATED FROM PLAYMATES AND CONFINED INDOORS ON A RAINY DAY. ONE QUESTION THAT REMAINS UNCHANGED OVER THE YEARS, "WHAT SHALL I DO NOW, MA?" FORTUNATELY MY MOTHER NEVER RAN OUT OF SUGGESTIONS. HERE ARE A FEW ECHOES:

"WHY DON'T YOU PLAY WITH YOUR BUTTON, BIRD EGG, STAMPS OR CIGAR-BAND COLLECTIONS?..... GO OUT IN

WOODSHED AND BUILD YOURSELF A PAIR OF STILTS...... MAKE A SLING SHOT......THIS IS JUST DANDY WEATHER TO MAKE CHRISTMAS PRESENTS! AUNT JANE LOVED THAT PADDED COAT-HANGER STUFFED WITH DRIED LAVENDER YOU AND I MADE LAST YEAR.....BOOT-JACKS ARE EASY TO MAKE AND GRANDPA SPLIT HIS ......READ SOME OF YOUR BOOKS AGAIN, BLACK BEAUTY, LITTLE LORD FAUNTLEROY OR THE THREE LITTLE PEPPERS.......I DON'T CARE! GO IN THE PARLOR AND LOOK AT THE PICTURES IN PILGRIM'S PROGRESS OR EVEN DANTE'S INFERNO!

"PUT ON YOUR FATHER'S IRRIGATING BOOTS AND MY SHAWL AND GO OUT IN THE BARN. SEE IF THAT RHODE ISLAND RED'S EGGS ARE STARTING TO HATCH. IF ANY OF THE CHICKS LOOK PUNY, BRING THEM IN AND I'LL DRY THEM OFF UNDER THE STOVE....BY THE TIME YOU'RE BACK I'LL HAVE THE SPONGE CAKE IN THE OVEN AND YOU CAN LICK THE BOWL AND SPOON.....AND DON'T TROMP WHEN YOU COME IN! THAT CAKE MIGHT FALL AND I'VE GOT A BATCH OF BREAD RISIN' ON BACK OF THE STOVE."

"HAVE YOU COUNTED YOUR SUNDAY SCHOOL CARDS LATELY? MAYBE YOU HAVE ENOUGH FOR A BIBLE?" OR MY MOTHER WOULD WARM THE WHOLE HOUSE WITH HER MELODIOUS VOICE, "COUNT YOUR MANY BLESSINGS, NAME THEM ONE BY ONE," OR "JESUS LOVES ME, THAT I KNOW, BECAUSE THE BIBLE TELLS ME SO."

OF ALL THE GOOD PEOPLE IN THE WORLD, WHY, AND SO OFTEN, MUST MOTHERS BE APPRECIATED ALWAYS TOO LITTLE AND FOREVER TOO LATE?

WE LIVED IN A MOST MODEST "BOARD AND BATTEN" HOUSE ON MILLER AVENUE. ABOUT 1900 MY FATHER PURCHASED TEN ACRES OF BARE LAND FROM THE 240 ACRE TANTAU RANCH. THE PRICE WAS $75 AN ACRE, TODAY WORTH 100 TIMES THAT. NOW SPRAWLING SUB-DIVISIONS SPREAD OVER THIS AREA AND A MILLION DOLLAR SCHOOL NOW COVERS OUR TEN ACRES.

AS INDICATED I WAS AN ONLY CHILD. I FORAGED

FOR MY PLAYMATES AS HOMES IN THIS SECTION WERE FROM A QUARTER TO A HALF MILE APART. MY BEST SOURCES WERE THE LARGE PORTUGUESE FAMILY "NEXT DOOR" AND THE COYKENDALL BOYS, RACHE AND KENNETH.

MY FAVORITE COMPANIONS WERE RACHE AND KENNETH WHO LIVED ON STEVENS CREEK ROAD. THEIR FATHER WAS A WEALTHY ORCHARDIST WHO OWNED AUTOMOBILES, YACHTS, CATTLE RANCHES AND ALWAYS THE LATEST MODEL AUTO. ALTHOUGH THEIR ECONOMIC STATUS WAS IN DIRECT CONTRAST TO OUR MODEST ONE, THE TWO BOYS AND I WERE INSEPARABLE PLAYMATES. WE HAD ONE MAGNETIC BOND, OUR CONSTANT DESIRE TO INVENT OR IMPROVISE ALL OF OUR ORIGINAL FORMS OF RECREATION.

WHILE MANY OF OUR INVENTIONS NEVER PROGRESSED BEYOND THE "ANTICIPATION" STAGE, WE DID HAVE ONE PROJECT WITH RATHER A SENSATIONAL, BOYISH ENDING. WE DECIDED TO BUILD A GIANT EIGHT FOOT KITE. TO INSURE SUCCESS, WE PATTERNED IT AFTER THAT OLD DEPENDABLE THREE STICK, SIX SIDED MODEL, USING LATH FOR FRAME AND LIGHT, OILED CANVAS FOR COVERING INSTEAD OF PAPER. WE WOUND YARDS AND YARDS OF SALVAGED, HAY-BALER, HEMP ROPE ON A HOMEMADE CRANK-REEL, AS SUBSTITUTE FOR THE USUAL KITE STRING.

WE CHOSE COYKENDALL'S DRY-YARD AS OUR LAUNCHING BASE. BEFORE THE DAYS OF DEHYDRATERS, ALL ORCHARDISTS HAD DRY YARDS FOR PROCESSING FRUIT. TRAYS OF LYE-DIPPED PRUNES WERE SPREAD ON THE GROUND TO ABSORB THEIR SUN-DRIED WRINKLES AND THEIR "SUNSWEET" QUALITIES. COYKENDALL'S HAD THREE ACRES OF DRY YARD WITH A STEEL TRACK FOR THE HAND PUSHED FLAT CARS. WE CHOSE THIS SITE BECAUSE WE SCENTED POSSIBILITIES. THE YARD HAD A LONG TRACK

AND ONE OF THESE FLAT CARS CARS WOULD EASILY ACCOMODATE THREE BOYS. THEN TOO, WE HAD A CAPTIVE AUDIENCE,— THE NEARBY PRUNE PICKERS AND DRY-YARD WORKERS. IN EVERY BOY THERE IS AN ABIDING DESIRE TO SHOW OFF. HERE LAY OUR OPPORTUNITY!

WE HAD UNDER-ESTIMATED THE PULLING POWER OF AN EIGHT FOOT KITE AND OVER-ESTIMATED THE STRENGTH OF THREE SMALL BOYS. WITH SKIDDING HEELS WE, (AND THE WINDLESS) WERE STARTING TO DRAG DOWN THE FIELD. NOW FLYING HIGH, THE KITE HAD ALL THE PULLING POWER OF A SPIRITED TWO-HORSE TEAM. NOW OR NEVER! WE SOMEHOW HOOKED THE ROPE TO THE LITTLE CAR AND LEAPED ON. JUST WHY WE FAILED TO PROVIDE SOME SORT OF BRAKE, OR REASON THAT ALL TRACKS MUST END, REMAINS UNANSWERED. WE HAD BECOME SO ACCUSTOMED TO FAILURE, WE NEVER EXPECTED THE UNUSUAL TO HAPPEN. IT DID. THE WIND SUDDENLY INCREASED AND WITH IT, OUR SPEED. WHILE WE THREE VOYAGEURS CLUNG TO EACH OTHER IN DELICIOUS EXCITEMENT, OUR LITTLE CAR RAISED ITS FRONT WHEELS COMPLETELY OFF THE STEEL TRACK AND AT A 30 DEGREE ANGLE WE SCREECHED DOWN THE YARD 40 MILES AN HOUR! (AS WE RETELL THIS STORY OVER THE PASSING YEARS, OUR SPEED INCREASES. QUIEN SABE? WITH LONGEVITY FAVORING WRITER, IT MAY SOME DAY STRETCH TO 70 MILES AN HOUR!)

"CUT THE KITE LOOSE, RACHE," I YELLED. BUT RACHE WAS IN NO POSITION TO EITHER FIND OR OPEN A KNIFE! SO TOO LATE! THE TRACK WAS ABOUT TWO BLOCKS LONG WITH A STURDY STACK OF TRAYS AS A TERMINAL. THE WIND INCREASED THE CAR'S ANGLE. WE HAD NO CHOICE

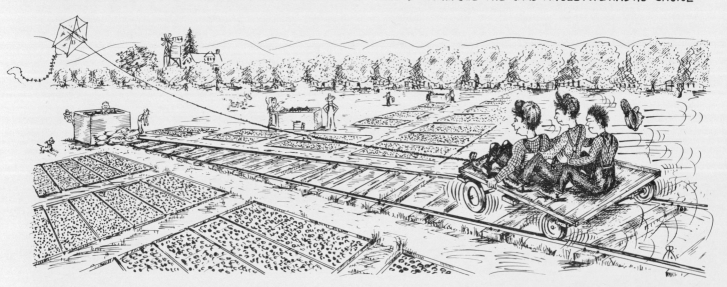

BUT LEAP OFF CAR ONTO THE TRAYS OF FRESH DIPPED PRUNES. WE SKIDDED TO A BOTTOM SPLINTERED STOP IN THE JUICY FRUIT WHILE THE KITE CONTINUED ITS MERRY COURSE. FINALLY IT LOOPED THE LOOP INTO AN OAK TREE SHADING THE CORRAL OF THE PORTUGUESE FAMILY'S BARNYARD. THE OAK TREE IS STILL STANDING (I HOPE) NOW OVERLOOKING THE CUPERTINO HIGH SCHOOL FOOTBALL FIELD.

ONE OF MY PORTUGUESE PALS TOLD US THEIR HORSE WAS SO FRIGHTENED HE BROKE DOWN THE CORRAL FENCE AND THEIR COW NOT ONLY WAS TERRIFIED, BUT "WENT DRY" AND WAS NEVER HER GENTLE SELF AGAIN.

MEANWHILE, WE PICKED THE SQUASHED PRUNES OUT OF OUR HAIR AND ELSEWHERE! LATER, MOTHERS WOULD REMOVE THE REDWOOD TRAY SPLINTERS FROM OUR POSTERIORS.

BUT WE HAD BEEN SENSATIONAL! REAL STARS! WE HAD ATTRACTED ATTENTION AND DISRUPTED ALL WORK WITHIN A MILE RADIUS. EVEN HORSE AND BUGGY TRAFFIC ON STEVENS CREEK ROAD HAD HALTED AND RURAL MAIL DELIVERY WAS DELAYED THIRTY MINUTES.

THIS DRAMATIC TRIUMPH SPURRED US TO SEEK LOFTIER FIELDS OF ACHIEVEMENT. A SHORT TIME BEFORE IN SANTA CLARA, A FEW MILES AWAY, MALONEY-MONTGOMERY HAD MADE THE WORLD'S PIONEER GUIDED GLIDER FLIGHT. THIS EVENT INSPIRED US TO ENTER THE AVIATION FIELD.

THE COYKENDALLS HAD AN IMMENSE HAY BARN WITH A GENTLE SLANTING SHAKE ROOF, JUST THE THING FOR A LAUNCHING FIELD. WE HURRIEDLY MADE GLIDER WINGS, USING LIGHT TRAY LUMBER WITH HANDY OLD HARNESS FOR WING FITTINGS AND BODY ATTACHMENT. AS WAS USUAL, WE SPENT AMAZINGLY LITTLE TIME WITH OUR "BLUE PRINTS AND CALCULATIONS," RELYING ON STRENGTH AND WEIGHT TO EASE THE STRESS AND STRAIN BUT IGNORING ALL NEEDS FOR LIFTING BUOYANCY. STILL ENVELOPED IN THE EXHILARATION OF OUR FORMER SUCCESS, WE COULD HARDLY WAIT TO BE "AIRBORNE". THE WINGS RECEIVED A HEAVY COAT OF PAINT. AFTER ALL, MIGHT WE NOT ENCOUNTER FOG OR RAIN AT HIGH ALTITUDES? THE WINGS COULD BE STRAPPED TO (MY) BACK OR ARMS, NOT TOO RIGIDLY OF COURSE; BECAUSE AFTER I HAD GAINED GREAT ALTITUDE, MIGHT I NOT DECIDE TO FLAP THEM;—JUST ENOUGH TO MAINTAIN FLIGHT BETWEEN THOSE LONG, SOARING INTERVALS?

AS MARK TWAIN WOULD SAY, "LET US GENTLY DRAW THE CURTAIN." ANTICIPATION CAN EXCEED REALIZATION.

EVERY BARNYARD HAD ACCOMPANING BARNYARD

FERTILIZER. COYKENDALLS HAD A LARGE STABLE AND THE WELL AGED ACCUMULATION ALMOST TOUCHED THE BARN EAVES. AND SO THIS MONUMENTAL MANURE PILE BECAME OUR IMMEDIATE EMERGENCY LANDING FIELD. ANYWAY, WE HAD A SAFE, SOFT, PUNGENT LET-DOWN!

OUR FIASCO CANCELLED OUT THE STATURE ATTAINED THROUGH THE KITE EPISODE. OUR FICKLE AUDIENCE LOST INTEREST IN US. THIS CAN BE DISHEARTENING TO SMALL BOYS SO WE PLAYED IT SAFE AND RETURNED TO OUR ONE RELIABLE SOURCE OF APPRECIATION, GRANDMA MCKEE, RACHE AND KEN'S GRANDMOTHER.

GRANDMA MCKEE WAS QUITE AGED AND LOOKED LIKE A TINY REPRODUCTION OF WHISTLER'S MOTHER SITTING ON THE BACK PORCH. WE FELT LIFE MUST BE DREARY AND DULL WITH SUCH A LIMITED VIEW. SO WE PERFORMED FOR HER ALMOST EVERY DAY. OUR DEAR, FRAIL FRIEND, SO INTERESTED IN OUR ACTIVITIES, WAS ALWAYS READY TO APPLAUD, LAUGH AT OUR ANTICS AND MAKE SUGGESTIONS FOR OTHER DRAMATIC PRODUCTIONS.

HER FAVORITE PLAY WAS THE "BATTLE OF BULL RUN" WHICH HAD A FLEXIBLE SCRIPT. WITH LITTLE THEME OR COSTUME CHANGE WE COULD SWITCH TO "CUSTER'S LAST STAND." OUR ARMY EXTRAS WERE ALL MEXICAN PRUNE PICKERS' CHILDREN. SO GRANDMA SMARTLY ADVISED WE MAKE IT "NATIONALITY AUTHENTIC" AND WITH A FORT OF PRUNE BOXES, ADD "FALL OF THE ALAMO" TO OUR REPERTOIRE.

THE "BATTLE OF BULL RUN" WAS A DRAMATIC SPECTACLE. SOMEHOW, RACHE HAD ACQUIRED A '44 REVOLVER WITH A SUPPLY OF BLANK CARTRIDGES. HE SAWED OFF THE LONG BARREL SO THAT IT MADE A TERRIFIC REPORT. NEXT WE MADE A CANNON BY MOUNTING A LENGTH OF SEWER PIPE ON TWO OLD WAGON WHEELS. WITH LITTLE PERSUASION WE ENLISTED OUR ARMY OF MEXICAN PRUNE-PICKERS' KIDS TO PLAY THE PART OF CHARGING REBELS. RACHE, KEN AND I WERE SOLE SURVIVORS OF A DECIMATED UNION ARTILLERY BRIGADE. WE WERE MAKING OUR LAST STAND BEFORE OVERWHELMING ODDS. STRANGELY, WE WERE ALL WOUNDED IN THE SAME SPOT; OUR BROWS BOUND WITH CATSUP-STAINED BANDAGES.

LED BY GALLANT OFFICERS MOUNTED ON BROOMSTICKS, THE HORDES OF SCREAMING, BAREFOOT CONFEDERATES WOULD CHARGE US, THROWING PRUNES OR OVER RIPE PEACH GRENADES. AS THE SAVAGE ENEMY ALMOST REACHED THE "CANNON'S MOUTH", RACHE WOULD THRUST THE '44 UP INTO THE SEWER PIPE AND PULLED THE TRIGGER SIX TIMES. THE ILLUSION WAS PERFECT,—THE NOISE, WAR-LIKE PERFECT-ION. TO COMPLETE THE PICTURE WE THREW HANDFULS OF FLOUR IN THE AIR FOR CANNON SMOKE. MORE CATSUP WAS DISTRIBUTED AMONGST THE MEXICAN ARMY BEFORE THEY FELL DEAD AT THE PROPER MOMENT. BEING MORTALLY WOUNDED EARLIER IN THE BATTLE, WE THREE LEADING ACTORS FINALLY SUCCUMBED WITH PROLONGED CONVULSIONS DIRECTLY BEFORE OUR AUDIENCE OF ONE, GRANDMA McKEE.

CHILDISH AUDIENCE, CHILDISH ACTORS, CHILDISH MEMORIES BUT OH, WHAT FUN, ALMOST FORGOTTEN, GENUINE FUN!

ATTENDING THEATER WAS A BOYHOOD HIGHLIGHT. THE JOSE, NOW SAN JOSE'S OLDEST OPERATING THEATER, WAS OUR SATURDAY MATINEE FAVORITE. HERE FOR "10-20-30¢", WE COULD SEE ED REDMOND'S PLAYERS. AS THE PLAY UNFOLDED I LIVED EVER EMOTION

I SAW. I SUFFERED, LOVED, HATED, DESPAIRED, BLINKED TEARS OR LAUGHED UNTIL THE FINAL CURTAIN. POPULAR PLAYS MIGHT INCLUDE, "SQUAW MAN", "BREWSTER'S MILLIONS", "GIRL OF THE GOLDEN WEST", "ALIAS JIMMY VALENTINE" AND "THE LITTLE MINISTER". PLAYS CHANGED EACH WEEK AND ACTORS WORKED HARD MEMORIZING TWO HOUR DIALOGUES. TO TOP THIS, SOME PLAYED TWO OR THREE CHARACTERS WITH QUICK COSTUME, BEARD OR WIG CHANGES. BELOW US, THE BOBBING HEAD OF THE PROMPTER IN HIS STAGE PIT JUST BEYOND OUR GENIAL, POPULAR ORCHESTRA LEADER, LEO SULLIVAN, THE LAWRENCE WELK OF THAT ERA.

THE VICTORY THEATER, PATRONIZED BY SAN JOSE'S ELITE, BROUGHT THE GREATEST GALAXY OF STARS THE TOWN HAD EVER SEEN. INCLUDED WERE ENRICO CARUSO, SARAH BERNHARD, MAUDE ADAMS, BILLIE BURKE, BARRYMORES, DAVID WARFIELD, GEORGE M. COHAN, FAVERSHAM AND THE FINEST OPERA COMPANIES. I THRILLED TO JOHN PHILIP SOUSA'S BAND, PRIMROSE MINSTRELS AND THE FAMOUS FEMALE IMPERSONATOR, JULIAN ELTINGE. THE VICTORY STAGE WAS ONE OF FEW IN THE WEST LARGE ENOUGH TO PRESENT SUCH SPECTACLES AS BEN HUR AND ITS CHARIOT RACE. (BY STRANGE COINCIDENCE, WHILE ABOVE WAS IN WRITING, THIS FIRE-BUFF AUTHOR "ANSWERED AN ALARM" TO WATCH OUR ENTERTAINMENT LANDMARK CONSUMED BY FIRE.)

LET US NOT OVERLOOK OUR "HIGH SOCIETY", THAT GROUP OF DISTINGUISHED MAIDEN LADIES, THE MORRISON SISTERS, WHO ALWAYS SAT IN THE SAME BOX. IT WAS THEIRS FOR LIFE BY DECREE OF THE VICTORY'S BUILDER, SENATOR PHELAN. ALL I COULD AFFORD WAS A 10¢ SEAT IN THE TINY SECOND BALCONY. STRAINING MY EYES TO SEE THE FAR DISTANT ACTION, HOW I WISHED I HAD A PAIR OF THOSE GOLD BOUND, ABALONE SHELL ENCRUSTED, PEARL HANDLE OPERA GLASSES. I NEEDED THEM SO MUCH MORE THAN THE MORRISON SISTERS!

AFTER THE SHOW WE WALKED ACROSS THE STREET TO SHORTY HIND'S FOR A MILK SHAKE. SHORTY HAD THE VERY LATEST EQUIPMENT. HE MIXED MILK AND FLAVORING (NO ICE-CREAM) WITH ICE THAT HE HAND-PLANED OFF A BIG CAKE UNDER THE COUNTER. THEN HE FASTENED THE CONTAINER INTO A BIG WHEEL. WHEN HAND CRANKED IT REVOLVED, VIOLENTLY AGITATING THE MIXTURE. THE RESULTING PRODUCT NEITHER LOOKED OR TASTED LIKE TODAY'S FORTY CENT, KNIFE-AND-FORK THICK MILK SHAKES. BUT CONSIDERING SHORTY'S PRICE OF FIVE CENTS, I GUESS WE GOT OUR MONEY'S WORTH.

IF OUR FOLKS WERE NOT WITH US, WE MIGHT "SNEAK A LOOK" IN THE LOUVRE, A "HIGH-TONED" SALOON CONNECTED WITH THE VICTORY AND PATRONIZED BY OUR HARD-HAT, BLUE-SERGE, PATENT LEATHER SET. ALL WE BOYS SOUGHT WAS A FURTIVE LOOK AT THOSE LIFE SIZE PAINTINGS BY OUR CELEBRATED VALLEY ARTIST, A.D.M. COOPER. HIS ALLEGORICAL SUBJECTS WOULD QUITE OFTEN INCLUDE EXTREMELY WELL DEVELOPED FEMALES, EVIDENTLY ENJOYING SOME TROPICAL CLIMATE REQUIRING LITTLE OR NO CLOTHING. MY FAVORITE WAS A LIFE SIZE, TORTURED MAIDEN TIED TO A WILD BUFFALO, RACING AHEAD OF A PRAIRIE FIRE. HER SCANT CLOTHING WAS MOST ARTISTICALLY DISARRANGED. TODAY, COOPER'S SCENIC AND EARLY WESTERN SUBJECTS ARE HIGHLY PRICED COLLECTORS ITEMS.

ONCE A LIVING EXAMPLE OF AMERICANA, THIS WAS THE ERA OF BIG TOP OUTDOOR CIRCUSES, BARNUM & BAILEY, SELLS-FLOTO AND THE RINGLING BROTHERS. LITTLE IS LEFT TO REMIND US OF THESE HAPPY SEASONAL EVENTS.

GONE ARE THE OLD VALLEY BARNS, PLASTERED WITH EXCITINGLY EXAGGERATED CIRCUS POSTERS. WINTER RAINS MAY HAVE LEFT THEM TORN AND JADED BUT TO A SMALL BOY, THEIR STILL GAY, TATTERED REMNANTS WERE REMINDERS OF PAST JOY AND PROMISE OF RETURN.

WE HAD OUR SHARE OF CIRCUS BUFFS UP AT 3 A.M. TO WATCH THE CIRCUS TRAIN UNLOAD AT SOUTH FIRST STREET. MANY A YOUNGSTER DREAMED OF JOINING AND WORKING HIS WAY UP FROM ELEPHANT WATER-BOY TO THAT MAN ON THE FLYING TRAPEZE. WHAT THRILLING ASPIRATION FOR A SMALL BOY DESTINED TO A SEEMINGLY ENDLESS CAREER OF PRUNE PICKING!

GONE IS THE CIRCUS STREET PARADE PRECEEDING THE PERFORMANCE; FREE TO ALL, INCLUDING MANY A WISTFUL FINANCIALLY EMBARRASSED YOUNG ONLOOKER. WE ALL STARED WIDE EYED AT THESE COLORFUL EXTRAVAGANZAS LED BY THE MAESTRO AND HIS GAUDY BAND WAGON FILLED WITH TENT PERFORMERS "DOUBLING IN BRASS". FOLLOWING CAME A CAVALCADE OF ANIMAL WAGONS, DAZZLING QUEENS IN DARING GARB, "REAL" CHARIOTS, CALLIOPE, CLOWNS WITH THEIR SIDE SPLITTING ANTICS AND FINALLY THAT LONG STRING OF SWAYING ELEPHANTS, EACH HOLDING THE PRE-CEEDING ONE'S TAIL BY HIS TRUNK. CIRCUSES APPARENTLY TRIED TO OUTDO THEIR COMPETITORS WITH NUMBER AND SIZES OF ELEPHANTS DISPLAYED IN PARADES. I RECALL ONE YEAR WHEN FOUR CIRCUSES CAME TO SAN JOSE, ALL OVERSTOCKED WITH ELEPHANTS. WHO REMEMBERS OUR ONE AND ONLY STREET-SWEEPER, CART, BROOM AND FRESH ROSE BUD STUCK IN HIS STRAW HAT? THAT WAS THE YEAR HE QUIT!

WE HAVE LOST SOMETHING RICH AND SATISFYING BY REPLACING THE OLD TIME CIRCUS WITH AUDITORIUM PRODUCTIONS. GONE ARE THOSE WOODEN TUBS FILLED WITH WEAK PINK LEMONADE WITH A FEW FLOATING LEMON RINDS AND A LIGHT COATING OF SAW DUST. GONE, THE BALLYHOOED SIDE SHOWS WHOSE CURIOUS WONDERS NEVER SEEMED TO MATCH THE POSTERS OR FULFILL THE "BARKER'S" PROMISES. EVEN THAT TANTALIZING "CIRCUS SMELL" IS GONE. IT WAS SUCH A PLEASANTLY UNPLEASANT ODOR, SO HAPPILY ENDURED.

I QUIT!

In the early 1900's San Jose belonged to a State League and played their games at Luna Park, almost forgotten recreation center on the end of 17th. Street. I remember Elmer Stricklett, a pitcher, who has been credited with introducing the spit-ball, now banned. Pitchers still sneak this elusive curve across, at least often enough to keep memories of Elmer's wet production alive.

There was Sodality Park on San Carlos Street at the S.P. overpass. Here in much later years, the immortal Babe Ruth, on tour, lofted ball after ball over the distant fence, the one with the Sloan's Liniment and Old Joe's Steam Beer sign.

Hal Chase, the greatest first baseman of all time, was our neighbor, and even his questionable part in the Black Sox scandal failed to dim my boyish admiration. Doomed then to oblivion of sand lot leagues, I watched him simultaneously play two infield positions. Never has there been a player to match Hal Chase and his ball-handling dexterity.

My father took me to the ball games although he had not the slightest idea what baseball was all about. Before moving West, he was a dawn-to-dark, hard working Kansas farmer in some remote district. In sharp contrast, here he was to see crowds of men who could all have been working instead of heartily enjoying themselves! To him, this was incredible! I think he was fascinated by all these idle people. He liked the peanuts and popcorn and spent most of the time simply watching the crowd. He left each game completely confused and still believing a team meant two horses, a foul had feathers and a baseball coach required four wheels.

Medicine shows attracted many a small boy.

Before the Pure Food and Drug Act, any so-called "Doctor" or "Professor" could peddle his bottles of colored water flavored with alcohol, quinine or a dash of red pepper, "cure-all" remedies for most minor ailments and far too many major ones.

There were usually two kinds of Medicine Shows, Wild West or Indian, with a scant crew dressed to fit the theme. Their tent and platform was set upon a vacant lot and an audience attracted by a dancer, sword-swallower, magician or ventriloquist. Then the "Healer" would dramatically extoll the curative power of his mysterious mixtures. Always planted in his audience was a "shill" who started the buying. My favorite "doctor" performed on a West Santa Clara vacant lot. He was such a glib, charming talker, even when he was so drunk he had to sit in a chair while delivering his lecture. One of his exhibits, or trophies, greatly enthralled me;— a collection of pickled tape-worms.

I remember two "Bigtime" medicine men, "The Great Ferdon" and "Kamama". Kamama claimed to be genuine three quarter Indian and fortunate heir to many secret tribal remedies, all with miraculous healing power. Such fakers dressed in outlandish costumes, hired open carriages and were driven up and down the main streets, standing, bowing, freely throwing kisses to the ladies and handfuls of small coins to the "poor children". Ah, but many a well known old timer had his fingers stepped on, in fact I could name a couple still bearing scars.

Agricultural Park, now the Hanchett Park district furnished entertainment for the lovers of speed. Usually financially embarrassed, I watched many of the races through a king-size knothole in a high board fence surrounding the track. By taking turns my pal and I glimpsed Barney Oldfield equal the

EXISTING WORLD'S RECORD OF 60 MILES AN HOUR! IMMEDIATELY AFTER ATTAINING THIS UNBELIEVABLE SPEED THE AUTO APPEARED TO BLOW UP IN A CLOUD OF WHITE SMOKE. BUT, AS WAS CUSTOMARY, A WAITING TEAM OF PERCHERONS OR CLYDESDALES, (WHAT MATTER?) HAULED THE SMOKING BEHEMOTH OFF THE TRACK. BARNEY, PUFFING HIS TRADITIONAL CIGAR, STRODE JAUNTILY AWAY, LIFTING HIS GOGGLES AND BOWING MOST GRACIOUSLY TO THE CHEERING CROWD. I DON'T KNOW WHAT HAPPENED NEXT; IT WAS MY PAL'S TURN AT THE KNOT HOLE.

ALSO IN AGRICULTURAL PARK WE SAW BUFFALO BILL'S WILD WEST SHOW. BUFFALO BILL, A MAGNIFICENT FIGURE WITH WHITE BEARD, LONG HAIR, BUCKSKIN COSTUME, RIDING A BEAUTIFUL WHITE HORSE, GAVE AN OUTSTANDING PERFORMANCE COMPLETE WITH ACTUAL FAMOUS WESTERN CHARACTERS AND REAL INDIANS. ON HORSEBACK HE WAS AN EXCELLENT SHOT, BREAKING GLASS BALLS THROWN IN THE AIR EVEN IF A FEW CYNICS MAINTAIN HE RESORTED TO BIRD SHOT LOADS. AS A MATTER OF FACT, WILLIAM CODY WAS AN OBSCURE BUFFALO MEAT HUNTER FOR THE U.S. ARMY. NED BUNTLINE, ORIGINATOR OF THE DIME NOVEL, RESCUED HIM FROM OBLIVION AND WITH ONLY PEN AND PUBLICITY, MADE HIM AN HEROIC FIGURE OF THE OLD WEST.

PER CAPITA, OUR SANTA CLARA VALLEY WAS PROVIDED AMPLY WITH PUBLIC PARKS AND RECREATION AREAS. LAND WAS CHEAP AND THIS ADVANTAGE WAS REALIZED. THESE OUTDOOR BEAUTY SPOTS WERE UNCROWDED, UNCOMMERCIALIZED, EASILY ACCESSIBLE VIA EITHER STEAM OR ELECTRIC RAILWAYS FOR MODEST 5 OR 10¢ CARFARES. POPULAR PARKS WERE ALUM ROCK, CONGRESS SPRINGS. SODALITY, LUNA, SCHEUTZEN AND THE SPARSELY INHABITED SARATOGA-STEVENS CREEK, LOS GATOS AREAS. RHEUMATISM SUFFERERS COULD ALSO FILL THEIR DEMIJOHNS AT AZULE, SODA ROCK OR GILROY HOT SPRINGS.

WE ALSO ENJOYED THE SARATOGA ANNUAL BLOSSOM FESTIVAL, USUALLY HELD IN MARCH WHEN THOUSANDS OF ACRES OF BLOSSOMING PRUNE TREES BLANKETED THE VALLEY LIKE GIANT WHITE DRIFTS OF POPCORN. A MINISTER, REV. EDWIN SIDNEY WILLIAMS, NICKNAMED

"SUNSHINE", ORIGINATED THIS DEFUNCT FESTIVAL. THE EVENT ATTRACTED PEOPLE FROM ALL PARTS OF CENTRAL CALIFORNIA. THE PENINSULAR RAILWAY'S "BIG RED" CARS CARRIED PASSENGERS ON "BLOSSOM TOURS" AS THEIR MANY ROUTES COVERED ALL SECTIONS OF THE SPECTACULAR VALLEY. HOW VIVIDLY I REMEMBER THE LONG PICNIC TABLES, GOOD FOOD, SACK-RACES, MAYPOLE DANCES AND ORATIONS.

UPROOTED PRUNE TREES, ENDLESS SUBDIVISIONS AND COLONIES OF APARTMENTS SPELLED DOOM FOR THIS EVENT. SOME DAY PROGRESS MAY NECESSITATE A TREASURE HUNT MAP SHOWING AT LEAST ENOUGH BLOSSOMS TO SUPPORT A SMALL HIVE OF BEES.

OPENING DAY FOR TROUT FISHING WAS THE PEAK OF ALL SPORTING EVENTS, AT LEAST FOR CERTAIN SMALL BOYS ON THE CUPERTINO WEST SIDE OF THE VALLEY. WE CROSSED OFF EACH DRAGGING DAY ON THE CALENDAR, PREPARED, PLANNED AND DREAMED WEEKS AHEAD. WE SAVED OUR MONEY TO BUY A TEN CENT LINE, A PACKAGE OF GUT HOOKS, TUBE OF SHOT FOR SINKERS, TWO LEADERS AND MAYBE A SPORTY GREEN WORM CAN THAT FASTENED WITH A BUILT-IN SAFETY PIN. IF I HAD SAVED EXTRA MONEY THAT YEAR I MIGHT BUY A JOINTED POLE AT SHILLING'S GUN SHOP ON POST STREET AND ALSO ASK TO AT LEAST LOOK AT THE WICKER FISH-BASKETS. USUALLY I WOUND UP USING A WET SALT SACK FOR THE TROUT AND SPENT THE MONEY ON A HUNK OF DRIED SALMON EGGS AND A ROYAL COACHMAN FLY HOOK. I REALLY ONLY WANTED THE ROYAL COACHMAN TO STICK IN MY STRAW HAT. IT GAVE ONE SUCH A SPORTY LOOK OF CAREFREE, WELL-TO-DO NONCHALANCE. ALSO ONE NEVER KNEW WHAT COMPETITIVELY BEDECKED FELLOW ANGLER MIGHT BE MET ALONG THE STREAM.

LIVING ON THE WEST SIDE, WE FISHED TWO SPRING-FED STREAMS, STEVENS CREEK AND PERMENENTE. UNLIKE TODAY, WITH "STANDING ROOM ONLY", WE OFTEN FISHED FROM DAWN TO DARK, MEETING ONLY THREE OR FOUR OTHER YOUNG IZAAK WALTONS.

WHEN I WAS TEN YEARS OLD I REMEMBER ONE SOLO TROUT FISHING TRIP TO THE HEADWATERS OF STEVENS CREEK. I HID MY BIKE NEAR SODA ROCK AND HIKED TO THE HIGHEST CAMPING SPOT CALLED "GRIZZLY FLAT. I FISHED ON THE WAY UP CATCHING FOUR OR FIVE TROUT WITH A (THEN AVERAGE) SIZE OF ABOUT FIVE INCHES.

REACHING GRIZZLY FLAT, I CEREMONIOUSLY

CHECKED THE ANCIENT, NOTORIOUS BUT SLIGHTLY DUBIOUS GRIZZLY BEAR CLAW MARKS ON THE BIG LAUREL TREE.

THEN I SETTLED DOWN TO ONE OF THE MAIN FEATURES OF THE TRIP, MY KING SIZE LUNCH MOTHER HAD, AS USUAL, PREPARED SO GENEROUSLY. FISHING EFFORTS COULD BE DISAPPOINTING BUT NEVER THOSE LUNCHES. IT WAS A REAL SMÖRGÅSBORD AND IF I WERE TO BE LOST, I HAD ENOUGH TO EAT FOR A WEEK. I COULD HAVE FED A SMALL HAY-BALER OR THRESHING MACHINE CREW.

ENHANCING MY DINING PLEASURE WERE MINIATURE WATERFALLS CASCADING DOWN A STEEP LITTLE RAVINE INTO BLACK POOLS OVERHUNG WITH FIVE-FINGER FERNS. HERE WAS A PERFECT SPOT TO REST, EAT AND DANGLE A LINE. FOLLOWING AN OVER-GROWN, ABANDONED LOGGING ROAD I COULD SEE A SMALL TRIBUTARY TRICKLING DOWN A STEEP, NARROW CANYON.

TO MY SURPRISE, I HEARD THE CLUMP OF HOOFS COMING DOWN THIS FORGOTTEN, OVERGROWN TRAIL. I COULD HARDLY BELIEVE MY EYES! APPEARING IN VIEW, A GAUNT AND FORLORN WHITE MULE WAS PUSHING HIS WAY THROUGH THE MANZANITA BUSHES. BEHIND THE LONG NECK AND FLOPPING EARS AND SITTING LOW IN THE MULE'S SWAY-BACK WAS AN ALMOST CONCEALED SMALL RIDER.

THEN I RECOGNIZED HIM! IT WAS "LITTLE DAVE", A HERMIT WOODCHOPPER, SHINGLE-SPLITTER AND CHAR-COAL-BURNER WHO LIVED AT THE SUMMIT HEADWATERS OF STEVENS CREEK. I HAD SEEN HIM AT THE WEST SIDE STORE. EVERY TWO MONTHS HE DROVE HIS MULE AND CART DOWN THE LONG GRADE FOR SUPPLIES. OF COURSE I DISTANTLY WATCHED HIS SHOPPING WITH NOSEY CURIOSITY. AS SOON AS ARCH WILSON, STOREKEEPER, SIGHTED LITTLE DAVE APPROACHING HE COULD START PUTTING UP THE ORDER BECAUSE IT WAS ALWAYS THE SAME. IT NEVER VARIED; SACK OF FLOUR, SIDE OF BACON, ARBUCKLE COFFEE, SALT, SUGAR, ROLLED OATS, COAL-OIL, STAR PLUG CHEWING TOBACCO, CHIPPED BEEF, PINK BEANS AND SULPHUR MATCHES. THEN HE ALWAYS ASKED ARCH HOPEFULLY IF THERE WAS ANY LEFT-OVER DOERR'S BAKERY PASTRY. THERE USUALLY WAS AN APPLE PIE, WELL AGED AND WITH THE CONSISTENCY OF A DISCUS. LITTLE DAVE IMMEDIATELY SPLIT THIS FIFTY-FIFTY WITH HIS MULE COMPANION.

SO HERE WAS MY FIRST CLOSEUP AND DAVE FILLED EVERY EXPECTATION. HIS LEGS WERE SO SHORT THE HIGH LACED BOOTS BARELY REACHED HIS KNEES. CLOTHES

FAIRLY CLEAN BUT HIS COWBOY HAT HAD LONG AGO LOST ITS VIM AND LOOKED LIKE A WILTED MUSHROOM. HE WAS ABOUT FIVE FEET TALL AND HAD AN ENORMOUS "HANDLE BAR" OR "WALRUS" MOUSTACHE THAT ENTIRELY OVERPOWERED THE REST OF HIS SMALL FEATURES. I KEPT WONDERING WHAT HE WOULD LOOK LIKE WITHOUT IT. BUT DAVE DID HAVE A PAIR OF TWINKLING, DEEP SET EYES, SO LIVELY ONE FORGOT ALL ELSE.

HE HAD PADDED THE MULE'S SHARP SPINE WITH A COUPLE OF BARLEY SACKS. TO ME IT STILL SEEMED SO PAINFULLY SHARP I WONDERED WHY LITTLE DAVE DIDN'T RIDE SIDE-SADDLE.

LIL' DAVE SLID OFF AND THREW THE BALE-ROPE REINS OVER A MADRONE LIMB. I COULD HARDLY BELIEVE IT BUT EVIDENTLY HE HAD BEEN FISHING THAT TINY TRIBUTARY! I COULD NOT KEEP MY EYES OFF HIS SPORTING EQUIPMENT AND HE, IN TURN, GAVE MY OUTFIT A LONG STARE. SUCH COMPARISON EMBARRASSED ME. I WAS FILLED WITH BOY LIKE PITY FOR POOR DAVE BECAUSE THIS HAPPENED TO BE MY FLUSH YEAR. I HAD A NEW $1.99 JOINTED POLE, A 35¢ REEL, A NEW WICKER BASKET AND THE ROYAL COACHMAN FLY-HOOK STUCK IN MY HAT HAD COMPANIONS THIS SEASON, TWO JAUNTILY DANGLING BLACK GNATS AND A 15¢ SPINNER.

LITTLE DAVE LEANED HIS POLE GENTLY AGAINST A REDWOOD. THE POLE WAS A LONG, FRESHLY CUT WILLOW SPROUT. HE HADN'T EVEN TROUBLED TO TRIM OFF SOME OF THE GREEN LEAVES! I HAD NEVER SEEN SUCH BIG BLACK HOOKS HE USED EXCEPT IN A 1900 SEARS CATALOGUE SELLING BY THE GROSS. I THINK THEY WERE DESIGNED FOR IGNORANT CATFISH IN MUDDY WATER. THEY HAD A SHORT SHANK, NO LEADER AND ONLY A ROUND EYE THREADED WITH A LINE LOOKING LIKE COMMON WHITE-STRING. I WONDERED HOW HE EXPECTED ANY SELF-RESPECTING, SPORTY STEVENS CREEK TROUT

TO GET ONE OF THOSE BIG HOOKS IN ITS MOUTH.

HE RATHER SHYLY APPROACHED ME. THIS ISOLATED, LONELY MEETING SEEMED TO TONGUE-TIE BOTH OF US. FINALLY I MANAGED TO GULP A "HELLO" AND RECEIVED A "ANY LUCK, BUD?"

I FELT SORRY FOR HIM AND HIS FISHING EFFORTS AND, WITH RELUCTANT PRIDE, SHOWED HIM THE FOUR, FIVE INCH TROUT. I HAD DAINTLY ARRANGED THEM ON AN EXTRA DEEP BED OF FERNS IN MY NEW STORE BASKET. LITTLE DAVE SAID NOTHING BUT GAVE ME AND MINE A LONG PECULIAR LOOK.

I INVITED HIM TO SHARE MY ENORMOUS LUNCH. AFTER SOME TIMID PERSUASION HE JOINED ME. HE ATE WITH SUCH GUSTO! AGAIN I WAS EMBARRASSED AND TRIED NOT TO LOOK AT HIM. THE FOOD SIMPLY DISAPPEARED BEHIND THAT PONDEROUS "WALRUS" MOUSTACHE. NO CHEWING ACTION WAS VISIBLE! MY ONLY ASSURANCE THAT HE WAS SWALLOWING WAS THE STEADY BOBBING OF HIS ADAM'S APPLE. WE DID NOT SPEAK UNTIL THE FOOD WAS ALL GONE. THEN I REMEMBER LITTLE DAVE MADE HIS LONGEST STATEMENT OF THE DAY. HE SAID, "SOMEHOW BEANS AND BACON EVER DAY GETS KINDA DULL. THIS HERE HOME COOKIN' TASTES MIGHTY GOOD COMPARISONED WITH BATCHIN' FOOD."

I THOUGHT OF MOTHER AND HOW DELIGHTED SHE WOULD BE WHEN INFORMED OF SUCH OBVIOUS APPRECIATION. IN FACT SHE WAS WHEN I TOLD HER. THEN I WISHED THAT I HADN'T! ON THE NEXT TRIP, MY BICYCLE PULLED SOME EXTRA WEIGHT. SHE INSISTED ON ADDING A CHERRY PIE AND A ROASTED HEN!

AFTER LUNCH LITTLE DAVE OPENED HIS POCKET KNIFE, LARGE ENOUGH TO CUT DOWN A SMALL TREE, AND CARVED OFF A CHEEKFUL OF STAR PLUG. HE STARTED TO OFFER ME SOME, THEN REALIZING MY AGE, JABBED HIS KNIFE IN THE DEEP LEAF MOLD TO CLEAN IT.

TURNING TO HIS DOZING MULE AND FROM THE HIDDEN SIDE, HE UNTIED A SOILED, WET FLOUR SACK. WITH A FARAWAY, VACANT LOOK UP INTO THE REDWOODS, HE RAN HIS SHORT ARM DEEP INTO THE WET DEPTHS AND FUMBLED FOR A MINUTE. NOW I KNOW THAT HE WAS MEASURING BY FEEL AND ALSO ESTIMATING SIZE OF MY BASKET.

FINALLY DAVE DREDGED OUT FOUR RAINBOW TROUT SO LARGE I TREMBLED AND MY EYES BULGED! NEVER IN MY WILDEST DREAMS HAD I IMAGINED SUCH FISH EXISTED IN THE SANTA CRUZ MOUNTAINS. I COULDN'T CLOSE THE BASKET LID SO DAVE TIED IT DOWN, THE TROUT TAILS DANGLING

DELIGHTFULLY FAR OVER THE EDGES, IN PUBLIC VIEW FOR MY HOMEWARD TRIP. ONE NEVER KNOWS WHO WILL BE MET OR HOW MANY UNEXPECTED DETOURS MIGHT BE NECESSARY.

SO CONCLUDED OUR MEETING. DAVE LED HIS MULE TO A REDWOOD STUMP AND WITH RHEUMATIC GROANS, CLIMBED ON. WHACKING HIS SORRY STEED WITH COMBINATION FISHPOLE AND WHIP, HE WAVED FAREWELL WITH THESE FINAL WORDS OF ADVICE, "FISH FOR THE BIG ONES, BUD, —WHERE YOU THINK THEY AINT."

THEN THE LITTLE MAN AND THE BIG MULE VANISHED INTO THE DARK REDWOODS. LITTLE? TO THE SMALL BOY; DAVE, INSTEAD OF FIVE FEET, WAS TEN FEET TALL!

WE MET AGAIN. HIS HOME WAS A LONELY CABIN AT THE VERY SOURCE OF STEVENS CREEK WHERE AN ARM SIZE STREAM OF CRYSTAL CLEAR WATER GUSHED FROM A GRANITE CLIFF. HE DIVERTED THIS NEWBORN BROOK TO WATER HIS BERRY PATCH. HE RECOGNIZED NEITHER HUNTING OR FISHING SEASONS. FOR DAVE, CIVILIZATION HELD NO CHAINS.

NEVER AGAIN WOULD I MEET A MAN WITH WANTS SO SIMPLE; ASKING ONLY FOR SOLITUDE, COMPANIONSHIP OF HIS MULE AND WHISPERING REDWOODS.

EUREKA!

STRANGE HOW MEMORIES OF YOUTHFUL EMBARRASSING MOMENTS KEEP CROPPING UP IN LATER YEARS.

THE FRUIT HARVEST WAS THE MAIN SOURCE OF EARNING PIN MONEY FOR YOUNGSTERS. THIS WAS USUALLY SPENT FOR AMUSEMENTS, TOYS, SOME CLOTHES AND IF A BANNER YEAR, BICYCLES. NOT ONLY WAS THE FRUIT AN ECONOMIC ADVANTAGE BUT IT PROVIDED US WITH MANY A HILARIOUS SUMMER.

APRICOTS WERE FIRST CUT IN HALF, PITTED, SPREAD ON TRAYS, SULPHURED AND PLACED ON THE DRYING YARD TO SUN DRY BEFORE THEY HIT THE MARKET.

HOW WE ANTICIPATED THE APRICOT SEASON AND OUR "CUTTIN' SHED JOB"! USUALLY THE ORCHARDISTS HIRED SCHOOL CHILDREN ALONG WITH A FEW ELDERS PLACED IN STRATEGIC POSITION TO CURB OUR EXUBERANCE.

WE WERE PAID 8¢ A BOX AND THE FRUIT BOXES WERE DOLED OUT TO US JUST AS THEY CAME OFF THE ORCHARD TRUCK, ELIMINATING PARTIALITY. THE LARGER THE APRICOTS, THE QUICKER WE COULD FINISH CUTTING A BOX OF "COTS". IF YOU WERE UNLUCKY ENOUGH TO DRAW A FIFTY POUND BOX OF "MARBLES" IT WAS A TRAGIC SITUATION REQUIRING SEVERAL HOURS FOR COMPLETITION. FURTHERMORE THE VICTIM OFTEN BECAME THE OBJECT OF RIDICULE OR PITY, DEPENDING ON MOOD OF US WITNESSING "IMPS OF SATAN".

THE ELDER (SOMETIMES CALLED FORELADY OR BOSS) ASSIGNED TO OUR LIVELY SECTION WAS MISS PEABODY, A LONE, NEIGHBOR SPINSTER. WE OFTEN WONDERED HOW SHE MANAGED TO BUTTON HER SHOES AS SHE WAS SO EXTREMELY SHORT, WEIGHING OVER 200 POUNDS. SHE EVEN HAD DIFFICULTY GETTING CLOSE ENOUGH TO THE FRUIT TRAY TO SPREAD HER APRICOTS.

THIS DID NOT MELLOW HER DIGNITY OR RESULT IN AN INFERIORITY COMPLEX! PRIM AND PURITANICAL IN A SUPERIOR MANNER, SHE FROWNED ON IDLE CHATTER, PUNS AND PRACTICAL JOKES AND HER SENSE OF HUMOR WAS TOTALLY LACKING. JUST ONE OF THOSE PIERCING, PENETRATING LOOKS WAS SUFFICIENT TO RESTORE ORDER. WE WERE AFRAID OF HER IN A HIDDEN, DISRESPECTFUL MANNER. WOULD NOTHING EVER HAPPEN TO "RUFFLE HER FEATHERS?"

THEN CAME THE *HAPPY DAY*, (THAT IS, HAPPY FOR US.) MISS PEABODY DREW A BOX OF APRICOTS SO SMALL THEY COULD HARDLY QUALIFY AS EVEN MARBLE SIZE! SHE SAID NOTHING, MAINTAINING A STOIC, FACIAL EXPRESSION. EACH URCHIN WAS BUSY AND OBSERVANT AS A ONE-EYED CAT WATCHING TWO RAT HOLES. FINALLY AT ABOUT THE END OF TWO HOURS WE DETECTED PERSPIRATION ON HER AUSTERE BROW. IT WAS THEN SHE PAINFULLY BENT OVER AS FAR AS HER OBESITY WOULD ALLOW AND PEERED HOPEFULLY INTO THE BOX OF INCREDIBLY SMALL FRUIT. REGAINING HER COMPOSURE AND BALANCE AND WITH A RARE BUT TRIUMPHANT SMILE, SHE LOUDLY PROCLAIMED,—

"THANK HEAVENS, FOR THE FIRST TIME, I DO BELIEVE I CAN AT LAST SEE PART OF MY *BOTTOM!*"

(OH, HAPPY DAY!)

144

Dear Reader,

The art work in this section can be classified as "cartoons" and "illustrations". A cartoon is now taken to be funny. An illustration is more sober, more explanatory. Some were drawn to fit the text of a particular book and others were momentarily inspired for amusement or scenic nostalgia. Several have been used in other publications and by author friends. Some became postcards or Christmas cards.

In particular, note the first auto ride, picturing Doc Durgin on Stevens Creek Road in 1900 and the San Jose junk collectors, otherwise known as the "Five Centies". Their load was worthless junk then; priceless antiques now! The page of cartoon drawings entitled "Just Dogs" portrays my canine companions of many years. I am always amazed at their incredible contortions! This series has never before been published. Neither has "The Butterfly-Better Fly" which was drawn for a little girlfriend who collected frog models. "A Weaver's Dream" was done in 1977 as part of some promotional art work for a local California Weavers' convention. Tired of looms, shuttles, etc., I drew this mildly insulting cartoon, Rube Goldberg style. But the weavers were not insulted!

Sarah Winchester's house was drawn from a popular photo made at the turn-of-the-century when the house was in "full flower". The "Doyle School" illustration was drawn from my class photo of 1901.

A page of assorted Dingbats has been included because I used them so extensively in all my books. A Dingbat is defined as "an ornamental design in conjunction with type" and Dingbats reached the peak of their popularity in the 1800's. For less than a dollar I bought two old 19th century books in a Salvation Army bookstore and found myself with enough Dingbats to give all ten books an "almost forgotten" atmosphere!

Yours Truly
Ralph Rambo

146

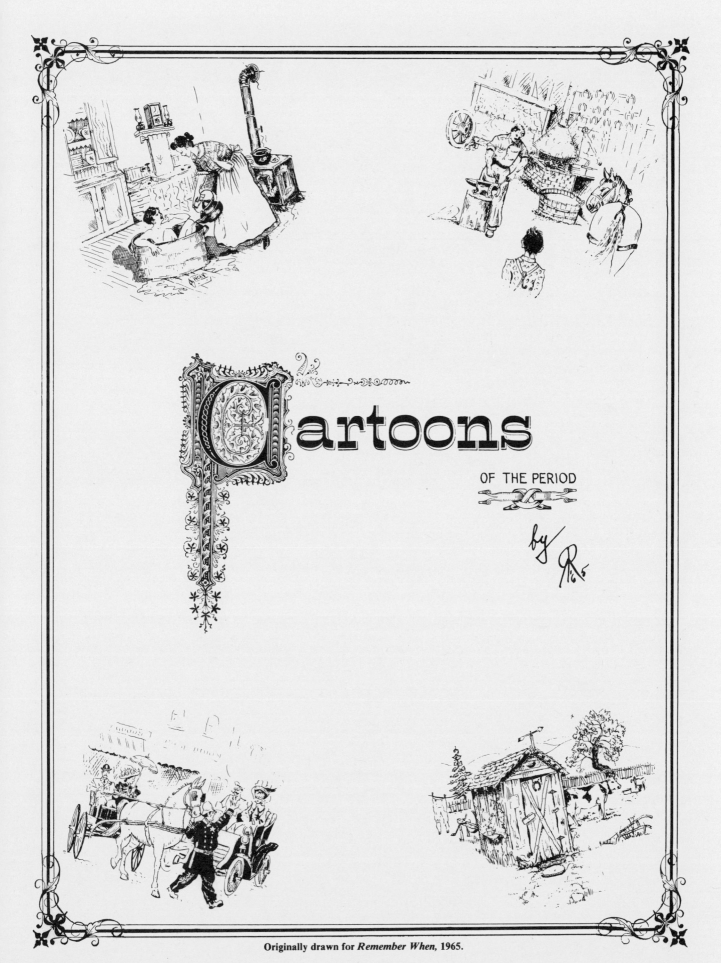

Cartoons OF THE PERIOD

by R.S.

Originally drawn for *Remember When*, 1965.

"WISTFUL THINKING"

Once a week facial operation, 1900.

Both cartoons originally drawn for *Remember When*, 1965.

Mrs. B.—wife of Dr. B.—drives down The Alameda in 1910 in her Baker electric.

Beginning of the end of horse-and-buggy days on old Stevens Creek *Road.*

Both cartoons originally drawn for *Remember When*, 1965.

One of the first electric street cars to run through San Jose, about 1880.

Actual first auto ride of artist with Cupertino's one and only M.D., "Doc Durgin", 1902.
That's a "one-lunger". (1900 slang for one cylinder)

Both cartoons originally drawn for Remember When, *1965.*

"JUNK Yesterday, ANTIQUES Today."

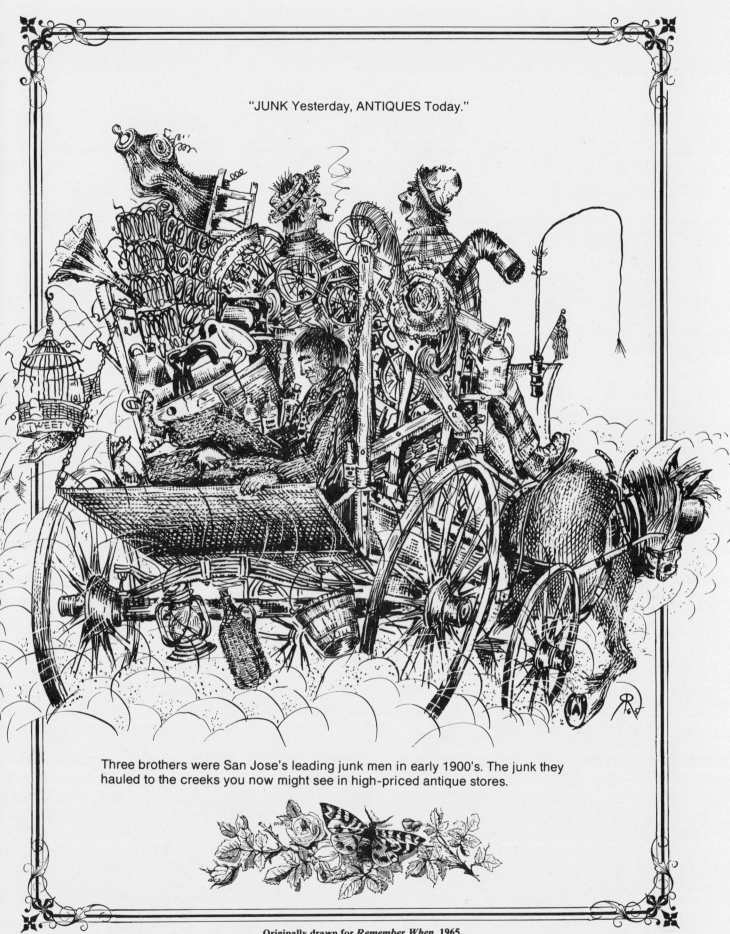

Three brothers were San Jose's leading junk men in early 1900's. The junk they hauled to the creeks you now might see in high-priced antique stores.

Originally drawn for *Remember When*, 1965.

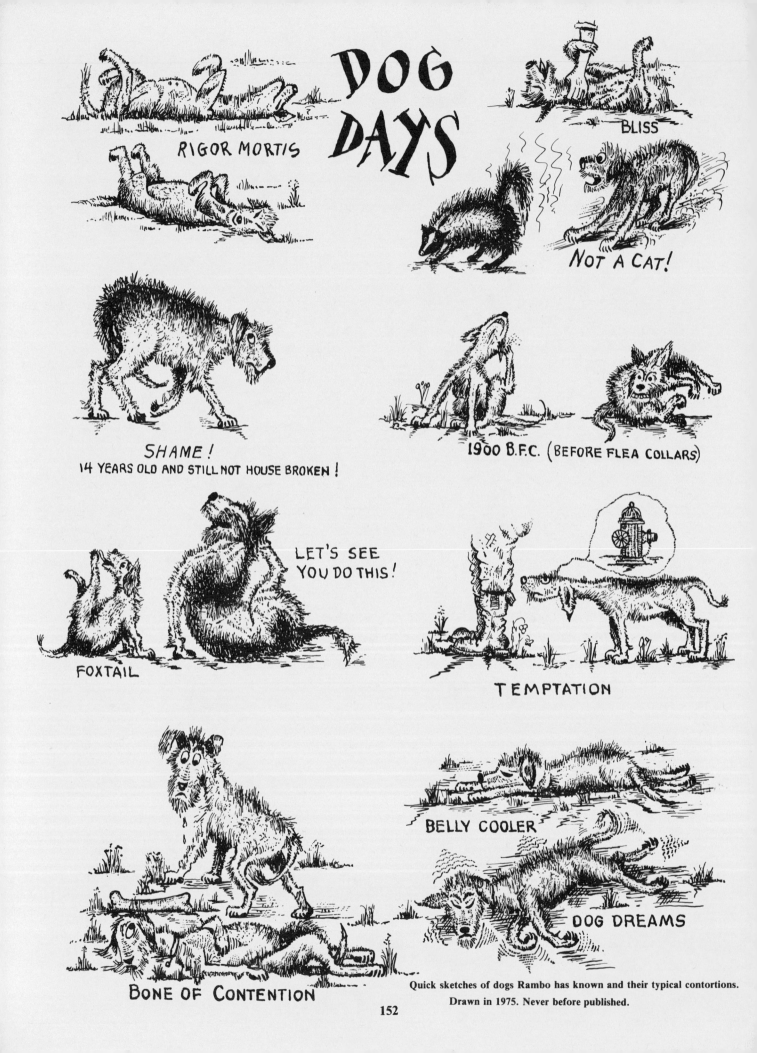

DOG DAYS

RIGOR MORTIS

BLISS

NOT A CAT!

SHAME!
14 YEARS OLD AND STILL NOT HOUSE BROKEN!

1900 B.F.C. (BEFORE FLEA COLLARS)

FOXTAIL

LET'S SEE YOU DO THIS!

TEMPTATION

BELLY COOLER

BONE OF CONTENTION

DOG DREAMS

Quick sketches of dogs Rambo has known and their typical contortions.
Drawn in 1975. Never before published.

BUTTERFLY–*BETTER FLY!*

Drawn in 1979 for a small girl who asked for it for her "butterfly picture collection"—or "frog picture collection." Never before published.

A WEAVER'S DREAM

Used by Northern California Conference of Hand Weavers' 25th Anniversary. For amusement it was sent to weavers' guilds all over the world.
Drawn in 1977. Not published, but loose prints made.

ALMOST FORGOTTEN PIONEERS

SECUNDINO ROBLES
1810 – 1890

CASTILIAN CALIFORNIO
MINER, TAVERN KEEPER, FATHER OF 29 CHILDREN, (1 WIFE) RUINED FINANCIALLY BY GREEDY 49'ER AMERICANOS.

MARCELLO
1780-1807
CORRECT

PROMINENT GIANT MISSION INDIAN
"AGE 125?" MISSION RECORDS ABOVE.

SLAPJACK HALL

SIMULATED PORTRAIT

GRANDMA BASCOM
CIRCA 1850

A MOST POPULAR SAN JOSE SETTLER
RAN A BOARDING HOUSE FOR DISTINGUISHED 49'ERS.
BASCOM AVENUE WAS NAMED FOR HER FAMILY.

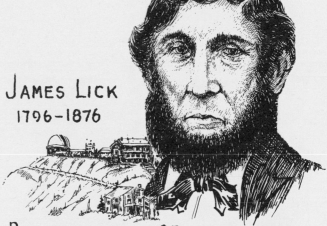

JAMES LICK
1796–1876

PIANO MAKER, BOUGHT S.F. SAND HILLS IN 1850.
FLOUR MILL OWNER, MILLIONAIRE, PHILANTHROPIST.
DONATED LICK OBSERVATORY, HIS ACTUAL TOMB.

CHARLES M. McKIERNAN
"MOUNTAIN CHARLEY"
1830-1902.

EARLY SANTA CRUZ MOUNTAIN SETTLER,
HUNTER AND FAMOUS FOR HISTORIC BEAR FIGHT.
BECAME PROMINENT LUMBERMAN.   (1854)

"CAPT." ELISHA STEVENS
1796–1876
FIRST MAN TO GUIDE WAGON TRAINS ACROSS SIERRAS'
DONNER PASS IN 1844. CREEK, BLVD., ETC.–NAMESAKES.

PORTRAITS & EXCERPTS FROM "ADVENTURE VALLEY" BY R

Portraits and excerpts from *Adventure Valley*, 1970. Never before published in this form.

Memory Lane

Typical one-room country school
Author's alma mater – Doyle-1894

O'Connor Sanitarium, 1889-1954
On San Carlos-now Sears

The horse had right-of-way
and this the only traffic jam

Butcher, baker, vegetable-man
Grocer, fish-man-delivered at your door

Typical old Valley cross-roads – "West Side"- now Cupertino,
in 1880's. Montgomery's store-Baer's blacksmith shop.

Likewise = "Meridian Corners", "Butchers Corners", "Robertsville" and "Rucker."

Drawn or selected for *Remember When* or *Almost Forgotten*, 1964-65.
Cupertino was drawn from an actual photograph.

Sarah Winchester

RAMBO

WINCHESTER MYSTERY HOUSE IN 1900
BUILT BY ECCENTRIC WIDOW OF WINCHESTER RIFLE MAGNATE. COST $5,000,000.
IN CONTINUOUS, WEIRD, EXPERIMENTAL CONSTRUCTION FROM 1884 TO 1922.
CONTAINS 130 ROOMS, 10,000 WINDOWS. YEARLY, OVER 100,000 TOURISTS VISIT THIS GHOSTLY MANSION.

SOUTH VIEW

"THE GUN THAT WON THE WEST"

Originally published in postcard form.

156

AUTHOR

BIG
JOE

ENTIRE EIGHT GRADES
OF DOYLE SCHOOL 1901
SKETCHED FROM AN OLD PHOTO.

This is a typical total assembly of a 1900 one-room country school. Rambo is wearing the then-popular sailor suit (see anchors). Originally appeared in *Remember When.*

GAME

Almost Forgotten Words

THE MORE REMEMBERED—THE OLDER YOU ARE!!

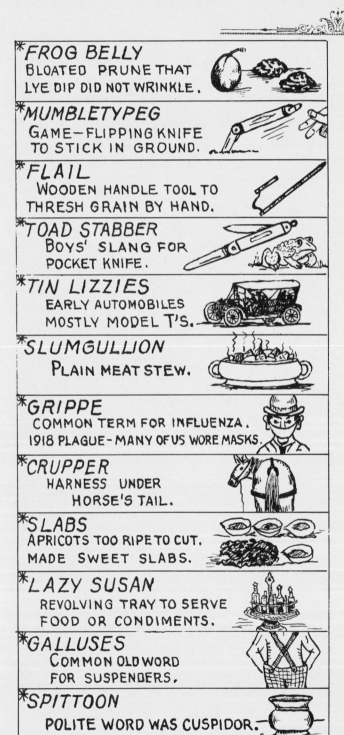

*FROG BELLY
BLOATED PRUNE THAT
LYE DIP DID NOT WRINKLE.

*MUMBLETYPEG
GAME—FLIPPING KNIFE
TO STICK IN GROUND.

*FLAIL
WOODEN HANDLE TOOL TO
THRESH GRAIN BY HAND.

*TOAD STABBER
BOYS' SLANG FOR
POCKET KNIFE.

*TIN LIZZIES
EARLY AUTOMOBILES
MOSTLY MODEL T'S.

*SLUMGULLION
PLAIN MEAT STEW.

*GRIPPE
COMMON TERM FOR INFLUENZA.
1918 PLAGUE—MANY OF US WORE MASKS.

*CRUPPER
HARNESS UNDER
HORSE'S TAIL.

*SLABS
APRICOTS TOO RIPE TO CUT.
MADE SWEET SLABS.

*LAZY SUSAN
REVOLVING TRAY TO SERVE
FOOD OR CONDIMENTS.

*GALLUSES
COMMON OLD WORD
FOR SUSPENDERS.

*SPITTOON
POLITE WORD WAS CUSPIDOR.

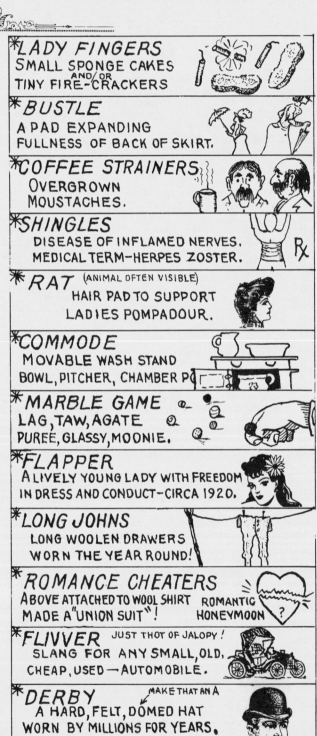

*LADY FINGERS
SMALL SPONGE CAKES
AND/OR
TINY FIRE-CRACKERS

*BUSTLE
A PAD EXPANDING
FULLNESS OF BACK OF SKIRT.

*COFFEE STRAINERS
OVERGROWN
MOUSTACHES.

*SHINGLES
DISEASE OF INFLAMED NERVES.
MEDICAL TERM—HERPES ZOSTER.

*RAT (ANIMAL OFTEN VISIBLE)
HAIR PAD TO SUPPORT
LADIES POMPADOUR.

*COMMODE
MOVABLE WASH STAND
BOWL, PITCHER, CHAMBER POT

*MARBLE GAME
LAG, TAW, AGATE
PUREE, GLASSY, MOONIE.

*FLAPPER
A LIVELY YOUNG LADY WITH FREEDOM
IN DRESS AND CONDUCT—CIRCA 1920.

*LONG JOHNS
LONG WOOLEN DRAWERS
WORN THE YEAR ROUND!

*ROMANCE CHEATERS
ABOVE ATTACHED TO WOOL SHIRT   ROMANTIC
MADE A "UNION SUIT"!   HONEYMOON

*FLIVVER   JUST THOT OF JALOPY!
SLANG FOR ANY SMALL, OLD,
CHEAP, USED—AUTOMOBILE.

*DERBY   MAKE THAT AN A
A HARD, FELT, DOMED HAT
WORN BY MILLIONS FOR YEARS.

Drawn in 1984. Never before published.

do you Remember game

TESTED YOUR "NOSTALGIABILITY" LATELY? MAYBE YOU'RE OLDER THAN YOU THINK! TO DISCOVER ANY FRIEND'S AGE, SIMPLY MULTIPLY HIS OR HER TOTAL CORRECT ANSWERS BY 2.5 (NOSTALGIC AGE!)

BELOW ARE THIRTY OBJECTS, ALL IN COMMON USE FIFTY OR SIXTY YEARS AGO BUT SELDOM SEEN OR USED TODAY. MOST ARE SIMPLE. LIST YOUR GUESSES BEFORE CHECKING ANSWERS AND YOU MUST BE SPECIFIC OR NO SCORE. EXAMPLES: NO.3 IS A MAN'S SHOE BUT WHAT STYLE SHOE?

NO. 17 IS MATCHES BUT WHAT KIND OF MATCHES? 10-15 RIGHT=FAIR,-BUT YOUNG. 15-20=GOOD,- STOLID MIDDLE AGED. 20-25=EXCELLENT;-GOT A TOUCH OF ARTHRITIS? 25-30=SUPERB!-APPLY FOR YOUR SOCIAL SECURITY! ALL CORRECT=GRAND!- YOU MUST HAVE AT LEAST 10 GRANDCHILDREN!

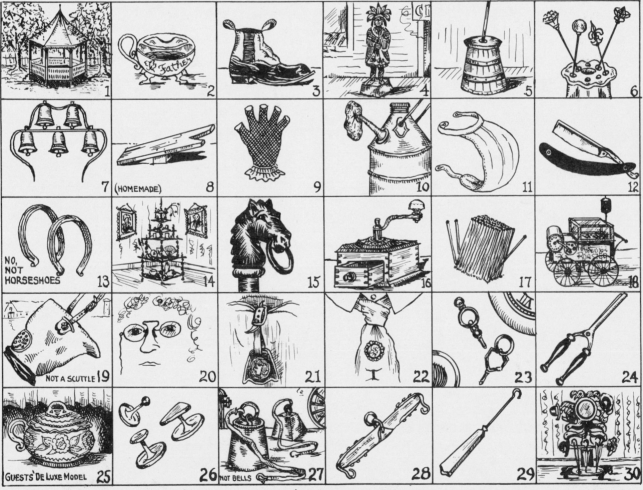

1 · 2 · 3 · 4 · 5 · 6
7 · 8 (HOMEMADE) · 9 · 10 · 11 · 12
13 (NO, NOT HORSESHOES) · 14 · 15 · 16 · 17 · 18
19 (NOT A SCUTTLE) · 20 · 21 · 22 · 23 · 24
25 (GUESTS' DE LUXE MODEL) · 26 · 27 (NOT BELLS) · 28 · 29 · 30

1=BAND-STAND, 2=MOUSTACHE CUP, 3=CONGRESS GAITER, 4=CIGAR STORE INDIAN, 5=CHURN, 6=HAT-PINS, 7=HARNESS BELLS, 8=BOOT-JACK, 9=LADY'S MITT, 10=COAL-OIL-CAN, 11=MAN'S DICKEY, 12=STRAIGHT EDGE RAZOR, 13=BIKE CLIPS OR PANTS GUARDS, 14=WHATNOT, 15=HITCH POST, 16=COFFEE MILL, 17=SULPHUR MATCHES, 18=PEANUT-VENDOR, 19= HORSE'S FEED BAG, 20=PINCE-NEZ, 21=WATCH-FOB, 22=STICK-PIN, 23=WATCH KEYS, 24=CURLING IRON, 25=CHAMBER POT, 26=COLLAR BUTTONS, 27=HITCHING WEIGHTS, 28=SINGLETREE, 29=BUTTON-HOOK, 30=HAT RACK-UMBRELLA STAND.

  ANSWERS Premature Peeking Prohibited

Drawn in 1965. Originally appeared in *Remember When*.

The biographer (in 1900)

and

A FEW PIONEER CHARACTERS
FOUND IN HIS LESS FORMAL
WRITINGS

A montage showing a few leading characters in Rambo's books.
Drawn as an illustrative page for the *Blue Book*, 1973.

FAMOUS OUTHOUSES

A Colorado miner in early days found a rich vein of gold or silver. He sold it for a fabulous sum and built one freakish mansion. Then he ordered a fancy privy to match his monstrosity. So this four-holer is said to have a center partition. Family sat in front, servants in back half. You can believe it or not.

The snowdrifts could be mighty deep? Maybe that's the reason for this two story backyard privy in Montana. It is joined by a bridge from an old hotel, convenient for upstairs guests. We join you in curiosity. What in the world was the floor plan ??

Above could be two of the most photographed outhouses in the U.S.A. Both are long retired from use yet well preserved, far from EXTINCT.

Never before published. Drawn in 1984.

Old Valley Ads

Ads cut from turn-of-the-century magazines. Includes four ads of well-known San Jose firms. Notice undertaker's small type "plug" at bottom. Assembled in 1973 for the *Pioneer Blue Book*.

Dingbats

Dingbats—an old word yet once with many applications, handy to apply to any object lacking a specific name. The writer gives it this page because in his ten books, dingbats certainly found their place.

The big Webster's dictionary gives it an air of mystery with the note "origin unknown". Applied to printing it is further defined as a "typographical ornament (as a star) used typically to an opening sentence or to make a break between two paragraphs."

These ornamental small vignette illustrations or so often elaborate designed initials were used in great quantity in the 1800's. They were easily collected by the writer from the enormous stock of unsold books. I believe they add an air of nostalgia to the majority of my writings.

Dingbats—"origin unknown". We like to guess who might have originated this word. Some bored typesetter of the 1860 era laboriously hand-setting a dull article or book needed a break. Time out to heavily decorate his page. Presto! He coined a word by calling for that type-case of "Dingbats". And a word was born that spread nationwide.

Many are remarkably designed extremely intricate drawings, engravings, etchings, even woodcuts well worth our modern admiration. A lost art? I am surprised that they aren't collected.

A159—2 for 45c

A160—35c

A161—2 for 45c

A164—6 for 35c

A162 2 for 40c

A163—2 for 45c

THE

A Grave Affair

W

Never before published. Assembled in 1984.

163

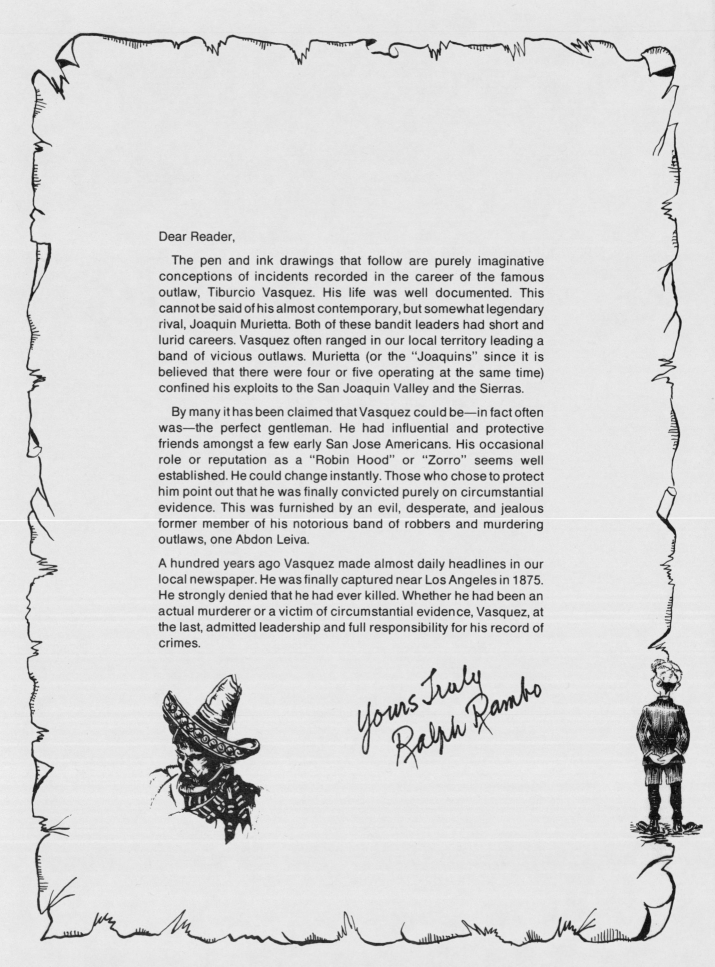

Dear Reader,

The pen and ink drawings that follow are purely imaginative conceptions of incidents recorded in the career of the famous outlaw, Tiburcio Vasquez. His life was well documented. This cannot be said of his almost contemporary, but somewhat legendary rival, Joaquin Murietta. Both of these bandit leaders had short and lurid careers. Vasquez often ranged in our local territory leading a band of vicious outlaws. Murietta (or the "Joaquins" since it is believed that there were four or five operating at the same time) confined his exploits to the San Joaquin Valley and the Sierras.

By many it has been claimed that Vasquez could be—in fact often was—the perfect gentleman. He had influential and protective friends amongst a few early San Jose Americans. His occasional role or reputation as a "Robin Hood" or "Zorro" seems well established. He could change instantly. Those who chose to protect him point out that he was finally convicted purely on circumstantial evidence. This was furnished by an evil, desperate, and jealous former member of his notorious band of robbers and murdering outlaws, one Abdon Leiva.

A hundred years ago Vasquez made almost daily headlines in our local newspaper. He was finally captured near Los Angeles in 1875. He strongly denied that he had ever killed. Whether he had been an actual murderer or a victim of circumstantial evidence, Vasquez, at the last, admitted leadership and full responsibility for his record of crimes.

Yours Truly
Ralph Rambo

HE GLORIED IN NOTORIETY

MANHUNT

WRONG STAGE — WRONG PASSENGER — AND A TONGUE LASHING

VASQUEZ the bandit

Original pen-and-ink drawings for above biography.

by R

BUT WHEN THE GIRL BURST INTO TEARS, ...

. . . . 47 MILES A DAY — FOR 60 DAYS.

FRIEND OR FOE ?

.......BUT THE TRAIN ROARED PAST!

...WAS HE BANDIT OR SHEEPHERDER?

CANTUA CANYON OPENED INTO THE SAN JOAQUIN VALLEY.

.....THEN MR. SUTHERLAND, WITH HIS HENRY RIFLE......

VASQUEZ WAS ELUSIVE AS QUICKSILVER

ABDON LEIVA — THE BETRAYED BETRAYER

JUAN SOTO—THE FIERCEST OUTLAW IN CALIFORNIA

GATEWAY INTO CANTUA CANYON

WITHOUT CAMERA OR DIRECTOR

...ON A WHITE HORSE — BUT IT WAS NOT VASQUEZ.

THE MARSHALL FACED THEM—ALONE.

..FOR VASQUEZ, MONOTONY WAS DEADLY

SENORITAS IN MANY A CANTINA—FROM SAN JOSÉ TO LOS ANGELES.

CANTUA CANYON—THE BANDITS' FORTRESS

......UNTIL THAT DAY—THEY HAD BEEN FRIENDS.

...... AND THE GREAT CHASE WAS OVER.

.... WOUNDED, HE RODE 70 MILES

SHERIFF'S OFFICE,
County of Santa Clara.

San Jose, March 18th 1875.

To A. C. Bassett Esq.

SIR.— Pursuant to the Statute in such cases you are hereby invited to be present at the execution of Tiburcio Vasquez, at the Jail of said County, in San José, on the 19th day of March, A. D. 1875, at 1:30 o'clock P. M.

J. H. ADAMS, Sheriff.

PRESENT AT JAIL ENTRANCE. NOT TRANSFERABLE

ONE OF THE 400 "INVITATIONS"

....IN A SANTA CLARA CEMETERY.

Dear Reader,

I cannot honestly assume the cloak of a true poet. Oh, I can take a short bow or nod for "Mystery Valley" because it doesn't remind me of any other poet's meter and I had all the little illustrations left over to embellish the page.

And no excuses for my "Ode to the Prune". If there is any reader alive and reading this ode or "pome" who picked prunes on sore, bended knees over adobe clods for ten hours and for 6¢ a 50-pound lug box, you can safely bet that he or she is saying "amen". I wrote this poem for the occasion of the dedication of Pellier Park in San Jose on November 29, 1977.

I was a little ashamed to abuse an old faithful like "The Night Before Christmas". This is a modernized pure parody. I wrote it 23 years ago! It made a huge 8½ x 11" Yuletide message. And yet, 23 years later, I didn't need to change a line. In fact, I believe it's a better fit, even for the Silicon Valley!

I do apologize to Longfellow and his protege, Hiawatha, for the familiar rhythm of my Tempus Fugit! Originally the title was "Sarah's Sad Solo". My idea of a pleasant afternoon is a slow stroll through the Pioneer section of our "Folk Hill Cemetery" (or equivalent) reading the moss-covered tombstones and mentally reviewing their well-recorded historic adventures or sordid reputations. For accompaniment, what better than the immortal shrieks of the graveyard peacocks and the eternal roar of Monterey Highway traffic?

Yours Truly
Ralph Rambo

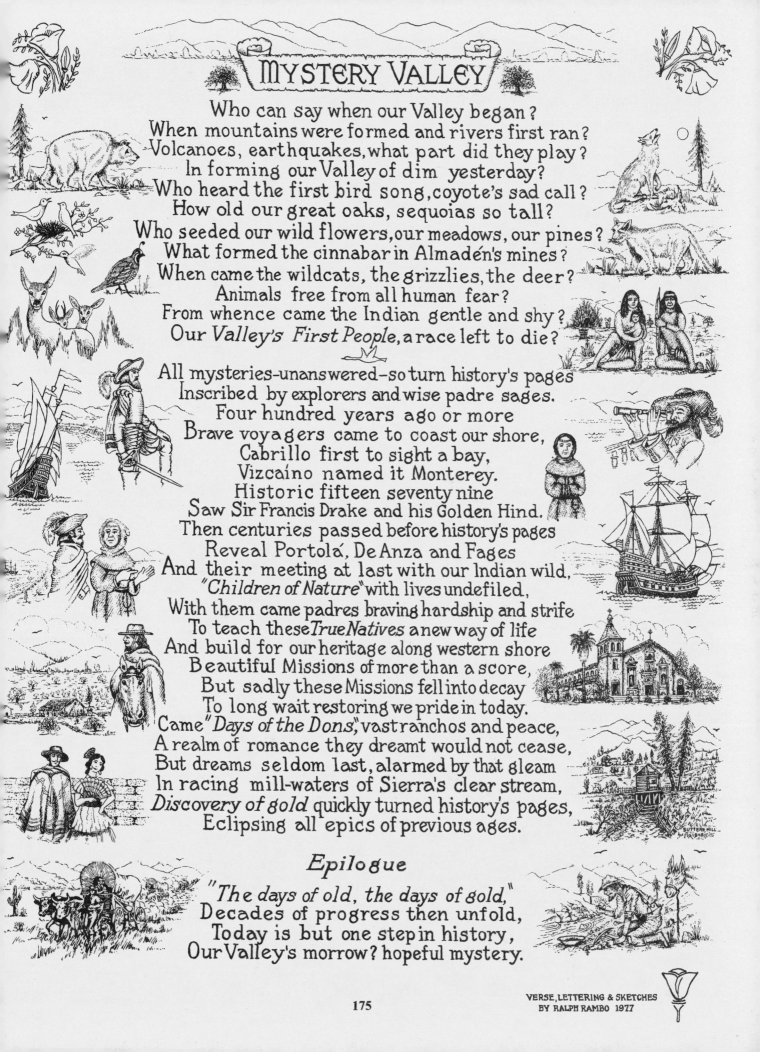

MYSTERY VALLEY

Who can say when our Valley began?
When mountains were formed and rivers first ran?
Volcanoes, earthquakes, what part did they play?
In forming our Valley of dim yesterday?
Who heard the first bird song, coyote's sad call?
How old our great oaks, sequoias so tall?
Who seeded our wild flowers, our meadows, our pines?
What formed the cinnabar in Almadén's mines?
When came the wildcats, the grizzlies, the deer?
Animals free from all human fear?
From whence came the Indian gentle and shy?
Our *Valley's First People*, a race left to die?

All mysteries-unanswered-so turn history's pages
Inscribed by explorers and wise padre sages.
Four hundred years ago or more
Brave voyagers came to coast our shore,
Cabrillo first to sight a bay,
Vizcaíno named it Monterey.
Historic fifteen seventy nine
Saw Sir Francis Drake and his Golden Hind.
Then centuries passed before history's pages
Reveal Portolá, De Anza and Fages
And their meeting at last with our Indian wild,
"Children of Nature" with lives undefiled,
With them came padres braving hardship and strife
To teach these *True Natives* a new way of life
And build for our heritage along western shore
Beautiful Missions of more than a score,
But sadly these Missions fell into decay
To long wait restoring we pride in today.
Came *"Days of the Dons,"* vast ranchos and peace,
A realm of romance they dreamt would not cease,
But dreams seldom last, alarmed by that gleam
In racing mill-waters of Sierra's clear stream,
Discovery of gold quickly turned history's pages,
Eclipsing all epics of previous ages.

Epilogue

"The days of old, the days of gold,"
Decades of progress then unfold,
Today is but one step in history,
Our Valley's morrow? hopeful mystery.

VERSE, LETTERING & SKETCHES
BY RALPH RAMBO 1977

"The Night Before...!"

Twas the night before Christmas and all through the house,
Not a critter was stirring, not even a louse,
The children were tucked in their Time-Payment beds,
While visions of sugar plums danced in their heads;
Sugarplums? Ha! my nostalgic friends,
They'd made out "lists" that would give you the bends!
We'd placed all the presents 'neath the 'luminum tree
And shook all the boxes with curious glee,
Then we checked our bank balance and I said to Rose
"*THAT* sure takes the bloom from MY wild Irish nose!"
Our Christmas-Gift list we gave a last check,
Yep, Uncle's forgotten, but ah what the heck?
The drugstore'll be open tomorrow I know,
We can pick up cigars for the old so-and-so.
Gay stockings were hung on the mantle with care,
Doomed to indifferent teen-agers' stare.
So,·· with sink full of dishes, we put out the cat,
Unwatered the dog and mumbled "that's that!"
Then mom in her curlers and me in my shorts
Took a last minute breather (and two Bourbon snorts),
"Jingle Bells" and "White Christmas" were tuned out with a snap,
And we settled ourselves for a long winter's nap.

When out on the lawn there arose such a chatter
I sprang from my bed to see what was the matter,
Away to the window I flew like a fiend,
Yanked up the Venetians, stuck my head through the screen,
"The moon on the breast of the new fallen snow
Gave a lustre of midday to objects below,"
('cept in Cal there's no snow and 'twas dark of the moon,
So dont get poetic, you long-legged goon!")
Now what to my wondering eyes *should* appear,
(but didn't)
Was a miniature sleigh and eight tiny reindeer,
I *DID* see Saint Nick, but 'twas only his GHOST,
A sad looking wraith, dejected the MOST!
That chatter? His dentures; the Old Boy was cold!
Bedraggled and skinny and pitifully old!
I cried out aghast at the spectral old Saint;
"How come you look so, er,—well; what you aint?"
"Where's Dasher, where's Dancer, where's Prancer and Vixen?
Where's Comet and Cupid and Donder and Blitzen?
Where's all that loot, that swag and the toys
For our Hi-Fi, Space-minded, girlies and boys?
How come there's no ashes, white fur or soot?
How come no fleet reindeer, how come you're on foot?

No cheeks like red roses, no nose like a cherry,
No twinkles, no dimples, and far, far from merry?
No stump of a pipe held tight in your teeth,
You're smoking Bull Durham and making that "wreath",
The beard on your chin's still as white as the snow,
But your mouth's puckered down, 'stead of up like a bow?
My gosh! you've lost weight and that slim little belly
Is sure a far cry from a "bowl full of jelly!"
As I am alive and memory still lives
For the sake of Sweet Christmas, dear Santa, *WHAT GIVES?*

With sad wink of an eye and a twist of his head,
Briefly, here's just what my Ghostly Friend said:

"The simple joys are gone forever,
Modern kids are just too clever,
The only ones that "believe" in Santy
Slyly upping parents' ante,
Shopping Centers, importations,
TV Santas, new sensations,
Competition's ruination,
Phony beards been my damnation.
Atom bombs that know no bounds
Forced my workshop underground,
Costlier toys and helpers' strike,
Eskimos demand wage hike,
Aged reindeer balk and freeze,
Young deer,--hoof-and-mouth disease!

Too much stupid world dissention,
Too much global intervention,
No Golden Rule or tolerations,
Understanding twixt the nations.

Tonight you may regret to hear it,-but
My ONLY *gift* is CHRISTMAS SPIRIT!
I've *changed* at last to an "ETHEREAL",
(Let mortals handle the "material.")
A SPIRIT, I, now and forever,
But Santa Claus forgotten? *NEVER!*

And he sadly exclaimed as he faded from sight

HAPPY CHRISTMAS to all, and to all a GOOD NIGHT!"

Note:—This was Rambo's 1961© Christmas card. Never before published.

Louis Pellier

Ode to the Prune

All hail to the name of Pelly-A,
(In French it's spelled another way,)
Horticulturist of historic note
Inspired, he to his brother wrote
"This Valley's rich and primed attune
To introduce our famed French Prune;
Stick scions in spuds to keep them wet,
We'll sprout a few—see what we get."
So his brother did with dubious doubt,
And a trunkful braved the Cape Horn route.
Little he knew that this just might
Create the "Valley of Heart's Delight".
The Prune was sweet, when dried would keep
And in bygone days was mighty cheap.
Presto! *dessert* from coast to coast
Served by many a boarding house host.
Cowboys' call for somethin' sweet
Was calmed with Prunes, chuck-wagon treat.
Prunes spread worldwide across the nations
Alleged to battle constipation.
Also the Prune had its springtime lure,
Ask one who rode the Blossom Tour,
Vast Valley bloomed in snow suburban
For a two-bit ride on the old Interurban.
But shaken when ripe from laden trees
A crawling Valley on sore knees
Picked Prunes amidst adobe clods,
Still well remembered—Oh Ye Gods!
NOW orchards long moved away,
Apartment houses now hold sway,
Worry no more about constipation,
Replace with groans about inflation,
The Prune indeed once had its day,
Now gone with the wind—like Pelly-A.

By an
ex-prune-picker
1900
R

178

 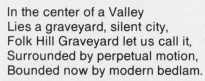 *tempus fugit*

In the center of a Valley
Lies a graveyard, silent city,
Folk Hill Graveyard let us call it,
Surrounded by perpetual motion,
Bounded now by modern bedlam.

Yet quiet Folk Hill still survives it
And in one secluded corner
Here still sleep our Valley's founders
Sleep despite engulfing "progress",
Screaming jets, unearthly noises,
Fearful quakes cannot disturb them,
Our Pioneers, forever peaceful.

And yet below one mossy tombstone
Stirred this certain restless Spirit,
"Sarah Bellum" read engraving, "1840-1900".
Peculiar Spirit, in life so curious
Eternal slumber distressed her sorely,
Inquisitive as she was when mortal,
Hungered for last inquiring eyeful,
One lingering view of her Old Valley.
Then at last she solved her problem!
Realized that as a phantom
She could practice LEVITATION!!

Surely she could plot her journey,
Who but she was more familiar?
Long she'd been a Valley teacher,
Graduate of old State Normal,
40 years she'd taught the Three R's
From West Side to Berryessa,
From Alviso to old Gilroy.

And so one morn she oozed her exit
Through the earth, her grassy blanket
(Calm yourself, oh dubious reader
Ghosts have power of penetration.)
Then, vapor-like she drifted skyward
'Til the Valley lay beneath her,
Same blue mountains closing round it,
Same salt marshes to the northward.

There, alas, nostalgia ended!
Sarah quickly lost her bearings,
Searched for one familiar landmark,
One faint hint of her Old Valley
What had time transformed below her?
"What," she cried, "In all Creation?"

Then Sarah swooped to lower levels,
Keenly seeking, ever hopeful
For that slightest indication
Of the Valley she remembered.

Chilling mists did her envelop
Strangely smelling and eye smarting,
Wrapped her shroud around more snugly
Knew she not of smog or sinus,
Blamed it on her fatal head cold.
(One that turned into pneumonia.)

Watery-eyed she scanned the City,
Storied concrete reaching skyward
Gone the Tower on old North Market,
City Hall and Old O'Connors,
Gone the yellow side-seat street cars,
Proud Vendome and S. P. depot,
Saint James Park, faintly familiar,
Once the Heart of "Garden City".

At last she saw remembered landmark,
Winchester House was freshly painted!
Then Sarah wafted toward the country,
Toward familiar farms and orchards,
Here Time again did harshly trick her,
In vain she sought that Separation
Where City ended, Country started,
Now they both were sadly scrambled!
Just scattered, teeming Shopping Centers,
Each a complete, bewildering City!
Woops! what was that pervading odor
Drifting skyward, onion flavored?
Knew she not the Valley's diet
Noontime lunch—a million burgers.

Where the Valley's famous prune trees?
Fruitful acres—solid concrete!
Once great oaks and rural crossroads
Giant freeways pierced the landscape,
Endless streams of steel and rubber,
Rush hour floods of human cargo,
Angry ants, their hill been stepped on,
Sarah murmured, "Why such hurry?
When all Eternity awaits them?"

Born too soon for tranquilizers
Such brief tour sufficed our Sarah,
As she dodged a plane's hot jet stream,
Singed her shroud and so alarmed her
Turned she gladly toward Old Folk Hill,
Toward her quiet marble orchard,
Slithered down to her companions,
Whispered to her slumbering neighbors,
"Sleep, old friends, do not awaken,
Here alone find peaceful refuge,
Here alone lies the OLD VALLEY."

By R.R. 1978

SCROOGE '81 MODEL

1981 GREETINGS
and a test on
HOW TO KNOW THAT YOU'RE GROWING OLDER

When your children begin to look middle aged.

When you turn off the lights for economy, not for romance.

When you tell the same story so often it only gets a few groans.

When a dripping faucet causes uncontrollable bladder urge.

When you start averaging up ages in paper's obituary list.

When only once a year you and the Christmas tree get lit.

When you subscribe to Modern Maturity instead of PLAYBOY.

When you're unaware of that drop of water under end of your nose.

When you pass the Milk of Magnesia stage and take Epsom Salts.

When you awaken you ache and what doesn't ache, doesn't work.

When dressed for jogging—those skinny legs!—you take a walk.

When you sink your teeth in a steak and they stay there.

When trimming your toenails amounts to major surgery.

When tying your shoes leaves you gasping for breath.

When your knees buckle but your belt wont.

When your back goes out more than you do.

TRY GERITOL

cartoons by above.

P. S. Many of above are familiar, appearing for instance in Ann Lander's column. But several are from the writer's aged experience. Happy Holidays Ralph

180

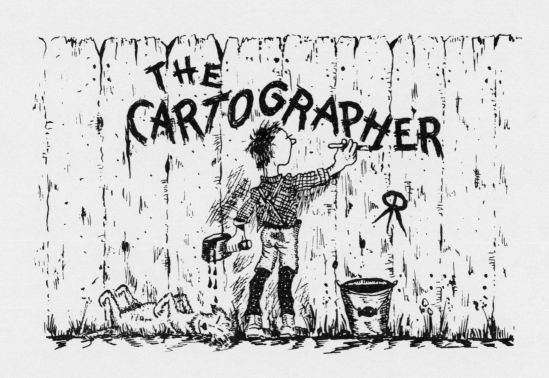

Dear Reader,

I waited 50 years to finally engage in a project long-contemplated (one that spare time never allowed) a cartoon map of the old Santa Clara Valley with scene set generally about the turn-of-the-century. It bears the title of this book *Pen & Inklings,* and can be found in both the front and back of this hardbound volume. The original map was done in black and red, best showing the pen and ink technique, and took about two months' work. It was a pleasure to produce and the public reaction was fantastic. The map was later produced in color and is the only one of my maps still in active publication.

The diseño or map of Rancho Santa Teresa was redrawn to supplement a book entitled "Santa Clara County Ranchos" written by Clyde Arbuckle, our noted Valley and Western historian. The original of the diseño is in the archives of the San Jose Historical Museum. Few, if any, of the original Ranchos were even roughly surveyed. On these immense tracts, the boundaries were often extremely vague and the property might be described as running from a certain tree to a large rock or waterway or other prominent landmark! With no cartographers or artists available, the diseños we have seen are neat but crude, occasionally carrying artistic colored calligraphy typical of the period. A diseño had to be furnished by every applicant for a Mexican or Spanish Grant along with an expediente, a descriptive application, plus the sum of $12 for as much as 40,000 acres!

The Peralta Maps were produced over a period of about 15 months. Along with Junior League of San Jose participation, important credit is due to Roberta Jamison who directed and coordinated the enormous and necessary amount of research. It was the writer's pleasure to convert this research into cartography, the "Scenic" and the "Location" maps. The Location Map shows the many adobes and also many of the original owners, all adobes located in relation to our present San Jose streets. The Scenic Map is the same, omitting the streets but with added detailed features and animation. Some of this is of course simulated or imagined, guided by existing adobes elsewhere or recorded historical descriptions.

To restore an 1887 frail and damaged map of Santa Clara County Country Schools I decided to redraw it with extensive illustrations and comment. I then ordered 1,000 for distribution to schools and friends. None were ever sold, and they are now practically out of print. I am told that only two or three of these original one-room schools are still in existence, being used as dwellings or barns.

In the pocket of this book you will find the "Old California Map" which was originally produced in numbered Limited Edition. It required about two or three months of unhurried research and drawing. One of the proudest moments of my life was when the City of San Jose chose to present this map to President Ford upon his visit to that city in 1976. I shook hands with him and saw him leave with my map in one hand and a book by Frances Fox in the other.

Yours Truly
Ralph Rambo

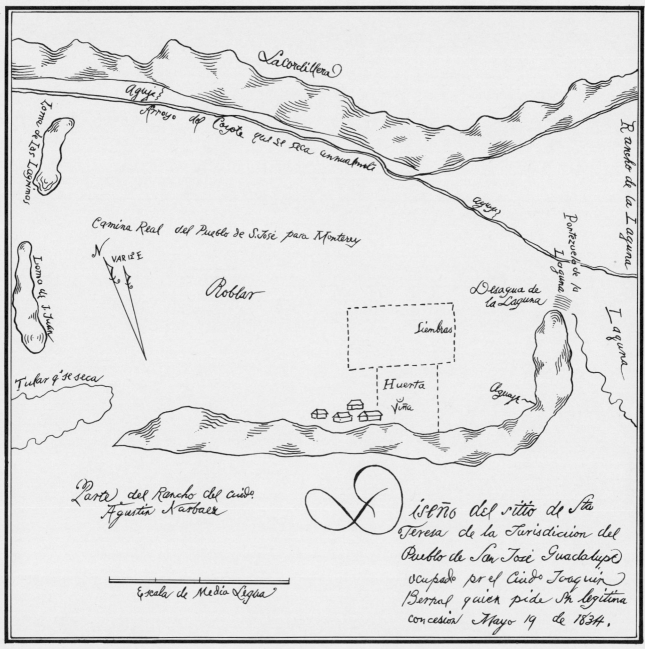

Facsimile of a diseño of the map showing La Cordillera, Arroyo del Coyote que se seca anualmente, Rancho de la Laguna, Camino Real del Pueblo de S. José para Monterey, Roblar, Siembras, Desagua de la Laguna, Pontezuela de la Laguna, Laguna, Huerta, Viña, Aguaje, Tome de las Lagunas, Loma de S. Juan, Tular q' se seca, Parte del Rancho del Ciud? Agustin Narbaez.

Diseño del sitio de Sta Teresa de la Jurisdicion del Pueblo de San José Guadalupe ocupado pr el Ciud? Joaquin Bernal quien pide Su legitima concesion Mayo 19 de 1834.

Escala de Media Legua

SAN JOSÉ — COYOTE CREEK — COYOTE
OAK HILL CEMETERY — EDENVALE — S.P.R.R. & MONTEREY ROAD
RANCHO SANTA TERESA — BERNAL

Clyde Arbuckle
HISTORIAN
Ralph Rambo
CARTOGRAPHER

Facsimile of a diseño of the Rancho Santa Teresa located about eight miles south of San José, bisected then as now by the El Camino Real. This 1834 diseño or map was drawn to accompany a textual description made up of boundaries simply defined by natural landmarks such as rocks, creeks and trees. These credentials formed a petition to the Mexican Government asking for legalized ownership. Don Joaquin Bernal applied for a square league or 4438 acres. In later years an accurate survey revealed his ownership of 9647.13 acres!

The rancho was well developed with yearly brandings of as many as 5000 head of cattle. There were four adobes, cultivated fields, an orchard, a vineyard and the famous Santa Teresa Spring, still flowing.

Today the original rancho boundaries of this typical California Don cover the entire Edenvale–Coyote region marked with such developments as IBM, and a steadily engulfing sea of tract homes.

Above is the exact reproduction of the original diseño or map—from the archives of the San Jose Historical Museum. Translations and explanations have been added.

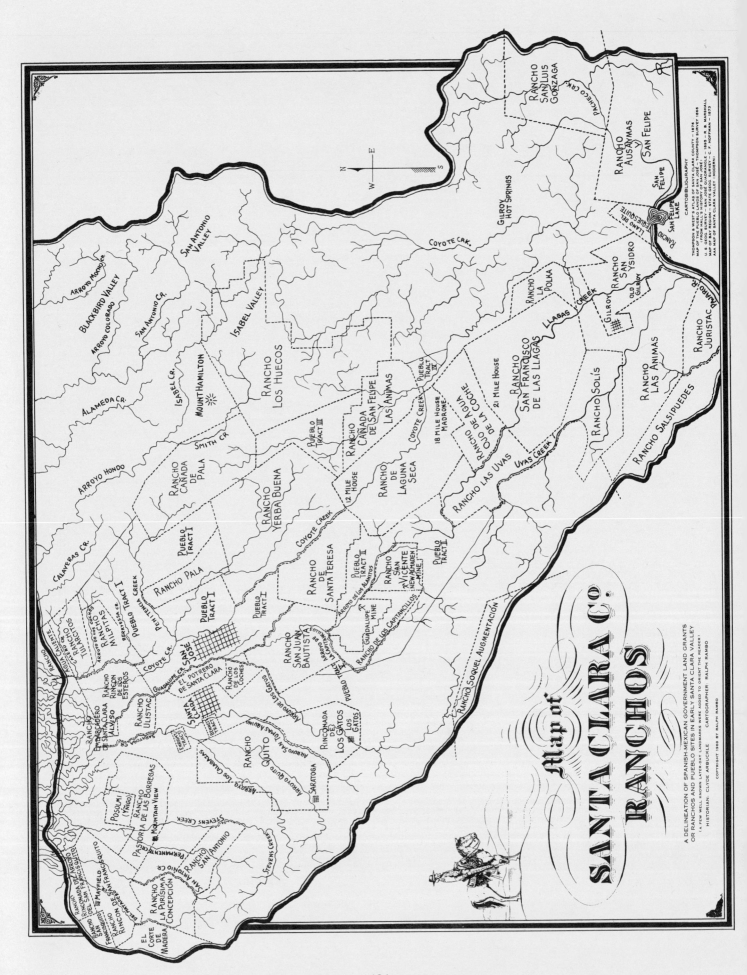

Map of SANTA CLARA CO. RANCHOS

A DELINEATION OF SPANISH-MEXICAN GOVERNMENT LAND GRANTS
OR RANCHOS AND PUEBLO SITES IN EARLY SANTA CLARA VALLEY
(A FEW WELL KNOWN LATER-DAY LANDMARKS WERE ADDED TO ORIENT THE READER)
HISTORIAN: CLYDE ARBUCKLE   CARTOGRAPHER: RALPH RAMBO
COPYRIGHT 1968 BY RALPH RAMBO

CARTOBIBLIOGRAPHY
THOMPSON & WEST CAPT4LAS OF SANTA CLARA COUNTY — 1876
MAP OF THE PUEBLO LANDS OF SAN JOSÉ — THOMPSON SURVEY 1866
(FROM HALL'S HISTORY OF SAN JOSÉ)
MAP OF THE PUEBLO LANDS OF SAN JOSÉ GUADANGLE — 1899 — R.B. MARSHALL
U.S. GEOL. SURVEY — SAN JOSÉ GUADANGLE — C.F. HOFFMAN — 1873
MAP OF BAY REGION — STATE GEOG. SURVEY
AKA MAP OF SANTA CLARA VALLEY (MODERN)

RANCHO SAN LUIS GONZAGA
RANCHO AUSAYMAS Y SAN FELIPE
SAN FELIPE
SAN FELIPE LAKE
LLANO DEL TEQUESQUITE
RANCHO JURISTAC
GILROY HOT SPRINGS
RANCHO SAN YSIDRO
OLD GILROY
GILROY
RANCHO LA POLKA
RANCHO SAN FRANCISCO DE LAS LLAGAS
RANCHO LAS ANIMAS
RANCHO SALSIPUEDES
RANCHO SOLÍS
21 MILE HOUSE
RANCHO LAS UVAS
18 MILE HOUSE MADRONE
RANCHO AGUA OJO DE LA COCHE
RANCHO CAÑADA DE SAN FELIPE Y LAS ANIMAS
RANCHO DE LAGUNA SECA
RANCHO SAN VICENTE
NEW ALMADEN MINE
PUEBLO TRACT IV
PUEBLO TRACT III
PUEBLO TRACT II
RANCHO YERBA BUENA
RANCHO LOS HUECOS
RANCHO CAÑADA DE PALA
RANCHO DE SANTA TERESA
PUEBLO TRACT II
RANCHO DE LOS CAPITANCILLOS
GUADALUPE MINE
RANCHO SAN JUAN BAUTISTA
ARROYO DE LOS ALAMITOS
PUEBLO TRACT I
RANCHO PALA
PUEBLO TRACT I
SAN JOSÉ
SANTA CLARA
EL POTRERO DE SANTA CLARA
RANCHO DE LOS COCHES
RANCHO SOQUEL AUGMENTACION
RINCONADA DE LOS GATOS
LOS GATOS
RANCHO QUITO
SARATOGA
RANCHO ULISTAC
EMBARCADERO DE SANTA CLARA
RANCHO RINCON DE LOS ESTEROS
RANCHO SANTA CLARA ALMSO
PUEBLO TRACT I
RANCHITOS TULARCITOS
RANCHITOS MILPITAS
AGUA CALIENTE
ARROYO DE LOS COCHES
BERRYESSA CR.
PENITENCIA CREEK
COYOTE CR.
GUADALUPE CR.
ARROYO SAN TOMAS AQUINO
ARROYO DE LOS GATOS
ARROYO LOS GUADALUPE
POSOLMI (YÑIGO)
RANCHO PASTORIA DE LAS BORREGAS
MOUNTAIN VIEW
STEVENS CREEK
PERMANENTE CR.
RANCHO SAN ANTONIO
SAN ANTONIO CR.
RANCHO LA PURISIMA CONCEPCIÓN
EL CORTE DE MADERA
RINCON DE SAN FRANCISQUITO
RANCHO DE SANTA FRANCISQUITO
RANCHO SAN FRANCISQUITO
RINCON DE ARROYO DEL SAN FRANCISQUITO
MAYFIELD
ARROYO MOCHO CR.
BLACKBIRD VALLEY
ARROYO COLORADO VALLEY
SAN ANTONIO CR.
SAN ANTONIO VALLEY
ISABEL CR.
ISABEL VALLEY
COYOTE CRK.
MOUNT HAMILTON
ALAMEDA CR.
ARROYO HONDO
SMITH CR.
CALAVERAS CR.
COYOTE CREEK
12 MILE HOUSE
LLAGAS CREEK
UVAS CREEK
PAJARO R.
N E S W

184

THE ABOVE MAP IS A REPRODUCTION OF A LARGER, COLORED EDITION THAT ACCOMPANIES "SANTA CLARA COUNTY RANCHOS." THIS WAS A 1968 REFERENCE 300K COMPILED BY HISTORIAN CLYDE ARBUCKLE, ILLUSTRATED BY RALPH RAMBO AND PRODUCED BY THE HARLAN-YOUNG PRESS, THERON FOX, PUBLISHER. A FIRST EDITION SOLD OUT IMMEDIATELY. THE CONDENSED CHART BELOW SHOWS THE 43 RANCHOS, PRONUNCIATION, TRANSLATION, EXACT ACREAGE, ORIGINAL GRANTEE AND FIRST PATENTEE, WITH DATES ACQUIRED.

A GRANTOR RANCHO WAS ACQUIRED FROM MEXICAN OR SPANISH RULERS, THE MEXICAN GRANTS BEING IN THE VAST MAJORITY. THE FEW SPANISH GRANTS WERE USUALLY REWARDS FOR MILITARY VALOR. A MEXICAN GRANT COULD BE OBTAINED BY ANYONE AND RAN IN SIZE FROM A HOUSE-LOT TO 40,000 ACRES. IT WAS ONLY NECESSARY TO FILE A ROUGH, UNSURVEYED BOUNDARY DESCRIPTION, PRESENT A CRUDE MAP AND DEPOSIT A FEE OF $12. AFTER THE U.S. HAD ACQUIRED CALIFORNIA, A U.S. PATENT WITH LAND SURVEY, CONFIRMED AN OWNERSHIP.

AGUA CALIENTE (Ah-gwah-Cahl'ee-ehn'tay) "HOT WATER" - 956.387 A.- GRANT BY GOV. ALVARADO TO FULGENCIO HIGUERA-1895. U.S. PAT. TO SAME-1858.

AUSAYMAS Y SAN FELIPE (Ah-sah-ee-mahs-ee-Sahn Fay-lee'pay) - 35,504.24 A.- GOV. FIGUERO TO AUSAYMAS AND ST. PHILIP-1833 - U.S. PAT. TO SAME-1859.

BENNETT TRACT - 355.03 A.- GRANT BY GOV. PICO TO NARCISO BENNETT-1845. U.S. PAT. TO MARY BENNET-1871.

CAÑADA DE PALA (Cahn-yah'dah-de-Pah'lah) 15,711.10 A. "SHOVEL GLEN" GRANT BY GOV. ALVARADO TO JOSÉ BERNAL - U.S. PAT. TO SAME 1863.

CAÑADA DE SAN FELIPE LAS ANIMAS (Lahs-Ah'nee-mahs) 8787 A.- GOV. CASARÍN GLEN OF ST. PHILIP AND THE SOULS - TO BOWEN & DALEY-1839- U.S. PAT. TO CHAS. WEBER 1866.

EL CORTE DE MADERA (El-Cohr-tay day Mah-day-rah) "PLACE WHERE TIMBER IS CUT" 13,316.05 A.- GOV. FIGUEROA TO PERALTA & MARTÍNEZ 1833 U.S. PAT. TO MARTÍNEZ-1858.

EL POTRERO DE SANTA CLARA "ST. CLAIRE'S COLT PASTURE" 1939.03 A. GRANT BY GOV. M. CHELTORENA TO JAMES FORBES 1844- U.S. PAT. TO COM. R.F. STOCKTON-1861.

EMBARCADERO DE SANTA CLARA (Ehm-bahr-cah-day-roh) "ST. CLAIRE'S EMBARKATION PLACE" 196.25 A. GOV. PICO TO BARCILA BERNAL-1845- U.S. PAT. TO HEIRS-1936.

ENRIGHT TRACT - 710 A. GRANT BY GOV. MICHELTORENA TO FRANCISCO GARCIA-1845. U.S. PAT. TO JAMES ENRIGHT 1866.

JURISTAC (Hoo-ree-stahk) "AT JURIS" (INDIAN) 4540.44 A. GRANT BY GOV. CASTRO TO ANTONIO AND FAUSTINO GERMAN-1835- U.S. PAT. TO J. SARGENT 1871.

LAGUNA SECA (Lah-goo-nah Say-cah) "DRY LAKE" 19,972.92 A - GRANT BY GOV. FIGUEROA TO JUAN ALVAREZ-1834- U.S. PAT. TO WM. FISHER'S HEIRS-1865.

LA POLKA "THE DANCE" 4166.78 A. GRANT BY GOV. FIGUEROA TO YSABEL ORTEGA 1833. U.S. PAT. TO BERNARD MURPHY -1849.

LA PURISIMA CONCEPCIÓN "THE HOLY VIRGIN" GRANT BY GOV. ALVARADO TO JOSÉ RAMÓN & JOSÉ GORGONIO-1846- U.S. PAT. TO JUANA MIRANDA-1871.

LAS ÁNIMAS "THE SOULS" 25,518 A. GRANT BY VICEROY FELIX MARQUINA TO MARIANO CASTRO. 1802- U.S. PAT. TO JOSEFA ROMERO-1835.

LAS UVAS (Oo-vahs) "THE GRAPES" 11,079.93 A. GRANT BY GOV. ALVARADO TO LORENZO PINEDA IN 1842 U.S. PAT. TO MARTIN MURPHY-1860.

LOS CAPITANCILLOS (Lohs Cah-pee-tahn-see-yohs) "THE LITTLE CAPTAINS" 4470.15 A. GRANT BY GOV. ALVARADO TO JUSTO LAROS-1842- U.S. PAT. TO CHAS. FOSSAT. 1871.

LAS COCHES (Coh-chays) "THE PIGS" 2219.34 A GRANT BY GOV. MICHELTORENA TO ROBERTO (INDIAN) 1844 U.S. PAT. TO ANTONIO SUNOL 1857.

LOS HUECOS (Hoo-ay-cohs) "THE HOLLOWS" 39,950.92 A- GRANT BY GOV. PICO TO LUIS ARENAS & ROLAND 1846- U.S. PAT. TO ROLAND AND HORNSBY-1876.

LLANO DEL TEQUESITE "ALKALI PLAIN" 39,950.92 A. (Yah'-no del Jeh-ke-is-kee'tah) GRANT BY GOV. CASTRO TO JOSÉ SANCHEZ-1835- U.S. PAT. TO VICENTE SANCHEZ-1871.

MILPITAS (Meel-pee-tahs) "LITTLE CORN FIELDS" 4457.66 A. GOV. CASTRO GRANT TO JOSÉ ALVISO IN 1835 - U.S. PAT. TO HIS HEIRS IN 1870.

OJO DE AGUA DE LA COCHE (Oh'-ho day Ahg'-wah day la Coh'-chay) "PIG SPRING" 8927.10 A. GRANT BY GOV. FIGUEROA TO HERNANDEZ-1835- PAT. TO MARTIN MURPHY-1860.

PALA (Pah'-lah) "SHOVEL" 4454 A. GRANT BY GOV. CASTRO TO JOSÉ HIGUERA-1835- U.S. PAT. TO CHARLES WHITE'S HEIRS-1868.

PASTORÍA DE LAS BORREGAS (Pah-toh-ree'ah day lahs Boh-ray'ghas) 9066.48 A. "EWE'S LAMB PASTURE" GOV. ALVARADO TO ESTRADA 1842- U.S. PAT. TO MARTIN MURPHY & CASTRO-1865-81.

POSOLMI (Poh-sohl'-mee) · INDIAN NAME · 1695.90 A. GRANT BY GOV. MICHELTORENA TO YÑIGO (INDIAN)-1844- U.S. PAT. TO ROBERT WALKINSHAW-1881.

QUITO (Kee'-toh) · TRANSLATIONS VARY · 13,309.85 A. GRANT BY GOV. ALVARADO TO JOSÉ NORIEGA AND JOSÉ FERNANDEZ-1841- U.S. PAT. TO FERNANDEZ HEIRS & MALVISO-1866.

RINCÓN DE LOS ESTEROS (Reen-cohn day los Eh-stay'-rohs) "ESTUARIES CORNER" 6352.90 A. GOV. ALVARADO TO Y. ALVISO-1838- U.S. PAT. TO WHITE, ALVISO & BERRYESSA-1842-'72-'73.

RINCÓN DE SAN FRANCISQUITO (Sahn-Frahn-sees-kee'-toh) "CORNER OF THE LITTLE ST. FRANCIS" 8418.21 A. GOV. ALVARADO TO JOSÉ PEÑA-1841- U.S. PAT. TO ROBLES BROTHERS-1863.

RINCÓN DEL ARROYO DE SAN FRANCISQUITO (Reen-cohn-nahl-del Ah-roy'-oh da Sahn-Frahn-sees-kee'-toh) 8418.21 A. GOV. ALVARADO TO MARÍA MESA-1841- U.S. PAT. TO SAME 1872.

RINCONADA DE LOS GATOS (Lohs-Gah'-tos) 6631.44 A. "CORNER OF THE CATS" GOV. ALVARADO GRANT TO PERALTA & HERNANDEZ-1840- U.S. PAT. TO HEIRS-1859.

SALSIPUEDES (Sahl-see-pway-dees) "GET OUT IF YOU CAN." 31,201.37 A. GRANT BY GOV. FIGUEROA TO JIMINEZ CASARÍN-1834- U.S. PAT. TO JAMES BLAIR-1861.

SAN ANTONIO (Sahn-Ahn-toh'-nee-oh) 444031 A. "ST. ANTHONY". GRANT BY GOV. ALVARADO TO MESA-1839 · PAT. TO DANA & ENCARNACIÓN-1866.

ST. FRANCISCO DE LAS LLAGAS (Yah'-gahs) 22,283.24 A. "ST. FRANCIS OF THE WOUNDS" GRANT BY GOV. C. CASTRO-1834- U.S. PAT. TO MARTIN MURPHY-1860.

SAN FRANCISQUITO "LITTLE ST. FRANCIS" 1471 A. GRANT BY GOV. ALVARADO TO ANTON BUELNA 1831 - U.S. PAT. TO MARÍA RODRÍQUEZ-1868.

SAN JUAN BAUTISTA (Sahn-Hoo-ahn Bah-hoo-tees'-tah) "ST. JOHN THE BAPTIST" 8877.54 A. GRANT BY GOV. MICHELTORENA TO AGUSTÍN NARVÁEZ-1844- U.S. PAT. TO A "POBLADOR"?

SAN LUIS GONZAGA (Loo-ees' gohn-gah gah) 48,827.43 A. "ST. ALOYSIUS GONZAGA" GRANT BY GOV. MICHELTORENA TO JUAN PEREZ PACHECO-1843 - U.S. PAT. TO SAME-1871.

SANTA TERESA (Tay-ray'-sah) "ST THERESA" 9,647.13 A. GRANT· GOV. FIGUERO TO JOAQUÍN BERNAL· 1834 U.S. PAT. TO AGUSTÍN BERNAL· 1867.

SAN VICENTE (Ve-sahn'-tay) "ST. VINCENT" 4438.36 A. GRANT BY GOV. ALVARADO TO JOSÉ BERRYESSA-1842- U.S. PAT. TO MARIA BERRYESSA-1868.

SAN YSIDRO (Ee-seed-roh) "ST. ISIDORE" 13,066.10 A. GRANT BY GOV. ARRILLAGA TO YGNACIO ORTEGA-1809- U.S. PAT. TO ORTEGA HEIRS· 1860-7-8.

SOLÍS (Soh-lees') UNCERTAIN FAMILY NAME· 8875.46 A - GRANT BY GOV. FIGUEROA TO MARIANO CASTRO 1834+ GOV. FIGUEROA TO M. CASTRO-1834· PAT. TO CASTRO HEIRS- 1859.

SOQUEL AUGMENTACIÓN (TRANS. UNCERTAIN) 32,702.41 A· (So-tal' Ohr-rorg-mohn-tah-see-ohn) - PART IN SANTA CRUZ COUNTY· GOV. FIGUEROA TO M. CASTRO-1834· PAT. TO HEIRS-1859.

TULARCITOS (Too-lahr-see'-tohs) 4394.35 A. "LITTLE TULE THICKETS"· GRANT BY GOV. PABLO DE SOLÁ TO JOSÉ HIGUERA 1821· U.S. PAT. TO HIGUERA HEIRS-1870.

ULISTÁC (Ooh-Lees-tahk') "AT ULIS" (INDIAN) 2200 A. GRANT BY GOV. PÍO PICO TO 3 INDIANS-MARCELO, PÍO & CRISTÓBAL-1845· U.S. PAT. TO JACOB HOPPE'S HEIRS-1868.

YERBA BUENA (Yehr-bah Bway-nah) 22342.64 A. "GOOD HERB" GRANT BY GOV. FIGUEROA TO ANTONIO CHABOLLA-1833· U.S. PAT. TO SAME-1859.

TO ABOVE LIST, ADD SMALL TRACTS, PUBLIC DOMAIN AND PUEBLO LANDS.

CATTLEMENS' BRANDS OF THE 1800'S SHOWN ABOVE ARE FROM THE ARCHIVES OF THE SAN JOSÉ HIST. MUSEUM.

BRANDED BY RAMBO-1970

LISTINGS ARE HOMES UNLESS OTHERWISE NOTED   ESTIMATED DATES OF CONSTRUCTION   UNKN:- UNKNOWN OWNER OR DATE OF CONSTRUCTION

Luis M. Peralta ① -PRE-1804. ② Peralta Indian dwelling-unkn. ③ Guadalupe Peralta-1852-55. ④ José Hernandez- unkn. ⑤ Alviso-Davidson-unkn ⑥ Pacheco-Davidson-unkn. ⑦ Sibrian-Castro-unkn. ⑧ Dolores Pacheco-unkn. ⑨ Notre Dame Convent-'30's. OR 40'S ⑩ David Davis-unkn. ⑪ Antonio Suñol Mill site-'30's. ⑫ Dickey-Mano-unkn. ⑬ Weeks-unkn. ⑭ Felipe Gongora-unkn. ⑮ Amesquita-Weeks-unkn. ⑯ Unkn.owner - unkn. ⑰ Adobe Washington Hotel-about-1850. ⑱ ⑲ Site of two adobes-probable '40's. ⑳ Columbet-probable '40's. ㉑ Bartolo Pacheco-Juana Pacheco-unkn. ㉒ D. Mesa-unkn. ㉓ Altamirano-unkn. ㉔ Mesa-unkn. ㉕ Sibrian-unkn. ㉖ Prado Mesa-unkn. ㉗ Adobe bldg-unkn. ㉘ Sepulveda-unkn. ㉙ Antonio M. Suñol-unkn. ㉚ Bernal-unkn. ㉛ José Noriega-unkn. ㉜ Garcia de Quevedo-unkn. ㉝ Pedro Sainsevain-unkn. ㉞ Montero-Moreno-Vioget-unkn. ㉟ Feliz-Garcia- de Saisset-Filipello-unkn. ㊱ Galindo-Burton-'20's. ㊲ Marmolejo-'40's. ㊳ ㊴ ㊵ Bldg. sites-prob.'40's. ㊶ Valencia-Fisher-'20's ㊷ Salvio Pacheco-Julian Hanks-'20's. ㊸ Justo Larios-prob.'40's. ㊹ Caldwell-unkn. ㊺ Ignacio Higuera-Francisco Diaz-prob.'20's ㊻ Bldg. site-unkn. ㊼ J. Bernal-prob.'40's ㊽ Flores-prob. '20's. ㊾ Site of Free Indians-prob.'30's. ㊿ Narvaez-Garcia-Juarez- before 1829. 51 Garcia-Jaboneria site-prob.'30's. 52 Narvaez-Galindo-Palomares-prob.'20's. 53 José M. Amador-unkn. 54 Welch-Castro -prob.'30's. 55 Alviso-Aloysin-Jones-1809 & 1835. 56 Barracks of the Guards-unkn. 57 Legislative Hall-1849. 58 Higuera-prob.'30's 59 Juan Bernal-unkn. 60 Ramon Bojorquez-prob.1810's. 61 Piñeda-Pico-1842-5. 62 Isaac Branham-1847-8. 63 Hoover-1847-8 64 A. S. Caldwell Planter's House-'40's. 65 Adobe Court House-1851. 66 County Jail-1854. 67 Young-unkn. 68 St. Joseph's Church-1803. 69 Leandro Rochin-pre 1827. 70 Adobe Office Bldg-unkn. 71 Black-'40's 72 Calvin Bldg. prob.'40's. 73 Adobe House-'40's. 74 Juzgado-1798-1850 75 J. S. Ruckel-bldg-unkn 76 Villagraña Bldg-1847. 77 Thomas Bowen-unkn. 78 Chas. M. Weber Store-unkn. 79 Lightston adt. to Weber Store-'47-8. 80 First Adobe Court House-1850. 81 Juan Soto-unkn. 82 83 Lightston Bldgs-1850. 84 J. D. Hoppe Bldg.-1850 85 Chabolla-Chattelle-unkn. 86 West Bldg.-'48. 87 Adobe Mansion House-'49-50. 88 Garcia-Mattei-'30's or '40's. 89 C. Dohring Bldg.-prob.'40's. 90 T. Campbell Bldg-prob'40's 91 Gregorio-unkn. 92 Rosa Gongora Bldg-1846-7. 93 Bowling Alley-prob.'40's 94 Antonio Chabolla-unkn. 95 Macario Saez-unkn. 96 José M. Flores-unkn. 97 Luis Chabolla-unkn. 98 Gonzales-Gongora-unkn. 99 Romano-unkn. 100 Daniel-prob.'40's. 101 102 103 Unknown owners and dates. 104 Swiss Hotel-adobe first floor-date of construction-unkn- (Birthplace of A. P. Giannini)-105 "Calaboose" (American Jail)-unkn. 106 107 108 109 110 -Owners and dates unknown.

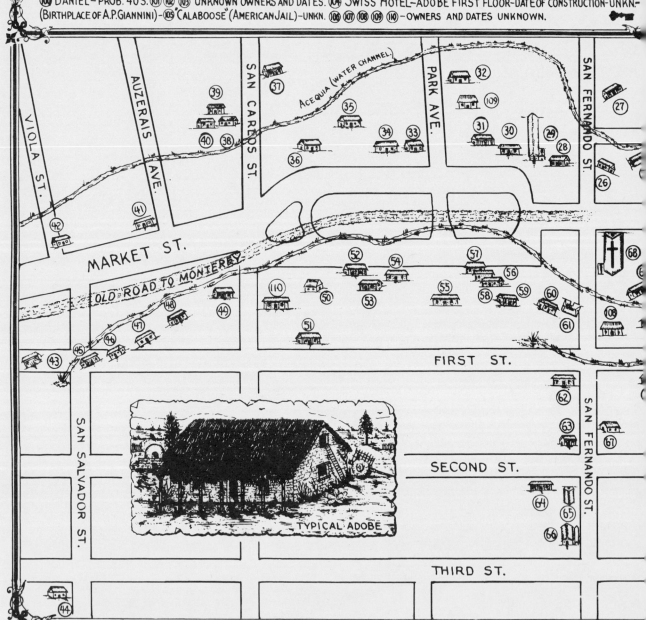

TYPICAL ADOBE

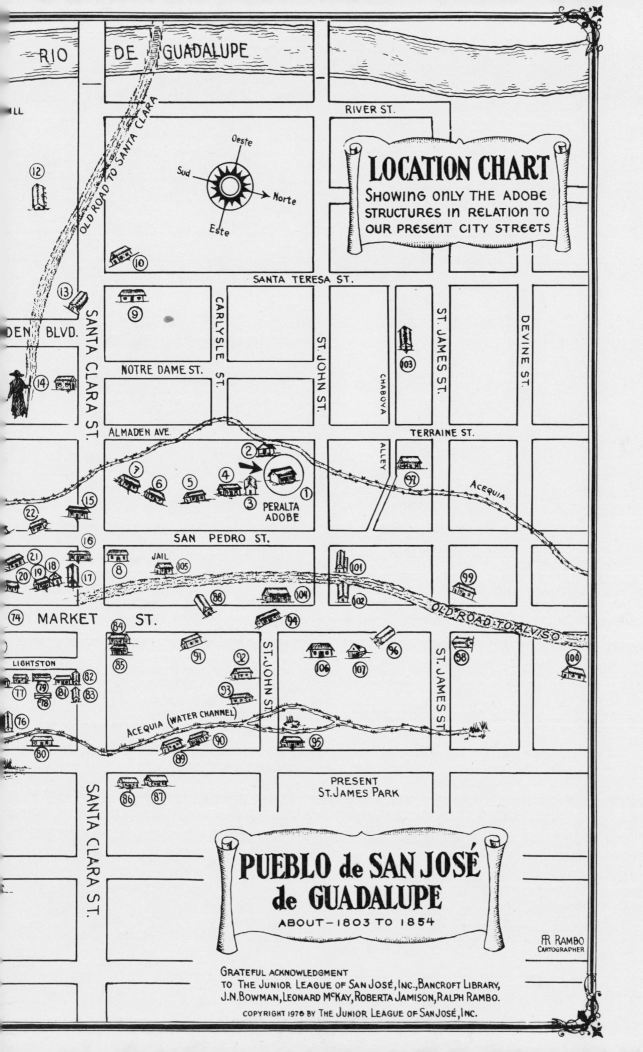

RIO DE GUADALUPE

RIVER ST.

Oeste

Sud

Norte

Este

LOCATION CHART
Showing only the adobe structures in relation to our present city streets

OLD ROAD TO SANTA CLARA

SANTA TERESA ST.

DEN BLVD.

SANTA CLARA ST.

CARLYSLE ST.

ST. JOHN ST.

CHABOYA

ST. JAMES ST.

DEVINE ST.

NOTRE DAME ST.

ALMADEN AVE.

TERRAINE ST.

ACEQUIA

PERALTA ADOBE

ALLEY

SAN PEDRO ST.

JAIL

MARKET ST.

OLD ROAD TO ALVISO

LIGHTSTON

ST. JOHN ST.

ST. JAMES ST.

ACEQUIA (WATER CHANNEL)

PRESENT ST. JAMES PARK

SANTA CLARA ST.

PUEBLO de SAN JOSÉ de GUADALUPE
ABOUT—1803 TO 1854

AR RAMBO
CARTOGRAPHER

Grateful acknowledgment to The Junior League of San José, Inc., Bancroft Library, J.N. Bowman, Leonard McKay, Roberta Jamison, Ralph Rambo.

Key to Names Associated with San José's Adobe Buildings

LISTINGS ARE HOMES UNLESS OTHERWISE NOTED   ESTIMATED DATES OF CONSTRUCTION   UNKN:- UNKNOWN OWNER OR DATE OF CONSTRUCTION

Luis M. Peralta (1) -Pre-1804. (2) Peralta Indian dwelling-unkn. (3) Guadalupe Peralta-1852-55. (4) José Hernandez-unkn. (5) Alviso-Davidson-unkn (6) Pacheco-Davidson-unkn. (7) Sibrian-Castro-unkn. (8) Dolores Pacheco-unkn. (9) Notre Dame Convent-'30's. or 40's (10) David Davis-unkn. (11) Antonio Suñol Mill site-30's. (12) Dickey-Mano-unkn. (13) Weeks-unkn. (14) Felipe Gongora-unkn. (15) Amesquita-Weeks-unkn (16) Unkn. owner -unkn. (17) Adobe Washington Hotel-about-1850. (18) (19) Site of two adobes-probable '40's. (20) Columbet -probable '40's. (21) Bartolo Pacheco-Juana Pacheco-unkn. (22) D. Mesa-unkn. (23) Altamirano-unkn. (24) Mesa-unkn. (25) Sibrian-unkn. (26) Prado Mesa-unkn. (27) Adobe bldg-unkn. (28) Sepulveda-unkn. (29) Antonio M. Suñol-unkn. (30) Bernal-unkn. (31) José Noriega-unkn. (32) Garcia de Quevedo-unkn. (33) Pedro Sainsevain-unkn. (34) Montero-Moreno-Vioget-unkn. (35) Feliz-Garcia-de Saisset-Filipello-unkn. (36) Galindo-Burton-'20's. (37) Marmolejo-'40's. (38) (39) (40) Bldg. sites-prob.'40's. (41) Valencia-Fisher-'20's (42) Salvio Pacheco-Julian Hanks -'20's. (43) Justo Larios-prob.'40's. (44) Caldwell-unkn. (45) Ignacio Higuera-Francisco Diaz-prob.'20's. (46) Bldg. site-unkn. (47) J. Bernal-prob.'40's (48) Flores-prob. 20's. (49) Site of free Indians-prob.'30's. (50) Narvaez -Garcia-Juarez-before 1829. (51) Garcia-Jaboneria site-prob.'30's. (52) Narvaez-Galindo-Palomares-prob.'20's. (53) José M. Amador-unkn. (54) Welch-Castro -prob.'30's. (55) Alviso-Aloysin-Jones-1809 & 1835. (56) Barracks of the Guards-unkn. (57) Legislative Hall-1849. (58) Higuera-prob.'30's (59) Juan Bernal-unkn. (60) Ramon Bojorquez-prob.1810's. (61) Piñeda-Pico-1842-5. (62) Isaac Branham-1847-8. (63) Hoover-1847-8 (64) A.S. Caldwell Planter's House-'40's. (65) Adobe Court House-1851 (66) County Jail-1854. (67) Young-unkn. (68) St. Joseph's Church-1803. (69) Leandro Rochin-pre 1827. (70) Adobe office bldg-unkn. (71) Black-'40's. (72) Calvin bldg. prob.'40's. (73) Adobe house-'40's. (74) Juzgado-1798-1850. (75) J.S. Ruckel-bldg-unkn (76) Villagraña bldg-1847. (77) Thomas Bowen-unkn. (78) Chas. M. Weber Store-unkn. (79) Lightston adt. to Weber Store-'47-8. (80) First Adobe Court House-1850. (81) Juan Soto-unkn. (82) (83) Lightston bldgs-1850 (84) J.D. Hoppe bldg-1850 (85) Chabolla-Chattelle-unkn. (86) West bldg:'48. (87) Adobe Mansion House-'49-50. (88) Garcia-Mattei-'30's or '40's. (89) C. Dohring bldg-prob.'40's. (90) T. Campbell bldg-prob'40's. (91) Gregorio-unkn. (92) Rosa Gongora bldg-1846-7. (93) Bowling Alley-prob.'40's. (94) Antonio Chabolla-unkn. (95) Macario Saez-unkn. (96) José M. Flores-unkn. (97) Luis Chabolla-unkn. (98) Gonzales-Gongora-unkn. (99) Romano-unkn. (100) Daniel-prob.'40's. (101) (102) (103) Unknown owners and dates. (104) Swiss Hotel-adobe first floor-date of construction-unkn- (Birthplace of A.P. Giannini)-(105) "Calaboose" (American Jail)-unkn. (106) (107) (108) (109) (110) -owners and dates unknown.

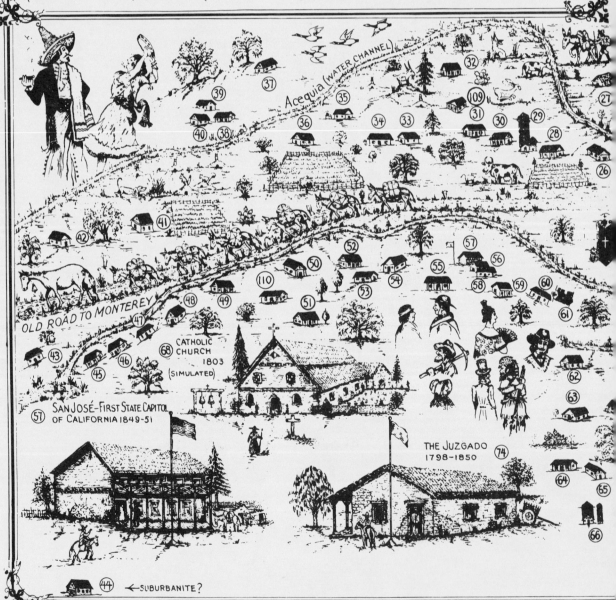

E. GUADALUPE

"los robles"

OLD ROAD TO SANTA CLARA

MILL

TEMESCAL

RANCHERIA

ONT 1776

Luis María Peralta

LUIS MARÍA PERALTA (1759-1851), A NATIVE OF TUBAC, MEXICO, (NOW IN ARIZONA), CAME TO CALIFORNIA WITH THE ANZA EXPEDITION OF 1775-76. WHILE SERVING IN THE ARMY (1781-1826) HE WAS APPOINTED *Comisionado* OF *Pueblo de San José* (1807-1822) AND LATER HELD THE OFFICE OF ELECTOR, TREASURER AND JUDGE UNDER MEXICO'S REGIME.

IN RECOGNITION OF MERITORIOUS SERVICES TO THE KING OF SPAIN, HE WAS AWARDED THE APPROXIMATE 48,000 ACRE EAST BAY RANCHO SAN ANTONIO BY GOVERNOR PABLO VICENTE DE SOLÁ IN 1820. YET HE CONTINUED LIVING IN HIS ADOBE WHILE HIS FOUR SONS OCCUPIED HIS SPANISH LAND GRANT, EQUALLY DIVIDED AMONG THEM IN 1842.

SEVENTEEN CHILDREN WERE BORN OF HIS MARRIAGE IN 1784 TO MARÍA LORETO ALVISO (1771-1836) BUT ONLY NINE REACHED MATURITY. WHEN HE DIED IN HIS ADOBE IN 1851 HIS ESTATE WAS VALUED AT $1,383,500.00. HIS HISTORICAL SIGNIFICANCE PROVIDES AN INDELIBLE LINK IN SAN JOSE'S RICH INDIAN, SPANISH, MEXICAN AND AMERICAN HERITAGE.

BY *Frances L. Fox*

PEAR ORCHARD

PERALTA ADOBE

JAIL

PUEBLO'S FIRST M.D. DR. BENJAMIN CORY 1848

TO THE MINES IN '49

OLD ROAD TO ALVISO

Acequia (WATER CHANNEL)

TYPICAL ADOBE

RAMBO CARTOGRAPHER

PUEBLO de SAN JOSÉ de GUADALUPE

ABOUT—1803 TO 1854

HISTORIC NOSTALGIA ADDED

GRATEFUL ACKNOWLEDGMENT TO THE JUNIOR LEAGUE OF SAN JOSÉ, INC., BANCROFT LIBRARY, J.N. BOWMAN LEONARD MCKAY, FRANCES FOX, ROBERTA JAMISON, RALPH RAMBO.

189

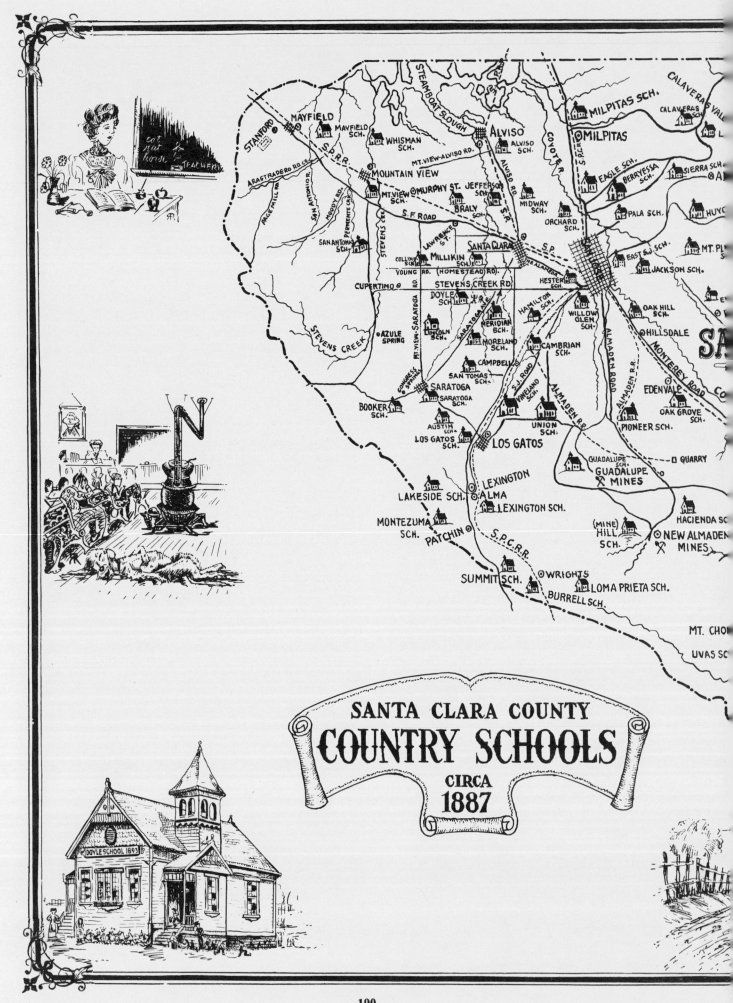

SANTA CLARA COUNTY COUNTRY SCHOOLS CIRCA 1887

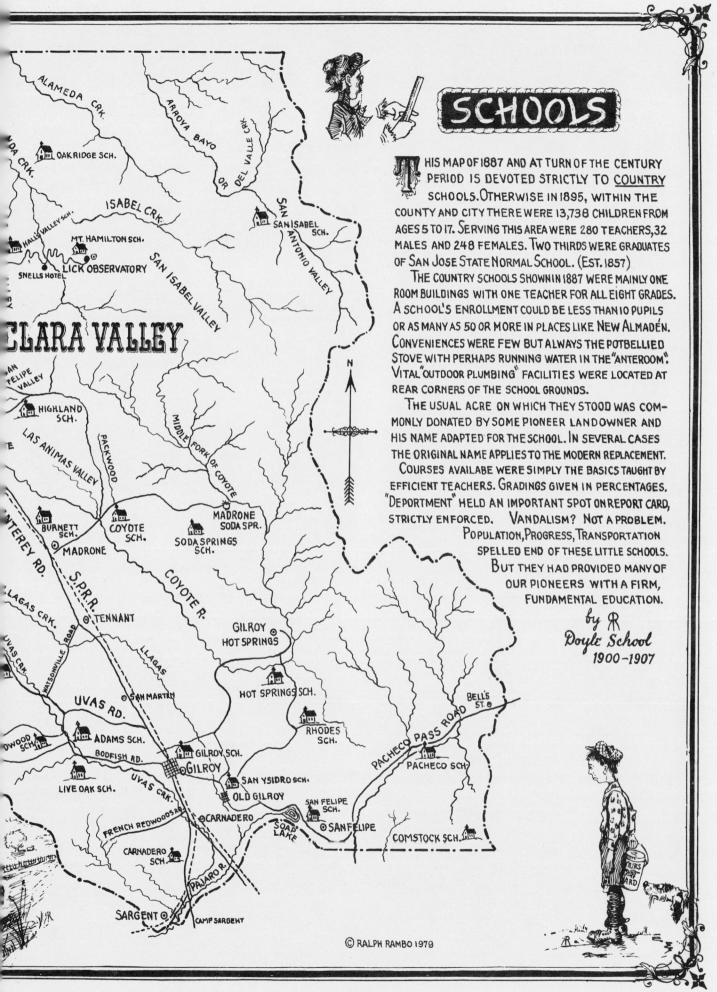

SCHOOLS

This map of 1887 and at turn of the century period is devoted strictly to COUNTRY schools. Otherwise in 1895, within the county and city there were 13,738 children from ages 5 to 17. Serving this area were 280 teachers, 32 males and 248 females. Two thirds were graduates of San Jose State Normal School. (Est. 1857)

The country schools shown in 1887 were mainly one room buildings with one teacher for all eight grades. A school's enrollment could be less than 10 pupils or as many as 50 or more in places like New Almadén. Conveniences were few but always the potbellied stove with perhaps running water in the "anteroom". Vital "outdoor plumbing" facilities were located at rear corners of the school grounds.

The usual acre on which they stood was commonly donated by some pioneer landowner and his name adapted for the school. In several cases the original name applies to the modern replacement. Courses available were simply the basics taught by efficient teachers. Gradings given in percentages. "Deportment" held an important spot on report card, strictly enforced. Vandalism? Not a problem. Population, Progress, Transportation spelled end of these little schools. But they had provided many of our pioneers with a firm, fundamental education.

by ℞

Doyle School
1900-1907

EPILOGUE

Only a few of us have the privilege of realizing, literally, a dream become a reality. To this writer, the publication of *Pen and Inklings* is just such a realization. I had hoped to believe that "life could begin at seventy" and, perhaps, last for another twenty years. But I had not anticipated this remarkable event.

Looking back, I can say that the word "work" never applied to those years of producing original stories, maps and cartoons. Instead, it was pure pleasure. There was the satisfaction of arousing OLD VALLEY memories, of recreating them, of illustrating them,—always with hopes they would find welcome reception among both pioneers and Valley newcomers alike.

Santa Clara Valley has a history of distinctive eras. We humans were few. Then came explorers, followed by the pioneers. Then came grazing herds of cattle, fields of grain, vineyards, a million fruit trees—the fruit basket of the world. Not a soul could then forecast, even imagine, the Silicon Valley of today. But we were happy with our simple way of life in the "Valley of Heart's Delight". And to us, it seemed so unchangeable, peacefully secure. How little did we know!

The writer has now, in ninety years, lived through several eras of transformation. No, I am not an exponent of the "Good Old Days", or a boresome member of the "It ain't like it usta be" club. I have come to enjoy the unexpected. On balance, the advantages of modern society clearly surpass the way of life in the bygone horse-and-buggy days.

A disclaimer is here in order. *Pen and Inklings* does not seek the status of an historical book. It has too many diversified ingredients—too remindful of old-fashioned beef stew, a little too heavy on the corn. There are traces of history in a few of the sketches—more, perhaps, in the illustrated maps. But the simple purpose was to compose a collected revival of memories; and for newcomers, a revealment of a Valley otherwise beyond imagination.

Fortunately, a reliable history was well documented in those earlier days by such historians as Bancroft, Hall, Sawyer, Foote, Guinn, Abeloe and others. And in my estimation, ranking above all others regarding our own Valley, we must include our close friend, Clyde Arbuckle. His amazing power of recall has no equal.

Nevertheless, in all this stored wealth of information there were, to this writer, two important omissions. Missing were the elements of nostalgia, the intimacies of that turn-of-the-century way of life; and the moments of humor that were a so, so important part of that life.

Hence there came to be *Pen and Inklings*. I hope that you have enjoyed them.

Yours Truly
Ralph R